THE

Garden Lovers' Guide

TO

BRITAIN

Kathryn Bradley-Hole

BBC BOOKS

ACKNOWLEDGEMENTS

This guide is my personal selection of the best Britain has to offer, and I have many people to thank for their local knowledge, hospitality, helpful suggestions and enthusiasm for this project. Particular thanks go to Adam Pasco and Séamus Geoghegan of BBC *Gardeners' World Magazine*, and Nicky Copeland and Khadija Manjlai at BBC Books, all of whom have given me unstinting help and encouragement. Richard Rosenfeld has done sterling work as copy-editor and Ben Cracknell has designed the pages and icons in an invitingly lively style.

My husband, Christopher, has been a 'guide, philisopher and friend' throughout; his support has been invaluable, as always.

Some years ago Sue Clifford and Angela King of Common Ground inspired me by their work. They have made us all aware of the importance of regional disinctiveness and I have tried to reflect some of that inspiration by including plants and people important to each region.

I would also like to thank: Geoff Amos, Stephen Anderton, Richard Ayres, David Beaumont, Peter Blackburne-Maze, Elizabeth Braimbridge, Jenny Broome, Neil and Jerry Campbell-Sharp, Georgina Capel, Nigel Colborn, Simon Dorrell, Valerie Finnis, Daphne Foulsham, Kate Garton, Jackie Gurney, Bob Harrison, Jane and Robert Hasell McCosh, Stephen Higham, Penelope Hobhouse, Malcolm Hutchinson, Carol Klein, Stephen Lacey, Roy Lancaster, Andrew Lawson, Val Lowther, Jim Marshall, Margaret Milton, Peter Pashley, Rosie Reed, Peter Reekie, John Sales, Myra Sanderson, Kathy Sayer, Peter Seabrook, Barbara Segall, Geoffrey Smith, William and Ruth Stearn, Anne Swithinbank, Christopher Thacker, Alan Titchmarsh, Rona Wallace, Charis Ward, Jim Ward, David Wheeler, Fred Whitsey, and all the garden owners, craftsmen, head gardeners and nurserymen and women, who have been incredibly generous with their time and knowledge.

COVER PHOTOGRAPHS

Front: above Beth Chatto Gardens, Essex (Jerry Harper); below Kifsgate Court, Gloucestershire (Jerry Harper)

Back: author photograph (courtesy of the author); above right photograph from the Garden Picture Library (Jacqui Hurst); inset Barnsley House Garden, Gloucestershire (Andrew Lawson); lower left Barnsley House Garden, Gloucestershire (Andrew Lawson); lower right photograph from the Garden Picture Library (John Glover)

Published by BBC Books, BBC Worldwide Limited, Woodlands, 80 Wood Lane, London W12 0TT

First published in 1998

ISBN 0 563 38754 8

Commissioning Editor: Nicky Copeland
Project Editor: Khadija Manjlai
Copy-editor: Richard Rosenfeld
Art Director: Jane Coney
Art Editor: Jane Parry
Designed by Ben Cracknell Studios
Maps: © MAPS IN MINUTES™ (1997) RH Publications

Set in Stone

Printed in Great Britain by Martins the Printers Limited, Berwick-upon-Tweed
Bound in Great Britian by Hunter & Foulis Limited, Edinburgh
Cover printed by Belmont Press, Northampton

Contents

Foreword

With such a rich heritage of gardens throughout our country, providing a living history of garden design through the ages, it is no surprise that visiting gardens is such a popular past time.

Gardens have often evolved in the most inhospitable regions, with limited money or resources, taming nature to produce scenes of breathtaking beauty. But in plenty of cases money has been no object, as entire landscapes have been remoulded, lakes excavated, and buildings and follies created. The end result? Some of the finest gardens in the world.

Throughout history, people and gardens have been closely linked. We can now marvel at the replanted Privy Garden of Henry VIII at Hampton Court, while sharing the gardening interests of our current Royal Family at Sandringham House, Norfolk, and at Highgrove, Gloucestershire. Start visiting such gardens and you will find yourself walking through a living *Who's Who?* of gardening and garden design. Spectacular gardens of the past, designed by Capability Brown, Geoffrey Jellicoe, Sir Edwin Lutyens and Humphry Repton have developed and matured much since their conception, while the gardens of Vita Sackville-West and Gertrude Jekyll, for instance, are often preserved in a form as close as possible to their original. You can also visit contemporary plantsmen and women, from Beth Chatto to Alan and Adrian Bloom, whose gardens attract visitors by the thousand each year eager to learn about new plants and the best ways to grow them.

Three things really excite me about visiting gardens, and from my contact with readers of *Gardeners' World Magazine*, I know they excite you too. First come the plants, which I try to identify despite their tongue-twisting Latin names, studying their shape and size, their associations with neighbours, and their preferences for, say, a shady spot under a tree, or the support of an old rustic arch in the sun. Rather than rely on memory, an enthusiast like me takes a camera and notebook to record every detail. Second are the special features, structures and design, and while some may inspire an odd corner of my own plot, most are there to be enjoyed and marvelled at, and to add to that ever-growing wish list of ideas for my dream garden. And third there are the people, not just fellow visitors but the owners and gardeners. Usually they are busying themselves with some essential chore, but most are happy to share a story about the garden or to pass on a few tips about a plant, which you might have struggled to grow for years, but which flourishes at the touch of their green fingers.

Gardens are as diverse as the interests of their owners, and the landscapes they occupy. Some are historical records still growing the very same plants raised from seed 60–70 years ago, brought back by the great plant hunters. Others may have been transformed from the most unpromising sites, being turned into the nearest image of paradise we will find on earth. And some have been carved out of a passion for a particular plant, becoming the site of a National Collection, a living museum of international importance.

With new gardens being created and opened all the time, visiting gardens is always full or surprises. Since gardens develop and mature, never standing still, seeing them at intervals through the year allows you to follow these subtle changes and bold, seasonal transformations. Many visitors will have travelled long distances, while others are inquisitive neighbours keen to find out what has been going on behind the boundary walls and fences. Thousands of pounds are raised for charity from many open gardens, much under the National Garden Scheme, with teas and plant sales adding to the overall enjoyment. On *Gardeners' World Magazine* we constantly receive a huge mail bag from readers, describing the wonderful new gardens they have discovered.

The value of any garden is in the eyes of the visitor. To some it involves learning about new plants, new plant associations or design features, while for others it is simply the sheer enjoyment, relaxation and contemplation, an escape from the hustle and bustle of the artificial word that surrounds us, and a chance to rekindle our relationship with the natural world.

Whatever your reason for visiting gardens, there is no better way to get the best from your day out than in the company of an experienced guide, a role that Kathryn

Bradley-Hole admirably fulfils in this book. Combining her plant knowledge and gardening experience with a love of gardens, their creation, and the stories behind them, she uncovers a wealth of gardens we can all enjoy.

Garden Lovers' Guide spans the entire country, presented by region and county, so that you can plan day trips and holidays, with a location map at the back of the book for quick reference. In addition to the gardens, you will find many nurseries and other places of interest found while researching this book, making it the most up-to-date, informative and inspiring guide you will ever find. Kathryn has also picked the brains of leading experts to find their favourite gardens, and the ones that feed their gardening passion.

I am sure you will enjoy the *Garden Lovers' Guide*, turning to it again and again to explore some of the hundreds of gardens described within its pages, and getting to know many of them personally on your gardening adventures.

Adam Pasco

Introduction

Visiting gardens, large and small, is one of the great pleasures of spending summer – or any other season – in Britain. It has often been my good fortune to visit and write about gardens professionally for the past 10 years, although I have toured them purely for pleasure for a good deal longer. My late mother was someone who enjoyed doing the rounds of stately homes, and I can remember, way back, being not greatly impressed by ornate plaster ceilings, portraits of swanky lords and ladies long gone, and dark wood carvings by Grinling Gibbons. As a child, I infinitely preferred wandering outdoors and nosing among the flowers, and that fascination has clearly withstood the test of time.

For the *Garden Lovers' Guide* I have travelled the length and breadth of the United Kingdom, covering many thousands of miles. I have met, along the way, a marvellously diverse range of people, all of whom share a common fascination and love for plants and gardens. I immediately think of Mark Robson, in Northumberland, who has been making a wondrous plantsman's garden at his parents' home since he was 15 years old. I think of Maitreya, a former Zen Buddhist monk, who has settled in Nottinghamshire and built by hand a tranquil Japanese garden that reminds him of his homeland. And of nurserywoman Jekka McVicar, who was a rock musician before she became captivated by culinary and medicinal herbs. I also think of Major Tony Hibbert, who retired in 1980 to Cornwall's south coast, only to begin an unexpected new career in his twilight years, restoring with gusto the all-but-lost Victorian garden of Trebah to its sub-tropical glory.

The *Garden Lovers' Guide* features, almost exclusively, gardens and nurseries that are *regularly* open, with just a few exceptions to this rule. It is therefore intended as a handy, glove-box guide in which you can quickly find places of interest in your area, or when taking a break elsewhere. Many of the National Trust's gardens are included, and I cannot stress too often the usefulness of having an NT membership card, which allows free entry to their numerous properties in exchange for the comparatively small annual fee. Certain gardens opening for the National Gardens Scheme (and Scotland's Gardens Scheme) are also included in this *Guide*. These organisations, which raise huge sums of money for Macmillan cancer relief and other worthy causes, deserve all possible support, and their well-known 'yellow books' are handy guides to thousands more gardens, which open perhaps just one or two afternoons a year for charity.

Lastly, I very much welcome your helpful comments on this first edition of the *Garden Lovers' Guide*. Your observations and contributions will help ensure that it continues to provide useful, entertaining information for everyone who loves plants and gardens.

How to Use This Book

Structure

The *Garden Lovers' Guide* is divided into the countries of England, Wales, Scotland and Northern Ireland, and subdivided into counties. Wales and Scotland, which have recently undergone extensive fragmentation (from the old counties into numerous unitary authorities), are arranged regionally, which will make more sense to the visitor. Within each county (or region) there is a scene-setting introduction, followed by main entries, which are organised alphabetically according to the nearest town or village. The index at the back of the book can also be used to locate a garden or nursery, when only the name is known.

Among the main entries there are boxed sections highlighting other places or features of note, including plants or people of local significance, locally made crafts from pots to trugs and a selection of special nurseries. At the end of each region the And Also... section is a round-up of other places worthy of mention.

Maps

The maps at the back of the book give approximate locations for all the entries in the *Guide*. When planning a tour of a region, however, you will also need a good road atlas showing more local detail than can be presented here. The maps are also useful because they show other nearby gardens, some in an adjacent county.

Plaques

Throughout the *Guide*, certain outstanding gardens and nurseries have been awarded a plaque. These places should not be missed when touring a particular region; the plaques are especially useful for pinpointing the best places to visit if time is limited.

Entries

Full addresses, telephone numbers, entrance fees (where applicable), directions and opening times are listed for each entry. Seasonal openings, such as 'March–Oct', are inclusive and run from the start of the first month to the end of the last. We have gone to great pains to ensure that details are up to date, and every entry has been checked with the owners at the time of going to press. However, if you are making a special journey to a garden or nursery, or planning a detailed itinerary, it is worth ringing beforehand to ensure that opening times have not suddenly been altered. Changes of ownership, a change of address, or route alterations due to road improvements can occur with little warning.

The best time of year for a visit is highlighted where appropriate. However, many gardens have something to offer throughout the year, and the garden's description will further pinpoint seasonal highlights. In order to make the most of each visit, facilities such as refreshments,

plants for sale, gift shops, wheelchair access and mail order services are clearly shown at the start of each main entry.

Entrance Fees

Charges for visiting gardens can vary greatly. The higher costs are given for tickets letting you into a stately home and the gardens. It is more usual, however, that cheaper tickets for the latter alone are available. As this is a garden visitors' guide, the emphasis is on the gardens, but where I have found the house to be particularly interesting, I have given it a mention too, and listed the ticket price for the interior. While the entrance fees quoted were correct at the time of going to press, on occasion you may find slight increases have been made at the start of the season.

Wheelchairs

Where available, wheelchair access has been noted at the start of each entry. Such notification indicates that the garden, or a significant part of it, can be negotiated by someone in a chair. It does not necessarily mean that there are full facilities, such as toilets, for disabled visitors, though they usually are present in the larger, more commercially run gardens, especially those attached to stately homes and National Trust properties.

Dogs

For various reasons dogs are practically never admitted to gardens, but sometimes guide dogs for the blind are permitted. It is worth checking ahead if you do have a guide dog.

Readers' Reports

We welcome your comments, good and bad, on any of the gardens, nurseries and other suppliers listed in the *Guide*, which will be helpful in compiling future editions. Also, if you know of any gardens or nurseries not currently in the *Guide* which warrant a mention, please send full details (including its complete name, postal address and telephone number) explaining why it should be included, and we shall follow it up. Send your letters to:

The Garden Lovers' Guide to Britain,
BBC Books,
Woodlands,
80 Wood Lane,
London
W12 0TT

ENGLAND

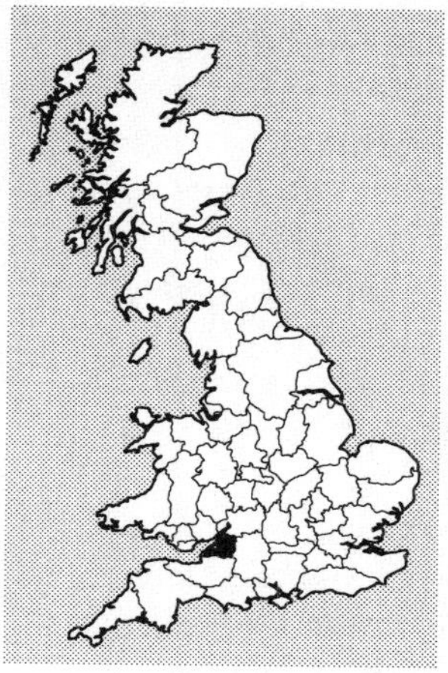

Avon district

MAP NO. 2

The area we have come to know as Avon over the last 20 years has recently been split up into four unitary authorities. However, for the purposes of the Guide it is convenient to keep Avon intact as an exceptionally rewarding region for garden visitors, plant enthusiasts and anyone who enjoys limestone landscapes and towns.

Taking in the elegant spa town of Bath and the historic sea port of Bristol, this area encompasses the lower reaches of the River Avon. It is rewarding for visitors who enjoy handsome architecture and gardens. Other highlights include Bath's sweeping Royal Crescent and Roman baths, built around a hot spring. Occupying fertile ground between the Mendip Hills to the south and the Cotswolds to the north, Avon is also a region which enjoys a fair share of interesting nurseries, so come armed with a cheque-book and plenty of car-boot space.

BATH

The American Museum, Claverton Manor

Bath BA2 7BD TEL. *01225-460503* OWNER *Trustees of the American Museum in Britain* HOURS *Late March–Oct, daily, except Mon, 2–5p.m., but Bank Holiday Suns and Mons, 11a.m.–5p.m.* ENTRANCE *£5, OAPs £4.50, children £2.50 (grounds £2.50, OAPs £2.25, children £2)* DIRECTIONS *3m SE of Bath, off A36 (not suitable for coaches), other route via Bathwick Hill, Bath*

SPRING SUMMER AUTUMN WINTER

Access | Gift Shop | Café

Claverton Manor is a handsome Georgian mansion of local stone in a glorious hillside setting, overlooking the valley of the River Avon and the picturesque Limpley Stoke Valley. Within its 55 acres, sloping lawns run up to the house, where a small parterre is laid out beside the stone terrace. This is the Colonial Herb Garden, with box-edged beds infilled with traditional dyers', culinary and medicinal herbs that were used by early American settlers. There are climbing roses and sun-loving shrubs against a tall balustraded wall near the house, but the main gardens and arboretum are set apart, further down the hill. The Mount Vernon Garden is enclosed by white palisade fencing and is a replica of George Washington's flower garden at Mount Vernon in Virginia. Filled with irises, columbines, salvias, geraniums, shrub roses and much else, it includes many of the plants that America's first president may have grown. Its brick-edged gravel paths lead to an attractive octagonal garden house, a reproduction of a similar building where Washington's step-grandchildren were schooled at Mount Vernon.

The arboretum is of special interest for its large collection of trees and shrubs of North American origin, including scarlet oaks, American hybrid magnolias, silver and sugar

ORGANIC HERBS BY POST

Jekka McVicar performed in a rock band and was a self-confessed hippie, 'every parent's nightmare', before she became hooked by the beauty and usefulness of herbs. After a brief spell working for a commercial herb nursery, she started a small business in the mid-1980s, growing and selling plants from her home. Business mushroomed, and today ***Jekka's Herb Farm*** *offers one of the largest selections of herbs and wildflowers in England, and her stand at the larger RHS flower shows is always worth investigating. (Recently I tried the delicious Vietnamese coriander,* Persicaria odoratum, *which Jekka recommends using with pineapple dishes, or for adding piquancy to salads.)*

The nursery is not open to visitors, but its mail order catalogue is extensive, and includes useful brief descriptions of the plants on offer. And there are plenty of them, around 500 different varieties, mostly sold as small plants, though some are available as seed. All are grown organically, to the standards of the Organic Food Federation. For a catalogue, send 4 × 1st-class stamps to ***Jekka's Herb Farm, Rose Cottage, Shellards Lane, Alveston, Bristol BS12 2SY (tel. 01454-418878).***

maples and many American roses. The garden's most unusual ornament is an Indian teepee of the Cheyenne tribe, a conical tent stretched over poles, decorated with buffalo designs.

While you are here, it is worth touring the manor, where there are fascinating exhibits of American domestic design (including quilts, stencils and Shaker furniture).

HAND-MADE TERRACOTTA POTS

Bill Donaldson, of ***Willow Pottery, Crosslease Farm, Woolley, Bath BA1 8AU (tel. 01225-859902), from Bath N on London Road, left onto old A46, left at pub, right at Woolley Lane, right into farm,*** *is a potter with a passion. After taking a degree in fine art at Leeds University, he worked with a clay producer, setting up a pottery in the heartland of the industry at Stoke-on-Trent. But in the mid-1980s he moved to Bath to set up his own pottery and has since developed a distinctive style, based on English traditional wares and motifs of the English countryside. Hares, dragonflies and bees ornament his early ranges, large fig pots are rimmed with appropriately figgy decoration, while his citrus pots are decorated with lemons.*

Well-made, hand-thrown pots such as these are fired at very high temperatures to cope with our climate. You will also find traditional Long-Toms, rhubarb forcers and alpine pans, and it is difficult to leave without weighing down the car boot with a selection of these tactile containers. Open Mon–Sat, 9a.m.–5p.m. Mail order catalogue available free.

BATH

Hannays of Bath

Sydney Wharf Nursery, Bathwick, Bath BA2 4ES TEL. *01225-462230* OWNER *V.H.S. and S.H. Hannay* HOURS *Early March–mid-Oct, Wed–Sun and Bank Holiday Mons, 10a.m.–5p.m.* ENTRANCE *Free* DIRECTIONS *in Bath, off A4 ringroad at bottom of Bathwick Roundabout, access via Sydney Mews (limited parking)*

SPRING SUMMER AUTUMN WINTER

Access Nursery

You will have to visit this fascinating ⅓-acre nursery, hidden in the middle of Bath, to acquire its plants (there is a catalogue – send £1.45 – but no mail order). Hannays sells around 1500 different plants, crammed into landscaped display beds so that you can see how they grow and behave. Sheilah and Spencer Hannay are also well-known plant hunters who cultivate many plants from seed, discovered on explorations from southern Africa to the Himalayas. Hardy geraniums are a speciality, plus unusual forms of phlomis, and there are many unusual plants on the list that suit dry conditions. For refreshment, head for the **Holburne of Menstrie Museum Tea House**, nearby.

BATH

Prior Park

Ralph Allen Drive, Bath BA2 5AH TEL. *01225-833422*
OWNER *The National Trust* HOURS *Daily, except Tues, 12–5.30p.m. or dusk if sooner; closed 25–26 Dec and 1 Jan*
ENTRANCE *£3.80, children £1.90, dogs not allowed*
DIRECTIONS *1m from city centre, by public transport only from central Bath as there is no parking nearby (bus 2, and Mon–Sat bus 4, from the bus station), or by taxi or hired bicycle. Access for disabled by reservation only: tel. 01225-833422*

SPRING SUMMER AUTUMN WINTER

Prior Park is for the enthusiast of the English 18th-century landscape garden, who will find it sublime, and for anyone wanting to stretch their legs on a hilly parkland walk. It also provides an airy escape from the traffic-filled streets of Bath, which can be seen in glorious views across the valley. At 28 acres it is comparatively small and intimate for a landscape garden, being largely the work of Alexander Pope, followed by Capability Brown (*q.v.*). After years of neglect the park was given to the National Trust in 1993 and has since been extensively restored at a cost of £½ million; its lakeside and woodland walks were opened up, and its fine features (including a handsome, colonnaded Palladian bridge) repaired.

The property was the creation of Ralph Allen, a larger-than-life gentleman and philanthropist of Bath (upon whom Henry Fielding based the wise and generous character of Squire Alworthy, in *Tom Jones*). He made a fortune by reorganising the cross-country postal system, and supplying the growing spa town with honey-coloured stone from his quarries at Combe Down and Bathampton. Architectural buffs will be enraptured by the classical stone house (now a school, closed to the public) with its rusticated arcades terminating in further large buildings. Allen intended it to be a Seat where his stone could be seen 'to much greater Advantage, and in much greater Variety of Uses than it had ever appeared in any other Structure.' Fortunately, in spite of two massive fires (in 1836 and 1991), the restored house is as imposing as ever, and its park is well on the way to providing it with gracious surroundings.

BRISTOL

University of Bristol Botanic Garden

Bracken Hill, North Road, Leigh Woods, Bristol BS8 3PF
TEL. *0117-9733682* OWNER *The University of Bristol*
HOURS *Mon–Fri, except Bank Holidays, 9a.m.–5p.m. (weekends only open to Friends of the Garden)* ENTRANCE *Donation* DIRECTIONS *From Clifton, cross the suspension bridge and take 1st right (North Road), garden entrance on left after ¼m; from M5 exit at Jct 19, then cross the bridge*

SPRING SUMMER AUTUMN WINTER

Set on a hill among substantial suburban houses near the famous suspension bridge, this unusual five-acre garden is a hidden-away gem in the city, and extraordinarily peaceful. Its sheltered position and extensive walling provide an ideal home for many plants of borderline hardiness, with plant collections from Australia, New Zealand and southern Africa. Although its function is primarily as a botanic garden for the university (and thus the layout is piecemeal), it is intimate enough and sufficiently packed with plants to provide an afternoon's entertainment for any keen gardener. There are bamboos and bulbs, a collection of hebes and wonderful glasshouses filled with orchids, bromeliads, succulents and other tropical greenery.

There is partial wheelchair access.

THE CHEDDAR PINK

Seedling trees and shrubs eke out a precarious living on the sheer limestone cliffs of Cheddar Gorge, England's own Grand Canyon. The chasms and caverns of this part of the Mendip Hills provide an awesome spectacle popular with visitors, while the springy, thyme-speckled turf above is the lone wild habitat of the Cheddar pink, Dianthus gratianopolitanus *(syn.* D. caesius*), one of Britain's most endearing wildflowers. Its clove-scented, deep rose-pink flowers were keenly sought by plant collectors and alpine gardeners during the 18th and 19th centuries. The Cheddar pink might easily have become extinct but for some tenacious and out-of-reach plants surviving in the most inaccessible crevices of the Gorge. Now a protected species, gardeners can find nursery-raised stocks through specialist alpine nurseries, including* **Arne Herbs** (q.v.) *at Chew Magna in this region.*

And also...

Arne Herbs, Limeburn Nurseries, Limeburn Hill, Chew Magna, Bristol BS18 8QW (tel. 01275-333399), offers around 600 culinary, aromatic and medicinal herbs by post (catalogue £2). A garden has recently been added to the Nursery. Visitors are welcomed, but an appointment is advisable. (Try to avoid visiting on Tuesdays if possible.)

Blackmore & Langdon, Stanton Nurseries, Pensford, Bristol BS18 4JL (tel. 01275-332300), specializes in phlox, begonias and, above all, delphiniums, for which stately plants the nursery has been famous since the early 1900s (July is therefore a rewarding time to visit). The catalogue (send a s.a.e.) lists old and new varieties, with informative notes, and there are also useful plant supports available by mail. Open Mon–Sat, 9a.m.–5p.m. and Sun 10a.m.–4p.m.

Cadbury Garden Centre, Smallway, Congresbury, Bristol BS19 5AA (tel. 01934-876464). It covers 15 acres of a former salad nursery and offers large stocks of typical garden centre ranges of plants and sundries, well displayed. Open Mon, 9.30a.m.–5.30p.m.; Tues and Thurs–Sat, 9a.m.–5.30p.m.; Wed, 9a.m.–8p.m; Sun, 10.30a.m.–4.30p.m.

David Bridgwater, Heather Cottage, Lansdown, Bath BA1 9BL (tel. 01225-463435), sells antiques, specializing in traditional garden architecture, ornaments and old garden tools, including metal watering cans, glass cucumber straighteners, and other fascinating gardening accessories. Visitors by appointment only.

The Kitchen Garden, Oldown Country Park, Tockington, Bristol BS32 4PG (tel. 01454-413605), attracts over 100,000 visitors per year, who come to see the fully working productive kitchen gardens, enjoy the 400 acres of woods and farmland and, best of all, take advantage of the extensive range of pick-your-own fruits and vegetables. Open May–Sept, Tues–Sun and Bank Holiday Mons, 10a.m.–6p.m.; Oct–April, Tues–Sun and Bank Holiday Mons, 10a.m.–5p.m. Entrance £4, OAPs/children £3.

Anyone with a penchant for passion flowers should visit the **Passiflora National Collection, Lampley Road, Kingston Seymour, Clevedon BS21 6XS (tel. 01934-833350)**, where nurseryman John Vanderplank cultivates over 200 species and varieties, both ornamental and edible, under glass. As well as hardy varieties, there are many suitable for the unheated conservatory or greenhouse and more tender specimens that require extra winter warmth. Open Mon–Sat, 9a.m.–1p.m. and 2–5p.m. (closed 25 Dec and 1 Jan); for mail order catalogue send 4 × 1st-class stamps.

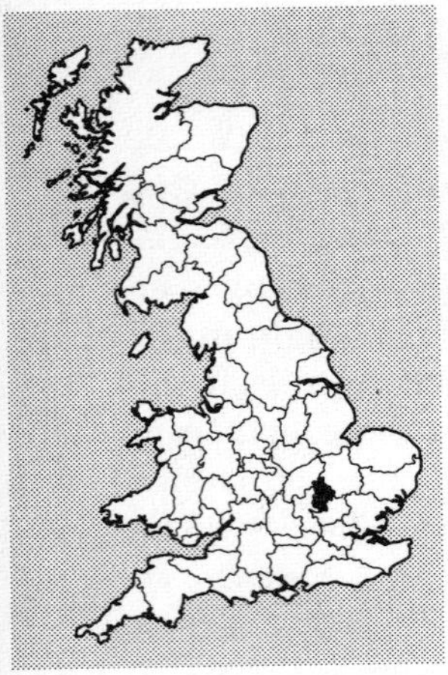

Bedfordshire

MAP NO. 3

The soil of rich clay which is a feature of this county gave rise to its centuries-old chief industries, brick-making and wheat-growing. It is a landscape of gentle undulations, sandwiched between a flat plain to the north, and a southern boundary of chalk hills. However, more people rush through this county en route to somewhere else than pause to look at it, which has been the case since the Romans extended Watling Street (now the A5) to link St Albans with Wroxeter and Wales. The M1 slices its way through the south of the county, leaving its tranquil gardens relatively unexplored.

OLD WARDEN

The Swiss Garden

Old Warden, Biggleswade SG18 9ER **TEL.** *01767-627666* **OWNER** *Shuttleworth Trust (leased to Bedfordshire County Council)* **HOURS** *Early March–Sept, Sat–Sun and Bank Holiday Mons, 10a.m.–6p.m.; Mon, Wed, Thur–Fri, 1.30–6p.m. (last adm. 5.15p.m.); Jan, Feb and Oct, Suns only, 11a.m.–3p.m.* **ENTRANCE** *£2.25, concessions/children £1.25, family £5, wheelchair-pushers free (no dogs allowed)* **DIRECTIONS** *2½m from Biggleswade, signposted from A1 (1m away) and from A600 (4m away)*

SPRING SUMMER AUTUMN WINTER

Access | Gift Shop

'Romantic' is the adjective most usually applied to the nine-acre Swiss Garden with its quaint Victorian cottage, dainty wrought-iron bridges, and wistful walks among cherry blossom and seas of daffodils. Spring is a wonderful time to visit because the pastel colours lend the garden a softness at this time, echoed by the meandering waters of the three irregular ponds.

It is an introspective garden, hidden from the outside world by gloomy shrubberies and large specimen conifers, many of the views angling inwards to the garden's *pièce de résistance*, a tiny, hilltop thatched cottage, appearing to be single-storey on one side, but with two visible from the other, where there is a partly concealed basement set in the hill. It is worth inspecting the building at close quarters to admire the patterned twigwork and pine cone decorations under the eaves of the verandah's roof, and the detailed craftsmanship within the cottage itself.

There are statues, urns, ornamental islands and marvellous specimen trees, but the other key feature at the garden's centre is the grotto and fernery – cool, damp and atmospheric, illuminated by shafts of sunlight through a moss-encrusted glass roof. The grotto is a cave-like structure of porous tufa stone, providing convenient cavities populated by ferns and ivies; the fernery is an important early example of cast ironwork with glass, dating from the early 1830s.

It is said that the garden was created by the 3rd Lord Longley, of the East India Company, for his mistress, and that it is haunted. Certainly, in spite of changing fortunes and recent restoration projects, this garden has managed to maintain its many attractive features and an eerie atmosphere of times past.

SILSOE

Wrest Park

Silsoe MK45 4HS **TEL.** *01525-860152* **OWNER** *English Heritage* **HOURS** *Early April–Sept, Sat–Sun and Bank Holiday Mons only, 10a.m.–6p.m.* **ENTRANCE** *£2.50, OAPs £1.90, children £1.30* **DIRECTIONS** *¾m E of Silsoe village, off A6*

SPRING SUMMER AUTUMN WINTER

Gift Shop Café

You could be forgiven for thinking you had been transported back to 18th-century France when visiting Wrest Park; its mansion is a 19th-century copy of a French chateau, set in palatial grounds with formal box parterres and a long water canal leading directly to a baroque pavilion, half a mile's walk from the house.

There are several distinct ages of garden design woven into the fabric of the park's 80 acres: the Long Water canal dates from the late 17th century, and is flanked by an early 18th-century woodland garden criss-crossed by straight rides, with smaller paths snaking their way through the trees, especially beautiful in spring and at leaf-fall in autumn. Capability Brown (*q.v.*) worked at Wrest in the mid-18th century, but his contribution was confined to far parts of the woodland garden, where he softened the contours of the formal canals surrounding the garden to provide a more naturalistic effect.

By the end of the same century Horace Walpole made no bones about the garden's outmoded formality, claiming it was 'very ugly in the old-fashioned manner, with high hedges and canals, at the End of the principal one of which is a frightful Temple...' New gardens, including the formal parterres, were added around the house when it was rebuilt in the 1830s, to the Francophile taste of its then owner.

Few visitors today would find the park ugly, or frightful, as Walpole did, and its peaceful greenery provides a perfect backdrop to its collections of statues and the elegant Chinese bridge. Do not miss the crumbling Bath House, a delightful fake ruin dating from 1770, sited at the water's edge, or the splendid French-style orangery which, in its heyday, is said to have housed the largest orange trees in England.

WHIPSNADE

Whipsnade Tree Cathedral

Whipsnade, Dunstable OWNER *The National Trust* HOURS *All hours* ENTRANCE *Free* DIRECTIONS *On W side of Whipsnade village, N of the village road*

SPRING SUMMER AUTUMN WINTER

While Whipsnade is best known for its zoo, the village possesses an unusual horticultural landmark. This extraordinary man-made woodland dates from the 1930s and is laid out in cathedral plan, with a nave and transepts, chancel, chapels and an outer cloister, all formed by trees. The brainchild of Edmund Kell Blyth, it was planted to commemorate the loss of his two boyhood friends during World War 1. Inspired by a visit to the newly built Liverpool Cathedral in 1930, Blyth embarked upon a plan to create his own cathedral, entirely of trees.

There is a chapel for each season: one of cherry trees for Easter, whitebeams (formerly elms) for summer, beech and cherry for autumn, and spruce firs for winter. The semi-circular chancel is of silver birch, and the cloister walk (with central dewpond) is formed from ash trees. The cathedral nave is of limes, while deodar cedars were chosen for the north transept, and horse chestnut for the south.

And also...

Bloms Bulbs, Primrose Nurseries, Melchbourne MK44 1ZZ (tel. 01234-709099), produces an explosively colourful, free catalogue for mail order bulbs listing over 400 varieties, with tulips a speciality.

Luton Hoo, Luton LU1 3TQ (tel. 01582-722955), is a fabulous mansion, most famous for its opulent Edwardian interiors (fashioned by the designers of London's Ritz Hotel) and, until recently, its collections of art and Fabergé jewellery. All this in the suitably ritzy grounds of a Capability Brown (*q.v.*) landscape park, with 10 acres of early 20th-century formal gardens (including a rose garden, water cascades and a rock garden) near the house. Open Easter–mid-Oct, Fri–Sun and Bank Holiday Mons, 12 noon–5.45p.m., and for pre-booked groups only, on Mon–Thurs. Entrance £6 (garden £3).

Over 100 varieties of herbs and wildflowers are on sale at **The Seed Sowers Training Project, Stables Christian Centre, Bolnhurst MK44 2ES (tel. 01234-376237).** The five-acre grounds include a woodland walk, shop and refreshments. Open April–Nov, Sat, 2–5p.m. Entrance free.

Willington Garden Centre, Sandy Road, Willington, Bedford MK44 3QP (tel. 01234-838777), is a substantial, well-stocked garden centre that has developed out of a 100-year-old nursery on the same site, and is still run by the same family. Open daily, April–Aug, 9a.m.–6p.m; Sept–March, 9a.m.–5p.m. (Fri all year from 9.30a.m.).

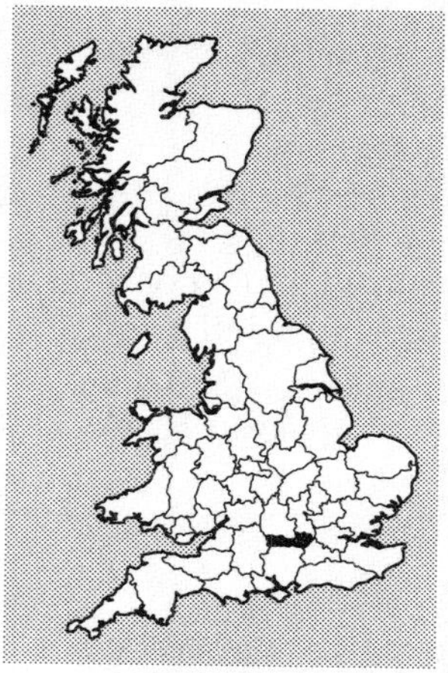

Berkshire

MAP NO. 2

Royal Berkshire takes in the vast park and ancient Windsor Castle, home of kings and queens. The county's landscape is varied, with the great meanderings of the River Thames snaking across the middle, through a broad plain of fertile pastures, and is speckled with glorious gardens. The swooping uplands of the Chilterns line the northern boundary, and in the west racehorses gallop the chalk downs around Lambourn, where bronze age remains pepper the grassy hills.

NEWBURY

Hollington Nursery and Gardens

Woolton Hill, Newbury RG20 9XT **TEL.** *01635-253908*
OWNER *Mr and Mrs S. G. Hopkinson* **HOURS** *Mid-March–Sept, daily, 10a.m–5.30p.m., Sun and Bank Holiday Mons, 11a.m.–5p.m.; Oct–Feb, restricted hours, please phone*
ENTRANCE *£1, OAPs 85p, children free (for gardens)*
DIRECTIONS *4m SW of Newbury, by A343; 8m from M4, exit at Jct 13 and use the A34 S, then the A343 towards Andover, Nursery on right*

SPRING SUMMER AUTUMN WINTER

Access | Gift Shop | Café | Plant Shop

Contained within the 18th-century brick walls of an old kitchen garden, this two-acre herb nursery (begun in 1976) has developed into a successful business alongside its numerous demonstration gardens, and is a delightful venue for mid-summer outings. Here are herbs used in imaginative ways – in a culinary garden, knot garden, paradise garden, and elsewhere with herbaceous flowers. Box topiaries and old-fashioned roses are well displayed too, being on sale in the nursery.

The proprietors, Simon and Judith Hopkinson, show how herbs and complementary plants can be used creatively in very small areas, and have divided up the walled plot into differently themed areas. Their Salad Days, held in June, are popular one-day courses on such topics as how to make a herb garden, and new ways of using home-grown herbs in the kitchen. The Salad Day that I attended was a hugely enjoyable outing, which inspired me with a new repertoire of delicious, herb-oriented recipes.

NEWBURY

Wyld Court Rainforest

Streatley Road, Hampstead Norreys, Thatcham, nr Newbury RG18 0TN TEL. *01635-200221* OWNER *Worldwide Land Conservation Trust* HOURS *March–Oct, daily, 10a.m.–5.30p.m.; Nov–Feb, daily, 10a.m.–4.30p.m. (closed 25–26 Dec). Last adm. ¾hr before closing* ENTRANCE *£3.50, concessions/children £3, under 14s £2 (under 5s free), family ticket £10 (all profits go to conservation work)* DIRECTIONS *M4 Jct 13 then go N on A34 and turn E onto B4009*

SPRING SUMMER AUTUMN WINTER

Access | Gift Shop | Café | Plant Shop

When it is cold or wet outside, a chance to retreat into the humid, enveloping warmth of a tropical glasshouse is particularly seductive, especially when the orchids or the giant waterlilies are in bloom. Wyld Court's glass-enveloped landscape covers 20,000 sq.ft and is as much an educational establishment as a practical home for tropical plants.

It is divided into three distinct, climatic areas with the temperature, humidity, ventilation and shade all monitored by computer. The Lowland Tropical area is the warmest, offering the deep shade and high humidity that nurtures lush, large-leaved anthuriums and alocasias. Fabulous orchids thrive in Amazonica, a brighter, less humid section, which is also home to *Victoria amazonica*, the extraordinary waterlily whose leaves can achieve an 8ft span in one season. The coolest house is Cloudforest with temperatures, similar to the Himalayan foothills, nurturing ferns, bromeliads and more orchids.

If you have children in tow, this is one garden they will really enjoy. Besides the spectacular plants, there are birds, fish and small mammals, demonstrating the symbiotic relationship between the flora and fauna of the rainforests.

THE LODDON LILY

*Resembling huge snowdrops, bearing sturdy white bell-flowers on 2–3ft high stems, the summer snowflake (*Leucojum aestivum*) is a captivating wildflower seen on some damp, southern river banks in May. It grows so plentifully on the sodden banks of the River Loddon in Berkshire that it has long enjoyed the popular title Loddon lily, forming white carpets among stands of willow. 'I have rarely seen anything more beautiful than a colony of the summer snowflake on the margin of a tuft of rhododendrons at Longleat,' declared William Robinson (*q.v.*) in his influential book* The Wild Garden *towards the close of the 19th century. 'Both the spring and summer snowflakes (*L. vernum *and* L. aestivum*) are valuable plants for wild grassy places, and the last grows freely in the good soil in the islets in the Thames near Wargrave.' At around the same time it was recorded that the flowers were used extensively for decorating Wargrave Church and that large quantities were gathered for sale in the streets of Oxford and for posies in local May Queen processions.*

*Robinson selected his own superior form of this handsome flower, naming it 'Gravetye Giant'. It is distinguished by its stout, strong stems and rich green, strappy foliage. Suppliers of 'Gravetye Giant' include Avon Bulbs (*q.v.*) and Hadspen Garden and Nursery (*q.v.*), both in Somerset.*

WINDSOR GREAT PARK

Frogmore

Windsor Castle, Windsor SL4 1NJ **TEL.** *01483-211535 (National Gardens Scheme)* **OWNER** *Her Majesty the Queen* **HOURS** *Open 1st Wed and Thurs in May for National*

Gardens Scheme, 10.30a.m.–7p.m. (last adm. 6.30p.m.) ENTRANCE *£2, house £3.* DIRECTIONS *Entrance via Park Street gate into Long Walk (follow AA signs)*

SPRING | SUMMER | AUTUMN | WINTER

Access | Café

'When we have done Broiling at Ascot, you shall cool yrself at Frogmore, where it looks very Ruralistic at present', wrote Queen Charlotte (wife of George III) to Lord Harcourt in 1793. In those days it was the venue for lavish entertaining, but is now largely kept out of the public eye, being a private home where the present Queen comes to relax and enjoy its peace. Queen Victoria also loved Frogmore, and she and Prince Albert are buried here, in an imposing marble mausoleum. Queen Victoria's mother lies in a smaller mausoleum in the grounds.

Nevertheless, its fame isn't just as a royal graveyard. Thirty-five-acre Frogmore has a delightful small park of immaculately kept gentle hillocks and bulb-filled lawns, sloping easily down to a meandering canal that winds its way through the gardens. Little stone bridges cross the waters, and there are attractive pavilions dotted about the grounds, including a pretty, hexagonal tea house draped

MRS SINKINS AND HER PINKS

The old-fashioned pink, Dianthus *'Mrs Sinkins', is a popular variety bearing attractively ragged white flowers with a heady, clove scent. Its origins go back to the Slough of more than 100 years ago, when John Thomas Sinkins ran the Slough Poor Law Institution, with his wife, Catherine, as matron. John was a flower fancier who bred a new garden pink which caught the eye of Charles Turner, of the Royal Nurseries, in Slough.*

Sinkins let the nursery raise the plant commercially on the condition that it was named after his wife. Supplies of Dianthus *'Mrs Sinkins' were made available to gardeners from the early 1870s onwards. Although its flowering period is brief, compared to more modern varieties, it is still valued, and appears in the coat of arms for Slough Borough.*

in Chinese wisteria. Nearby are two ancient holm oaks under which Queen Victoria used to set up a tent, where she painted in summer. Although Frogmore gardens are opened rarely, for charity, they have tranquil beauty and are well worth visiting.

WINDSOR GREAT PARK

The Savill Garden

Windsor Great Park, Windsor SL4 2HT **TEL.** *01753-860222* **OWNER** *Crown property* **HOURS** *March–Oct, daily, 10a.m.–6p.m., Nov–Feb, daily, 10–4, closed 25–26 Dec* **ENTRANCE** *£3.50, OAPs £3, children free* **DIRECTIONS** *3m W of Egham by A30 and Wick Road, signposted; from M25 Jct 13 (3m away) follow Egham Road*

SPRING SUMMER AUTUMN WINTER

Access | Gift Shop | Café | Plant Shop | DON'T MISS

Only 35 of Windsor Great Park's 4500 acres are taken up by this popular garden which is one of my favourite springtime haunts. It is a woodland garden *par excellence*, with fine magnolias, rhododendrons, pieris and dogwoods filling out a middle layer under tree canopies of oaks and pines.

The garden also features a large collection of daffodil cultivars, individually grouped and well labelled, but even more attractive are the grassy slopes when covered with hoop-petticoat narcissi (*N. bulbocodium*), and patches of the dainty *Narcissus cyclamineus*. Informal gravel paths wind through the Dry Garden, where there are further colourful plantings of spring bulbs and Mediterranean plants. In the damper valleys, bright yellow kingcups and lysichitons line the bogs and streams among unfurling fronds of ferns. One of the garden's finest trees, an unusual Chilean *Podocarpus* in the herbaceous area, was quite unintended; it was a discarded nursery seedling that took root here 60-odd years ago. A modern glasshouse was added in 1995 to house more tender rhododendrons, and plants of the southern hemisphere.

WINDSOR GREAT PARK

The Valley Gardens

Windsor Great Park, Windsor SL4 2HT TEL. *01753-860222* OWNER *Crown property* HOURS *Open all year, daily, 8a.m.–7p.m. or sunset if sooner; possible closure in bad weather* ENTRANCE *£3 for car and occupants (coin machine)* DIRECTIONS *3m W of Egham by A30 and Wick Road, signposted*

SPRING SUMMER AUTUMN WINTER

This is a huge garden within Windsor Great Park, extending to around 400 acres on the northern shores of lake Virginia Water. Mature trees planted in the 1750s date from the time of William, Duke of Cumberland, the son of George II, which now provide some of the majestic framework to be enjoyed on the wooded slopes.

Rhododendrons flourish on the local, acid soil of Bagshot sand where they can be found in great variety decking the hillsides in drifts of shocking pink and orange, purple and delicate yellow. The Punch Bowl – a natural amphitheatre of great beauty – is the main area for spring's kaleidoscopic azalea show. The soil is also suitable for heathers displayed in the Valley Gardens in vast numbers, beyond the pinetum. As well as native species and varieties, there are imported heathers that bring colour into the gardens at every stage of the year. There are also important collections of hollies, dwarf conifers and magnolias within the gardens.

And also...

Dorney Court, Dorney, Windsor SL4 6QP (tel. 01628-604638). This quaintly creaking Tudor manor of pink bricks and old oak timbers oozes character surrounded by wonderful yew topiary and ancient Buckinghamshire woods. Open July–Aug, Mon–Thurs, 1–4p.m. Entrance £4.50, OAPs £4, children £2.50. Of more interest to gardeners, however, is the **Bressingham Plant Centre (tel. 01628-669999)** in the grounds, featuring a wide range of plants raised by Blooms of

Bressingham, notably perennials and conifers (open daily, except 25 and 31 Dec, 9a.m.–5.30p.m.). Entrance free.

Foxgrove Plants, Foxgrove, Enborne, Newbury RG14 6RE (tel. 01635-40554), specializes in snowdrops which are sold 'in the green' (when in leaf) so that they have a better chance of establishing than if sold as dry bulbs. Snowdrop catalogue published each Feb (£1). They also offer a range of alpines and small hardy plants (catalogue £1). There is no mail order service, but orders can be placed to collect from the various RHS shows around the country. Open all year, Wed–Sun and Bank Holiday Mons, 10a.m.–5p.m.; closed in Aug.

Waltham Place, White Waltham, nr Maidenhead FL6 3JH (tel. 01628-825517), has 20 acres of organic gardens, including walled gardens, bluebell woods, fine specimen trees and a lake. Open April–Sept, Wed, 2–5p.m. (when plants and dried flowers are for sale at the property's farm shop) and Fri 2–5p.m. and Sat 10a.m.–1p.m.

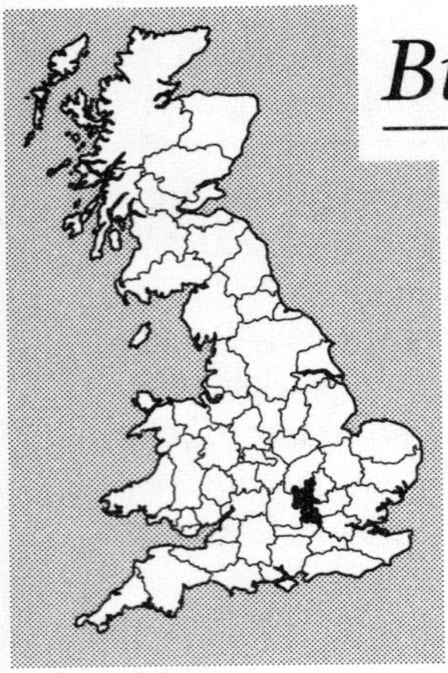

Buckinghamshire

MAP NO. 5

The northern part of this county embraces the flat and fertile Vale of Aylesbury (renowned for rearing the eponymous white ducks). It is distanced from the encroachment of north London's outer suburbs by the uncompromising high chalk ridge of the Chiltern Hills, among which are scattered numerous attractive villages. In past centuries, the region's beech woods were coppiced or pollarded for firewood, and subsequently their timbers were used by wood-turners for chair-making. In the south, Burnham Beeches is the most famous wood in the Chilterns. Many of its trees are stout and ancient pollards, of massive girth and enormous character, bearing twisted and misshapen trunks.

AMERSHAM

Chenies Manor House

Chenies, nr Amersham WD3 6ER TEL. *01494-762888*
OWNER *Lt-Col. and Mrs MacLeod Matthews* HOURS *April–Oct, Wed–Thur, 2–5p.m. (last adm. to house 4.15p.m.); also Bank Holiday Mons, 2–5p.m.* ENTRANCE *(house and garden) £4.50, children £2.20; (garden only) £2.20, children £1*
DIRECTIONS *In Chenies village, off A404 between Amersham and Rickmansworth; from M25 Jct 18 follow signs to Amersham for 2m*

SPRING SUMMER AUTUMN WINTER

Access | Gift Shop | Café | Plant Shop | DON'T MISS

When Elizabeth and Alistair MacLeod Matthews bought the red-brick Elizabethan manor in the 1950s, practically nothing remained of the four-acre Tudor garden that had once surrounded it. They therefore made their own gardens of topiaries and colourful flowers, in the spirit of Tudor formality if not in detail, for this garden has its own style and is not a slave to historical dogma. Neat lawns beside the house lead to a trelliswork screen of dark green ivy, beyond which is a brilliantly colourful sunk garden, filled with tulips in spring, and dahlias and other bedding flowers in summer.

There is an interesting physic garden of medicinal and culinary herbs, a turf maze, a productive and very attractive kitchen garden, a pleached lime tunnel, and a narrow *allée* lined with velvet-smooth cypress hedging, proving that × *Cupressocyparis leylandii* need not be a monstrous hedger, provided it is regularly tamed with shears. The White Garden, especially effective in the twilight of summer evenings, is planted with white cosmos and marguerites, grey-leaved and variegated plants and stout topiary birds in yew. All is immaculately maintained by Elizabeth MacLeod Matthews and one helper.

BUCKINGHAM

Stowe Landscape Gardens

Stowe, Buckingham MK18 5EH **TEL.** *01280-822850* **OWNER** *The National Trust* **HOURS** *Late March–mid-April, daily; mid-April–early July, Mon, Wed, Fri, Sun; mid-July–early Sept, daily; mid-Sept–end Oct, Mon, Wed, Fri, Sun; end Dec–Jan, daily. All 10a.m.–5p.m., or dusk if earlier; last adm. 1hr before closing* **ENTRANCE** *£4.40, children £2.20* **DIRECTIONS** *3m NW of Buckingham via Stowe Avenue, off A422; from M40 Jct 9 use A421, turn towards Brill in Kingswood*

SPRING SUMMER AUTUMN WINTER

Gift Shop

Café

It is said that England's greatest contribution to world art is the landscape garden. And Stowe is great. Like Castle Howard (*q.v.*) in Yorkshire, it is a heroic landscape on the grandest scale, with a ½-mile beech and chestnut avenue leading from the Buckingham entrance to a triumphal arch, from where you can look upon the 375-acre garden laid out around the magnificent mansion which is now Stowe School. The list of landscapers who helped is impressive; Sir John Vanbrugh, Charles Bridgeman and William Kent were involved in the early work; Lord Cobham, the owner, involved himself in the development of the grounds; he employed the young Capability Brown (*q.v.*) who became head gardener in 1741 (at the age of 25) and laid out the Grecian Valley. Stowe's waters, vistas, numerous garden buildings and undercurrents of allegory make an exhilarating visit, beautiful and atmospheric in every season.

BERNWODE PLANTS

Large quantities of herbs and unusual hardy perennials are the speciality of ***Bernwode Plants, Kingswood Lane, Ludgershall, Aylesbury HE1 89RB (tel. 01844-237415/ 0860-798115), 11m W of Aylesbury, then 1m SE of Ludgershall off the Wotton road, from A41 turn towards Brill in Kingswood****. I first met Derek and Judy Tolman 10 years ago, when they had recently quit city life in favour of the Good Life to set up their nursery. Its list is now extensive, and has recently expanded to include a selection of old apple cultivars and other fruits. Plants are available by mail and the catalogue (send 8 × 1st-class stamps or £2) is exceptionally well produced, with many interesting descriptions, especially where plants have historical interest. Open March–Oct, Tues–Sun and Bank Holiday Mons, 10a.m.–6p.m., or dusk if earlier.*

TAPLOW

Cliveden

Taplow, Maidenhead SL6 0JA **TEL.** *01628-605069* **OWNER** *The National Trust* **HOURS** *Easter–Oct, daily, 11a.m.–6p.m., Nov–Dec, daily, 11a.m.–4p.m. Closed Jan–Feb* **ENTRANCE** *£4.80, children £2.40* **DIRECTIONS** *2m N of Taplow off A4 on B476; from M4 Jct 7 take the A4, then follow signs*

SPRING SUMMER AUTUMN WINTER

Access | Gift Shop | Café

You can almost smell the money in this well-heeled area embracing the upper Thames. Fabulous houses lie behind high gates and, towering over them all, like a temple of Mammon, sits Cliveden, perched on its chalk eyrie in 10 acres of gardens. The house (now a luxurious hotel) was built by Sir Charles Barry in 1850, but was bought by William Waldorf (1st Viscount) Astor in 1893. Astor brought a balustrade from the Villa Borghese in Rome, several ancient Roman sarcophagi, vast urns and statuary, and laid out a serene topiary garden and an oriental-style water garden. An intimate rose garden hidden in the woods was designed by Sir Geoffrey Jellicoe.

A broad, lawned platform below the house is planted with a formal box parterre, infilled with seas of mauve nepeta, and grey santolina and senecio which, while somewhat uninspired, does not detract from the main point of this area – its spectacular views of the Thames and surrounding landscape. There are plenty of shady walks on hot summer days, and rough steps descend the cliff to the river.

WEST WYCOMBE

West Wycombe Park

West Wycombe HP14 3AJ **TEL.** *01628-488675* **OWNER** *The National Trust* **HOURS** *April–late May, Sun and Wed, 2–6p.m.; Easter, May and Spring Bank Holiday Suns and Mons, 2–6p.m.; June–Aug, Sun–Thurs, 2–6p.m. Last adm. 5.15p.m.* **ENTRANCE** *£2.50, children £1.25 (£4.20, children £2.50, includes house, June–Aug)* **DIRECTIONS** *On A40, from M40 Jct 4 take A404 N, then A40 to West Wycombe*

SPRING SUMMER AUTUMN WINTER

Access

Here is an 18th-century landscape garden of sublime tranquillity, dotted with classical statues and pavilions, and an exquisite music temple, serenely reflected in the waters of a large lake. There are plantations of fine trees contrasting with open lawns, quaint timber bridges cross the streams, and you can be thrilled by the sound of a magnificent, flint-enclosed gushing cascade.

Can it be that this park is the creation of the same man who founded the infamous Hell-Fire Club? It is. 'Fornication, adultery, whore-mongering, drunkenness, blasphemy, gambling, and atheism were thought, by the pious, to be increasing at an alarming rate in the 18th century', explains Eric Towers in his book *Dashwood: the Man and the Myth.* At the same time, Sir Francis Dashwood, from 1735 until his death in 1781, worked on his 350-acre garden, creating a formal landscape in the early years which was overlaid with softer contours as the naturalistic influences of Capability Brown (*q.v.*) became *de rigueur*. Little has altered since, although the National Trust's summer evening concerts are not quite the Bacchanalian revelries the park witnessed in its youth.

WING

Ascott

Wing, nr Leighton Buzzard LU7 0PS TEL. *01296-688242* OWNER *Sir Evelyn de Rothschild and The National Trust* HOURS *April and Sept, Tues–Sun, 2–6p.m. Early May–late Aug, every Wed, and last Sun in each month, 2–6p.m. Open Good Friday but closed Bank Holiday Mons* ENTRANCE *£4, children £2*

SPRING SUMMER AUTUMN WINTER

Access

This 40-acre garden is so redolent of the Victorian age when it was created that you might expect to see ladies tightly waisted and bustled, taking a leisured perambulation (with parasol in hand) through the park.

It was laid out in the late 19th century by Leopold de Rothschild, with the help of the Veitch Nursery of Chelsea. It is famous for its trees, topiaries and formal seasonal bedding, all signature features of the Victorian age. One area, hedged in golden-leaved yews and golden holly, draws in the yellows of the cornfields lying in the Vale of Aylesbury beyond the garden's boundaries. Another topiary area conveys the sentiments of the age with a sundial (its gnomon in green and golden yew) surrounded by the hedged inscription 'Light and shade by turn but love always'. The Roman numerals of the sundial are fashioned in clipped box.

And also...

Bekonscot Model Village, Warwick Road, Beaconsfield HP9 2PL (tel. 01494-672919), is huge fun. It is the oldest model village in the world, covering 1½ acres, and is planted with over 8000 conifers and 2000 miniature shrubs; 200 tons of stone have been used to make its rockeries. It offers a nostalgic glimpse of English village life in the 1930s in a series of cameo scenes, with cricket on the village green, the local hunt riding by, and the sounds of the choir emanating from the church, all within a quaint garden setting. Open mid-Feb–Nov, daily, 10a.m.–5p.m. Entrance £3.60, children £1.80, concessions £2.50.

Buckingham Nurseries and Garden Centre, Tingewick Road, Buckingham MK18 4AE (tel. 01280-813556), specializes in trees, shrubs and conifers suitable for hedging (whatever sort of hedge you want, you will almost certainly find it here). The prices are very reasonable, especially for bare-rooted plants available for autumn–winter planting. The Nursery provides a free catalogue. Open all year, Mon–Fri, 8.30a.m.–6p.m., and Sun, 9.30a.m.–6p.m. (closes at 5.30p.m. in winter).

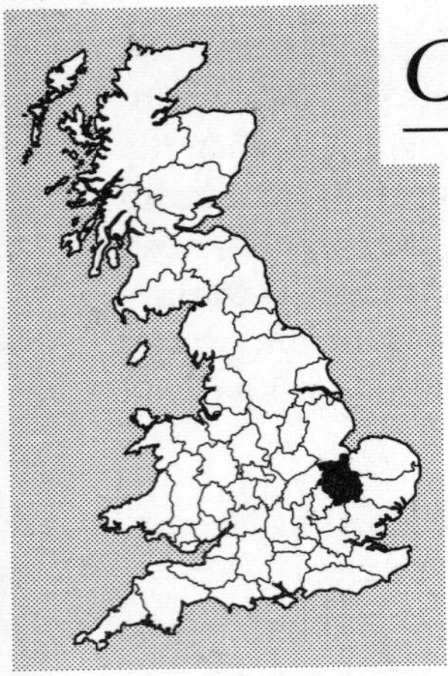

Cambridgeshire

MAP NO. 6

This small, relentlessly flat county is part of the East Anglian fenlands, a region of dark, alluvial soil and lonely marshes, criss-crossed by drainage ditches, with the level horizon intermittently broken by the shimmering silhouettes of willows. The Romans first tried to drain the fens, but it was not until the arrival of Dutch engineers in the 17th century that the landscape became useful pasture, speckled with windmills driving huge pumps. The River Ouse winds a lazy route across the county, dividing north from south. The historic university city is crammed with beautiful buildings and bicycles, the favoured mode of transport by students and staff alike.

CAMBRIDGE

Cambridge University Botanic Garden

Cory Lodge, Bateman Street, Cambridge CB2 1JF **TEL.** 01223-336265 **OWNER** University of Cambridge **HOURS** Open all year, daily, except 25–26 Dec, 10a.m.–4p.m. (6p.m. in summer) **ENTRANCE** £1.50, children/OAPs £1 **DIRECTIONS** Entrance on Bateman Street, 1m S of city centre

SPRING SUMMER AUTUMN WINTER

NPC

Any time of year is a good time to visit this diverse garden, set in a rectangular site of nearly 40 acres in the city's southern suburbs. Its many mature trees, including handsome cedars and pines, bring height and a sense of enclosure into this level site, and its winding paths ramble pleasantly through a series of areas, including herbaceous beds, systematic order beds (where plants are grouped according to their botanical families), and an ecological area. The best features are the rock and water gardens (with a beautiful madrona tree) beside a naturalistic lake, and the clutch of glasshouses nurturing desert and Mediterranean plants, tropical flowering plants, palms and rainforest trees, orchids and cacti. The glasshouses make a warmly welcoming refuge in winter, but outdoors the mid-winter gardens are colourful with stems of dogwoods, willows and brambles among bright-foliage conifers.

FENLAND SWEET PEAS

Fragrant sweet peas were in great demand 100 years ago. ***Unwins Seeds, Histon, Cambridge CB4 4LE (tel. 01223-236236),*** *is one of the nurseries which has specialized in these flowers since the early 20th century, when William Unwin, an enthusiast, issued his first modest seed list of home-raised varieties. Their list today includes over 50 varieties, covering all available colours and shades. The free colour catalogue also covers a wide seed list of other flowers and vegetables. Mail order only.*

HEMINGFORD GREY

The Manor

Hemingford Grey, nr Huntingdon PE18 9BN **TEL.** *01480-463134* **OWNER** *Mr and Mrs P. S. Boston* **HOURS** *Open all year, 10a.m.–6p.m. House visits by appointment only* **ENTRANCE** *(garden only) £1.50, children 50p (parties can book to see the house, £3 and £1.50)* **DIRECTIONS** *At Hemingford Grey, off A14, 3m SE of Huntingdon. Park in village and enter via towpath on River Ouse*

SPRING | SUMMER | AUTUMN | WINTER

Foreign visitors to Hemingford Grey call it a 'delicious slice of England', and I have to thank Jim Ward, editor of *Garden News*, for alerting me to the delights of this four-and-a-half-acre garden. The house was built around 1130 and is reputedly the oldest, continuously inhabited house in the country, with much of its moated Norman structure intact. It became famous in the 1950s, when Lucy Boston wrote a series of children's books about Green Knowe (modelled on Hemingford Grey), that acquired a worldwide following.

Lucy Boston died in 1990, aged 97, but her daughter-in-law, Diana Boston, is working hard to maintain the Green Knowe legacy in the house and garden. The latter boasts herbaceous borders in traditional style, with an old-fashioned mix of delphiniums, pinks, lavender, phlox and, especially, roses. Lucy Boston only planted roses that were known prior to 1900, and around 200 of them are still here. Garden visitors enter via a small gate, attracted by the cascades of mid-summer roses in bloom. There are also splendid yew topiary 'cottage loaves', with cross finials on top.

LODE

Anglesey Abbey and Garden

Lode, Cambridge CB5 9EJ TEL. *01223-811200* OWNER *The National Trust* HOURS *Late March–mid-Oct, Wed–Sun and Bank Holiday Mons, 11a.m.–5.30p.m., last adm. 4.30p.m. (house open 1–5p.m.). Also garden only, early July–mid-Sept, daily, Oct–Dec, Thurs–Sun* ENTRANCE *£5.80, children £2.90, but Sun and Bank Holiday Mons £6.80, £3.40 (garden only £3.40, £1.70)* DIRECTIONS *In village of Lode, 6m NE of Cambridge on B1102, signposted from A14 2m away*

SPRING SUMMER AUTUMN WINTER

Access | Gift Shop | Café | Plant Shop | DON'T MISS

Ninety-eight acres of windswept Cambridgeshire fenland may seem an unpromising site for a garden, but the Anglesey estate, sold in 1926 to Huttleston Broughton, the first Lord Fairhaven, had two things in its favour: the romantic remains of an Augustinian abbey, and the tremendous vision of Lord Fairhaven who had the means to lay out a magnificent park.

Be prepared for a good long walk, if you want to see it all. Vast avenues and vistas were created to provide the perfect setting for the owner's collection of 18th- and 19th-century statuary. The Emperors' Walk, for example, runs a straight quarter mile. It was formed to display a dozen busts of Roman emperors carved from Carrara marble. The Coronation Avenue of magnificent chestnut trees extends for more than half a mile.

There are also fine flower gardens, including a D-shape traditional herbaceous border, wonderful at mid-summer, sheltered by tall beech hedges. A formal area of symmetrical beds, enclosed by precision-cut yew hedges, is fragrant with bedded out hyacinths in spring, which are replaced by blocks of scarlet and golden dahlias for a late summer display.

FRAGRANT FIELDS OF HYACINTHS

Picture a vast plain, with pastel rainbow stripes running like colourful ribbons into the distant horizon. For a brief spell in late March and early April, this transformation occurs on the dark, peaty fenlands of Waterbeach, when the National Collection of hyacinths is in bloom, its heady perfumes fleetingly carried away by the winds. Farmer Alan Shipp turned to hyacinths in the mid-1980s, and part of his 100-acre holding is now devoted to these exotic bulbs, instead of the more prosaic wheat, sugar beet and potatoes that surround them.

Today's garden hyacinths trace their ancestry to the wild Hyacinthus orientalis *of Asia Minor, first grown in Europe in 1573 by botanist Carolus Clusius in Vienna. On moving to Holland, Clusius took his bulbs with him and within the space of 100 years they had spawned a lucrative industry. Two hundred years after Clusius planted his first bulbs, there were 351 cultivars for sale, and by the mid-1800s 2000 varieties had been bred. Now there are only perhaps 240, for many old strains are extinct, and the* ***National Collection, 9 Rosemary Road, Waterbeach CB5 9NB (tel. 01223-571064/860069)*** *extends to 110. They can be seen on just one open weekend, usually at the end of March.*

SHEPRETH

Crossing House Garden

Meldreth Road, Shepreth, Royston SG8 6PS **TEL.** *01763-261071* **OWNER** *Mr and Mrs D. G. Fuller and John Marlar* **HOURS** *Open all year, daily, dawn to dusk* **ENTRANCE**

Donation DIRECTIONS *8m S of Cambridge, ½m W of A10, follow signs to Shepreth*

SPRING SUMMER AUTUMN WINTER

DON'T MISS

Here is one railway level crossing where you will never get bored while waiting for the express trains between Cambridge and London to fly past. The commuters on board get a jolt, too, when they reach Shepreth, for the colourful Crossing House Garden looms into view, with its tapestry of flowers strung along the railwayside.

Margaret and Douglas Fuller came to The Crossing House in 1959, when Douglas was appointed crossing keeper. Nowadays the crossing is automatically operated, but the Fullers have remained in their eccentric, wedge-shape plot and continue to tend a ¼-acre garden crammed with all manner of decorative trees and shrubs, roses, perennials and colourful annuals (they reckon to have around 5000 different plants). There are beds, a lawn edged with dwarf box, topiary in box and yew, three small greenhouses packed with orchids and alpines, and much more. Fortunately, the Fullers like trains although Margaret preferred the days of the steam engines 'when people waved out of the windows'.

SHEPRETH

Docwra's Manor

Shepreth, Royston SG8 6PS TEL. *01763-260235/261557* OWNER *Mrs John Raven* HOURS *Open all year, Wed and Fri, 10a.m.–4p.m.; also 1st Sun of month April–Oct, 2–5p.m. and NGS charity open days* ENTRANCE *£2, £3 for special openings, extra for tour* DIRECTIONS *In Shepreth village, opposite war memorial*

SPRING SUMMER AUTUMN WINTER

Access Plant Shop

Plants have a free rein in this delightfully informal two-and-a-half-acre garden, made over the last 40 years by the late John Raven (a scholar and botanist) and his wife, Faith. An enormous range of plants is gathered here, with particular emphasis on those hailing from dry habitats such as the Mediterranean. The garden is divided into a series of enclosed areas, separated by walls and hedges which provide some wind shelter; within, self-sown plants enhance the garden's feeling of natural abundance. The emphasis on species, rather than garden hybrids, is refreshing and instructive.

WISBECH

Peckover House

North Brink, Wisbech PE13 1JR **TEL.** *01945-583463* **OWNER** *The National Trust* **HOURS** *House and garden early April–end Oct, Sat–Sun, Wed and Bank Holiday Mons, 2–5.30p.m. (last adm. 5p.m.). Garden only Mon–Tue, 2–5.30p.m.* **ENTRANCE** *£3, children £1.25 (on garden only days £2, children £1)* **DIRECTIONS** *On N bank of River Nene, in Wisbech (B1441), ¾m from A47 (limited parking available 10 mins from House)*

SPRING SUMMER AUTUMN WINTER

Access Café

Graceful Georgian houses lining the River Nene at Wisbech belonged to merchants who traded on the then navigable waters, when the town was a thriving port. Peckover House is a classic example, formerly belonging to a prosperous Quaker family, and its garden is a rare and spacious survival of a Victorian layout, covering two acres. Within you will see a rustic summerhouse, yew topiaries, fine specimen trees, including an old *Ginkgo biloba* and fan palms on broad lawns, summer bedding and a fine orangery complete with ancient orange trees. The potted plant displays of ivies, ferns, aspidistras, primulas, geraniums, gloxinias and Malmaison carnations are a notable Victorian feature in the glasshouse.

And also...

Bulbeck Foundry, Reach Road Industrial Estate, Burwell CB5 0AH (tel. 01638-743153), manufactures English lead statuary, such as fountains, urns, planters and troughs in a range of traditional designs, and also undertakes restoration work of lead antiques. Catalogue free on request. Open Mon–Fri, 8.30a.m.–5.30p.m., but phone before visiting.

Elm House Nursery, PO Box 25, Wisbech PE13 2RF (tel. 01945-581511) specializes in young (plug) plants by mail. Chrysanthemums are a speciality, but there are also osteospermums, scented-leaf pelargoniums, fuchsias and garden pinks, and a good range of plants for containers and hanging baskets.

Elton Hall, Elton, Peterborough PE8 6SH (tel. 01832-280468). The gardens contain herbaceous borders, old roses and fine trees. Open Spring Bank Holiday Sun and Mon; June, Wed; July and Aug, Wed, Thurs, Sun and Aug Bank Holiday Mon (parties by appointment on other days), 2–5p.m. Entrance (house and garden) £4.50, children (15 and under) free (garden £2.50). The **Bressingham Plant Centre (tel. 01832-280058)** at Elton Hall opens daily, 9a.m.–5.30p.m. (closed 25–26 Dec), offering alpines, conifers, climbers and herbaceous perennials in the old walled kitchen garden. Entrance free.

Columbines, granny's bonnets, granny's nightcaps – call them what you will, aquilegias are enchanting flowers of damp meadows, woodlands and alpine pastures, tremendously varied in shape, colour and size. John Drake keeps a National Collection of them in his attractive, windy garden outside Cambridge at **Hardwicke House, Fen Ditton CB5 8TF (tel. 01223-292246)**, open by appointment and for the National Gardens Scheme. Aquilegia plants and seeds are also available by mail (catalogue 70p).

The Herbary, Mile End Road, Prickwillow, Ely CB7 4SJ (tel. 01353-688392), sells fresh-cut culinary herbs, edible flowers and speciality leaf-salads by mail, amounting to around 20 varieties. The price list is free.

Monksilver Nursery, Oakington Road, Cottenham CB4 4TW (tel. 01954-251555), is a plant connoisseur's dream nursery full of rare and choice plants, tantalisingly seldom open to visitors but redeemed by a mail order catalogue (6 × 1st-class stamps). Herbaceous perennials, particularly pulmonarias, lamiums, mildew-resistant monardas and galeobdolon feature, with new plants from recent Far Eastern expeditions, and unusual shrubs. Open March–June, and Oct, Fri–Sat only, 10a.m.–4p.m.

Wimpole Hall, Arrington, Royston SG8 0BW (tel. 01223-207257), is the largest country house in Cambridgeshire, an imposing 18th-century mansion set in park landscaped first by Charles Bridgeman (in the 1720s) followed by Capability Brown (*q.v.*) and Humphry Repton (*q.v.*), with a model farm attached. There are many wonderful trees in the 350-acre park, and its colourful parterre garden was recently restored by the National Trust. Garden open late March–Oct, Tues–Thurs, and Sat–Sun, 10.30a.m.–5p.m., and daily July–Aug. Also Bank Holiday Mons. Entrance £2, children £1 (£5.20 and £2.25 for hall and garden).

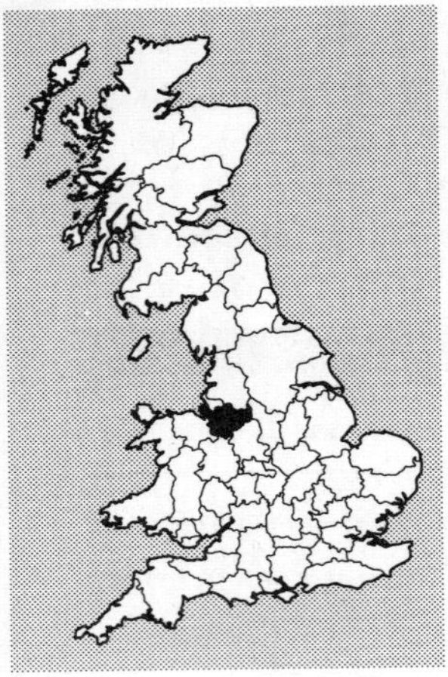

Cheshire

MAP NO. 5

The fertile Cheshire plain is rich farming country, with hedged and tree-lined pastures, watered by countless small canals and meres. Much of the county is spread over low ground, with gentle undulations here and there, and trees grow well in this region of rich soil and relatively high rainfall. It changes character to the east, where steep moorland rises on the edge of the Pennine range and sheep graze the hillsides. The ancient and prosperous city of Chester was founded by the Romans, who built the foundations of its two-mile city wall.

ALTRINCHAM

Dunham Massey

Altrincham WA14 4SJ **TEL.** *0161-941 1025* **OWNER** *The National Trust* **HOURS** *Garden: early April–early Nov, daily, 11a.m.–5.30p.m. (last adm. 5p.m.); park: all year, daily* **ENTRANCE** *Garden £3, children £1.50; park only £2.80 per car* **DIRECTIONS** *3m SW of Altrincham, off A56, signposted*

SPRING SUMMER AUTUMN WINTER

Access | Gift Shop | Café

The 30 acres of fine gardens are embraced by a 350-acre park within a vast estate. The gardens demonstrate the layered effect of different periods: there is an Elizabethan mount, a moat lake, an 18th-century orangery, well-preserved Victorian pleasure grounds with extensive shrubberies, and an Edwardian parterre.

Its appeal lies in the skilful blending of these elements, especially the streamside and woodland plantings. The rhododendron collection, ribbons of cobalt blue meconopsis, and contrasting swathes of pink persicaria are some of the spring-into-early-summer enchantments. The standard of upkeep is also exceptionally high.

KNUTSFORD

Tatton Park

Knutsford WA16 6QN **TEL.** *01565-654822* **OWNER** *The National Trust* **HOURS** *April–Sept, park daily, 10a.m.–6p.m., garden Tues–Sun, 10.30a.m.–5p.m.; Oct–March, park Tues–Sun, 11a.m.–5p.m., garden Tues–Sun, 11a.m.–4p.m.* **ENTRANCE** *Park £2.80 per vehicle, garden £2.80, children £1.80* **DIRECTIONS** *3½m N of Knutsford, 4m S of Altrincham, 5m from M6 Jct 19. Well signposted on A556*

SPRING SUMMER AUTUMN WINTER

Gift Shop · Café · DON'T MISS

This 60-acre garden is a sumptuous period piece, summing up many of the gardening ideals of the 19th century. Its neo-classical mansion of pinky-grey sandstone gazes over terraced lawns to a swanky Italianate parterre (probably designed by Sir Joseph Paxton) filled with seasonal bedding plants. There are two very fine glasshouses – an orangery built in 1818 that is still used for nurturing citrus fruits, and a handsome fernery which houses a collection of prehistoric-looking dicksonia tree ferns from the antipodes. There are further formal flower gardens, with mixed shrub and herbaceous borders, rose beds and neatly clipped yews.

The most celebrated part of Tatton Park is its Oriental Garden, laid out in 1910 by Japanese landscapers, with a still, dark pool fed by four streams. It is richly planted with azaleas and acers, ferns, irises, willows and mosses. Flat stone bridges cross the waters leading to a ceremonial tea-house with a thatched roof. It is a place of abundance and tranquillity, surrounded by some of the magnificent trees of the park.

MALPAS

Cholmondeley Castle

Malpas SY14 8AH **TEL.** *01829-720383* **OWNER** *The Marchioness of Cholmondeley* **HOURS** *April–Sept, Wed–Thurs, 12 noon–5p.m.; Sun, Good Fri and Bank Holiday Mons, 12 noon–5.30p.m.* **ENTRANCE** *£2.50, OAPs £2, children 75p* **DIRECTIONS** *Off A49 Tarporley–Whitchurch road*

SPRING SUMMER AUTUMN WINTER

Access | Gift Shop | Café | Plant Shop | DON'T MISS

Cholmondeley Castle is an early 19th-century gothic creation of pink and grey sandstone, with pointed windows and battlemented roof. It sits on the summit of a gently rising hill, surrounded by 30 acres of tree-filled gardens, looking benevolently onto its own cricket-ground and 300-year-old cedars. There are some formal gardens near the house, with roses and herbaceous borders, but the woodland and water gardens are the really enchanting part of Cholmondeley.

There are magnolias and weeping beeches, thickets of bamboo and glorious rhododendrons and azaleas. Late spring is the best time to see them, when you will also be enchanted by the pocket-handkerchief tree, *Davidia involucrata,* in bloom, in a sea of white narcissi and bluebells. The Temple Garden is like a willow-pattern design come to life, with islands in a serpentine lake, bridges and

THE MARTON OAK

The great oak at Marton, three miles north of Congleton on the A34, is one of the largest old oak trees in the country and perhaps it takes the record for being the strangest. Its trunk long ago split vertically into four separate pieces, with a girth totalling 58 feet at the foot of the tree. According to local lore, when the tree split it made a convenient pound in which a local farmer kept his bull. It now provides an unusual enclosure for a wendy house, which has been erected right inside the trunk at ground level.

waterfalls, twisty-branched cedars and tiered Scots pines. Not consciously oriental, but conveying the tranquillity of an Eastern garden. The traditional kitchen garden is run organically, with neat rows of vegetables and caged fruits, and there is a section offering home-grown azaleas and other ornamental plants for sale.

NANTWICH

Bridgemere Garden World

Bridgemere, Nantwich CW5 7QB TEL. *01270-521100* OWNER *John Ravenscroft* HOURS *Open all year, daily, except 25–26 Dec, 10a.m.–8p.m. (5p.m. winter)* ENTRANCE *£1.50, OAPs/children £1* DIRECTIONS *On A51 S of Nantwich*

SPRING SUMMER AUTUMN WINTER

Access | Gift Shop | Café | Plant Shop | Nursery | DON'T MISS

The owners claim Bridgemere offers the greatest gardening day out in Europe; that is a lot to live up to, but it is certainly the most impressive garden centre I have seen anywhere, well organised with a huge range of stock, including many choice and unusual plants. Beyond is a large area devoted to 20 display gardens, including well-landscaped rock and water gardens, a sumptuous rose garden, gardens of herbaceous flowers and annuals, rhododendrons, winter gardens, and several Chelsea flower show exhibits, rebuilt here. There are also huge displays of conservatory and houseplants, a children's play area and spacious restaurant.

NESTON

Ness Botanic Gardens

Ness, Neston L64 4AY TEL. *0151-353 0123* OWNER *University of Liverpool* HOURS *March–Oct, daily, 9.30a.m.–dusk; Nov–Feb, daily, 9.30a.m.–4p.m.* ENTRANCE *£4, OAPs/students £3.50, children under 18 free if*

accompanied, unaccompanied £3.50. Guide dogs only
DIRECTIONS *Signposted off A540 Chester–Hoylake road*

SPRING SUMMER AUTUMN WINTER

Access Gift Shop Café Plant Shop

This interesting garden is owned and run by Liverpool University, yet it retains much of the ambience of the private, domestic garden that it once was. It was started in 1898 by Arthur Bulley, a Liverpool cotton broker and founder of the seed merchants Bees of Chester. A keen collector of plants from distant parts of the world, Bulley launched the plant-hunting careers of George Forrest and Frank Kingdon-Ward by helping to finance their seed-collecting expeditions to western China. Consequently, oriental trees and shrubs, including magnolias, rhododendrons and Himalayan birches are well represented here, and Kingdon-Ward's exquisite blue Himalayan poppies, *Meconopsis betonicifolia*.

The undulating site at Ness enjoys fine views across the Dee estuary to the Clwyd hills, and its 62 acres embrace a variety of soil types. There is a good collection of roses, an azalea border, a vast herbaceous border, a large rock garden and one of the best heather gardens in the country which is at its most brilliant in late summer.

NORTHWICH

Arley Hall

Great Budworth, Northwich CW9 6NA TEL. *01565-777353*
OWNER *Viscount Ashbrook* HOURS *April–Sept, Tues–Sun, 1–5p.m.* ENTRANCE *£3.60, OAPs £3, children £1.80*
DIRECTIONS *5m W of Knutsford*

SPRING SUMMER AUTUMN WINTER

Gift Shop Café Plant Shop DON'T MISS

On my first visit to Arley Hall I had the great good fortune to be shown its grounds by the late Lady Ashbrook, who had run the 12-acre gardens since 1939, and by Tom Acton, her head gardener who arrived in 1940. Both of them knew every plant, and the experience of seeing the gardens through their eyes (each of them having been there for more than 50 years) was unforgettable.

Most of the garden's present layout was done by Lady Ashbrook's great-grandparents in the 1840s. They made Arley's famous double herbaceous borders in 1846, when Queen Victoria had been on the throne less than 10 years. 'It was called the Alcove Walk,' said Lady Ashbrook, 'because the term "herbaceous border" hadn't yet been invented.' The two rows of mixed perennial flowers are almost certainly the first herbaceous borders ever planted, and they have changed relatively little over 150 years.

They are reached via the straight Furlong Walk, which runs for ⅛ mile above a ha-ha overlooking the fine park. The rest of the gardens are less labour-intensive than in Victorian days, but still include topiarised holm oaks, a herb garden, scented garden, roses and shrubberies, a vinery, and woodland grove of ornamental shrubs and trees, underplanted with spring bulbs. An annual garden festival is held here over a weekend in late July, when the borders are going full tilt.

STOCKPORT

Lyme Park

Disley, Stockport SK12 2NX **TEL.** *01663-762023* **OWNER** *The National Trust* **HOURS** *Park daily, gardens April–Oct, daily, 11a.m.–5p.m (Wed–Thurs, 1–4p.m.) ; Nov–mid-Dec, Sat–Sun only, 12 noon–3p.m.* **ENTRANCE** *Garden £2, children £1, car £3.30* **DIRECTIONS** *6½ m SE of Stockport on A6, just W of Disley*

SPRING SUMMER AUTUMN WINTER

Access | Gift Shop | Café

The grounds of Lyme Park are for ever etched in millions of viewers' minds as Pemberley, home of Mr Darcy in the BBC's popular adaptation of *Pride and Prejudice*. According to Vicky Dawson, the property manager, visitors of all nationalities want to know where Mr Darcy went for a dip, and whether they can see his wet shirt. (Alas, we can't.)

The property is one of the National Trust's most dazzling jewels, with a huge palladian mansion and 17 acres of fabulous gardens within a 1400-acre landscaped park grazed by red and fallow deer. It also enjoys breathtaking views of the Pennines and the lowland Cheshire plain. There is a formal, patterned Dutch garden with ivy-edged beds, infilled with bright spring and summer bedding. A sunken garden on the north side is more discreetly planted with trees and shrubs. An early 19th-century orangery houses a splendid fig tree and two enormous camellias, dating from Victorian times, plus a scattering of other fragrant and leafy conservatory stalwarts. Outside are terraced beds and a rose garden, leading on to less formal grounds with lawns and woodland. The lake and lime avenue are remnants of a 17th-century garden that has been absorbed into the gentler contours of the great 18th-century park.

And also...

Cheshire Herbs, Fourfields, Forest Road, nr Tarporley CW6 9ES (tel. 01829-760578), is a specialist herb nursery selling pot-grown plants (around 180 different herb varieties), with a small shop on the premises selling herb-related products and gifts. Herb seeds only are sold by mail order (catalogue on request). Open all year except the Christmas–New Year period, daily, 10a.m.–5p.m.

Spring and autumn are the best times to visit **Granada Arboretum, Jodrell Bank, Macclesfield SK11 9DL (tel. 01477-571339)**. Occupying a level site of 35 acres, it has National Collections of malus (crab apples particularly) and sorbus (mountain ash). There are also many alders, birches, pines and other trees and a large collection of heathers. Open mid-March–late Oct, daily, 10.30a.m.–5.30p.m. Nov–mid-Mar, Sat–Sun only, 11a.m.–4.30p.m. Entrance £4, OAPs £2.80, children £2, family ticket £11.50 (includes visits to science centre and planetarium).

Late May, rhododendron time, is when **Hare Hill Garden, Garden Lodge, Over Alderley, Macclesfield SK10 4QB (tel. 01625-828981)**, is at its most splendid. Covering 10 acres, it has a walled former kitchen garden, now grassed over and planted with flower borders and tender shrubs trained on the walls. Unusual hollies feature in its woodland. Open April–Oct, Wed–Thurs, Sat–Sun and Bank Holiday Mons, 10a.m.–5.30p.m.; also daily for 3 weeks from mid-May–early June, for rhododendrons. Entrance £2.50, children £1.25.

Little Moreton Hall, Congleton CW12 4SD (tel. 01260-272018), owned by the National Trust, has a one-and-a-half-acre formal garden surrounding one of the most celebrated timber-framed houses in England (the property was used in the TV filming of Daniel Defoe's *Moll Flanders*). Its knot garden is based on an Elizabethan design and there are historic herbs, vegetables and herbaceous flowers. Open mid-March–end Oct, Wed–Sun, 12 noon–5.30p.m.; Bank Holiday Mons, 11a.m.–5.30p.m.; Nov–mid-Dec, Sat–Sun, 12 noon–4p.m. Entrance £4, children £2, family ticket £10.

Peover Hall, Over Peover, Knutsford WA16 9HW (tel. 01565-722656), has five walled gardens within its 15 acres. They include a White Garden with box topiary, a lily-pond court, a rose garden, herb garden and pink-flower garden, surrounded by an 18th-century landscape garden with fabulous trees and pretty pavilion. There is also a woodland dell with rhododendrons and magnolias, and a pleached hornbeam walk by the churchyard. Do not miss the magnificent stables with carved stalls and an ornate plaster ceiling. Open May–Sept, Thurs and Mons (but not Bank Holidays), 2–4.30p.m. Entrance £2, children £1.

Stapeley Water Gardens, London Road, Stapeley, Nantwich CW5 7LH (tel. 01270-623868), displays huge ranges of waterlilies and other aquatic plants in both outdoor and indoor water gardens. Although a tourist spectacle, it is also somewhere to buy anything and practically everything to make ponds and water features at home. Open all year, daily, except 25 Dec, 9a.m.–6p.m.

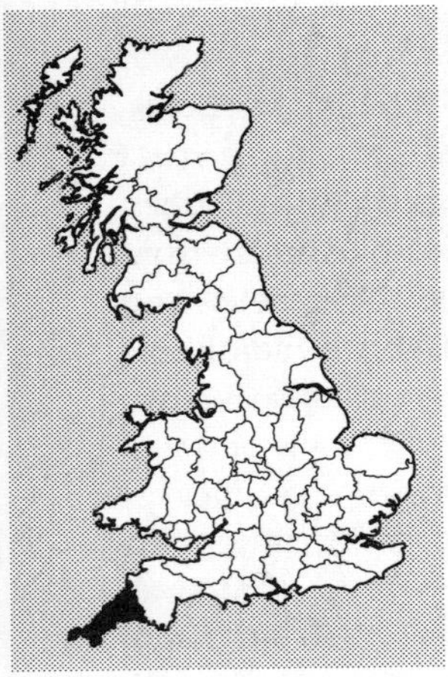

Cornwall

MAP NO. 1

Resembling a long, bony foot stepping gingerly into the deep Atlantic, the rugged Cornish peninsula sits in splendid isolation in England's extreme south-west. Its wind-blasted cliffs are carpeted with tough heathers and thrift; the 'nut-smell of gorse and honey-smell of ling / Waft out to sea the freshness of spring' as John Betjeman observed.

Plunging, sheltered valleys provide homes for spectacular exotics such as tree ferns from Australasia, and lofty rhododendrons and magnolias from the slopes of the Himalayas. For centuries the county's wealth stemmed from tin-mining and shipping, and the coastal area around the port of Falmouth is rich in famous sub-tropical gardens that have been maturing for 100 years or more. Cornwall celebrates its horticultural diversity in its own Festival of Gardens, when around 60 properties open their gates to the public (some for only a day or two) between mid-March and the end of May.

FALMOUTH

Glendurgan

Mawnan Smith, nr Falmouth TR11 5JZ **TEL.** *01326-250906* **OWNER** *The National Trust* **HOURS** *March–Oct, Tues–Sat and Bank Holiday Mons (closed Good Friday), 10.30a.m.–5.30p.m. (last adm. 4.30p.m.)* **ENTRANCE** *£3.20, children £1.60 (under 5s free), family ticket £8* **DIRECTIONS** *4m SW of Falmouth, ½m SW of Mawnan Smith on road to Helford Passage*

SPRING SUMMER AUTUMN WINTER

Gift Shop | Café | Plant Shop

Both Glendurgan and its next-door-neighbour, Trebah (*q.v.*), were created in the 1830s by the Fox family, Quaker merchants with shipping interests in Falmouth. The 26-acre gardens descend dramatically from their respective hilltop houses, through sheltered valleys to the Helford waters beyond. Glendurgan boasts a pair of vast tulip trees, a highly unusual laurel maze, glorious spring displays from magnolias, rhododendrons, primroses, bluebells and daffodils and woodland walks down to the hamlet of Durgan (where there are National Trust cottages to rent), at the water's edge.

Poolside gunneras with their vast, spiny parasol leaves are another feature of Glendurgan, and winding paths on each side of the steep valley allow intermittent, focused views of the garden spread out below. The recently built visitor centre cum entrance will be welcomed by many, although I felt it, and the rather manicured garden paths, rather diminished the garden's previously more spirited atmosphere.

FALMOUTH

Trebah Garden

Mawnan Smith, nr Falmouth TR11 5JZ **TEL.** *01326-250448* **OWNER** *Trebah Garden Trust* **HOURS** *Open all year, daily, 10.30a.m.–6.30p.m. (last adm. 5p.m.)* **ENTRANCE** *£3.20, children (age 5–16) £1; Nov–Feb £1 and 50p* **DIRECTIONS** *4m SW of Falmouth, 1m SW of Mawnan Smith (signposted from A39/A394 Treliever Cross roundabout; 500yds W of Glendurgan Garden)*

SPRING SUMMER AUTUMN WINTER

Gift Shop · Café · Plant Shop · DON'T MISS

When Major Tony Hibbert and his wife bought Trebah in 1980, they envisaged spending their retirement 'sipping gin and tonic on the terrace and doing a spot of sailing' in the Helford Estuary at the bottom of the garden. The local Gardens Trust soon informed them, however, that they possessed an important historic garden with many rare plants thought lost in the undergrowth for 40 years.

Sportingly, the Hibberts began restoring their 25-acre ravine, which descends 200ft from the 18th-century house down to a private beach.

It is now, says Tony, 'like a corner of the Himalayas only better cared for', with a stream cascading over waterfalls, ponds of giant Koi carp surrounded by exotic waterside plants, towering rhododendrons of scarlet and pastel shades, and two acres of brilliant blue and white hydrangeas. Trebah has glades of 100-year-old giant tree ferns, which form the biggest collection in Europe, and also boasts vast clumps of 18ft-high *Gunnera manicata* with leaves 10ft across. Unlike many gardens regularly open to the public, Trebah is allowed a hint of wildness and eccentricity, which contributes greatly to its appeal. There are garden trails and a thrilling Tarzan's Camp for children, and a good plant sales area.

MARAZION

St Michael's Mount

Marazion, nr Penzance TR17 0HT **TEL.** *01736-710507* **OWNER** *The National Trust and Lord St Levan* **HOURS** *April–Oct, Mon–Fri, 10.30a.m.–5.30p.m. (last adm. 4.45p.m.), Nov–March, Mon, Wed and Fri (subject to weather and tide), guided tours only (ring first). Also open for charity most summer weekends, when NT members are asked to pay for admission* **ENTRANCE** *April–May, gardens only £1.50, castle and gardens £3.90, children £1.95, family ticket £10* **DIRECTIONS** *½m from the shore at Marazion, ½m S of A394. Foot access over cobbled causeway at low tide (unsuitable for wheelchairs and prams, etc.). In summer there is a ferry, weather permitting (for ferry info. tel. 01736-710265)*

SPRING SUMMER AUTUMN WINTER

Café Plant Shop

Limited access adds to the Mount's air of isolation and mystery. The Revd William Borlase wrote in 1762 that it was 'Anciently only a monastery, in tumultuous and warlike times a fort and a monastery together, since the Reformation a fort only, and now neither fort nor monastery, but a neat comfortable and secure dwelling house'.

The forbidding granite house sits on top of the rocky outcrop, and much of the garden is made from small terraces reached by narrow, ascending paths on the cliff face. Head gardener Roy Powell was a merchant seaman before he switched to terra firma and horticulture. Yet even now he is almost at sea, cast away on this precipitous island where much of the gardening has to be done by abseiling down the cliff faces.

Although exposed to constant winds and salt-laden air, sub-tropical flowers abound throughout the year, having rooted themselves into the rocky crevices. Pelargoniums, fuchsias, osteospermums, hebes and euryops thrive on the usually frost-free slopes; Hottentot figs and around 30 different mesembryanthemums broadcast their vivid, daisy-like flowers from the crevices. Red-hot pokers have spread like wildfire on the lower slopes, and spring sees the island under a quilt of wild daffodils.

PENZANCE

Morrab Gardens

Morrab Road, Penzance **TEL.** *01736-362341* **OWNER** *Penwith District Council* **HOURS** *Daily all year, 9a.m.–dusk* **ENTRANCE** *Free* **DIRECTIONS** *In Penzance town centre, close to the seafront*

SPRING SUMMER AUTUMN WINTER

Access

Penzance enjoys views of Mount's Bay and St Michael's Mount (*q.v.*) from its long promenade, while its narrow streets and Regency squares boast some charming architecture. *Morrab* is Cornish for 'sea-shore' and these three-acre gardens, close to the town centre and seafront, were developed by Penzance Corporation in 1889 as a public amenity following a nationwide competition. It was won by a London landscaper who received a prize of £21 and the pleasure of seeing his designs realised.

Morrab Gardens retain much of their Victorian aura, with winding paths and plenty of traditional benches on which to eat sandwiches and take in the view. Large cabbage palms, Abyssinian bananas, sophoras and libertias are among the exotic features of this surprising and pleasing urban park.

PENZANCE

Trengwainton

Nr Penzance TR20 8SA TEL. *01736-363021 or 68410* OWNER *The National Trust* HOURS *Early March–Oct, Wed–Sat and Bank Holiday Mons, 10.30a.m.–5.30p.m. (5p.m. in March and Oct), last adm. ½hr before closing* ENTRANCE *£3, children (under 16) £1.50* DIRECTIONS *2m NW of Penzance, ½m W of Heamoor on B3312, or ½m off A3071*

SPRING SUMMER AUTUMN WINTER

Access | Gift Shop | Café | Plant Shop

Large, rare magnolias, camellias and rhododendrons planted earlier this century contribute to the magnificence of Trengwainton. A gurgling stream runs close to the carriage drive, its banks planted with skunk cabbages whose smell is an acquired taste, strongest in spring when the cowled flower spikes appear. These banks also feature white arum lilies, masses of primulas – crimson *P. pulverulenta* and *P. japonica*, and yellow *P. helodoxa* – and shady tree ferns from Australia.

The 25-acre south-facing site, looking over Mount's Bay (with a view of St Michael's Mount in the distance) particularly favours tender plants such as the vivid blue Chatham Island forget-me-nots. Brick-walled gardens, built in the 19th century, feature unusual, sloping beds, built to raise early produce for the kitchen. They now provide a sheltering home for plant rarities.

MAGNOLIA MAGIC

Exquisite and fragrant-flowered magnolias are among the oldest plants on Earth, having changed little in 100 million years. They thrive in the acidic soils and humid, rain-speckled atmosphere of Cornwall, the oldest specimens offering their glorious, waxy-petalled blooms from lofty branches, best seen in the great valley gardens which often allow good views from above. The first magnolia, M. virginiana, *arrived in England from Virginia in 1688. The shiny-leaved evergreen* M. grandiflora *followed in the early 18th century, but it was not until 1789 that the first Chinese magnolias reached these shores and nearly 100 years later that* M. stellata *arrived from Japan. Among the most spectacular plants in this genus are* M. campbellii, *brought from China in 1864, and* M. sargentiana robusta, *with pendent, large-petalled flowers 23cm (9in) in diameter, one of many outstanding species introduced by the plant-hunter E.H. Wilson (q.v.) in 1908.* M. denudata, *with elegant, pure white goblet flowers, has been cherished in China for at least 1400 years, being grown in temple gardens as a symbol of candour, purity and the feminine (Yin) principle.*

REDRUTH

Burncoose Nurseries and Garden

Gwennap, Redruth TR16 6BJ **TEL.** *01209-861112* **OWNER** *C.H. Williams* **HOURS** *Daily all year, 9a.m.–5p.m. (Sun 11a.m.–5p.m.)* **ENTRANCE** *£2* **DIRECTIONS** *3m S of Redruth on A393, between Lanner and Ponsanooth (signposted)*

SPRING SUMMER AUTUMN WINTER

Access Café Nursery

This is a must for plant lovers. Well-displayed, well-grown shrubs and trees in stock include many rare and slightly tender species unlikely to be found elsewhere in British nurseries. Varieties of camellia, leptospermum, magnolia, hydrangea and pittosporum are very well represented, as are Japanese acers and bamboos. A peaceful, 30-acre woodland garden (awash with bluebells in spring) adjoins the nursery, featuring broad collections of acid-loving shrubs and around 25 species of bamboo.

ST AUSTELL

Caerhays Castle Garden

Caerhays, Gorran, St Austell PL26 6LY TEL. *01872-501310* OWNER *F.J. Williams* HOURS *Mid-March–early May, Mon–Fri, 11a.m.–4p.m.* ENTRANCE *House and garden £6, garden only £3, children £1.50* DIRECTIONS *In Caerhays village, 10m S of St Austell on the coast by Porthluney Cove (parking at beach car park)*

SPRING SUMMER AUTUMN WINTER

Café Plant Shop

A thrilling place for springtime woodland walks, where it is essential to peer into the treetops and discover pale-pink magnolia flowers the size of dinner plates, all the more glorious against a clear blue sky.

The romantic, early 19th-century gothic castle of Caerhays was built for the Trevanions by John Nash. However, John Trevanion's fortune ran out before the landscaping could be completed, and he fled to Paris to escape his creditors. Subsequently, the wealthy Williams family, with mining interests in the county, bought the castle and began to plant the garden. It is now famous for being intimately connected with the intrepid explorations of E.H. Wilson (*q.v.*) and George Forrest (*q.v.*) who brought back wondrous new shrubs and trees from the Far East. Like so many Cornish gardens, its woodland stretches down to the sea, and is filled with plants which date particularly from 1896, when J.C. Williams retired from politics to garden in earnest.

The 100-acre garden's impressive collection includes vast magnolias dating from this period (notably *M. campbellii* ssp. *mollicomata* and *M. veitchii*) and the famous *williamsii* hybrid camellias, bred by J.C. himself, who also did valuable work in hybridising daffodils and rhododendrons.

ST IVES

The Barbara Hepworth Museum and Sculpture Garden

Barnoon Hill, St Ives TR26 1TG **TEL.** *01736-796226* **ADMINISTERED BY** *The Tate Gallery, St Ives* **HOURS** *Oct–March, Tues–Sat, 11a.m.–5p.m., April–Sept, Mon–Sat , 11a.m.–7p.m., Sun and Bank Holiday Mons, 11a.m.–5p.m.* **ENTRANCE** *Museum only £3, concessions £1.50, Tate Gallery only £3.50, concessions £2, combined ticket £5, concessions £3* **DIRECTIONS** *In the centre of St Ives (sign-posted). Parking in public car parks some distance away*

SPRING SUMMER AUTUMN WINTER

Gift Shop Café

From the 19th century onwards the picturesque fishing village of St Ives, clustered on a steep hillside, became a colony for artists seeking inspiration from the landscape and the sea (don't miss the new Tate Gallery nearby on the seafront, which also serves good food in its roof terrace café).

The sculptress Barbara Hepworth is among the many famous people who took up residence in St Ives; her studio is now a fascinating museum, with many of her nature-inspired sculptures displayed among the cabbage palms and exotic flowers in her ¼-acre walled garden.

'Here in Cornwall,' she wrote, 'I have a background which links with Yorkshire [her birthplace] in the natural shape of stone structure and fertility, and it links with Italy because of the intensity of light and colour. Here I can carve out of doors all the year round – a background for which I am grateful – for I have always been preoccupied with man's position in landscape and his relation to the structure of nature.'

The garden presents a marvellous, atmospheric Mediterranean-style setting for Hepworth's work, with winding paths threading through thickets of bamboo, flowering cherries, camellias, myrtles, a ginkgo tree and ground-covering geraniums. Hepworth's bright studio opens into the garden and is kept as it was at her death in 1975, with work in progress on a trestle table surrounded by tools and plaster-stained overalls hanging on pegs behind.

OLD GARDEN ARTEFACTS

Keith Webb and Mary Porter run ***Farm and Garden Bygones at Padstow Antiques, 21–23 New Street PL28 8EA (tel.01841-532914) (Padstow Antiques and their display garden are just above St Petroc's Hotel, at the end of the one-way system).*** *Their stock includes a large range of old granite troughs, millstones and staddle stones, old garden tools, wooden barrows, statuary and plenty of old terracotta oil jars imported from Spain, Greece and Morocco. Open all year, Mon–Sat, 10a.m.–5p.m., but Keith says phone first if you're making a special visit as they close the shop when they're out buying new stock.*

TRESCO

The Tresco Abbey Gardens

Tresco, Isles of Scilly TR24 0QQ **TEL.** *01720-422849* **OWNER** *Mr R. A. Dorrien Smith* **HOURS** *Open all year, daily, 10a.m.–4p.m.* **ENTRANCE** *£5, accompanied children free; weekly tickets (7 days) £10* **DIRECTIONS** *From Penzance Heliport by helicopter (for reservations tel. 01736-363871), from St Mary's island by launch or by steamer from Penzance to St Mary's (tel. 0345 105555)*

SPRING SUMMER AUTUMN WINTER

Gift Shop · Café · Plant Shop · DON'T MISS

Cast away at sea, 28 miles from the craggy cliffs of Land's End, the Isles of Scilly endure, enriched by their tempestuous maritime surroundings. Augustus Smith, a young landowner from Hertfordshire, took out a lease on these remote isles in 1834 and immediately built his new home, Tresco Abbey (alluding to the nearby ruined Benedictine priory). The house exterior was described by a

Celebrity Choice

Roy Lancaster, plant hunter, author and television presenter

'For me there are two great things in the world: mountains and the sea. Mountains are my favourite – you have to climb them, to explore them. And that is why I like **Trebah** (q.v.)*. It's not mountainous, of course, but the depth of the valley is very much like a mountainside, and it has very good mountain flora, especially its Himalayan and Chinese content – the big rhododendrons, bamboos, a huge* Davidia involucrata*, one of my favourite trees. It's a primeval world. It is also about foliage, and scale. To stand by the house at Trebah and look down the valley, glimpsing what appears to be the sea at the bottom, is very exciting. Then there is the huge gunnera grove in the valley. The path through it is very carefully cleaned up around the plants so you can see the huge rhizomes, very primeval looking indeed, and I love the lurid green light that shines through the gigantic leaves when you are standing under them. The plant content at Trebah takes in so many elements I've enjoyed in wild places. It's a rough, jagged garden, and one I love visiting.'*

visitor in 1843 as having 'a very respectable, if not picturesque appearance, with just enough workmanship to prevent it looking commonplace, but not enough to give it that cold, formal, workhouse-like appearance which is the great defect of more magnificent mansions'.

Smith also started in haste on the 16-acre gardens, and a vast range of exotic plants from the southern hemisphere is now grown here, including scarlet banksias from Western Australia, king proteas from South Africa (regularly in bloom), together with New Zealand flame trees, silver trees from Cape Province, and metallic-turquoise puyas from Chile. They thrive under the warming influence of the Gulf Stream and the south-facing slope on which the gardens lie.

According to Mike Nelhams, the curator, wind shelter is the critical factor. It is provided by thickets of cypresses, pines, eucalyptus and evergreen oaks to supplement Smith's original plantings of Monterey cypress which are reaching the end of their life. A steep, stone stairway (lined with Canary Islands palm trees and hedgehog-like furcraeas from Mexico) cuts through the middle of the garden, ascending the hill to provide access to the garden's richly planted terraces. Succulent aeoniums cover rocky cliff walls, joined by brilliant mesembryanthemums and spiny agaves. A recently made Mediterranean garden and a fascinating collection of ornate figureheads salvaged from ships wrecked long ago add to the allure of this unique place. A day trip is interesting, but a longer stay (there are self-catering cottages, a hotel and an inn on the island) reveal more of the island's charms.

TRURO

Trelissick

Feock, nr Truro TR3 6QL TEL. *01872-862090* OWNER *The National Trust* HOURS *Early March–Oct, Mon–Sat, 10.30a.m.–5.30p.m., Sun, 12.30a.m.–5.30p.m. (5p.m. in March and Oct), last adm. ½hr before closing. Woodland walks only, throughout year* ENTRANCE *£4, children £2, family ticket £10* DIRECTIONS *4m S of Truro, on both sides of B3289, above King Harry Ferry (for cars and pedestrians)*

SPRING SUMMER AUTUMN WINTER

Access · Gift Shop · Café · Plant Shop

The blissfully peaceful 25-acre garden of Trelissick is set on a majestic eminence above a broad estuary known as the Carrick Roads, a deep water anchorage for Falmouth Harbour. Large ships and tankers often provide curious eye-catchers from the upper slopes of the garden.

Trelissick's undulating park was planted in the 1820s by Ralph Allen Daniel, who was so rich (from tin-mining) that he was known as 'Guinea-a-minute' Daniel. It is said he could ride all the way to Truro without leaving his property. Fruit trees were added by a later owner, but most of the present garden is early 20th-century planting and features massed hydrangeas, rhododendrons and camellias (*de rigueur* in this county), underplanted with cyclamen and erythroniums, a dell with bog-loving plants and fine tree ferns. The extensive woods are streaked magenta by the abundant foxgloves in late spring. Near the entrance, a splendid gothic water tower with pointed roof and circular rooms would suit latter-day Rapunzels, and can be rented from the Trust.

And also...

Around 3000 different plants are offered at the **Duchy of Cornwall Nursery, Penlyne, Cott Road, Lostwithiel PL22 08W (tel. 01208-872668).** The emphasis is on the acid-loving or slightly tender plants that thrive in Cornwall, including hydrangeas, myrtles, echiums and Australasian shrubs. The nursery is well run and prints a catalogue, £1, but there is no mail order.

The 'lost' gardens of **Heligan**, **Pentewan, St Austell PL26 6EN (tel. 01726-844157)**, were buried under brambles and the rampant evergreenery of rhododendrons when Tim Smit, a former archaeologist turned rock music producer, first visited (machete in hand) eight years ago. The 57-acre gardens had been untouched since 1914 when the Tremayne family left and the house was commandeered by the War Department. Extensive restorations since 1991 have seen the reinstatement of walled kitchen gardens (with melon and pineapple pits), a vinery, grotto, extensive rockery, Italian garden with pool, and summerhouse, and much more. A wilder, lost valley with lakes is now being reclaimed in this imaginative and awesome project. Open all year, daily, 10a.m.–6p.m. (last adm. 4.30p.m). Entrance £4.50, OAPs £4, children £2, family ticket £12.

The garden at **Lamorran House**, **Upper Castle Road, St Mawes TR2 5BZ (tel. 01326-270800, or evening 01872-530204)**, is the passion and creation of Robert Dudley-Cooke, who has filled his steep, four-acre hillside with intimate glades featuring over 500 azaleas, 250 rhododendrons, sumptuous collections of plants from the southern hemisphere, Italian-style masonry and tranquil pools. Open April–Sept, Wed and Fri 10a.m.–5p.m. and by appointment. Entrance £2.50.

Trerice, at Kestle Mill, Newquay TR8 4PG (tel. 01637-875404), on six acres of land, is a small and secluded Elizabethan manor, surrounded by herbaceous borders and cottage garden plants, and an orchard planted in formal 17th-century style. The former stable hay loft contains a fascinating museum of early lawnmowers.

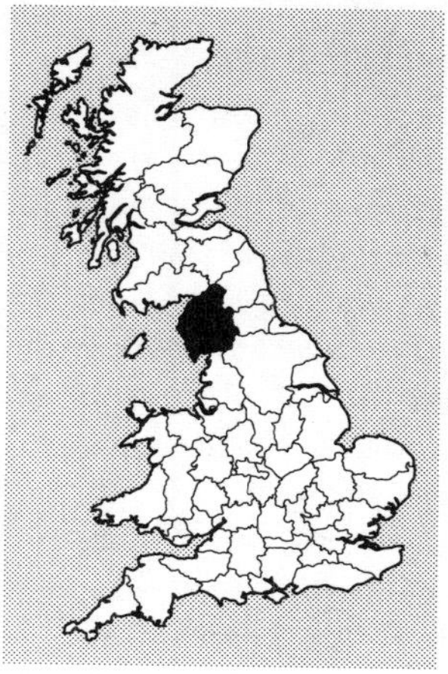

Cumbria

MAP NO. 7

The dramatic landscapes of the Lake District are unforgettable, with high, volcanic peaks in the central region reflecting in deep meres under ever-changing skies. The heathy uplands of the fells are the domain of tough sheep and the resourceful curlew, while abundant local sandstones and slates have fashioned farmsteads and field boundaries for many centuries. It is a region of high rainfall, and of such scenic beauty that the most famous lakes and towns are tourist honeypots, best avoided in high season. The 70ft waterfall of Aira Force tumbles down a wooded gorge to feed the lovely lake of Ullswater; a spring walk nearby, among the daffodils, inspired William Wordsworth to write his best-known poem.

AMBLESIDE

Rydal Mount

Rydal, Ambleside LA22 9LU TEL. *015394-33002*
OWNER *Rydal Mount Trust* HOURS *March–Oct, daily, 9.30a.m.–5p.m.; Nov–Feb, daily, except Tues, 10a.m.–4p.m.* ENTRANCE *£1.50 (house and garden) £3.50, concessions £3, children £1* DIRECTIONS *8m from M6 Jct 36 on A591, 1m N of Ambleside, 14m from Kendal*

SPRING SUMMER AUTUMN WINTER

Gift Shop

The home of William Wordsworth from 1813 until his death in 1850, the slate-roofed white cottage sits snugly in the hillside enjoying distant views of Windermere from the upper windows, where the poet had his study. Wordsworth was a keen gardener who designed not only the four and a half acres surrounding his home, but also the gardens of many friends and neighbours.

At Rydal Mount, still much as he designed it, Wordsworth followed his philosophy that a garden should be informal, harmonise with the surrounding landscape and include 'lawn, and trees carefully planted so as not to obscure the view'. There are long terrace walks following the contours of the rising ground behind the house and further walks winding through woodland and shrubberies. Wordsworth also built a rough-stone rustic summerhouse on the upper terrace, from where you can still enjoy views of Rydal Water and the distant heather-clad hills. The garden retains much of the atmosphere of an early 19th-century residence in the Picturesque style, and its enthusiastic curators, Peter and Marian Elkington, have uncovered further walks and water-courses that had long been lost in dense undergrowth. A handsome fern-leaved beech is one of many fine trees planted by the poet.

ALPINES IN THE PENNINES

There is a wonderful, scenic drive from Penrith up to ***Hartside Nursery Garden, nr Alston CA9 3BL (tel. 01434-381372), down a stony track, 1¼m SW of Alston, on E side of A686, use Jct 40 of M6,*** *with a chance to pause for excellent organic food at the bakery in Melmerby, on the way. The road winds its lonely route through the high moors of the Pennines, offering magnificent views of the Vale of Eden, which you leave behind as you climb. In fact, Hartside is very close to the Northumberland border and this inland site, around 1100ft above sea level, makes it perhaps the highest and bleakest nursery in the country.*

Expect exceptionally hardy plants from this family-run nursery which specializes in unusual alpines, primulas, dwarf conifers, ericaceous shrubs and ferns, which can withstand local winter temperatures as low as -23°C (-80°F). It isn't what you would call a neat nursery, with weeds threading their way among the pots in the small display area, where there are plenty of rarities. Owner Sue Huntley is an enthusiastic grower who exhibits at many of the top RHS shows around the country. If you cannot get here, there is a mail order catalogue (send 4 × 1st-class stamps). Open March–Oct, Mon–Fri, 9a.m.–4.30p.m.; Sat–Sun and Bank Holiday Mons, 12.30–4p.m.

GRANGE-OVER-SANDS

Holker Hall

Cark-in-Cartmel, Grange-over-Sands LA11 7PL **TEL.** *015395-58328* **OWNER** *Lord and Lady Cavendish* **HOURS** *End March–Oct, daily, except Sat, 10a.m.–6p.m. or dusk if earlier. Last adm. 4.30p.m. when house closes* **ENTRANCE** *£3.15, children over 6 £1.80, family ticket £9.25 (extra to see house, motors, birds of prey)* **DIRECTIONS** *4½m W of Grange-over-Sands off B5278, signposted; 15m from M6 Jct 36 on A590, then signposted*

SPRING SUMMER AUTUMN WINTER

Access · Gift Shop · Café

DON'T MISS

By any standards this unusual and spectacular garden is thrilling, because you are instantly aware of its high quality in design and maintenance. From a modest garden entrance at one side of the house, you come into the Elliptical Garden, a symmetrical, formal area laid out in 1993. Local materials such as slates and cobblestones from the nearby coast are used in the hard landscaping and planting is of mixed shrubs and herbaceous perennials. There are ripples of blue catmint and fascinating delphinium 'cages' made yearly from hazel rods cut on the estate.

The Summer Garden beyond features a tunnel of Portuguese laurel casting shade along the central path, topiarised above clean stilt trunks. There are fragrant shrubs, lilies, roses and lavender, and the box-edged beds are filled with seasonal flowers. In contrast, the wildflower meadow beyond is home to 24 species of perennial native wildflowers, a glorious sight before hay cutting.

Long grasses and wildflowers are encouraged to great effect elsewhere in the gardens, among the numerous specimen trees that have been planted over the centuries. A fountain is surrounded by the lofty, twisted trunks of *Rhododendron arboreum* (hugely decorative when its deep pink petals carpet the ground), which was planted by Lord Burlington around 1840. A magnificent stepped water cascade to one side is a fairly recent addition, inspired by an ancient Indian water garden in Rajasthan. Across the lawns from the top of the cascade, you reach the small, intimate rose garden, a formal area with trellised gazebos supporting climbing varieties. Throughout the 25 acres there are many interesting, unusual trees and shrubs, making this is a garden to return to, as new projects are continually executed.

KENDAL

Levens Hall

Kendal LA8 0PD TEL. *015395-60321* OWNER *Mr C. H. Bagot* HOURS *April–mid-Oct, Sun–Thurs, 10a.m.–5p.m. (house, 12 noon–5p.m.)* ENTRANCE *£3.80, children £2.10 (house and garden £5.20, £2.80), family ticket £11 (house and garden £15)* DIRECTIONS *5m S of Kendal by A591 and A6; from M6 use Jct 36, then A591 or A6*

SPRING SUMMER AUTUMN WINTER

Access Gift Shop Café Plant Shop DON'T MISS

The astonishing topiary garden draws most visitors to Levens. There are yews and box trees cut into all manner of quixotic shapes – huge pyramids, top hats, tipsy leaning spirals, chubby little birds and many other, non-representational bulging forms that have evolved over centuries.

The topiaries have grown out of formal, box-edged parterres that were laid out in the 17th century, and the spaces between the box hedges are filled with seasonal bedding plants in bold blocks of colour, adding a vivid counterpoint to the greenery of the topiary. Historically, it is interesting because it is a very rare example of the work of Guillaume Beaumont, a French landscaper much in vogue in the late 17th century. His large beech hedges remain intact as does the ha-ha (a dry ditch, forming a concealed boundary), which is thought to be the first in this country. Golden-leaved yew topiaries were added in the Victorian age. Elsewhere in the 10-acre garden there are pleasing herb and rose gardens, herbaceous borders and an orchard which is magnificent at blossom time, when the fruit trees rise out of a sea of scarlet 'Apeldoorn' tulips.

The surprisingly cosy grey stone hall itself dates from the 13th century, with later additions. It is well worth seeing, especially as certain upper windows give an interesting perspective on the topiaries below.

KENDAL

Sizergh Castle

Sizergh, nr Kendal LA8 8AE **TEL.** *015395-60070* **OWNER** *The National Trust* **HOURS** *April–Oct, Sun–Thurs, 12.30–5.30p.m. Last adm. 5p.m. (castle opens 1.30p.m.)* **ENTRANCE** *£4, children £2 (garden £2 and £1)* **DIRECTIONS** *3¼m S of Kendal, NW of interchange A590/A591*

SPRING SUMMER AUTUMN WINTER

Access | Gift Shop | Café

According to Malcolm Hutchinson, Sizergh Castle's long-serving, loquacious head gardener, you should see the gardens in reverse order to the one suggested in the official guide. You will be surprised as each new vista unfolds as you walk through the rose garden, the formal lawns of the Dutch garden towards the castle and lake. The magnificent rock garden then becomes the climax of the visit, as it should. It dates from 1926, when such conceits were deeply fashionable. Built with beautiful weathered local stones, it covers nearly one acre of ground and is planted with Japanese acers, now handsomely gnarled and characterful in their maturity, accompanied by assorted small conifers, primulas and a huge collection of hardy ferns.

PENRITH

Acorn Bank Garden

Temple Sowerby, Penrith CA10 1SP **TEL.** *017683-61893* **OWNER** *The National Trust* **HOURS** *Late March–Oct, daily,*

10a.m.–5.30p.m. (last adm. 5p.m.) **ENTRANCE** *£2.10, children £1* **DIRECTIONS** *1m N of Temple Sowerby, 6m E of Penrith, from Penrith use Jct 40 of M6, then A66*

SPRING SUMMER AUTUMN WINTER

Access | Gift Shop | Plant Shop

Around 250 different herbs are grown in the two and a half acres of sunny, sheltered walled gardens at Acorn Bank, in the broad vale of the River Eden. The herb garden is a small part of the walled area, but is home to an interesting, well-labelled collection of medicinal and historic herbs, including woad, which the ancient Britons used as blue dye, tattoo-like patterns on their skin, and Florentine irises, whose roots are used in perfumery. Also within the walled area is an orchard of local old apple varieties such as 'Keswick Codlin' growing in long grasses and meadow flowers. Wildflowers, especially daffodils, populate the glorious oak woodland walks on steep banks rising from the waters of Crowdundle Beck. It is a peaceful gem of a garden, not far from Wetheriggs Country Pottery (*q.v.*) and Larch Cottage Nurseries (*q.v.*).

PENRITH

Dalemain

Dalemain Estate, Dacre, Penrith CA11 0HB **TEL.** *017684-86450* **OWNER** *Mr R. B. Hasell McCosh* **HOURS** *Late March–early Oct, Sun–Thurs, 11.15a.m.–5p.m.* **ENTRANCE** *£3, children free (house and garden £5, children £3)* **DIRECTIONS** *On A592 3m SW of Penrith; from M6, 4m away, use Jct 40, then A592, left at roundabout*

SPRING SUMMER AUTUMN WINTER

Access | Café | Plant Shop

A smart Georgian facade of pink sandstone greets visitors to Dalemain, although behind it lies an Elizabethan manor

WETHERIGGS HISTORIC POTTERY

*At **Wetheriggs Country Pottery, Clifton Dykes, nr Penrith CA10 2DH (tel. 01768-892733), at Clifton Dykes, signposted on local roads, from M6 (2m away) use Jct 40, take A66 towards Appleby, then A6 towards Shap, left towards Clyburn, then 1½m on left,** you can see the only surviving steam-powered pottery in the country, with its nearby clay pit, settling pans, steam house, pug-mill and beehive kiln. Much of the stock is glazed domestic ware, still made to traditional designs that have been produced here for over 135 years. The greatest interest for gardeners, however, lies in the terracotta hand-thrown flowerpots, alpine pans, strawberry and herb pots, rhubarb forcer jars and Long-Toms. It is also possible to order 9in and 12in Victorian flowerbed edging tiles which are still made to the original designs. The arch design tiles were made for gardens backing onto the Settle–Carlisle railway, while another pattern features a shamrock, thistle and rose, reflecting the region's proximity to Scotland and Ireland. Open daily, but may close weekdays in winter, 10a.m.–5.30p.m. (closed 25 Dec and 1 Jan).*

house, a medieval hall and a 12th-century peel tower, a strategic tower typical of the Border lands. An amalgamation of periods and styles exists in the 10-acre gardens, too, for the early knot garden near the house is surrounded by 17th-century terraced walks, around which lies an 18th-century park. The garden's Tudor gazebo looks over ancient woods to Dacre Beck and an old coach road; there are high brick and stone Tudor walls enclosing an orchard, beside which are gently sloping lawns and flower borders which have been largely replanted in the last four decades.

Overlooking the park, the first terrace you encounter has a long, herbaceous border which terminates in the shade of a vast silver fir tree, *Abies cephalonica*, almost certainly one of the first of its kind to have been planted in this country. The wild garden below features mown paths through massed daffodils and rhododendrons, and breathtaking drifts of blue Himalayan poppies in late May which thrive in the sheltered site and acid soil.

Within the walled garden, some of the gnarled apple trees that were purchased in 1782 still bear fruit while a path beside them is being developed into a rose walk, with old-fashioned varieties planted over rustic arches, and in

SEEDS OF WONDER BY MAIL

If you enjoy growing plants from seed, you will be endlessly tempted by the ranges offered annually in the catalogue of ***Chiltern Seeds, Bortree Stile, Ulverston LA12 7PB (tel. 01229-581137).*** *Around 4500 different items are available, covering all manner of annuals, herbaceous perennials, trees, shrubs, conifers, British wildflowers and herbs. There are also exotic seeds such as Japanese cut flowers, oriental and uncommon vegetables, Australian and New Zealand plants, and many oddities that can be grown from seed as house or conservatory plants. Although unillustrated, the free catalogue (a tall, narrow volume of nearly 300 pages) is a great read, with tempting descriptions and cultivation notes.*

long beds to either side. The garden's development in the decades after the Second World War was largely the work of the late Sylvia McCosh, who documented much of her work at Dalemain in two enjoyable books, *Between Two Gardens* and *North Country Tapestry*. Inspired by these writings, her daughter-in-law, Jane Hasell McCosh, is now actively involved in maintaining and replanting the gardens, which look forward to a rosy future.

PENRITH

Hutton-in-the-Forest

Penrith CA11 9TH **TEL.** *017684-84449* **OWNER** *Lord and Lady Inglewood* **HOURS** *Gardens daily, except Sat, 11a.m.–5p.m.; house May–Sept, Thurs–Fri, Sun and Bank Holiday Mons, 1–4p.m.* **ENTRANCE** *£2. House and gardens £3.50, children £1.50* **DIRECTIONS** *6m NW of Penrith, on B5305, 3m W from Jct 41 of M6*

SPRING SUMMER AUTUMN WINTER

Café

Traditional herbaceous borders in the opulent, Edwardian style are backed by yew hedges running through the delightful walled garden at Hutton-in-the-Forest. There are old-fashioned purple lupins, bearded irises, campanulas, phlox, lady's mantle and oriental poppies. Beyond the walls, the gardens drop away in terraces from the mansion house, merging into woodlands and the medieval Forest of Inglewood.

There are stout topiaries, planted a century ago, while the Low Garden is a spectacular Victorian plantation of yews and other conifers, with large rhododendrons, cut through by formal rides. This area, the ponds and cascade beyond became neglected and overgrown during the 20th century and they are gradually undergoing restoration and some replanting.

WINDERMERE

Holehird

Patterdale Road, Windermere LA23 1NP TEL. *015394-46008 (tel. unmanned in winter)* OWNER *Lakeland Horticultural Society* HOURS *Daily, dawn to dusk* ENTRANCE *Donation* DIRECTIONS *1m N of Windermere by A592; from M6 (12m away) take A591 to Windermere, then A592 (¾m away)*

SPRING SUMMER AUTUMN WINTER

Access NPC

The Lakeland Horticultural Society has its base at Holehird, three and a half acres of sloping grounds which enjoy spectacular views of Lake Windermere and some of England's highest mountains beyond. The walled garden covers just over one acre of thoroughly well-tended borders and lawns, maintained by the Society's volunteer members. Beyond lies a magnificent rock garden which makes full use of the natural stone outcrops on the high ground. The plantings of heathers are particularly effective, and are best seen in high summer and autumn. There are National Collections of astilbes, hydrangeas and *Polystichum* ferns and there is also a large collection of hostas.

The gardens were originally planted with choice specimen trees including rare conifers, and a formerly magnificent handkerchief tree which has recently had to be heavily pruned. They date from plant-hunting expeditions to the Far East in the 19th century, and add considerably to the character of this impressive garden.

And also...

Graythwaite Hall, Ulverston, Hawkshead LA12 8BA (Tel. 015395-31248), is a pleasant, hidden-away place to visit in late spring when its tree-packed slopes are brightly jewelled with rhododendrons in bloom. The local architect Thomas Mawson was hired to landscape six acres of grounds around the house from 1889 to 1895, which he did in the contemporary Arts and Crafts style. There are formal terraces near the house giving way to a woodland garden with stream, leading to a naturalistic pool. Open April–Aug, daily, 10a.m.–6p.m. Entrance £2, children free.

Anyone looking for sculptural inspiration for their garden will enjoy rambling in the seven square miles of **Grizedale Forest.** Maps can be purchased at the Visitor Centre (signposted locally, tel. 01229-860010) pinpointing the fascinating wood and stone sculptures by artists such as Giles Kent, Richard Harris, Andy Goldsworthy and Sally Matthews, etc.

The imposing stone and stained-glass entrance to **Larch Cottage Nurseries, Melkinthorpe, Penrith CA10 2DR (tel. 01931–712404)**, leads into a fascinating sales and display area with naturalistic pools, a herb garden, pergola walk, Japanese dry garden and arcaded stone 'ruins', built in recent years. Plants for sale include a large range of cottage garden perennials, plus a broad choice of shrubs, alpines, roses and aquatic plants. There is also a first-floor coffee shop for refreshments, and imaginative light meals. Open daily, 10a.m.–7p.m; 10a.m.–5p.m. in winter (closed weekends Jan–Feb). Entrance free.

Muncaster Castle, Ravenglass CA18 1RQ (tel. 01229-717614), has an aura of gothic chill. Visit in spring, when its important collection of rhododendrons is in bloom, some of them cascading down a deep ravine. During the 19th century, Muncaster's was considered the largest collection of species rhododendrons in Europe and had a further injection of plants in the 1920s and 1930s, when many more new species were introduced and others were bred here. Substantial investment is currently under way to restore the 77 acres of gardens to their former glory and prominence. The grassed Terrace Walk, with panoramic views of Eskdale and the fells beyond, is memorable. Muncaster Castle also has an owl centre, which is the headquarters of the World Owl Trust. Open daily, 11a.m.–5p.m. Entrance £3.50, children £2. (Castle open March–Oct, Sun–Fri, £5.20 and £3.10.)

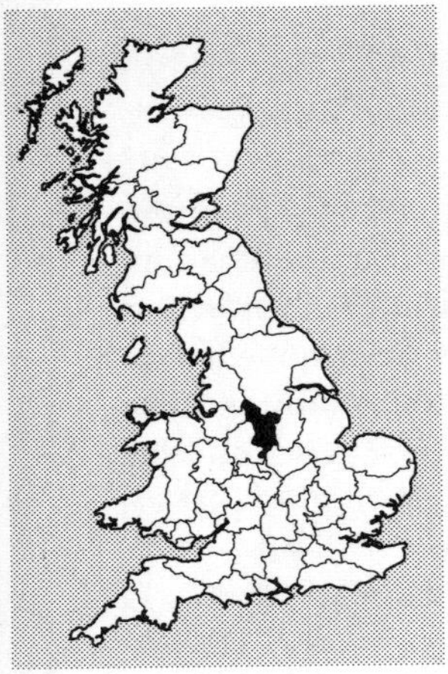

Derbyshire

MAP NO. 5

Some of the country's most awesome landscape belongs to Derbyshire. The Pennine range, England's mountainous backbone, starts here on its northward journey to the Scottish border. There are the grouse-grazed highlands of the Peak District, with purple heather-clad moors and spectacular crags, tranquil reservoirs like inland seas and hillside pastures contained in a mesh of stone walls. In the south, heavy industry and mining have played their hand, bringing riches to some. Derbyshire boasts several of England's stateliest homes, the most glorious of which is Chatsworth, near the market town of Bakewell, home of the eponymous almond tart.

BAKEWELL

Chatsworth

Bakewell DE45 1PP **TEL.** *01246-582204* **OWNER** *Chatsworth Settlement Trustees* **HOURS** *Mid-March–Oct, daily, 11a.m.–5p.m.* **ENTRANCE** *£3.50, concessions £3, children £1.75, family ticket £9* **DIRECTIONS** *8m N of Matlock, signposted from M1, off B6012. To see waterworks in action, ring to check times and dates*

SPRING SUMMER AUTUMN WINTER

Access | Gift Shop | Café | Plant Shop

DON'T MISS

Gardening on the grand scale does not come much grander than at Chatsworth, the home of the Duke of Devonshire. The palatial mansion sits in a 100-acre garden, surrounded by a vast estate with glorious views of the surrounding hills. This garden says power, money, grandeur and water, which gets spectacular treatment in several different areas.

Most stunning is the great cascade, a broad stairway of water which tumbles gently down a grassy hill, from various spouts and dolphins arranged on, and around, a handsome pavilion at the top of the slope. The water re-emerges elsewhere in the garden to feed the sea-horse fountain on the south lawn and then another fountain before reaching the river. More water dribbles down an artificial, natural-looking, 45ft-high waterfall known as Wellington. There is also a fake willow tree (modelled on one dating from 1692) which spurts surprise showers from its branches at the discreet turn of a nearby valve, and the great Emperor Fountain and canal, a centrepiece dating from 1702, which throws up a 200ft vertical jet.

Capability Brown (*q.v.*) made substantial alterations to the formal 17th-century gardens, and by the time Horace Walpole visited in 1768 he found them 'much improved ... many of the foolish waterworks being taken away ...' Astonishingly, the water supplying the cascade and the Emperor Fountain is supplied by natural pressure from four large reservoir lakes, all man-made, on the plateau above the woods. There is much else to see here too; rose gardens, flower borders, Paxton's rockeries and a long wall of glasshouses, a fine maze, magnificent trees, a wonderful woodland garden, serpentine hedges and a kitchen garden.

TISSINGTON'S FAMOUS FLOWER

Among the speedwells, Veronica gentianoides *makes an excellent front-of-border perennial, sending up spikes of late-spring/early-summer blooms of clear, pale blue above a clump of glossy green foliage. Its desirable white-flowered form, 'Tissington White', has its origins in the Peak District village of Tissington, where it was found in the front garden of an estate cottage. The plant had spread to line both sides of a path, and was locally known as Prince of Wales feathers. A few years ago it almost disappeared when the garden was tidied up for a new occupant. Fortunately, a few plants were rescued by local plantswoman Anne Liverman, who recognised its garden-worthiness and brought it into cultivation. A few nurseries now stock it, including* ***Tissington Nursery, Tissington, Ashbourne DE6 1RH (tel. 01335-390650),*** *where Derek Watkins filled me in on its history. The nursery, in the walled former kitchen garden of Tissington Hall, is open March–Oct, Wed–Sun and Bank Holiday Mons, 10a.m.–6p.m. Send 2 × 1st-class stamps for a mail order catalogue.*

For me, it is still the water that captivates, but everyone should find something magical here.

CHESTERFIELD

Hardwick Hall

Doe Lea, Chesterfield S44 5QJ **TEL.** *01246-852353* **OWNER** *The National Trust* **HOURS** *April–Oct, daily, 12.30–5p.m, Wed–Thurs, and Sat–Sun* **ENTRANCE** *House and garden £5.80, children £2 (garden £2.50 and £1)* **DIRECTIONS** *Signposted from Jct 29 of M1, 3m away*

SPRING SUMMER AUTUMN WINTER

Access · Gift Shop · Café · Plant Shop

DON'T MISS

Bess of Hardwick, Countess of Shrewsbury, is one of history's larger-than-life characters – a sort of Pamela Harriman, in spades. Born plain Elizabeth Hardwick in 1527, the daughter of an obscure Derbyshire squire, married four times, on each occasion to a husband wealthier and more powerful than the last, she outlived them all. At the time of her death she was the richest woman in England

THE BLOODY CRANESBILL

It seems unkind, or at least inaccurate, to call this spectacular native geranium 'bloody', for its cheerful flowers are actually a strikingly extrovert magenta, on a low, spreading hummock of a plant.

In bloom for a long period through the summer, Geranium sanguineum *is a signature plant of Derbyshire's dales and other limestone regions. Its deep pinkness is set off beautifully by the greyness of the stones among which it creeps, and the leaves take on burnished tints as cooler weather arrives with the autumn. Many named garden cultivars have been bred from the species, offering a range of flower tints from dark to pale pinks, red-veined and pure white varieties, such as the popular* G. s. *'Album'. The cultivar 'Cedric Morris' bears particularly large magenta flowers and* G. s. *var.* striatum *bears pretty, candy-pink petals pencilled with contrasting red veins. Easy to grow and propagate and ideal for borders and rock gardens, the bloody cranesbill and its cultivars are widely available through nurseries specializing in hardy perennials.*

after the Queen, with 100,000 acres and an annual income of £10,000, a huge fortune at the time.

We have her to thank for beautiful 'Hardwick Hall, more glass than wall', around which lies just the skeleton of her early 17th-century garden. But no matter; the present eight-acre gardens are formally laid out, in sympathy with the building, rather than being historically correct. There are wonderful yew hedges and hornbeam avenues, one of the largest and most beautifully planted herb gardens in Britain, a nuttery, old fruit trees, Gertrude Jekyll-style abundant flower borders, and fine parkland trees. It is a place to enjoy many times, not least up to the hall's rooftops where the initials ES are still proudly silhouetted in fretted stone against the sky.

TICKNALL

Calke Abbey

Ticknall DE7 1LE TEL. *01332-863822* OWNER *The National Trust* HOURS *April–Oct, Sat–Wed, 11a.m.–5.30p.m. (last adm. 5p.m.)* ENTRANCE *£2.20, children £1.10 (house, £4.90, children £2.45, family ticket £12.25)* DIRECTIONS *10m S of Derby in village of Ticknall*

SPRING SUMMER AUTUMN WINTER

Access | Gift Shop | Café

Magnificent limes line the sweeping drive through the 25-acre park at Calke Abbey and the setting, of gently undulating pastures, curvaceous lakes and ancient woodland, is captivating, full of the atmosphere of times past. The olden days are even more evident in the house (which must be seen); it is a time capsule that had been barely disturbed for 100 years when the National Trust took over the property, and they have gone out of their way to keep it that way, largely resisting the temptation to spruce it up.

Outdoors, the walled flower and kitchen gardens are hidden away up the hill, where they would not intrude on the 18th-century landscape. In the 1770s Sir Henry Harpur even built a tunnel between the servants' quarters in the house and the walled garden, so there would be no vulgar views of staff fetching food for the kitchen. Here there are flowers, Victorian bedding schemes and vegetables, but the high point is the exceedingly rare auricula theatre, of tiered shelves set in the garden wall, for displaying auriculas in bloom in spring, followed by pots of pelargoniums in summer.

DRESSING WELL IN DERBYSHIRE

Well-dressing is a decorative floral custom unique to a cluster of Derbyshire villages, particularly in the Buxton region, known for its famous spring water. The custom is believed to have originated in pagan times, although the first record of well-dressing (or its revival) dates from the early 1600s, at Tissington.

In limestone areas such as this, where water drains quickly through the porous stone, villages and homesteads were typically situated around reliable water sources. Decoration of the wells became a way of giving thanks for the precious gift of water and ensuring supplies for the future.

The dressing of wells is a skilled art, whereby villagers create pictures, usually of biblical scenes, from flower petals, mosses, lichens, leaves, bark and other natural materials, to make vivid and colourful designs. Traditionally, the men build the board base, onto which the flowers and other materials are pressed into soft clay by the village women. The ornaments last for up to a week, adorning wells in villages such as Tissington, Worksworth, Monyash, Tideswell, Eyam and Whitwell.

And also...

Plantsman-explorer Roy Lancaster alerted me to the treasures on sale at **Bluebell Nursery, Annwell Lane, Smisby, Ashby-de-la-Zouch LE65 2TA (tel. 01530-413700/01283-222091).** Its catalogue (£1.50) is full of obscure shrubs and trees, such as *Sinocalycanthus chinensis*, a rare Chinese relation of American allspice, and the red-and-white-flowered *Mahonia gracilipes*, a dwarf, suckering shrub, also from China. A young, four-acre woodland garden is now open once a month through the season, under the National Gardens Scheme. Nursery open daily except Christmas period, March–Oct, 9a.m.–5p.m.; Nov–Feb, 9a.m.–4p.m. (Sun all year 10.30a.m.–4.30p.m.).

Dam Farm House, Yeldersley Lane, Ednaston, Ashbourne DE6 3BA (tel. 01335-360291). I am told it has a wonderful, plant-packed two-acre garden made since 1980 by Jean Player, a scion of the Loder family which has made several of the great gardens of Sussex. There are mixed borders, a scree garden, and rare plants propagated for sale to interested visitors. Open April–Oct, private visitors and groups by appointment, also for several afternoons in summer for the National Gardens Scheme.

Elvaston Castle Country Park, Borrowash Road, Elvaston DE72 3EP (tel. 01332-571342), is interesting because of its history and connection with William Barron, a pioneer of tree transport. No expense was spared in making the gardens between 1830 and 1850, when thousands of mature specimen trees and large, fully formed topiaries were brought in from great distances. Open all year, daily, dawn–dusk (the Old English Garden, 9a.m.–5p.m.). Entrance free (60p–£1.20 charge for parking).

Haddon Hall, Bakewell DE45 1LA (tel. 01629-812855), is a thoroughly romantic medieval castle (used in filming Zeffirelli's *Jane Eyre* in 1995), with lofty gardens dating from the 17th century. 'A gloomy and solemn silence pervades its neglected apartments, and the bat and the owl are alone the inmates of its remaining splendour' claimed Rhodes's travel guide *Peak Scenery* in 1819. Today, restored, it is noted for its roses planted into stepped, south-facing limestone terraces descending to the fast-flowing River Wye. Open April–Sept, daily, 11a.m.–5p.m. Closed Sun in Aug. Entrance (hall and gardens) £4.75, OAPs £3.90, children £2.95.

For all manner of greenhouse and propagating equipment, including staging, potting benches, propagators, heaters, watering systems and cloches, you will seldom need to look further than **Two Wests and Elliott Ltd, Unit 4, Carrwood Road, Sheepbridge Industrial Estate, Chesterfield S41 9RH (tel. 01246-451077).** The two Wests – Christopher and Josephine – started the business in 1975; Elliott is the black labrador which graces the pages of their comprehensive mail order catalogue (free on request). Open all year, Mon–Fri, 8.45a.m.–5.15p.m.

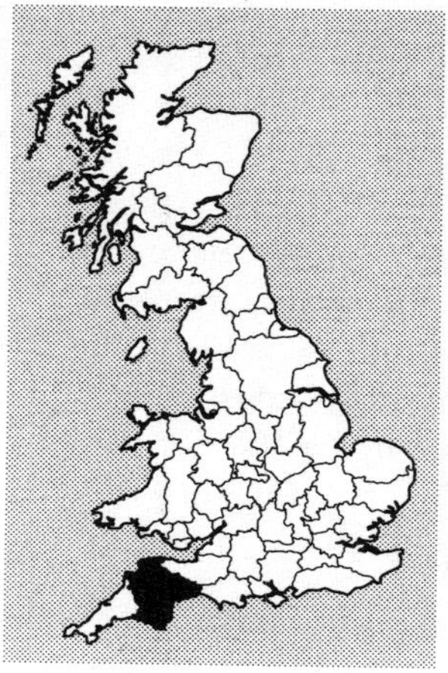

Devon

MAP NOs 1–2

A county of rich, rolling pastures, edged by two wonderful coastlines and encompassing the rugged moorland expanses of Dartmoor, Devon is varied and endlessly scenic. Its south-eastern coast is particularly favoured with sandy beaches and a mild climate, ingredients that have led it to be called the 'English Riviera', with favoured resorts at Dawlish, Torquay and Paignton. The National Trust owns, and preserves for the nation, a good deal of property in Devon – around 5500 acres of Dartmoor, more than 80 miles of coastline, and a cluster of magnificent houses and gardens. Here, perhaps more than anywhere, the cost of a membership card can quickly repay itself while you see the best of what Devon has to offer.

BARNSTAPLE

Marwood Hill Gardens

Barnstaple EX31 4EB TEL. *01271-342528* OWNER *Dr J. A. Smart* HOURS *Open all year, daily, except 25 Dec, dawn–dusk* ENTRANCE *£2* DIRECTIONS *4m N of Barnstaple, signposted from A361 (Barnstaple–Braunton road) for cars and coaches, or B3230 for cars only. Limited parking at roadside*

SPRING SUMMER AUTUMN WINTER

Access · Café · Plant Shop · NPC

DON'T MISS

Marwood Hill is renowned for its huge range of plants and breathtaking spectacles of spring and summer blossom. However, I visited last year in early November and found the garden still flourishing, with many plants gloriously in bloom (including the National Collection of *Tulbaghia*) and the added bonus of fantastic autumn tints from its large collection of trees and shrubs.

It is a plantsman's garden, informal in layout, spread over 20 acres of sloping ground. The owner, Dr Jimmy Smart, has been developing the garden for nearly 50 years. Now in his 80s, Dr Smart was frantically potting-up roots of assorted agapanthus in the potting shed when I called and the speed with which he accomplished the task would put many a young nurseryman to shame. Much of the garden is now mature too, with fine trees covering the south-facing hillside that sweeps down to a series of stream-fed lakes.

The old walled garden near the entrance is an intensively active nursery and plant sales area and includes a camellia greenhouse. Its stone walls are clothed in tender shrubs such as abutilon and *Cestrum* 'Newellii', and choice climbers such as the prolifically flowering, cowslip-scented *Clematis rehderiana*. Beyond the walls a scree garden is packed with alpines, and terraced beds in the upper garden are crossed by narrow turf paths among small shrubs and herbaceous plants in variety. I had never seen *Euphorbia stygiana* before,

Celebrity Choice

***Anne Swithinbank, television presenter and panellist on Radio 4's* Gardeners' Question Time**

'I thoroughly recommend **Bicton** (q.v.)*, especially for family visits. My husband and I have been there with my parents and our children, and it really does have enough to interest all three generations. If you take the train ride, which is fun, you can see all the grounds, including the pinetum with its metasequoias and a beautiful umbrella pine,* Sciadopitys verticillata*.*

'The children love the ducks and the adventure playground, and the fountain has always been working – you feel that someone really looks after the place. The planting everywhere is very well executed: the summer bedding is good and the containers well planted. There's a collection of passiflora, and the conservatory is lovely, from an architectural point of view. It's nice to go where there is some diversion, and where there are things to interest other members of the family who may not be as much into the plants as I am.'

but its thick, waxy leaves and fat but spreading stems make it an appealing subject for a garden in sub-tropical mode. It is the sort of place where you can get distracted by all sorts of things before even reaching the pools and stream in the valley bottom.

By the water are grassy walks among ferns and assorted eucalyptus, beds of hostas and heathers, and a wonderful weeping form of Bhutan pine. The richly planted bog garden has a large stand of gunnera at one end. The soggy banks of the stream are where you will find candelabra primulas in variety, plus the National Collections of *Astilbe* and *Iris ensata*, the rather flat-bloomed Japanese irises in lovely pastel shades.

The north-facing slope on the far side of the bog garden is home to even more trees and shrubs, with mown paths suggesting a route up the hill for the energetic, plant-thirsty visitor. By the way, teas are served at Marwood Hill, but only on Sundays and Bank Holidays, from April to September, or for parties by prior arrangement.

BROADCLYST

Killerton

Broadclyst, nr Exeter EX5 3LE **TEL.** *01392-881345* **OWNER** *The National Trust* **HOURS** *Garden open all year, daily, 10.30a.m.–5.30p.m. (dusk in winter); house open mid-March–end Oct, daily, except Tues, 10.30a.m.–dusk* **ENTRANCE** *Garden £3.50 (£1 Nov–Feb); house and garden £5* **DIRECTIONS** *7m NE of Exeter on W side of B3181 Exeter–Cullompton road*

SPRING SUMMER AUTUMN WINTER

Access | Gift Shop | Café | Plant Shop | DON'T MISS

The 21-acre garden at Killerton is enjoyable in all sorts of ways. Its summer beds and borders near the house are exuberantly planted with peonies, shrub roses and assorted Mediterranean plants, with plenty of late-flowering perennials taking over for end-of-season colour. Its woodland gardens beyond are crammed with all manner of beautiful trees, many of them grown from seed brought back from plant-hunters' expeditions in the 19th and early 20th centuries. In spring, the rhododendrons, azaleas and magnolias are remarkable, and the woodland banks are host to carpets of primroses, bluebells, cyclamen and narcissi. The Bear's Hut, near the rock garden, is a delightful rustic building with a patterned floor partly made from the knuckle-joints of long-deceased deer. The peach-coloured house is lovely, too; its elegant rooms are light and spacious, and there are historic costume exhibitions. You can also eat well here in the restaurant (open same days as the house).

BUDLEIGH SALTERTON

Bicton Park Gardens

East Budleigh, Budleigh Salterton EX9 7DP **TEL.** *01395-568465* **OWNER** *Mr and Mrs Stevens* **OPEN** *Easter–late Oct, daily, 10a.m.–6p.m. (or dusk if sooner)* **ENTRANCE** *£4.95, OAPs £3.75, children £3.95* **DIRECTIONS** *On A376 2m N of Budleigh Salterton*

SPRING SUMMER AUTUMN WINTER

Access · Gift Shop · Café · Plant Shop

The blatantly commercial entrance to Bicton Park can be a little off-putting if you are coming expecting to see tranquil gardens; but do not be deterred, because the 50-acre grounds beyond are magnificent, with interesting features remaining from the different styles which have prevailed over the centuries.

The early 19th-century Palm House is one of the finest in the country, a filigree web of iron and glass, extraordinarily complex in the design of its three-domed roof. It is home to a range of tropical plants, as are the other, more prosaic glasshouses at the top of the walled Italian Garden. Here are broad lawns with formal flowerbeds displaying some of the best – and best-cared-for – seasonal bedding schemes you will see anywhere. The sculpted grass banks and water canal at the further end are survivors from a formal design of the early 18th century, and around it lies the park and splendid pinetum. There are urns and statues, a pretty, early-Victorian Shell House made of flint stones (reached via an unusual rock garden), and many fine and unusual trees. The miniature-gauge railway and extensive children's play facilities ensure that enjoyment can be had here by people of all ages.

A PLEASANT SELECTION OF SALVIAS

Plantswoman Christine Yeo is passionate about salvias (sages) in their seemingly endless forms and holds the National Collection at ***Pleasant View Nursery, Two Mile Oak, nr Denbury, Newton Abbot TQ12 6DG (tel. 01803-813388), 2m from Newton Abbot, off A381 at Two Mile Oak Cross.*** *It is a collection that has been gathered over the past 20 years and amounts to over 200 different varieties.*

Salvias belong to the Labiatae *family, together with other herbs such as rosemary, lavender, mint and thyme. They have aromatic and sometimes very attractive foliage, and the range of flower size and colour is diverse, including vivid cobalt blues, pale sky blue, mauves and purples, pink, scarlet, orange, yellow and white. Hardy species tend to start flowering from May, and may repeat-flower later in summer; half-hardy and tender species generally bloom from July onwards, continuing until November or later, if the season is mild. Most perform best on light, well-drained and slightly limy soil in a sunny position; very few will tolerate moist conditions or wet combined with frost. Both plants and seeds are available from the nursery and by mail; Christine Yeo has also written an excellent, colour-illustrated booklet on salvias (£5.45 incl. p&p). Open mid-March–mid-Oct, Wed–Sat, 10a.m.–5p.m.; garden open May–Sept, Wed and Fri only, 2–5p.m. Entrance £1.50, children 25p.*

DARTINGTON

Dartington Hall

Dartington, Totnes TQ9 6EL TEL. *01803-862367* OWNER *Dartington Hall Trust* HOURS *Gardens open all year, daily, dawn–dusk; groups (10 or more) by appointment only* ENTRANCE *Donation (£2 a head suggested)* DIRECTIONS *2m NW of Totnes, E of A384*

SPRING SUMMER AUTUMN WINTER

Access Plant Shop

Although the Hall dates from the 14th century, the 28-acre garden has a curiously Art Deco, asymmetrical quality to it, but that is not so surprising, as much of the present layout dates from the 1920s and thirties. Spring is the most enchanting time when the long camellia walk is in bloom, the banks are awash with flowering hellebores, crocuses and daffodils, and when the splendid magnolias reach their peak of loveliness.

It is a fascinating garden; grand in its execution, with giant, turf steps ascending the hillside, and a magnificent stone stairway links the woods (and a Henry Moore statue) above with the lawns below. Around the Hall, the treatment is formal, with straight paths, flower borders and clipped

FLOWERPOTS AND MORE

If you are touring the north Devon area, it is well worth calling at ***Brannams Pottery, Roundswell Industrial Estate, Barnstaple EX31 3NJ (tel. 01271-343035), on the south-west side of Barnstaple, close to the roundabout junction of B3232 and A39 Barnstaple–Bideford road****. It is a huge pottery, but don't be intimidated by the industrial scale – visitors are welcome.*

There are guided pottery tours to see pot-throwing (you can even try making your own), a pottery museum with displays documenting the history of Brannams Pottery (founded in 1879) and a restaurant offering light meals and snacks. A huge range of terracotta pots is sold. Some are cheap-and-cheerful, machine-made and imported items, but there are also thick, swagged pots, traditional Long-Toms, bulb bowls, square planters and ornately decorated troughs. Brannams also imports a range of salt-glazed and decorated oriental pots which make ideal containers for acers, hostas and bamboos.

The pottery shop (which stocks a huge range of domestic/kitchen ware) includes a 'seconds' area with assorted garden pots where you may pick up a bargain. Open all year. Shop and restaurant: Mon–Sat, 9a.m.–5p.m. (shop also open Sun, Easter–Oct); pottery tours: Mon–Fri, usually 10a.m–4.15p.m. Entrance: adults £3.50; OAPs £2.90; children (over 5) £2.25; family ticket £8.50; groups of 12 or more: adults £3 each, OAPs £2.50 each, children £1.75.

yews. It becomes wilder and more woodish as you leave the Hall behind; good use is made of the undulating terrain and its lovely views of the Devon countryside.

Several well-known, 20th-century designers contributed to its making, including H. Avray Tipping in the late 1920s, followed by the American landscape architect Beatrix Farrand; in the 1940s and fifties garden designer Percy Cane became involved.

DREWSTEIGNTON

Castle Drogo

Drewsteignton EX6 6PB **TEL.** *01647-433306* **OWNER** *The National Trust* **HOURS** *April–late Oct, daily, except Fri, 11a.m.–5p.m.* **ENTRANCE** *Castle and gardens £5.20, family ticket £13, garden/grounds only £2.40* **DIRECTIONS** *5m S of A30 Exeter–Okehampton road via Crockernwell, or A382*

SPRING SUMMER AUTUMN WINTER

Access · Gift Shop · Café · Plant Shop · DON'T MISS

Castle Drogo is in a very dramatic setting, enjoying panoramic views of the rugged northern fringes of Dartmoor. Although it is a medieval fortress in spirit, the stern, granite house was built by Sir Edwin Lutyens from 1910–1930 for Julius Drewe, a wealthy client who had made his money from a chain of grocery stores.

To see the 12-acre garden in the correct sequence you should walk up the driveway to the castle and then double back, first taking in the rhododendron valley to the north-west, if you are here in spring. The main gardens are laid out in a series of ascending terraces, with an arrow-straight path leading directly through the centre. Crisp yew hedges enclose them, echoing the stout walls of the castle. From granite steps and a pretty gateway you enter the Rose Garden, a formal area of hybrid tea and floribunda roses, on either side of which are marvellous herbaceous borders. Shady loggias in the corners are interestingly fashioned from parrotia trees, trained over wire ropes and iron girders.

The next level features a corridor walk through spring-flowering shrubs, acers and shrub roses, leading to a huge, circular croquet lawn enclosed by yew. Lutyens' genius is present throughout the gardens; in his treatment of the hierarchy of spaces, their perfect proportions, and the winding paths through the borders – a brilliant counterpoint to the overall linear design. The detail planting, which is also good, was by another early 20th-century designer, George Dillestone.

While here, do see the castle, which is wonderfully bright and airy, despite its low proportion of windows, another example of Lutyens' brilliance.

GREAT TORRINGTON

Rosemoor Garden

Great Torrington EX38 8PH **TEL.** *01805-624067* **OWNER** *The Royal Horticultural Society* **HOURS** *Open all year, daily, except 25 Dec, 10a.m.–6p.m. (Oct–March, 10a.m.–5p.m.)* **ENTRANCE** *£4, children (6–16) £1* **DIRECTIONS** *1m SE of Great Torrington on B3220*

SPRING SUMMER AUTUMN WINTER

Access · Gift Shop · Café · Plant Shop · NPC

This is the stronghold of the Royal Horticultural Society in the south-west. Rosemoor is, in fact, two gardens, the early section being chiefly an eight-acre woodland garden with rhododendrons and other choice shrubs and trees that thrive on acidic soil, with more formal plantings near the house, made by Lady Anne Palmer in the 1960s. The second, 32-acre garden adjoins it (via a subterranean passage), and has been laid out in recent years since Lady Anne gave the property to the Society in 1988.

There are fine rose gardens, herbaceous borders, a cottage garden, demonstration kitchen gardens, water and bog gardens, a herb garden and colour-themed areas. The Society holds regular courses, lectures and demonstrations throughout the year, and the set-up is particularly well planned for visitors, with a well-stocked shop and plant centre and licensed restaurant. Lady Anne's garden holds important National Collections of dogwoods and hollies.

KINGSWEAR

Coleton Fishacre

Coleton, Kingswear, Dartmouth TQ6 0EQ TEL. *01803-752466* OWNER *The National Trust* HOURS *March, Sun, 2–5p.m., April–Oct, Wed–Fri, Sun and Bank Holiday Mons, 10.30a.m.–5.30p.m.; also Suns in March, 2–5p.m.* ENTRANCE *£3.50, children £1.70, pre-booked parties of 15 or more £2.80 each* DIRECTIONS *3m from Kingswear, off Lower Ferry Road*

SPRING SUMMER AUTUMN WINTER

Café | Plant Shop | DON'T MISS

Sailing, sunshine and south Devon's fashionable resorts brought Rupert D'Oyly Carte, son and heir of the musical impresario partner to Gilbert and Sullivan, to this region. In 1925 he had a delightful house built of local stone, on an enchanting, south-facing valley. Around it the 22-acre garden is laid out in a series of beautifully planted terraces.

This garden offers a very satisfying blend of architectural and natural elements. There are dry-stone walls, circular waterlily pools and a narrow water-rill near the house; but all of that soon gives way to a free-form, organic pattern of winding paths and shrubberies. Countless little streams feed luxuriant waterside plantings of irises, ferns and oriental primulas. Rhododendrons thrive, and the mild climate nurtures a huge collection of half-hardy plants from Australasia and South Africa. The Rill Garden is brilliant in high summer, with bright orange and scarlet-flowered cannas joined by salvias and assorted African daisies. Coleton Fishacre is tucked away down narrow lanes but is well worth seeking out for its beauty and tranquillity.

TIVERTON

Knightshayes Court

Bolham, Tiverton EX16 7RG TEL. *01884-254665* OWNER *The National Trust* HOURS *April–Oct, daily (house not open Fri, except Good Friday), house and garden, 11a.m.–5p.m.; shop, 10.30a.m.–5.30p.m.* ENTRANCE *£3.50; house and garden £5.10* DIRECTIONS *2m N of Tiverton; turn R off Tiverton–Bampton road (A396) at Bolham*

SPRING SUMMER AUTUMN WINTER

Access | Gift Shop | Café | Plant Shop | DON'T MISS

Passions for golf and gardening do not often go hand-in-hand; each activity demands too much time for them to co-exist. But the wonderful garden at Knightshayes proves the exception to the rule. It was largely the inspiration of Lady Heathcoat-Amory who, as Joyce Wethered, was distinguished in the 1920s as the finest woman golfer in the country – four times British Open Champion and five times English Champion. (Henry Cotton declared that 'no golfer, male or female, has stood out so far ahead of his or her contemporaries'.) However, from the 1950s, Lady Amory exchanged the hickory shafts of her golf clubs for the elm of her garden spade, and delved into the woodland of her husband's home at Knightshayes Court.

The existing canopy of oak and beech was thinned out (at around two acres per year) to make a spectacular and exotically planted 30-acre garden in which the Amorys developed lovely rambling walks among rhododendrons, Japanese acers, magnolias and assorted rare trees and shrubs, underplanted by carpets of bulbs. Especially breathtaking in both spring and autumn (and coolly green, with subtle floral highlights through the summer), Knightshayes' woodland garden is among the best of its type in the country.

Beside the house (a Victorian pink-sandstone monstrosity), formal terraces are planted with sun-loving shrubs above rolling lawns and parkland. Several yew-hedged compartments contain assorted mini-gardens featuring alpines, perennials and a serene, circular lily-pool. Hedging is used exceptionally well at Knightshayes, and one memorable hedgetop sports a topiarised scene of fox and hounds, dating from the 1920s.

UMBERLEIGH

Glebe Cottage Plants

Pixie Lane, Warkleigh, Umberleigh EX37 9DH TEL/FAX *01769-540554* OWNER *Carol Klein* HOURS *Open Easter–Oct, Tues–Fri, 10a.m.–1p.m.* ENTRANCE *Free for nursery, £1.50 for garden, children free* DIRECTIONS *Between Umberleigh and South Molton, south of B3227. From Chittlehampton head S towards Chittlehamholt (nursery is signposted locally). At Swing Gate Cross turn left onto track to Glebe Cottage Plants by the nursery sign*

SPRING SUMMER AUTUMN WINTER

Plant Shop Nursery

So often it is the small, hidden-away nurseries that prove the most rewarding and Glebe Cottage Plants is no exception. It is remotely located, down a long and narrow typical Devon lane made long ago for the odd farm cart. Tall hedgerows thick with brambles and ferns (and primroses in spring) prevent you from looking anywhere but forwards (or backwards) until you reach a farm gate, and a further track which leads down a sloping pasture to the nursery.

Vermilion-haired nurserywoman Carol Klein is renowned for her fabulous and beautifully arranged plant displays which frequently win gold medals at Chelsea and other major flower shows. Her forthright and engaging style has also earned her a second career as a television gardening expert, giving practical advice on Channel 4's *Garden Party*, and advocating wildflower planting in her own recent series, *Wild About the Garden*.

Carol's nursery is a haven for plant lovers, for she seeks out the unusual, especially where hardy perennials are concerned. 'To get in our list, a plant has to be gardenworthy, interesting and beautiful,' says Carol. Hear, hear. There are pulmonarias, anemones and hardy geraniums in variety, and a substantial list of penstemons, including many that were favoured by plantswoman Margery Fish of East Lambrook Manor (*q.v.*). Carol counts Margery Fish and Beth Chatto (*q.v.*) among the most important influences in her own gardening style, which is naturalistic and uncorseted, with special pleasure taken in self-sown plants.

In her earlier career, Carol taught fine art, and her strong sense of colour and form are put to good use in her own, steeply sloping one-acre garden beside the nursery, which is partly terraced and sunny, partly woodland, with rambling paths among spring flowers. There is an excellent nursery catalogue (£1.50 plus A5 s.a.e.) but mail order is no longer offered, so arrive with plenty of car-boot space. If you are after something in particular, it is wise to phone ahead in the off-peak season as many plants are kept at a holding nursery elsewhere.

And also...

Ann and Roger Bowden, Sticklepath, Okehampton EX20 2NL (tel. 01837-840481) live 700ft up, on the northern edge of Dartmoor, where they specialize in hostas, of which they hold a National Collection amounting to over 500 different varieties. A large number (but not all) are on sale in their excellent mail order catalogue (send 3 × 1st-class stamps), which is sumptuously illustrated. You can also visit the nursery by appointment only, and their display garden of hostas opens several times in summer for the National Gardens Scheme (see the yellow book for details). Entrance £1, children free.

The National Trust's **Buckland Abbey, Yelverton PL20 6EY (tel. 01822-853607)**, was founded by the Cistercian order, and later became the home of Sir Francis Drake. Beyond its 13th-century barn is a delightful walled herb garden featuring 52 box-edged compartments of random pattern, each one containing a different herb, and stone paths winding through. The main abbey gardens are chiefly sloping lawns, dotted with specimen trees.

Open April–Oct, daily, except Thurs, 10.30a.m.–5.30p.m.; Nov–March, Sat–Sun, 2–5p.m., last adm. 45 minutes before closing. Entrance £4.30, children £2.10, grounds only £2.20. (The Garden House, below, is nearby.)

Full use is made of the water running through **Docton Mill, Lymebridge, Hartland, Bideford EX39 6EA (tel. 01237-441369)**. It makes an idyllic and naturalistic garden of mixed shrubs, bulbs and waterside perennials. The eight-acre garden is at ease with its tranquil setting in a quiet valley near the sea. Open March–Oct, daily, 10a.m.–5p.m. Entrance £2.50, children 50p.

The tipsy seven acres of **The Garden House, Buckland Monachorum, Yelverton PL20 7LQ (tel. 01822-854769)**, reveal a plantsman's garden of great variety, laid out within and around ancient walls. Plants are carefully selected for harmonising effects of their foliage and flowers, well cared for and well labelled. Open March–Oct, daily, 10.30a.m.–5p.m. Entrance £3, OAPs £2.50, children £1.

Overbecks Museum and Garden, Sharpitor, Salcombe TQ8 8LW (tel. 01548-842893), occupies a steeply sloping, six-acre site with spectacular views of the Salcombe estuary. Due to the mild climate, there is more than a touch of the French Riviera in its planting, with fan palms, banana trees, cannas and eucalyptus contributing magnificent foliage. Hydrangeas, day lilies, red-hot pokers and sunflowers contribute to its glorious summer spectacle. Garden open all year, daily, 10a.m.–8p.m. (or dusk if earlier). Entrance £2.40 (more to see museum, which has more limited opening times).

There is no mail order from **Peveril Clematis Nursery, Christow, nr Exeter EX6 7NG (tel. 01647-252937)**, but a visit is well worthwhile. There are varieties you will not find anywhere else (including many that were bred here) and some lovely, rare species clematis. Nurseryman Barry Fretwell offers well-grown and very reasonably priced stock, and the garden beside the nursery shows many clematis in action, draping walls, trees, shrubs and timber structures, often prettily paired with contrasting roses. Open March–Oct, daily, except Thurs, 10a.m.–1p.m., 2–5p.m., Sun 10a.m.–1p.m. only.

Plant hunter and speciality seed merchant Ray Brown runs **Plant World Botanic Gardens, St Marychurch Road, Newton Abbot TQ12 4SE (tel. 01803-872939).** The display gardens are ingeniously divided into world habitat zones, and unusual plants are available from the specialist nursery. Open Easter–Sept, daily, except Wed, 9.30a.m.–5p.m.

Suttons Consumer Products Ltd, Hele Road, Torquay TQ2 7QJ (tel. 01803-614455), is an old-established seed merchant with a large and sumptuously illustrated colour catalogue of flower and vegetable seeds, and garden sundries. Also produces an autumn catalogue of spring bulbs, perennial plants and soft fruits. Catalogues free on request.

If you never know what to do with all those windfalls, or regularly have a glut of berry fruits, it is worth considering ways of using or preserving the produce. **Vigo Vineyard Supplies, Station Road, Hemyock EX15 3SE (tel. 01823-680230),** sells a range of traditional fruit presses and crushers (ideal for making apple and pear juice), and a stainless-steel Finnish juice steamer for currants and other berry fruits, all by mail order, catalogue on request. Open weekdays, 9a.m.–5p.m.

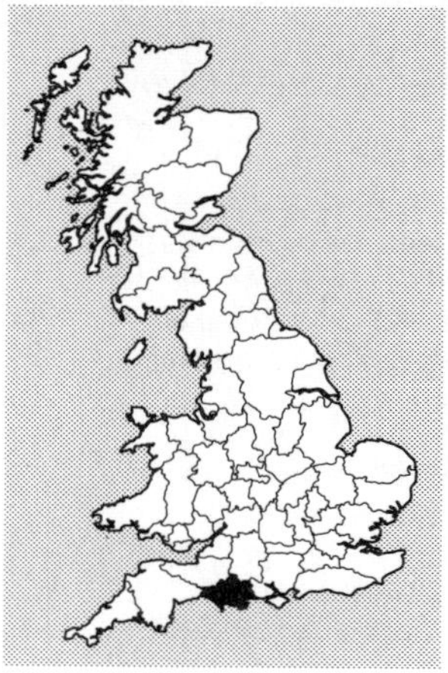

Dorset

MAP NO. 2

This small county embraces green and undulating chalk downs, such as the anciently forested Cranborne Chase, and windswept sandy heathland, immortalised as Thomas Hardy's brooding Egdon Heath, 'a thing majestic without severity, impressive without showiness, emphatic in its admonitions, grand in its simplicity'.

Its coast is balmy, with cosy seaside resorts, such as fossil-rich Lyme Regis, where Jane Austen enjoyed the bay, 'animated with bathing machines and company', and John Fowles's French lieutenant's woman cogitated on the Cobb. Queen Victoria recommended the 'very salubrious air' of pine-encrusted Bournemouth to Disraeli, and its riverside gardens are just a fraction of the town's commitment to horticultural display. Dorset's gardens reflect its varied terrain, from the flint-and-cob walls and yew hedging in the chalkands, to the exotic bedding displays of the coastal resorts.

ABBOTSBURY

Abbotsbury Sub-tropical Gardens

Abbotsbury, nr Weymouth DT3 4LA TEL. *01305-871412/ 871344* OWNER *Ilchester Estates* HOURS *Open all year, daily, 10a.m.–5p.m. (10a.m.–3p.m. Nov–Feb), closed 25–26 Dec and 1 Jan* ENTRANCE *£4.20, OAPs £3.80, children (under 15) £1.50 (under 5s free), parties of 10 or more £3.80 each* DIRECTIONS *9m SW of Dorchester, 9m NW of Weymouth, off B3157*

SPRING SUMMER AUTUMN WINTER

Access | Gift Shop | Café | Plant Shop

If you approach Abbotsbury from the Bridport coast road to the west, you won't fail to spot a dense jungle standing

SEXY HAND-MADE POTS

Jonathan Garratt's fascinating yard at ***Hare Lane Pottery, Cranborne BH21 5QT (tel. 01725-517700), 2m E of Cranborne towards Alderholt****, is crammed with pots of all shapes and sizes, with familiar Long-Toms, rhubarb forcers and alpine pans, as well as a range of beautiful one-off pots in his own design. Garratt draws inspiration from prehistoric and traditional pots from France, West Africa and the Far East to make some striking and innovative containers with attractively textured patterns. The pots divide, he says, into two kinds, 'one is about function, the other about sex and romance'. Rhubarb forcers and your average Bill-and-Ben flowerpot clearly fall into the functional category; the sensual shapes, primitive patterning and rich glazes of his other ranges are useful too, but more tactile and interesting.*

The clay is dug from a local pit and the kiln is fired around eight times a year. The kiln holds a month's work, and takes 17 hours to fire, entirely with wood; it then cools for four days. Pot colours vary according to the heat in the kiln, from warm reds and oranges through brown to purple-black. 'I don't produce a price-list, maddeningly for everyone,' says Garratt, 'because I sell chiefly from here and change the designs very frequently.' Open all year, daily, but telephone to check times.

proud of the surrounding grasslands in the coastal plain below. This is Abbotsbury's 20-acre sub-tropical garden, a haven of hothouse plants growing in the protecting embrace of a hollow in the chalk and limestone hills.

Inside, the shrieking peacocks and aviary of tropical birds bring complementary sounds to the exotic surroundings of fan palms, phormiums and yuccas. Among the garden's prize specimens is a Caucasian wingnut tree, the largest in Britain. The valley garden has woodland walks which are dazzling at azalea time; in summer they maintain a cool atmosphere under the canopy of mature palms, oaks and eucalyptus.

Streams filled with waterside plants meander lazily through a chain of ponds and simple timber bridges, and through seemingly endless jungle. By late summer the hydrangea walk is in its element, and by climbing a series of log steps to the Coronation Walk, you can admire their carpet of changing colours from above. An excellent range of plants, particularly Australasian and mild-climate species, is on sale in the plant centre.

BOURTON

Chiffchaffs

Chaffeymoor, Bourton, Gillingham SP8 5BY TEL. *01747-840841* OWNER *Mr and Mrs K. R. Potts* HOURS *End March–Sept, Wed and Thurs, 1st and 3rd Sun in month, Bank Holidays, 2–5p.m. Also open by appointment. Nursery open March–Nov, Tues–Sat, 10a.m.–5p.m.* ENTRANCE *£2, children 50p* DIRECTIONS *3m E of Wincanton. Leave A303 (Bourton bypass) at sign marked Bourton and continue to W end of village. Take lane signposted Chaffeymoor. Chiffchaffs and Abbey Plants ¼m on right*

SPRING SUMMER AUTUMN WINTER

Plant Shop

Ken and Gudrun Potts's 11-acre garden and nursery sits right on the borders of Dorset, Somerset and Wiltshire, and has developed around ancient stone cottages with views over the Blackmoor Vale to Bulbarrow Hill. Fine trees include the paperbark maple, a weeping wych-elm and a dawn redwood, for Ken Potts was a forester before he became a nurseryman.

Most of the garden is on free-draining greensand and the woodland dell, with its pockets of natural peat, has been developed with acid-loving shrubs. Giant gunneras thrive, unfurling their vast leaves. Around the house, stone walls and crunchy gravel paths wind through colourful borders of cottagey plants, helianthemums and old-fashioned roses, against an evergreen framework. Many plants seen in the gardens are sold in the Abbey Plants nursery that the Potts run on the same site.

CRANBORNE

Cranborne Manor Gardens and Garden Centre

Cranborne, Wimborne BH21 5PP TEL. *01725-517248* OWNER *The Viscount and Viscountess Cranborne* HOURS

March–Sept, Wed, 9a.m.–5p.m., garden centre open all year, daily, 9a.m.–5p.m., Sun 10a.m.–5p.m. ENTRANCE *£3, OAPs £2.50* DIRECTIONS *From A354, midway between Salisbury and Blandford, take B3081 SE and follow signs for Cranborne. House is on left as you enter Cranborne; entrance is via the Garden Centre*

SPRING SUMMER AUTUMN WINTER

Plant Shop · Garden Centre · DON'T MISS

This, I must confess, is one of my all-time favourite gardens; it seems to have everything, in perfect scale. The manor house is one of the prettiest in the country, being not too grand, and is exquisitely proportioned. The original manor was built in 1207 as a hunting lodge for King John and was remodelled in Tudor times. It passed to Robert Cecil, 1st Earl of Salisbury, in the early 17th century and his descendants still live here.

A fine beech avenue runs down a gentle slope from the road to the twin pepperpot gate-houses. The house sits snugly in its 11-acre grounds, which were laid out in Robert Cecil's time under the instructions of John Tradescant the Elder, who brought back rare plants and bulbs from the Continent. A Jacobean mount (built for viewing the

DISCREET PLANT LABELS

If you despair of remembering the names of the plants in your garden, but do not want to fill it with garish white plastic labels, you will be pleased to know about ***MacPennys Products, 154 Burley Road, Bransgore, nr Christchurch BH23 8DB (tel. 01425-672348).*** *Their labels are a discreet black, with a scratchable surface onto which you etch the name with a fine metal scriber. Labels come in various sizes including a range with hanging wires for trees and shrubs, and are available by mail order. MacPennys is also a long-established nursery, with a broad general range of plants for sale, including some rare and unusual varieties (which also available by mail, send an A4 s.a.e. and 50p for a catalogue). Nursery open daily, except 25–26 Dec and 1 Jan, Mon–Sat 9a.m.–5p.m., Sun 2–5p.m. The adjoining four-acre woodland garden, converted from an old gravel pit, is also open for charity.*

owner's rolling acres), and the walled and hedged enclosures, reflect the intimate garden style prevailing at that time.

Broad stretches of grass under fruit and forest trees are spangled with narcissi, cowslips, primroses, orchids and fritillaries in their thousands through spring. A rose and wisteria-covered pergola runs beside the old kitchen garden; there are pleached limes, a garden of old roses and pale flowers, and a herb garden with windows cut into an old yew hedge to give views of the countryside beyond.

The River Crane, from which Cranborne gets its name, runs along the northern edge of the garden; it is a winter bourne that dries out in summer. Pause to admire the nearby ancient flint-and-cob walls.

Part of the old walled garden has been turned into a well-stocked garden centre, specializing in old-fashioned roses, herbs, fruit trees and garden ornaments.

EDMONDSHAM

Edmondsham House

Edmondsham, nr Wimborne BH21 5RE TEL. *01725-517207* OWNER *Mrs J. Smith* HOURS *Easter Sun and Mon, May and August Bank Holiday Mons, April–Oct, Wed and Sun, 2–5p.m. Also by appointment* ENTRANCE *£1, children 50p* DIRECTIONS *1¼m from Cranborne, between Cranborne and Verwood, off B3081*

SPRING | SUMMER | AUTUMN | WINTER

Access | Plant Shop

A stone's throw from Cranborne, the handsome, gabled house at Edmondsham stands on the site of a manor which was once seized by William the Conqueror, who gave part of it to his queen, Matilda. There are some fine specimen trees in the six-acre grounds and a former medieval cock-fighting pit, but for me, the chief interest is the kitchen garden, where head gardener Andrew Haynes conquers plant pests entirely organically.

Within the brick-and-cob walled enclosure there are wall fruits and ancient espaliered apples, arched tunnels of runner beans and neat lines of chemical-free vegetables and salads. The dense rows of pot marigolds look wonderfully cheerful in their brilliant gold and orange hues, but their real purpose is to keep the cabbage root fly away. Since Andrew began planting his brassicas in small gaps between the marigolds, they have not been troubled by these pests. He is also a great believer in the efficacious effects of liquid feed made from the rotting leaves of Russian comfrey (despite its rank odour), and will gladly pass on nuggets of organic gardening lore to those who are interested.

A straight path running through the walled garden is flanked by deep herbaceous borders planted for a long season of colour; in high summer watch out for the large, bright blue trumpets of *Nicandra physalodes*, a very unusual but highly poisonous relative of the tomato. Its sturdy, black stems, handsome foliage and lantern-like seedheads are also very attractive.

Celebrity Choice

Penelope Hobhouse, gardening author and internationally renowned garden designer

'I love ***Athelhampton*** (q.v.) *near Dorchester. It has a wonderful design dating from the 1890s by Inigo Thomas. The atmosphere and architecture of the garden are superb, but I do rather give thumbs down for the planting, however, which is a bit of a muddle. But as a garden I like and admire it a lot. The pyramidal yews are wonderful, and they inspired me to plant some like them in my own garden.*

'I also love John Hubbard's garden at ***Chilcombe House, Chilcombe, nr Bridport DT6 4PN (tel. 01308-482234), 5m E of Bridport, off A35,*** *which is laid out in a series of rooms, very charming, with loose planting. It is planted in a very unselfconscious way. John is an artist and has an eye for combining plants. The garden has really good, strong structure, and exuberant planting, and I especially like the orchard with its roses.' Open June, Weds only, 2–6p.m. Entrance £2.50, children free.*

POOLE

Compton Acres

Canford Cliffs Road, Poole BH13 7ES TEL. *01202-700778* OWNER *L. Green* HOURS *March–Oct, daily, 10a.m.–6p.m. (last adm. 5.15p.m.)* ENTRANCE *£4.50, OAPs £3.50, children £1* DIRECTIONS *1½m W of Bournemouth by A35 and B3065, well signposted*

SPRING SUMMER AUTUMN WINTER

Access · Gift Shop · Café

Compton Acres offers 9½ acres of sheer, unadulterated garden tourism. It is a theme park of a garden, chiefly laid out between the two world wars. The south coast visitors love it, and so do I, because it is executed with great conviction. The bold colours of the planting are invigorating, from the spring azaleas and coppery foliage of the Japanese garden to the corseted bedding schemes around the Italian lily-pool with gushing fountains.

The Heather Dell, under wind-pruned pines, gives just a hint of what was once here; the garden is built on the sandy heathland that has all but disappeared under 20th-century development. The house was built in 1914 but immediately after the First World War its rich new owner, Thomas William Simpson, created several gardens linked by winding paths on the south-facing slopes overlooking Poole's yacht-speckled harbour. No expense was spared, either, in transforming its rough slopes of heather, bracken and briars into a lush and terraced landscape. The bill came to £220,000 (more than £2 million in present-day terms). Statues of bronze, marble and lead, ornate fountains and exotic trees and shrubs were imported to transform the site. The Japanese garden was designed and built by Japanese craftsmen, with genuine oriental artefacts including a stepped temple, imperial tea house, dragon gates and stone lanterns. Compton Acres is a place to enjoy the thrill of gardens in all their variety, and marvel at the single-mindedness of its makers.

PUDDLETOWN

Athelhampton House and Gardens

Athelhampton, nr Puddletown, Dorchester DT2 7LG **TEL.** *01305-848363* **OWNER** *Patrick Cooke* **HOURS** *Late March–late Oct, daily except Saturday, 10.30a.m.–5p.m.* **ENTRANCE** *Gardens only £2.80, children £1.50 (under 5s free), house and gardens £4.80, OAPs £4.50, concessions £2.80, children £1.50* **DIRECTIONS** *1m E of Puddletown, on A35*

SPRING SUMMER AUTUMN WINTER

Access Café

Puddletown is deep in Thomas Hardy country, and doubled as Weatherbury in *Far From the Madding Crowd*. Hardy's father was the local stonemason and carried out repairs at Athelhampton; the manor provided the setting for some of the writer's work. The fine 12-acre gardens are due to Alfred Cart de Lafontaine, a rich bachelor who bought the estate in 1891; he promptly employed Inigo Thomas, an advocate of formal garden design, to lay out the 20-acre grounds.

Thomas created a masterly series of self-contained spaces entirely in sympathy with the house and its surroundings. From the Corona – a circular area enclosed by scalloped walls of rich, ochre Hamstone topped by slender obelisks – tempting gateways lead into other spaces: to the house forecourt, the private garden with its croquet lawn and central canal, the pool garden known as the Lion's Mouth, and to the Great Court. The latter features a dozen vast yew pyramids on smooth lawns. Beyond, a raised terrace has a pavilion at each end, decorated with stone faces: a smiling one in the west signifying the joy of summer and a scowling one in the east for winter. Later additions include a Cloister Garden of pleached limes around an octagonal pool, and a garden of white and pale flowers.

The 15th-century house is built on the legendary site of King Athelstan's palace and suffered a fire in 1992, but has fortunately been sympathetically restored.

WIMBORNE

Knoll Gardens

Stapehill Road, Hampreston, nr Wimborne BH21 7ND TEL. *01202-873931* OWNER *J. and J. Flude, N. Lucas* HOURS *March, Wed–Sun, 10a.m.–4p.m., April–Oct, daily, 10a.m.–5.30p.m., Nov–21 Dec, Wed–Sat, 10a.m.–4p.m.* ENTRANCE *£3.25, OAPs £2.90, children £1.70, family ticket £7.90* DIRECTIONS *Between Wimborne and Ferndown off Ham Lane, B3073, signposted*

SPRING SUMMER AUTUMN WINTER

Access | Gift Shop | Café | Plant Shop | NPC

Knoll Gardens is a strange place, piecemeal rather than designed, but with plenty to interest the plantsman or gardener, for it crams over 4000 different species into a compact six-acre site, without feeling cramped.

An immaculate gravel entrance drive leads past impressive displays of fuchsia- and pelargonium-filled hanging baskets; inside, lawns and winding paths lead under mature oaks, eucalyptus and robinia trees to various themed areas. The water garden is a bold feature with lily-ponds and cascades, and beyond is a bedded-out formal parterre with dragon fountain. A straight strip of lawn, bordered either side with a thick ribbon of scarlet begonias, gives the impression of a formal carpet rolled out for an official function.

The garden's National Collection of phygelius, the Cape figwort, began nearly 30 years ago, when the popular hybrid, *P.* 'African Queen', was raised here. It is displayed in the brilliant summer borders, among dahlias, cannas and marguerites; there are also many interesting shrubs, including ceanothus in variety, and *Crinodendron patagua* from Chile, with white bell flowers. Trehane Nursery (*q.v.*) is next door.

And also...

There are pond plants in abundance at **Bennett's Water Lily Farm, Water Gardens, Putton Lane, Chickerell, Weymouth DT3 4AF (tel. 01305-785150)**, with its six acres, and some 100 varieties of waterlilies. The flowering season is from June to September, with early summer a good time to visit if you want to stock up with pond plants and other aquatic supplies. There are also tropical water plants for conservatory pools and a tea room, open through the season. Their stocks are available by mail. Open April–Oct, Tues–Sat, 10a.m.–5p.m. Also Sun April–Aug, 10a.m.–5p.m. Send 3 × 1st-class stamps for catalogue.

Global Orange Groves UK, Horton Road, Horton Heath, nr Wimborne BH21 7JN (tel. 01202-826244), specializes in citrus fruits for the conservatory or greenhouse. Their stocks are available by mail. Spanish peaches, apricots and olive trees are also now available. Open seven days a week, 10.30a.m.–5p.m. Send s.a.e. for catalogue.

C.W. Groves & Son, West Bay Road, Bridport DT6 4BA (tel. 01308-422654), is a traditional, family-run nursery-turned-garden centre, which has been trading since 1866. As well as providing a good general range of plants, Clive and Diana Groves specialize in violas, particularly Victorian varieties, which are only sold by mail (send a s.a.e. for the catalogue). The show garden features some of the nursery's stock, and there is a demonstration vineyard, roses and asparagus beds. Open daily all year, 8.30a.m.–5p.m. (Sun, 10.30a.m.–4.30p.m.).

In 1880 General Pitt Rivers laid out **The Larmer Tree Victorian Pleasure Gardens at Tollard Royal (tel. 01725-516228 or 01725-516453)** for the recreation of people in neighbouring towns and villages. The chief interest is the eclectic collection of buildings he acquired and arranged around a broad lawn. They include an Indian room, a Roman temple, an open-air theatre and a richly carved building from Nepal; the surrounding 13-acre gardens are being developed and restored. Open mid-July–Aug, Sun–Thurs and Bank Holidays, 11a.m.–6p.m. Entrance £3, children £1.

Parnham House, Beaminster DT8 3NA (tel. 01308-862204), is famous for the timber workshops of John Makepeace, where hand-crafted furniture is made in an entirely appropriate setting in this 14-acre park with its silent, wooded landscape. The formal gardens are dominated by stout cones of yew, marching around the lawns below the terrace in front of the house. Parnham boasts attractive herbaceous borders, too: one a cool collection of pinks, blues, silvers and whites, the other red-hot with dahlias, achilleas and schizostylis, both planted by Jenny Makepeace in 1984 and '85. Open early April–late Oct, Tues–Thurs and Bank Holidays, 10a.m.–5p.m. Entrance £4, children £2.

Trehane Nursery, Stapehill Road, Hampreston, nr Wimborne BH21 7NE (tel. 01202-873490), is renowned for camellias and blueberries. Both plants need a free-draining acid soil to thrive, and this part of Dorset has it in abundance. The nursery is in a sheltered spot with a stream running through, fed by natural springs; the water has a pH of 4.8, ideally suited to these plants. You can buy plants but there is also a mail order service. Open all year, Mon–Fri, 9a.m.–4p.m., and weekends in spring and autumn, 10a.m.–4p.m.

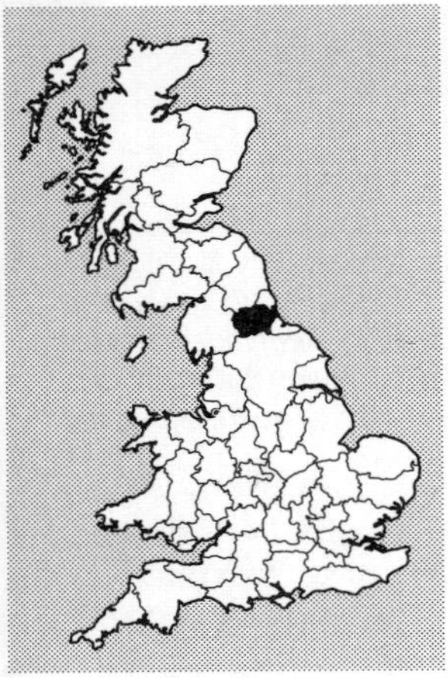

Durham

MAP NO. 7

This is a land of fortresses on rocky outcrops, steeped in histories of border wars, and princes and powerful bishops. Old Durham city, with its vast and splendid Norman cathedral (where the Venerable Bede was laid to rest), lies within a hairpin loop of the River Wear. To the south-west, the Tees Valley embraces some of the country's finest landscape and a sprinkling of attractive, unspoilt villages. Upper Teesdale is famed for its traditionally managed pastures, a wealth of natural limestone flora, and the unique Teesdale violet.

DURHAM

University Of Durham Botanic Garden

Hollingside Lane, Durham DH1 3TN TEL. *0191-374 7971* OWNER *Durham University* HOURS *Open all year, daily, 9a.m.–4p.m. Visitor Centre open April–Oct, daily, 10a.m.–5p.m.; Nov–March, daily, 1–3.30p.m., except Christmas Day and bad weather* ENTRANCE *£1, OAPs 50p, children free* DIRECTIONS *A167 from Durham, left at roundabout signposted towards Durham, right at College*

SPRING SUMMER AUTUMN WINTER

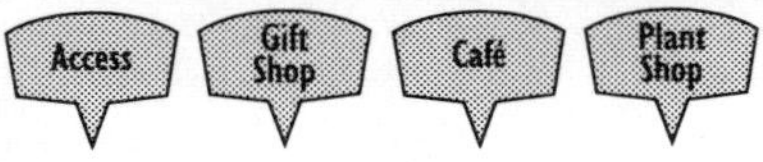

Just a mile from the city's centre, this garden covers around 18 acres, principally used for academic teaching and research. A striking feature near the entrance is the Prince Bishop's Garden, featuring recent, carved statues of six of the county's most prominent historical figures. (Alas! All are male – the north is clearly a stronghold of male chauvinism – but surely Cicely Neville, the Rose of Raby, should be there?

RARE AND UNUSUAL PLANTS

Dirk van der Werff is a plant enthusiast who has used his hobby to found a fascinating and invaluable subscription-only journal for plantaholics. Five years ago he thought of producing an occasional newsletter giving out obscure plant information to like-minded people. New, Rare and Unusual Plants: A Journal for Plant Enthusiasts *is the result, now in its fourth year of production. It is distributed quarterly for a global market of around 1400 subscribers.*

'Information was scarce about [new] plant species which had been collected, where new cultivars appearing in nurseries had come from and old named plants which had been rediscovered,' says Dirk. 'I try to act as a signpost as much as anything else – directing people to where they can find more plants.'

The A5 journal, partially illustrated with colour photographs, is packed with features by nurserymen, plant hunters and others, covering such topics as: the best Japanese anemones, new thyme cultivars, the latest in hardy geranium breeding and new plants from America.

When not hard at work in his own garden or producing this great little journal, Dirk works as a picture editor for a regional evening newspaper. Subscription enquiries should be directed to Aquilegia Publishing, 2 Grange Close, Hartlepool TS26 0DU, tel/fax 01429-423165. E-mail:dirk@aquil.demon.co.uk.

She was the wife of Richard of York who bore two kings, Edward IV and Richard III.) Beyond lie the glasshouses, featuring climates for desert plants and those hailing from the humid tropics. There is a small rose garden and adjoining alpine garden, and a garden of heathers and conifers set in wavy ground whose topography was produced by hundreds of years of ridge-and-furrow ploughing.

The main features, however, are the woodland garden of primulas, giant lilies and blue poppies among the rhododendrons which are best seen in spring, and the North American Arboretum at its most colourful in autumn. Unlike other botanic gardens, where plants are normally grouped according to their botanical families, in this arboretum the trees are planted in groups that would be found growing together naturally in the wild. Thus, those of California are grouped together, separate from those of Canada. A Himalayan dell features white-stemmed birches of the Far East, graceful Bhutan pines and deodar cedars.

And also...

Durham College of Agriculture and Horticulture, Houghall, Durham DH1 3SG (tel. 0191-386 1351), covers 24 acres of training grounds for students, encompassing many different horticultural disciplines. There are glasshouses, rock and heather gardens, woodland plants, herbaceous grounds, a water garden and arboretum. There are also National Collections of meconopsis and sorbus species. Open daily, all year, 9a.m.–4.30p.m. Entrance free.

Pockerley Manor, at The North of England Open Air Museum, Beamish DH9 0RG (tel. 01207-231811), features ¼-acre terraced gardens re-created to look as they might have done 200 years ago. Three terraces descend the hill, featuring a formal parterre, a vegetable garden of historic varieties, and an orchard. The discovery of the 1820 lists of Gateshead nurseryman William Falla, then one of the largest commercial nurseries in Britain, provide invaluable data on locally grown plants. Open April–late Oct, daily, 10a.m.–5p.m. (10a.m.–6p.m., mid-July–Aug) (last adm. 3p.m.). Entrance summer £7, OAPs and children £5; mid-July–Aug £8 and £5; winter £3 and £2.

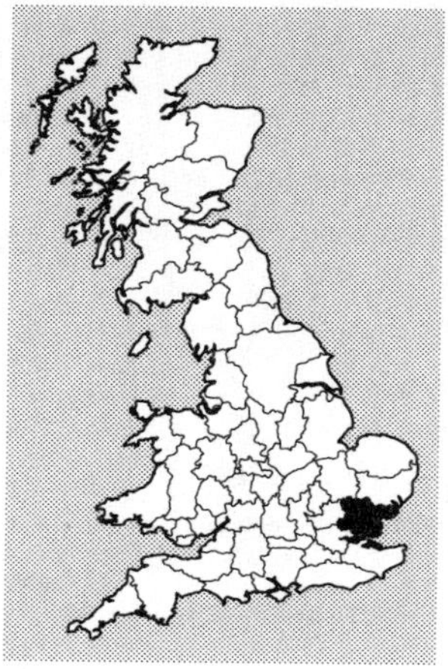

Essex

MAP NO. 3

Essex has many different faces. There is the urban sprawl in the south and west that has encroached from north-east London, there are the broad mudflats and silty marshes of the Thames estuary, and the famous old seaside resorts of Southend, Clacton, and Frinton-on-Sea. Inland Essex, away from the docks and industrial sprawl, is surprisingly rural – much of it low, level ground with the skyline pierced by the silvery silhouettes of great willow trees. The Stour Valley, on the boundary with Suffolk, is scenic country, often painted by John Constable. Nowhere does this region present real hills, although there are subtle undulations to the north of the county, an area which boasts many pretty villages. Colchester, however, stands on a ridge and was strategically important in Roman times.

CHELMSFORD

Hyde Hall RHS Garden

Rettendon, Chelmsford CM3 8ET TEL. *01245-400256*
OWNER *The Royal Horticultural Society* HOURS *Late March–Oct, Wed–Sun and Bank Holidays, 11a.m.–6p.m. (closes 5p.m. Sept–Oct)* ENTRANCE *£3, children (6–16) 70p*
DIRECTIONS *6m SE of Chelmsford, signposted from A130*

SPRING SUMMER AUTUMN WINTER

Access | Café | Plant Shop | NPC

This is a real enthusiasts' garden, begun in 1955 by Dick and Helen Robinson, who passed the property on to the Royal Horticultural Society in 1992. It has always been a garden of richly diverse horticulture: in its 24 acres there are pools, woodland areas and mixed borders of shrubs, roses, trees and bulbs. There are substantial collections of roses, irises, South African plants, viburnums, conifers, daffodils and much else, too.

When the Robinsons came to the windswept, upland farm, there were precious few trees and no garden at all. It was developed gradually, in a piecemeal way, and the spaciousness of the site has allowed it to convert, without too much trouble, into a major horticultural attraction. Development continues under the Society's direction and, most recently, the lower pond has been enlarged to provide enhanced displays of waterlilies and naturalistic swaths of waterside plants.

MISS WILLMOTT AND HER 'GHOST'

Sea hollies, or eryngiums, are popular herbaceous plants, valued for their spiky flowers which make excellent specimens when dried. Some species have an unusual, metallic blue sheen to both stems and flowers, others are green or grey, but attractively statuesque. Eryngium giganteum *is a desirable biennial sea holly, gleaming silver-grey and often called 'Miss Willmott's Ghost'.*

The name refers to Miss Ellen Willmott (1858–1934), a headstrong heiress with formidable horticultural knowledge, especially where roses were concerned. She lived at Warley Place, near Brentwood, where her considerable fortune was lavished on the garden and thousands of pounds were spent yearly on new plants. (In its heyday, Warley Place was internationally famous and employed 104 uniformed gardeners and displayed unrivalled plant collections, beautifully grown.)

It is said that the eponymous eryngium earned its name from the way that Miss Willmott scattered its seeds in the gardens of people she visited. The resulting plants were, so to speak, her slowly germinating calling-cards.

The fortune, alas, expired before Miss Willmott did, and Warley Place and its awesome gardens no longer exist, except as a woodland nature reserve.

COLCHESTER

The Beth Chatto Gardens

Elmstead Market, Colchester CO7 7DB TEL. *01206-822007* OWNER *Beth Chatto* HOURS *March–Oct, Mon–Sat, 9a.m.–5p.m.; Nov–Feb, Mon–Fri, 9a.m.–4p.m., closed Bank Holidays* ENTRANCE *£2.50, accompanied children free* DIRECTIONS *7m E of Colchester, ¼m E of Elmstead Market on A133*

SPRING SUMMER AUTUMN WINTER

Plant Shop | Nursery | Mail Order

DON'T MISS

Beth Chatto is one of the most inspiring gardeners I have had the good fortune to meet, and anyone who gardens in difficult conditions (especially in drought areas) can be uplifted by a visit here. From 1960 onwards, on waste ground considered unfit for farming, Beth began to make a garden following ecological principles by choosing plants to suit the prevailing conditions. She was inspired by her husband's detailed knowledge of wild plants and their habitats.

The result is a wonderful, six-acre garden, still evolving, with moisture-loving plants providing an exquisite foliage tapestry around pools and springs. Elsewhere, there are richly planted borders where the soil is fertile but well drained; areas of dry shade under trees are planted with appropriately undemanding subjects and bulbs. The relatively recent Gravel Garden is especially instructive, as it is never watered, and this is in drought-ridden East Anglia. It is a beautiful, flower-filled tapestry of colours through the seasons. Key plants here include pink and mauve alliums, poppies, mulleins, assorted grasses, lavenders, sages, verbenas and African lilies. The adjoining nursery is another feast, with a huge range of well-grown plants, which are also available by mail (the excellent, descriptive catalogue costs £2.50).

GREAT DUNMOW

The Gardens of Easton Lodge

Little Easton, Great Dunmow CM6 2BB TEL. *01371-876979* OWNER *Mr and Mrs B. Creasey* HOURS *Easter–Oct, Sat–Sun, 2–6p.m., Feb–Mar (for snowdrops), Sat–Sun, 12 noon–4p.m. (subject to weather)* ENTRANCE *£2.75, OAPs £2.50, children under 12 free* DIRECTIONS *1m N of Great Dunmow off B184, signposted*

SPRING SUMMER AUTUMN WINTER

Access Café Plant Shop

DON'T MISS

The owners prefix the property as 'The Forgotten' Gardens of Easton Lodge, but perhaps not for too much longer, for a fascinating project of repair and restoration is now under way. But first, a little background. Originally an Elizabethan estate with 800 acres of deer park, it was home to the fabulously rich Daisy, Countess of Warwick, who was a mistress of the Prince of Wales during Queen Victoria's reign. Daisy employed Harold Peto (*q.v.*) to landscape the gardens in 1902 which he did by providing balustraded raised beds, a rectangular pool, a brick-and-stone pavilion, lawns with arched pergolas and trelliswork, a fantastic Italian garden with 100-ft-long lily-pool surrounded by Ham stone terraces and balustrades, a maze, a tree-house and a Japanese garden with a tea house by the lake. Alas, after the Countess's death in 1938 the property deteriorated, and in the war the park was obliterated to make an airfield for bombers. The main house was demolished and the gardens abandoned in 1950.

THE SAFFRON WALDEN CROCUSES

The picturesque and ancient town of Saffron Walden is famous for its colour-washed houses and decorative plasterwork (pargeting). It is also intimately connected with crocuses, for it derives its very name from the saffron crocus, Crocus sativus. *These corms are among the oldest of all cultivated flowers. They ornamented vases of ancient Crete, c.1500 B.C., and saffron features in the Greek herbal of Dioscorides. Saffron was used medicinally and for dying wool, and the Romans may well have brought it to England. There is no record of its being grown here commercially until the 14th century however, when many small fields around Saffron Walden were used for the purpose.*

According to one account, a pilgrim in the Holy Land 'stole an head of Saffron, and hid the same in his Palmers staffe ... and he brought this root into this realme, with venture of his life'. Cultivation ceased to be commercial from the 1750s, when cheaper Spanish imports could be bought, but the flower remains significant locally, and is displayed in the town's coat of arms and in carvings in the parish church.

Part of Peto's heroic scheme has now been restored (including the terraced beds, formal pool and pavilion), and scrub and tree clearance has revealed the crumbling remains of the Italian garden. All is done on a very tight budget with much help from volunteers, and it will be fascinating to see more of this extraordinary garden reappear, year by year.

GREAT SALING

Saling Hall

Great Saling, Braintree CM7 5DT TEL. *01371-850243* OWNER *Mr and Mrs Hugh Johnson* HOURS *May–July, Wed, 2–5p.m., parties by written permission* ENTRANCE *£2 for NGS charity* DIRECTIONS *Great Saling is 2m from A120 (turn N at the Saling Oak)*

SPRING | SUMMER | AUTUMN | WINTER

This is the lovely, Dutch-gabled home of the erudite wine and tree expert Hugh Johnson, whose books on both subjects are best sellers. 'Trees are tremendously exciting; there is something about the permanence of wood that really appeals to me, rather like maturing wines,' Hugh told me.

Beside the house and its splendid conservatory the gardens are walled and formal, with topiarised box and juniper trees, ancient apples and rectangular beds infilled with glorious mixtures of herbaceous plants and shrub roses. Further from the house the planting is more relaxed, with a large area of almost level ground planted as an arboretum. There is a slender Japanese garden with acers and a stream, a Shinto shrine, and sensuously curvaceous mounds of clipped box huddled together; there is also an informal pool, ornamented by a group of Himalayan birch trees, with gleaming white stems. The plant collection, particularly of trees and shrubs, is extensive, and the 12-acre grounds include an ancient duck-pond and a moat.

SAFFRON WALDEN

Audley End

Saffron Walden, CB11 4JF **TEL.** *01799-522842* **OWNER** *English Heritage* **HOURS** *April–Sept, Wed–Sun and Bank Holidays, 10a.m.–6p.m. (house open 12 noon–5p.m.); last adm. to grounds 5p.m.* **ENTRANCE** *£3.30, OAPs £2.50, children £1.70 (more to see house)* **DIRECTIONS** *1m W of Saffron Walden on B1383*

SPRING SUMMER AUTUMN WINTER

Gift Shop Café

Audley End is a splendid Jacobean mansion set in a fine 99-acre, 18th-century park that was transformed from an earlier, formal layout by Capability Brown (*q.v.*). It is regarded as one of his most successful pastoral landscapes, with woodland groves, an elegant bridge by Robert Adam, temples and wonderful vistas. The River Cam weaves through its rolling lawns; many wonderful mature trees enhance the silhouette of this garden on level ground. A

Celebrity Choice

Peter Seabrook, author, journalist and presenter of* Peter Seabrook's Gardening Week *on BBC1

'I am always very impressed with **Glen Chantry** (q.v.) *because it has a variety of interesting features on a scale that makes sense to most gardeners. The garden demonstrates good horticultural skills, and the way the plants are grown makes a refreshing change. Within the small garden there is a rockery, a water feature, a shade border and several shrub roses. It is on a hillside, with less than perfect soil, but the planting associations are very well thought out, especially the way the tulips are imaginatively mixed with other plants.*

'Just over the border from here, in Suffolk, I love the little walled garden at **Sun House***, Long Melford* (q.v.)*. It is a nice garden, of reasonable scale, all done by the owner Mrs Thompson, who has a theatrical background, I believe. At any rate, there is a touch of theatrical flair in her planting, and in the way she uses the shrub roses, irises, peonies and tulips. Each area of the garden has its season, and here again is a garden that shows good cultural skills.'*

magnificent Victorian parterre of flowers in geometrically arranged beds beside the house dates from 1830. The beds make a formal pattern cut into the lawn and were restored in recent years, having disappeared due to lack of labour for their upkeep in the Second World War. Now they provide a brilliant summer spectacle of mixed herbaceous perennials, bulbs and tender bedding plants, including lychnis and acanthus, sisyrinchiums, violas, lilies and peonies.

WICKHAM BISHOPS

Glen Chantry

Ishams Chase, Wickham Bishops CM8 3LG TEL. *01621-891342* OWNER *Mr and Mrs Staines* HOURS *April–mid-Oct, Fri–Sat, 10a.m.–4p.m.; also on selected Suns and Mons April–Sept, and for pre-booked groups of 15+ (tel. for details)* ENTRANCE *£1.50, children 50p* DIRECTIONS *9m NE of Chelmsford off A12, take the Witham turn-off, 2m SE of Witham; turn left off B1018 towards Wickham Bishops, past golf course, over river bridge and left up track by Blue Mills*

SPRING SUMMER AUTUMN WINTER

Access · Plant Shop · Nursery · DON'T MISS

Most of the wonderful three-and-a-half-acre garden at Glen Chantry is informally arranged, with broad areas of grass winding between large island beds which are packed with choice plants. Amazingly, the garden was started by Sue and Wol Staines just over 20 years ago, on a very dry and windswept site in the driest corner of England. The soil is free-draining and stony, and to compensate for the relatively low rainfall, the beds are heavily mulched annually with composted waste and manure.

Planting is in bold drifts, with ornamental grasses used creatively for their foliage colours and wispy effects. There are hostas and hellebores, irises, peonies, poppies and a huge range of plants bringing continued changing effects all year round. Special features include a wonderful rock garden flowing away from the house down to a richly planted bog garden and lily-pool, and a more formal white garden. The adjoining nursery opens when the garden does, and specializes in a developing range of the more unusual perennials and alpines. There is an excellent catalogue (send 4 × 1st-class stamps), but no mail order.

And also...

Cants of Colchester, Nayland Road, Mile End, Colchester CO4 5EB (tel. 01206-844008), is the oldest of Britain's rose nurseries which has raised countless well-known varieties, including the highly successful 'Just Joey'. Bare-rooted plants are sold by mail from Nov–March (free catalogue on request), but container-grown roses are available to callers from April–July. Open July–Sept, daily dawn–dusk; telephone first and make an appointment.

Crowther Nurseries and Landscapes, Ongar Road, Abridge RM4 1AA (tel. 01708-688581), is a smallish nursery and garden centre with popular ranges of plants and sundries. It also has an adjoining demonstration garden which is linked to the BBC Radio Essex gardening programmes, and regular gardening talks are given here by broadcaster Ken Crowther, who is also the proprietor. Open all year, except Christmas period, daily, 9a.m.–5.30p.m. Entrance free.

Flora Exotica, Pasadena, South Green, Fingringhoe, Colchester CO5 7DR (tel. 01206-729414), offers carnivorous plants, by mail order only (catalogue £1.50). Stock includes a wide range of hardy and tropical orchids and many rare and unusual herbaceous plants.

The Gibberd Garden, Marsh Lane, Gilden Way, Harlow CM17 0NA (tel. 01279-442112), covers nine tranquil acres on a gently sloping site, with wooded glades, streams and pools, a waterfall and carefully placed sculptures. It was the home of Sir Frederick Gibberd, the modernist architect who designed Harlow New Town, early buildings for Heathrow Airport, Liverpool's Roman Catholic cathedral and the Northumbrian reservoir, Kielder Water. Open April–Sept, Sun only, 2–6p.m.

Langthorns Plantery, Little Canfield, Dunmow CM6 1TD (tel. 01371-872611), stocks an enormous range of plants, especially hardy herbaceous perennials. Alpines, trees and shrubs are also supplied. There is a £1 catalogue, but no mail order. Open all year except Christmas/New Year period, daily, 10a.m.–5p.m. Entrance free.

Ken Muir, Honeypot Farm, Rectory Road, Weeley Heath, Clacton-on-Sea CO16 9BJ (tel. 01255-830181), specializes in fruit, particularly strawberries (his Chelsea show displays are too tempting for words), raspberries, blackberries, currants and a range of tree fruits, especially by mail. Send 3 × 1st-class stamps for a catalogue. Open all year, daily, 10a.m.–4p.m. (closed Christmas).

Trevor Scott, Thorpe Park Cottage, Thorpe-le-Soken CO16 0HN (tel. 01255-861308), specializes in ornamental grasses in a big way. 'Grasses can make superb accents, either standing tall above lower plants, or subtly quiet amongst dissimilar foliage. They can be massed in billowing volumes or spaced apart so that grasses with ample forms provide a sculptural weight; those with narrow forms, flowing lines,' says Scott. His catalogue (send 5 × 1st-class stamps) lists hundreds of varieties, for different effects. There is no mail order. Directions will be given when you make an appointment. Entrance free.

Suffolk Herbs/Seeds by Post, Monks Farm, Pantlings Lane, Kelvedon CO5 9PG (tel. 01376-572456), produces a fantastic, free mail order catalogue of herb, wildflower, vegetable, green manure crop and ancient grain seeds (e.g. quinoa, grown by the Incas); also Chinese and oriental vegetables, organic seeds and products, and a small range of gardening tools.

Warley Rose Gardens, Warley Street, Great Warley, Brentwood CM13 3JH (01277-221966), is a specialist rose grower offering a broad range (over 400 varieties), including climbers and ramblers, hybrid teas and floribundas, shrub, miniature and patio roses. Free catalogue on request. Open all year, Mon–Sat, 9a.m.–5.30p.m. Rose fields in bloom, July–Sept.

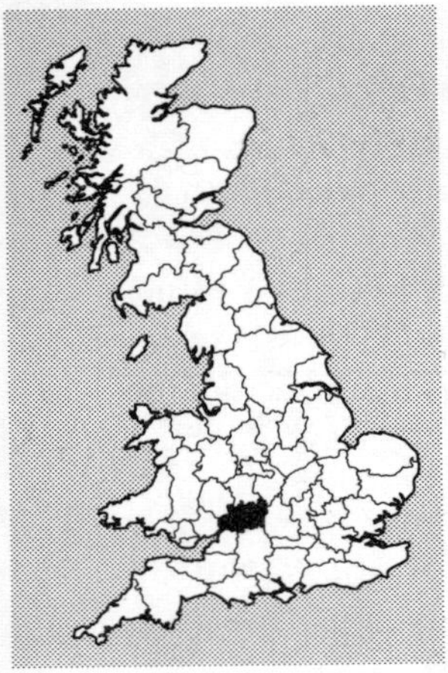

Gloucestershire

MAP NO. 2

The limestone hills of the Cotswolds give Gloucestershire much of its character. They have provided the pleasing undulations in the landscape, and also the wonderful stone that has built many of the county's handsome villages and churches. There are stately homes and royal residences dotted about its dignified countryside, and Gloucestershire certainly has a healthy slice of good gardens, making visiting weekends worthwhile in every season. Designers, architects, artists and others sympathetic with the Arts and Crafts movement of the late 19th and early 20th centuries found the unpretentious vernacular architecture of the Cotswold villages to their taste, and gardens such as those at Snowshill and Rodmarton Manors exemplify the style brought outdoors.

BARNSLEY

Barnsley House Garden

Barnsley, nr Cirencester GL7 5EE TEL. *01285-740281* OWNER *Mr Charles Verey* HOURS *All year, Mon, Wed–Thurs, Sat, 10a.m.–6p.m.* ENTRANCE *£3, OAPs £2, children free, Dec–Jan free* DIRECTIONS *4m NE of Cirencester on B4425 in Barnsley village*

SPRING SUMMER AUTUMN WINTER

Access | Plant Shop

This is the famous four-acre garden of the even more famous *grande dame* of gardening, Rosemary Verey, garden adviser to the Prince of Wales, Elton John and others. My first visit some years ago coincided with laburnum time (at the end of May), when Mrs Verey's famous laburnum tunnel was in full bloom, underplanted by alliums, dark columbines and contrasting foliage of deadnettles, and it was breathtaking. It is still the time I like best in this garden, when the late spring bulbs are joined by early perennials. The peonies, lupins and poppies beautifully mix with sturdy topiaries and formal hedging.

There are intensively gardened mixed borders, strong vistas and contrasting sweeps of lawn, a Tudor-style knot garden, a shrubby and flowery wilderness and, across the farm track, a formal and beautifully kept kitchen garden/potager.

BROADWAY

Snowshill Manor

Broadway WR12 7JU **TEL.** *01386-852410* **OWNER** *The National Trust* **HOURS** *April–Oct, daily, except Tues, 1–5p.m. (closed Good Friday). Grounds and visitor facilities open 12 noon* **ENTRANCE** *(House and grounds – timed ticket system for house) £5.50, children £2.75, family ticket £13.80; (gardens only) £2.50, children £1.25* **DIRECTIONS** *3m SW of Broadway, approach only from turning off A44 by Broadway Green. New car park and entry (500 yards away) – no entry from Snowshill village*

SPRING SUMMER AUTUMN WINTER

Gift Shop Café DON'T MISS

To foreign eyes, and even British ones, Snowshill Manor seems the quintessential English country garden, backed by stone walls, filled with cottage garden plants in great profusion. Poppies, lady's mantle and penstemons spill over its narrow gravel paths, aubrieta tumbles off the walls, and roses and vines run rampant. White pigeons flutter above the mossy, stone-tiled roof of the substantial medieval dovecote, and beyond are sneak views of the rolling Cotswold pastures.

It is a highly architectural garden, its two acres having been planned in the first instance by M.H. Baillie Scott, an architect working in the Arts and Crafts style in the 1920s, whose intentions were simplified and made less formal by the owner, Charles Wade, who was also an architect. Its little walled enclosures, corridors and flights of steps were laid out with precision, and the incidental timber work – doors, benches, niches and so on – were (and continue to be) picked out in a bold French blue that complements both the flowers and the honey-grey local stone. There are daffodil-packed lawns rolling down the hill in a smooth, green counterpoint to the formal stonework, and everything is now managed organically, in sympathy with the bucolic flavour of the place.

CHIPPING CAMPDEN

Hidcote Manor Garden

Hidcote Bartrim, Chipping Campden GL55 6LR TEL. *01386-438333* OWNER *The National Trust* HOURS *April–Oct, daily, except Tues and Fri, 11a.m.–7p.m. (closing 6p.m. in Oct); also Tues, June–July; last adm. 1hr before closing* ENTRANCE *£5.30, children £2.60, family ticket £13.20* DIRECTIONS *At Hidcote Bartrim, signposted from B4632 Stratford–Broadway road*

SPRING SUMMER AUTUMN WINTER

Access | Gift Shop | Café | Plant Shop | DON'T MISS

Hidcote Manor is one of Britain's most famous and influential gardens, made in the early years of the 20th century by Major Lawrence Johnston. Like Sissinghurst (*q.v.*) in Kent, it is essential visiting for anyone with more than a superficial interest in gardens, partly because its impact on 20th-century garden-making has been profound, partly because it is a great garden.

Having been given the hamlet of Hidcote Bartrim, the manor house and 280 acres of farmland by his mother in 1907, Major Johnston set about creating his 10-acre garden masterpiece. It is divided into hedged rooms and green corridors in a thoroughly disciplined way, but within each area the chosen planting conveys a different feel. The restful green simplicity of grass and plain hedges of one area lead

'CHINESE' WILSON AND HIS PLANTS

If you have Clematis armandii, C. montana rubens, *kiwi fruits, a paperbark maple (*Acer griseum*), or the deeply fragrant* regale *lilies in your garden then you have reason to thank Ernest 'Chinese' Wilson (1876–1930), who was born at Chipping Campden. These are just a few of the beautiful plants that he introduced to our shores following his intrepid expeditions to the Far East in the early years of the 20th century. Wilson's journals note the perilous nature of his task in searching out new plants: 'Well, if they take a fancy for my head during the night I do not see what is to prevent them from taking it,' he recorded on a trip to the mountains of Formosa. 'Gathered around several fires were two score half-naked ex-head-hunters, armed with bows and arrows, long knives and guns, who had struggled all day ... carrying our belongings.' Wilson nearly lost his life in collecting* Lilium regale *but ironically, having survived landslides, armed rebellions and snowstorms during his expeditions, he died in a car crash on a suburban highway near Boston.* ***The Ernest Wilson Memorial Garden, High Street, Chipping Campden GL55 6AF (tel. 01386-852630),*** *features a collection of his plants. Open all year, daily, dawn to dusk. Entrance by donation. At the north end of High Street.*

to intensive, colourful planting in another. There is a famous White Garden with topiary birds; an equally famous pair of red borders featuring seasonal red flowers and bronze foliage, terminating in handsome brick gazebos; a circular pool garden almost entirely filled with water; a garden of fuchsias; a Long Walk serenely grassed and hedged; woodland and stream gardens crossed by winding paths and much more. Each season has its merits, so return often – there are always new surprises.

CHIPPING CAMPDEN

Kiftsgate Court

Chipping Campden GL55 6LW **TEL.** *01386-438777*
OWNER *Mr and Mrs J. Chambers* **HOURS** *April–May, Aug–Sept, Wed–Thurs, Sun and Bank Holiday Mons, 2–6p.m.; June–July, Wed–Thurs, Sat–Sun, 12 noon–6p.m.*
ENTRANCE *April–May, Aug–Sept, £3; June–July, £3.50;*

children £1 **DIRECTIONS** *3m NE of Chipping Campden, close to Hidcote Manor (q.v.)*

SPRING SUMMER AUTUMN WINTER

Plant Shop

Famous for the rampant 'Kiftsgate' rose, which effortlessly clambers through large trees and over a tithe barn, showering everything in white blossoms in July, this is a six-acre garden of dramatic statements. Its house sits at the top of a steep escarpment, peering through the trees to the Vale of Evesham. The garden runs downhill in a series of terraces and zigzag walks, with enclosed areas at the top padded out by lush plantings of shrubs and seasonal flowers, giving way to more natural fusion with the landscape as the paths progress down the steep slope. There are other lovely roses here, including a long path hedged either side by pink-and-white *Rosa gallica* 'Versicolor' (a.k.a. *Rosa mundi*) which terminates by a seat, interestingly framed by an arch fashioned in trained and pruned whitebeam. It is a pleasant, living, family-run garden as it has been for three generations, and there are some interesting plants for sale near the entrance.

COWLEY

Cowley Manor

Cowley, Cheltenham GL53 9NL **TEL.** *01242-870540*
OWNER *The Cowley Manor Partnership* **HOURS** *March–Oct, daily, except Fri and Mon (but open Bank Holiday Mons), 10a.m.–6p.m.* **ENTRANCE** *£3.50, OAPs £3, children under 18 free* **DIRECTIONS** *In Cowley village, off A435 Cheltenham–Cirencester road*

SPRING SUMMER AUTUMN WINTER

Plant Shop

FABULOUSLY FRAGRANT CARNATIONS

There are many different carnations, but none compare with the sumptuous, peony-like blooms and heady, clove fragrances of the Malmaison race, admired in the 19th century but only recently brought back from obscurity by enthusiast Jim Marshall. ***Marshall's Malmaisons, 4 The Damsells, Tetbury GL8 8JA (tel. 01666-502589),*** *specializes in these plants, which produce tall stems and classic cut flowers, ideal for ornate arrangements.*

The Malmaison carnation originated in France, but its cultivation was perfected in Britain. The variety 'Souvenir de la Malmaison' (also known as 'Old Blush') was so named because it resembled the flowers of the Bourbon rose of that name. Other early varieties include 'Princess of Wales', with rose-pink flowers, 'Duchess of Westminster', also a strong pink, 'Tayside Red', and 'Thora', a pale blush, fading to white. They like the cool, airy conditions of a well-ventilated conservatory or glasshouse. Water sparingly over winter, and use a weak liquid feed from April when new growth has started. Shade is needed to avoid bleaching the flowers once buds begin to open. Most Malmaisons will propagate by stem cuttings taken from March–September. Open by appointment only.

More than 100 years ago the polemical gardening writer William Robinson (*q.v.*) suggested that many plants, usually grown in the constraint of a border, could successfully be let free, to grow alongside native grasses and wildflowers to create, in fact, a 'wild garden'. Since then, few people have seriously experimented with the approach, but it is one that is now being given rein at Cowley Manor, where the 50-acre grounds have been undergoing radical replanting and renovations in recent years.

Much of the Victorian structure of the garden – its Italianate terracing and waterworks – dates from the late 1890s, when James Horlick, purveyor of the eponymous bedtime drink, bought the property. Succeeding years have seen several changes of ownership, and plantsman-designer Noel Kingsbury is now experimenting with Cowley's pleasing landscape to produce naturalistic, flower-filled theme 'meadows' using herbaceous perennials, ornamental grasses and wildflowers. It is early days yet, but this seems a worthy and ecologically friendly approach that is likely to capture the imagination of more gardeners as time progresses. There are areas for moisture-loving plants, borders on dry soil, managed pastures, and a lovely valley of wild orchids, kingcups and meadowsweet.

TETBURY

Hodges Barn

Shipton Moyne, Tetbury GL8 8PR TEL. *01666-880202* OWNER *Mrs Charles Hornby* OPEN *April–mid-Aug, Mon–Tues and Fri, 2–5p.m.* ENTRANCE *£2.50, children free* DIRECTIONS *3m S of Tetbury on Malmesbury side of Shipton Moyne, a few hundred yards after leaving village*

SPRING SUMMER AUTUMN WINTER

You really get the feeling of a well-loved, personally looked-after garden at Hodges Barn. It is renowned for its extensive use of climbing and shrub roses (the late Charles Hornby was passionate about them), and Amanda Hornby will often be seen tending the gardens herself, which she does with limited help, or offering helpful advice to visitors. The Barn itself (now a sumptuous home, not open) was originally an elaborate dovecote, built in 1499 to provide food for a nearby mansion house which no longer exists. The eight-acre gardens surrounding it are divided by ancient, Cotswold-stone field walls and mature hedges. Spring ushers in naturalised bulbs and blossoming cherries, crab apples and magnolias. The many roses take over from early summer, joined by relaxed plantings of herbaceous flowers and fragrant shrubs. There are skilfully planted pots of hydrangeas, fuchsias and scented-leaf plants beside the loggia, and a woodland area backing onto sheep pastures devoted to choice shrubs and more shrub roses.

TETBURY

Westonbirt Arboretum

Westonbirt, Tetbury GL8 8QS TEL. *01666-880220* OWNER *Forestry Commission* HOURS *Open all year, daily, 10a.m.–8p.m. (or dusk if earlier). Visitor Centre open all year, daily, 10a.m.–5p.m.* ENTRANCE *£3.20, OAPs £2.20, children £1* DIRECTIONS *3m S of Tetbury on A433*

SPRING SUMMER AUTUMN WINTER

Access | Gift Shop | Café | Plant Shop | NPC | DON'T MISS

Wear stout shoes for a jaunt at Westonbirt (it covers 600 acres) which you can enjoy in any season. There are 18,000 trees, representing 4000 species brought from all over the world, and every visit will inspire new impressions. Spring sees the magnolias, rhododendrons, azaleas, dogwoods and wildflowers (especially bluebells) in bloom.

In summer the shade of broad-leaved trees and open lawns provide endless picnic venues, and the air is heady with lime-blossom. Autumn is the peak visiting season for tinted leaf displays rivalling (and, some say, improving upon) New England in the Fall; this is when the leaves of acers, exotic oaks, sweet gum, dogwoods, etc. turn to brilliant golds and scarlets with the onset of colder weather. In winter the deep green and golden silhouettes of the conifers bring a startling contrast to the twiggy, hazy outlines of their unclothed neighbours. There are 17 miles of trails, and the arboretum holds National Collections of acer (maples) and salix (willows).

WINCHCOMBE

Sudeley Castle and Gardens

Winchcombe GL54 5JD TEL. *01242-602308* OWNER *Lady Ashcombe* HOURS *March, daily, 11a.m.–4.30p.m., April–Oct, daily, 10.30a.m–5.30p.m.* ENTRANCE *£4.10, OAPs £3.80, children £2.20 (extra to see castle)* DIRECTIONS *8m NE of Cheltenham, on B4632 (A46)*

SPRING SUMMER AUTUMN WINTER

Gift Shop | Café | Plant Shop

Sudeley Castle oozes history; it was Crown property during the Wars of the Roses, and after the death of Henry VIII was given to Thomas Seymour who married Henry's widow, Katherine Parr. Queen Elizabeth was entertained here in the 1590s and Charles I stayed at the castle during the English Civil War.

The 15-acre gardens are romantically exuberant, but take their inspiration from the formal and symmetrical patterns of original Tudor garden plans. Wisterias and species roses feature in the Tithe Barn Garden; the White Garden features roses in abundance with white-flowered spring bulbs and summer perennials; the Queen's Garden is enclosed by fantastic yew tunnels, 160 years old, and has formal beds of old roses and herbs. Spring bulbs ornament a garden dedicated to an ancient mulberry tree, and there are further knot gardens and roses, and a new Henry Doubleday Victorian vegetable garden.

And also...

Batsford Arboretum, Moreton-in-Marsh GL56 9QF (tel. 01608-650722), offers wonderful walking through 50 acres of diverse trees which have been planted on its undulating hillside since the 1880s. An especially good place for autumn jaunts, the arboretum is also speckled with interesting statuary, including subjects brought from the Far East. Open March–early Nov (ring for Nov closing date), daily, 10a.m.–5p.m. Entrance £3.50, OAPs/children (11–15) £3 (under 11s free). The garden centre by the car park is open all year, and is well stocked with shrubs, trees, alpines and flowering plants.

Art and nature come together in the **Forest of Dean Sculpture Trail** (off B4226 between Coleford and Cinderford). There is a marked route of around five miles through the vast forest that blurs Gloucestershire's border with Wales. It is clearly not a garden but, like Grizedale Forest (*q.v.*) in Cumbria, can give anyone a new perspective on using natural materials in a decorative way in the garden, albeit in reduced scale. Open all year. Entrance free.

There are around 3000 different pots on display at **The Old Bell Pottery, High Street, Lechlade GL7 3AD (tel. 01367-252608)**. Some are thrown on site by potter Keith Broley, others he has bought from suppliers across Britain, Europe and the Far East, and displayed in his pot and topiary garden, at prices ranging from under 50p to over £400. Open all year, daily, 9.30a.m.–6p.m.

Splendidly gabled and mullioned **Owlpen Manor, Uley, Dursley GL11 5BZ (tel. 01453-860261)**, is the quintessentially English Cotswold country house. It is set in a picturesque valley, below its yew-garlanded church and a rising wood of beeches. The formal, two-acre terraced gardens date from the 16th and 17th centuries, and maintain the spirit of ages past. They feature yew topiaries, box parterres, old roses and herbs; interest is added by the nearby medieval tithe barn and old mill and mill-pond, and there is a licensed restaurant, tel. 01453-860816, open from 12 noon. Open April–Oct, Tues–Sun and Bank Holiday Mons, 2–5p.m. Entrance £3.75, children (5–14) £2, family ticket £10.50 (house and garden); garden and grounds only: £2.50, children £1.

Painswick Rococo Garden, The Stables, Painswick House, Painswick, Stroud GL6 6TH (tel. 01452-813204), had been lost in woodland and undergrowth until, in 1983, its owner Lord Dickinson began to rootle around trying to find its early 18th-century layout and buildings. Now, almost fully restored, its 10 acres offer splendid walks along snaking paths to investigate its pools, temples, alcoves and gothic retreats. The snowdrop carpets in February are especially magnificent. Open mid-Jan–Nov, Wed–Sun, 11a.m.–5p.m. Also daily, July–Aug. Entrance £3, OAPs £2.70, children £1.60.

The four-acre garden of **The Priory, Kemerton GL20 7JN (tel. 01386-725258)**, is renowned for its richness of colour, especially in late summer, from herbaceous borders packed with sumptuous dahlias, rhubarb chard, heleniums, Michaelmas daisies and crocosmia. There is a pale border of graduated hues, with silver foliage plants and feathery cosmos, and a renowned red border of sultry, deep purple foliage including ricinus and cotinus, and deep red dahlias in profusion. The hidden-away June garden features old roses and pastel-coloured perennials. Open June–late Sept, Thurs only, 2–6p.m. Entrance £2 (£1.50 in June).

There is a really strong feeling of the late 19th-century Arts and Crafts style as advocated by William Morris and his contemporaries at **Rodmarton Manor, Rodmarton, Cirencester GL7 6PF (tel. 01285-841253)**. This lovely eight-acre Cotswold garden is laid out in hedged rooms around an idyllic stone manor house. It is undergoing gradual restoration and renovation and features yew topiaries, pleached limes, stone troughs of alpines, double herbaceous borders, and a walled garden where I bought a vigorous scarlet-flowered pelargonium, having seen it flourishing in the glasshouses. Open mid-May–end Aug, Sat only, 2–5p.m. Entrance £2.50, children (under 16) free.

At **Ruardean Garden Pottery, Ruardean, Forest of Dean GL17 9TP (tel. 01594-543577)**, master potter John Huggins specializes in frost-proof terracotta plantpots for the garden in a large range of styles. Also hand-made rhubarb and sea kale forcing jars with lids, for blanching the stems in the traditional way. Mail order is available (send s.a.e. for a catalogue). Open all year, Mon–Sat, 9a.m.–5.30p.m. (also Suns, March–Sept, 1–5p.m.).

Westbury Court Garden, Westbury-on-Severn GL14 1PD (tel. 01452-760461), is a rare example of a 17th-century Dutch-style garden, laid out on level ground, with water canals, yew hedges and topiary. The five-acre garden was laid out between 1696 and 1705, and has undergone extensive restoration since the 1970s, with plantings appropriate to the period and the rebuilding of a lovely brick pavilion offering first-floor views from its tall windows. The walled garden features old fruit and flower varieties. Open April–Oct, Wed–Sun and Bank Holiday Mons, 11a.m.–6p.m. (closed Good Friday). Entrance £2.70, children £1.35.

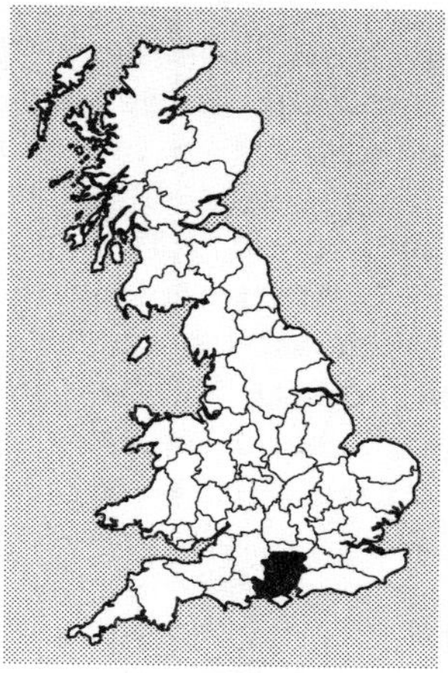

Hampshire

MAP NO. 2

Mostly scenic but partly industrial (in its southern ports), embracing the high chalk hills of the North and South Downs, with vast tracts of forested heaths and fertile lowland farms, Hampshire is like England in miniature. There are houses built of solid ironstone, and others fashioned from flints and local clay bricks. The famous chalk streams running off the Downs provide some of the best trout fishing in the land, lying in some of the loveliest landscape. The New Forest is home to wild deer and itinerant ponies, and much of its 90,000 acres makes rewarding walking, whether on open heath or through beech and oak wood. Hampshire's gardens are just as varied, too, and its fertile soils have found favour with a number of notable nurseries.

ALRESFORD

Hinton Ampner

Bramdean, nr Alresford SO24 OLA **TEL.** *01962-771305* **OWNER** *The National Trust* **HOURS** *(Garden only) late March–Sept, Tues–Wed, Sat–Sun and Bank Holiday Mons, 1.30–5p.m.* **ENTRANCE** *£3, children £1.50* **DIRECTIONS** *On A272, 1m W of Bramdean village, 8m E of Winchester. Leave M3 Jct 9 and follow signs to Petersfield*

SPRING | SUMMER | AUTUMN | WINTER

Access | Café

The 18th-century brick mansion of Hinton Ampner is not open to viewing, but is set in wonderful grounds, with outstanding views of its own park and very fine Hampshire countryside. The 12-acre gardens have formal terracing near the house with lawns, excellent topiary and lovely flower borders. In front of the house the stairway balustrades are garlanded with pink roses, and self-sown erigerons and lady's mantle provide a relaxed counterpoint to the austerity of the terrace. There are long, grassy walks terminating in statues, and well-thought-out routes that lead to intimate areas and surprise views. The Dell at Hinton Ampner is a former chalkpit planted with assorted trees and shrubs that were initially chosen for their ability to thrive in the strongly alkaline conditions of the pit. Beyond it is a fragrant philadelphus walk with tall box hedging and assorted flowering shrubs. All in all, a very enjoyable place to spend an afternoon.

THE BEAUTY OF BOX

Elizabeth Braimbridge, of Langley Boxwood Nursery, Rake, nr Liss GU33 7JL (tel. 01730-894467), *ring for directions and opening times, started to grow box 15 years ago, when she wanted some for hedging but could not find a supplier anywhere. Her nursery is now known internationally for its wide range (she sells around 60 different species and varieties of these understated plants and holds the National Collection). 'One thing people always want to know is when they should trim the bushes,' she says. 'I like to prune just before growth begins, when the buds begin to move in March. Later, if they are a bit shaggy, I give them another trim in late June, when the earlier growth has hardened.' Although it is fine to leave pruning to just one session, in August, it should be finished before the end of August to allow any new growth some time to harden off before the frosts arrive. As well as having substantial stocks of hedging and topiary, the nursery stocks dwarf, large-leaved, small-leaved, weeping, fastigiate, extra hardy, slightly tender, and variegated cultivars which have been sourced from all over the world. Send 4 × 1st-class stamps for a mail order catalogue. Open by appointment only.*

EXBURY

Exbury Gardens

Exbury, nr Southampton SO4 1AZ TEL. *01703-891203* OWNER *E.L. de Rothschild* HOURS *March–Oct, daily, 10a.m.–5.30p.m. (sunset if earlier)* ENTRANCE *£4.50, OAPs £4 (£3.50 Wed–Thurs), children £3.50* DIRECTIONS *From*

Totton (W of Southampton) 14m to Exbury village by A326 and B3054

SPRING | SUMMER | AUTUMN | WINTER

Access · Gift Shop · Café · Plant Shop · DON'T MISS

Late April and early May is the peak time to visit Exbury's 200 extraordinary acres. This is when you will see most of the garden's thousands of rhododendrons and azaleas in bloom, and the sight is breathtaking. The gardens were made by Lionel de Rothschild (*q.v.*), a scion of the famous banking family, in the years between the two World Wars. The local mild climate, natural oak wood and light, acidic soil proved ideal for rhododendrons, and Lionel de Rothschild spared no expense in making a garden that was to contain around one million plants, with 22 miles of irrigation pipes and sprinklers to avoid problems in a drought. He took great interest in the plant hunting expeditions to the Far East by George Forrest, Frank Kingdon-Ward and others, and bred 1210 rhododendrons himself, the best 462 of which were named and registered.

Wear comfortable shoes and set aside a day to enjoy Exbury's 20 miles of rambling pathways, its pools, springs and quiet glades. Early spring sees many camellias and the

LIONEL DE ROTHSCHILD'S WORLD OF PLANTS

*Lionel de Rothschild, the charismatic creator of Exbury's famous rhododendron grounds, grew up among fine gardens. He was born at Ascott (*q.v.*) in Buckinghamshire, and from an early age was interested in flowers. Although famous for his home-raised rhododendrons, they were not his only passion. During the 1920s and thirties he also planted an arboretum at Exbury, which he intended should display every hardy tree that could be grown. (His adviser was W.J. Bean, the famous tree expert and curator of Kew Gardens.) There were also acres of greenhouses on the estate, where pride of place was given to a huge orchid collection. Lionel became almost as famous for his orchids as for the rhododendrons, his hybrid cymbidiums being particularly prized.*

large-leaved rhododendrons such as *R. sinogrande* and the Exbury-raised 'Fortune' in bloom; May sees the fragrant azaleas joined by flowering dogwoods, candelabra primulas and fresh-leaved acers. There is a small, summer garden of roses, but autumn is good for foliage tints in the woodlands. There is also a two-acre rock garden, lovely in April, with dwarf rhododendrons and associated plants.

LYNDHURST

Furzey Gardens

Minstead, nr Lyndhurst SO4 37GL TEL. *01703-812297* OWNER *Furzey Gardens Charitable Trust* HOURS *Open all year, daily (except 25–26 Dec), 10a.m.–5p.m. (or dusk in winter)* ENTRANCE *£3, OAPs £2.50, children £1.50 (reduced prices in winter)* DIRECTIONS *At Minstead, 8m SW of Southampton, 1m S of A31, 3½m NW of Lyndhurst*

SPRING SUMMER AUTUMN WINTER

Gift Shop Plant Shop

Furzey is an eight-acre garden of great subtlety and charm. It was made in the 1920s out of rough heathland, in the middle of the New Forest. The planting style is of very informal shrubberies and open lawns covering the garden's south-facing slopes, using a large variety of acid soil-loving plants. The late spring show of azaleas is spectacular, with flowers in pink and tangerine hues. There is a good collection of birch trees, including *Betula lenta*, with toffee-coloured peeling bark, and the heather collection is extensive, bringing colour all year round. On the lower ground there is a lovely pond with rustic bridges and a stream, with associated waterside plants such as skunk cabbages and candelabra primulas.

Early spring sees the grass carpeted in snowdrops, crocuses and daffodils and the autumn tints of the shrubberies are spectacular, with plants such as enkianthus and amelanchier turning to brilliant reds and golds.

Celebrity Choice

Alan Titchmarsh, presenter of BBC2's* Gardeners' World *from his home at Barleywood, Hampshire

'The National Trust's property at **Hinton Ampner** *(q.v.) is, if you like, my local stately home. The brick Georgian house is a beauty and the garden complements it rather well. It is just 20 minutes' drive away from my home, so when I go there I like to dream a little of what it must have been like to be lord of all you surveyed. Its garden has been rejuvenated in recent years, with lovely, luxurious plantings. There are great beds of dahlias and more informal, lush planting, a dell garden, some very good yew topiary and, above all, wonderful views of rolling fields of pasture and wheat. I'd visit Hinton Ampner even if it had no garden at all, just for the views. This garden has a very satisfying component of formal and informal elements, and there's so much there, it takes a while to explore.*

'I have also always had a fondness for **Greatham Mill, Greatham, nr Liss GU33 6HH (tel. 01420-538245).** *The garden was made by the late Mrs Pumphrey, a lovely lady who was great fun and had a wonderfully relaxed way of planting. There is an old mill house draped in wisteria, with a river running through the grounds. The planting is very informal, but well chosen. Mrs Pumphrey's son and daughter-in-law are now rejuvenating the garden, and long may it continue to bring pleasure to all.' Open April–Oct, daily, 10a.m.–6p.m. Entrance £2, children free.*

ROMSEY

Mottisfont Abbey Garden

Mottisfont, nr Romsey SO51 0LJ TEL. *01794-341220*
OWNER *The National Trust* HOURS *April–Oct, Sat–Wed, 12 noon–6p.m. (or dusk if sooner). In rose season, early June–early July (ring to check the dates), daily, 11a.m.–8.30p.m. (last adm. 1hr before closing)* ENTRANCE *£4, children £2, mid-summer rose season £5, children £2.50* DIRECTIONS *4m NW of Romsey, ½ m W of A3057*

SPRING SUMMER AUTUMN WINTER

Access · Gift Shop · Café · Plant Shop · NPC · DON'T MISS

These are really lovely gardens in one of Hampshire's most idyllic locations, beside a fast-flowing tributary of the River

Test. The clear waters skirt a lawn which is host to a vast plane tree – the largest of its kind in the country and, according to some authorities, probably also the largest tree of *any* kind in this country. There are wild areas frothed up with cow-parsley in spring, and more formal gardens beside the abbey, designed in the 1930s by Sir Geoffrey Jellicoe, featuring a pleached lime avenue underplanted with early bulbs.

However, the walled, former kitchen garden is the essential, early summer feature of the 25-acre gardens. Within its red-brick walls lie four square lawns around a central fountain, flanked by herbaceous borders and a staggering collection of old-fashioned roses. Knee-high box edging lines the perimeter gravel paths, and lends a note of order among the unruly profusion of shrub roses. They are displayed in great variety, in countless shades of pink and crimson, forming opulent bushes, garlanding the old fruit trees and clothing the garden walls. Their June flowering is accompanied by white-flowered foxgloves to terrific effect. Another walled garden beyond features further rose and herbaceous plantings.

ROMSEY

The Sir Harold Hillier Gardens and Arboretum

Jermyns Lane, Ampfield, nr Romsey SO51 0QA **TEL.** *01794-368787* **OWNER** *Hampshire County Council* **HOURS** *April–Oct, daily, 10.30a.m.–6p.m.; Nov–March, daily, 10.30a.m.–5p.m. (closed 25–26 Dec)* **ENTRANCE** *£4, OAPs £3.50, children £1 (reduced rates in winter)* **DIRECTIONS** *3m NE of Romsey by A31 (signposted)*

SPRING SUMMER AUTUMN WINTER

Access Café Plant Shop Nursery

Within the 166 acres of undulating ground there is a staggering collection of around 12,000 different plant species and varieties (with the emphasis on trees and shrubs), and a total of approximately 42,000 plants. Although it is lovely at all times of year, I have emphasised its autumn and winter appeal as this is one of the most interesting and rewarding gardens you can visit out of season. There are the fantastic ranges of leaf tints and berries setting fire to the autumnal landscape; winter highlights include the scents of mahonias, the beauty of sculptural trees, colourful bark, shapely conifers, and the icing effect of hoar-frost on grasses and assorted twiggery.

There is a long herbaceous border for summer interest, a water and bog garden, a scree bed and collection of heathers. The renowned nurseryman, Sir Harold Hillier, began planting his arboretum in 1953, and its standing as one of the most important hardy plant collections in the world is unchallenged.

SELBORNE

The Wakes (Gilbert White's House)

Selborne GU34 3JH TEL. *01420-511275* OWNER *Oates Memorial Trust* HOURS *Garden open Jan–mid-March, Sat–Sun, mid-March–Dec, daily, 11a.m.–5p.m.* ENTRANCE *£3.50, over-60s and students £3, children £1* DIRECTIONS *On B3006, 4m S of Alton, 8m N of Petersfield*

SPRING SUMMER AUTUMN WINTER

Access | Gift Shop | Café | Plant Shop

The Wakes was the home of the Revd Gilbert White (1720–1793), celebrated naturalist and author of *The Natural History and Antiquities of Selborne*. This seminal work gives uniquely detailed information on the local landscape and the flora and fauna within it, and has been published in 100 editions, in five languages. White enjoys less fame as a gardener, but in fact his five-acre garden is also one of the best documented of the 18th century, due to the meticulous records he kept for 42 years, most notably in *The Gardener's Kalendar* and subsequently in *The Naturalist's Journal*.

In 1990 a decision was made to restore the gardens which had all but vanished since White's day, through the ravages of time and various changes of ownership. White embraced the views of his contemporary, William Shenstone, where gardens were concerned, believing the ground should be divided into three separate areas comprising a kitchen garden, a parterre or flower garden, and a 'landskip' or picturesque garden with follies, woods and vistas. White's orchard has recently been replanted with Portugal quinces, Dutch medlars, red filberts and old varieties of apples and pears that White had once grown. Vegetable and flower gardens have also been recreated more or less according to White's specifications, and herbs and cottage garden flowers are once again being cultivated near the house. (The house is interesting, too, with natural history exhibits and furnishings in period style.)

There is a lovely walk nearby, created with zigzag paths by White and his brother in 1753, ascending the hill to Selborne Common, a wooded area of outstanding natural beauty.

STOCKBRIDGE

Longstock Park Nursery and Gardens

Longstock, nr Stockbridge SO20 6EH TEL. *01264-810894* OWNER *John Lewis Partnership* HOURS *Nursery and walled garden: April–Sept, Mon–Sat, 8.30a.m.–4.30p.m.; Sun, 2–5p.m. Water gardens: 1st and 3rd Sun of each month, 2–5p.m.* ENTRANCE *Nursery/walled garden free; water gardens £2, children 50p*

SPRING SUMMER AUTUMN WINTER

Access Café Plant Shop Nursery DON'T MISS

I had the great fortune to tour Longstock's gardens and nursery one happy mid-summer day in the company of Roy Lancaster and the garden's estimable curator, David Stuart. The nursery, which is open daily, has a broad and discerning range of plants, including many different kinds of waterlilies, bog primulas, clematis, penstemons, irises, hardy geraniums, buddleias and viburnums. Adjacent is a beautiful walled garden with a 100-yard-long traditional herbaceous border, and an equally long rose pergola, decked with climbing roses and many choice clematis. Notable in this area was *Phygelius* 'Winchester Fanfare', of soft, pinky colouring, growing 6ft or so, trained to the wall; Roy was ecstatic to see *Ostrowskia magnifica* (an unusual, white-flowered relation of the campanula) blooming in the border. Beyond is a large collection of buddleias (viewable by appointment).

The famous seven-acre water gardens of Longstock are nearby, occasionally open to the public. There is nothing quite like them, but the effect is rather as if you had walked into a studio full of Claude Monet's paintings of waterlily pools. Neatly cut turf paths wind around a series of pools and streams, and wooden plank bridges criss-cross the clear waters. The banks are filled with astilbes, ferns, mimulus, hostas and primulas, the whole effect being utterly peaceful and enchanting. The Longstock estate was bought in 1946 by John Lewis, who passed it on to the John Lewis Partnership.

And also...

Apple Court Nursery, Hordle Lane, Hordle, Lymington SO41 0HU (tel. 01590-642130), is renowned for its extensive ranges of hostas, grasses, ferns and day lilies. It also holds National Collections of woodwardia, rohdea and hosta, and there are splendid display borders and a show garden. Open Feb–Oct, Thurs–Mon, 9.30a.m.–1p.m., 2–5p.m. Also daily July–early Aug.

Braxton Gardens, Braxton Courtyard, Lymore Lane, Milford-on-Sea SO41 0TX (tel. 01590-642008), is set within a half-acre walled garden and courtyard, with a lily-pool and dovecote, around the red-brick barns of a Victorian farmyard. Besides the knot garden and broad range of herbs, there are old-fashioned roses. Herbs and herb products are sold in the shop and adjacent plant centre. Open all year, daily, 9a.m.–5p.m. (Suns, 10a.m.–5p.m., 24 Dec, 9a.m.–2p.m., closed 25–26 Dec and 1 Jan). Telephone to check opening times in winter. Donations to National Gardens Scheme.

You can buy all manner of fruit at **Family Trees, PO Box 3, Botley SO3 2EA (tel. 01329-834812)**, which stocks good ranges of dessert apples, pears, plums and peaches, both trained and untrained. Also hedging, old roses and some woodland trees. The catalogue is free on request (mail order: min. £35). Open mid-Oct–end April, July–Aug, Wed and Sat only, 9.30a.m.–12.30p.m.

Hardy's Cottage Garden Plants, The Walled Garden, Laverstoke Park, Laverstoke, Whitchurch RG28 7NT (tel. 01256-896533), offers good ranges of herbaceous perennial plants, such as hardy geraniums, phloxes and penstemons. There is a catalogue (send 3 × 1st-class stamps), but no mail order. Open March–Oct, daily, 9a.m.–5.30p.m.

Longthatch, Lippen Lane, Warnford, Southampton SO32 3LE (tel. 01730-829285), is renowned for its hellebores in spring, accompanied by other early plants such as primulas and pulmonarias. It is a three-and-a-half-acre plantsman's garden beside the River Meon, with lovely pools and riverside plantings, and many unusual trees and shrubs, around a thatched 17th-century house. Open March–Aug, Wed, 10a.m.–5p.m., and regularly during the spring–summer season for the National Gardens Scheme on certain Sundays (ring for details, or see the NGS yellow book); also by appointment with the owners. Entrance £1.50.

Arthur Nash, 46 Mulfords Hill, Tadley RG26 3JE (tel. 01189-815591), makes and sells besoms (those useful lawn sweepers that look like witches' brooms), either direct or by mail order, but telephone to check opening times before calling.

New Springs Aquatic Nursery, 24 Winchester Street, Whitchurch RG28 7AL (tel. 01256-892837), has been operating since 1984 on the site of former watercress beds. It specializes in true aquatics, emergents and marginal plants, and dispatches small plants by post. Send a 1st-class stamp for a catalogue. Open by appointment.

The Tudor House Garden, Tudor House, Bugle Street, Southampton SO14 2AD (tel. 01703-635904), is a well-made, thoroughly researched reconstruction of a formal Tudor garden with knot, fountain, secret garden and plantings of appropriate herbs and flowers, all confined to a very small plot. Open all year, Tues–Fri, 10a.m.–5p.m.; Sat, 10a.m.–4p.m.; Sun, 2–5p.m. Entrance free.

The Vyne, Sherborne St John, nr Basingstoke RG24 9HL (tel. 01256-881337), is a handsome house with 17 acres of extensive lawns, a lovely lake, fine trees and a herbaceous border; a pleasant and peaceful place to while away a couple of hours. Open weekends in March, then April–Oct, daily, except Mon and Fri, 12.30–5.30p.m. Also open Good Fri and Bank Holiday Mons, but closed Tues following. Entrance £2, children £1 (grounds).

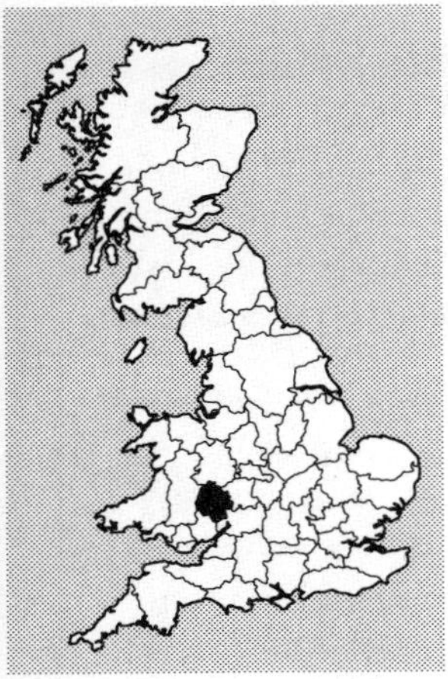

Herefordshire

MAP NO. 5

Sitting on the border of Wales, and enjoying startling views of the mountains, Herefordshire is deeply rural, with strong farming traditions on its gentle green hills. You notice how well trees grow here on the fertile soils, whether they are massive oaks sprung out of hedgerows, or more exotic species planted in the region's fine gardens. The proliferation of springs, generally mild climate (warm in summer to ripen fruit) and frequency of rain has also encouraged a thriving cider industry for many centuries. The most famous producer is Bulmers (founded in 1887), and as Percy Bulmer's mother once wisely said, 'If you are going into business, let it be food or drink – they never go out of fashion.'

ABBEY DORE

Abbey Dore Court Garden

Abbey Dore, Hereford HR2 0AD **TEL.** *01981-240419* **OWNER** *Mrs C. Ward* **HOURS** *(Garden only) March–mid-Oct, daily, except Wed, 11a.m.–6p.m. Other times by appointment to see hellebores* **ENTRANCE** *£2, children 50p* **DIRECTIONS** *Off B4347, 3m W of A465, midway between Hereford and Abergavenny*

SPRING SUMMER AUTUMN WINTER

Access | Gift Shop | Café | Plant Shop

Meeting Charis Ward was the highlight of my tour of Herefordshire. She is a formidable plantswoman and great company. She also clearly commands the respect of her neighbours, the army, since they ceased practising helicopter manoeuvres on the afternoon of my visit, at her request. (Perhaps they had decided to brush up on spying

A WORLD OF CARNIVOROUS PLANTS

The mysterious world of carnivorous plants has largely eluded me, or it did, until I met Paul Gardner, of **Marston Exotics, Brampton Lane, Madley, Hereford HR2 9LX (tel. 01981-251140), just off the A465; take the right turn after Belmont Abbey; 1m from village of Madley.** *Paul has a train-spotter-like passion for insect-eating plants, and an infectious enthusiasm, developed over the 10 years that he has been growing them. Here are Venus fly-traps, sundews, pitcher-plants and butterworts in great variety – ideal fly-catchers for house and greenhouse, provided you bear in mind their needs. They all thrive when standing in peaty soil in rainwater (or distilled water), simulating the bogs which are their habitat; hard, alkaline water is poisonous to them. Cutting off the flower buds maintains the plants' vigour, but you shoud never feed with fertilizers; the plants get their food by digesting flies.*

Contrary to popular belief, Venus fly-traps are not short-lived, but often die because people are tempted to trigger the hairs in the trap to watch it close. If there is no fly to digest, the plant is weakened. Anyone keen on natural control in the greenhouse or conservatory should try Pinguicula moranensis caudata, *a Mexican butterwort, 'the best control I know for whitefly, midges and compost flies,' Paul adds. A tip: do not ask what happens to the indigestible remains of flies caught in pitcher plants – you will be shown them! Open all year, Mon–Fri, 8a.m.–4.30p.m.; and Sat–Sun Mar–Oct. Entrance free. Plants also by mail order.*

instead, as the helicopters started up again the moment I got back to my car.)

The gardens spread for five acres along both banks of the River Dore in a peaceful, wooded valley. The entrance is through a stable yard, into a former walled kitchen garden, which is now largely given over to herbaceous plants, especially euphorbias, peonies and hardy geraniums – their pastel colours mingle in big, blowsy drifts, contrasting with a formal orchard beyond. A right-hand turn leads to the lawn beside the house, planted with two prominent wellingtonia trees, and a lower lawn, enclosed by mixed plantings of trees, shrubs and perennials.

Most beguiling on a hot afternoon is the shady River Walk, among dogwoods, hostas and ferns, to the music of birdsong and the fast-flowing Dore. There are also double borders featuring a progression of purple, golden and grey-leaved plants with colour-coordinated flowers, and a meadow area with a pond and rock garden. The house (not open) was an inn until the mid-19th century, when it was converted into a gentleman's residence. The Wards have lived here for 30 years; when not rearranging the plants in her beloved garden, Charis Ward disappears indoors to rearrange her Persian rugs, her other passion.

HEREFORD'S APPLE HERITAGE

Foxwhelp, Brown Snout, Bloody Turk and Sheep's Nose may sound like the province of the doctor and vet, but they are in fact some of the old varieties of cider apple that once flourished in Herefordshire's orchards, and which are now rare.

The region's tradition of cider-making began long before Roman times; throughout history it was drunk in castles, manors and farms, and was a popular substitute for imported wine during the Napoleonic Wars. You can still see cider orchards dotted about the countryside, but much of the old orchard land is now used for arable farming, and the tradition of producing local farmhouse cider has virtually disappeared. There are, however, several local initiatives to find and replant old varieties, and you can taste some of the results at ***Dunkertons Cider Mill, Hays Head, Luntley, Pembridge HR6 9ED (tel. 01544-388653), signposted from Pembridge, nr Leominster,*** *which also serves delicious food. Open Mon–Sat, 10a.m.–6p.m. If you want to grow your own old-fashioned cider crop, contact* ***Deacon's Nursery*** *(q.v.) on the Isle of Wight, or* ***Keepers Nursery*** *(q.v.) in Kent, for trees by mail order.*

HAMNISH

Strawberry Cottage Garden

Hamnish, Leominster HR6 0RH **TEL.** *01568-760319* **OWNER** *M. and H. Philpott* **HOURS** *Last Sun in April–mid-Sept, Thurs–Fri, Sun and Bank Holiday Mons, 11a.m.–5p.m. and by appointment* **ENTRANCE** *£2, children free, concessions for groups* **DIRECTIONS** *3m E of Leominster, off A44; signposted*

SPRING SUMMER AUTUMN WINTER

Café Plant Shop DON'T MISS

A long, rough track leads from the road up to – you begin to think – goodness knows where, but then you reach Strawberry Cottage, perched on a steep, south-facing hill. The garden enjoys spectacular views (as do the airborne buzzards which regularly nest in the old stone quarry nearby), and the Philpotts have turned their two acres into a richly planted, varied series of gardens.

Natural springs trickle down a rock bank planted with spring bulbs, primulas, astilbes, mimulus and much else in front of the house. Sloping away to the rear are mixed borders, a clear, spring-fed pool, sheltered arbour and terrace, wildlife/wildflower garden, rose garden, colour-themed herbaceous grounds and cottage garden with annual flowers. There are many unusual but garden-worthy plants, and Heather Philpott has grown most of them from seed. Here is a colourful, peaceful and very personal long-season garden, much enjoyed by its visitors.

PRESTEIGNE

Bryan's Ground

Stapleton, Presteigne LD8 2LP TEL. *01544-260001* OWNER *D. Wheeler and S. Dorrell* HOURS *May–Sept, Sat–Sun and Mon, 2–5p.m., groups at other times by appointment* ENTRANCE *£2, children 50p* DIRECTIONS *From Presteigne town centre take unclassified road heading N over River Lugg, then first right, for 1 mile. Bryan's Ground is a yellow house set back from the road*

SPRING | SUMMER | AUTUMN | WINTER

Café · Plant Shop · DON'T MISS

The house that David Wheeler and Simon Dorrell moved into in 1993 is in the style of the Arts and Crafts architect, Voysey, and is what they describe as 'Surrey stockbroker-style, transported, incongruously, to the borders of Wales'. Literally to the border, for their boundary, the River Lugg, is also the national boundary; they can paddle over to Wales at the end of their garden. The river bank provided flat, smooth, worn cobblestones which are effectively used in an unusual stone-and-twig parterre beside the front door. In front is an orchard of apple trees, bred locally, leading to the road.

When they arrived, much of the garden was already divided into 'rooms' by stout yew hedges, put in by the Arts and Crafts architects who built the house. Within them, and in the walled kitchen garden, David and Simon have made new, symmetrical gardens in what you might call the Tudor-style with a twist. The rose garden is very formal, with beds cornered by pyramidal yews trained in wooden obelisks. The walled garden layout is derived from plans in Thomas Hill's book, *The Gardener's Labyrinth*, of 1577, its potager enclosed by fancy trellis with carved birds on top, à la Hill. There is a marvellous restored greenhouse, a box-edged sunk garden, a wood, and much more.

Around five of their 25 acres are being developed as garden, the rest is pasture. Each part of the garden has a different name: Crackenthorpe, for example, is a narrow strip of lawn flanked by two borders of sumptuous purples and reds, leading to a delightful pavilion Simon built with salvaged masonry from demolition work at Cardiff docks. In all, Bryan's Ground is a plant-filled, beautifully executed garden, made with liberal doses of humour as well as plantsmanship.

And also...

Arrow Cottage Garden, Ledgemoor, Weobley HR4 8RN (tel. 01544-318468), is a two-acre plantsman's garden divided into many different, colour-themed areas. Water abounds in the garden, via a stream, fountain and stepped rill lined with potted agapanthus. All is immaculately kept. Open April–Sept, Wed–Fri and Sun, 2–5p.m. Closed Aug. Entrance £2, no children.

Brobury House, Brobury HR3 6BS (tel. 01981-500229), has woodland gardens in an idyllic position above the River Wye. Its fascinating gallery housing over 100,000 antique prints for sale includes botanical illustrations. There is also pristine B&B accommodation in the house. Open all year, Mon–Sat, 9a.m.–4.30p.m. (4p.m. in winter). Entrance £2.50.

Horseway Herbs, Staunton-on-Arrow, Leominster HR6 9HS (tel. 01544-388212), is a small, informal herb nursery in the long, narrow back garden of a cottage at the west end of Staunton village. Open April–Oct, daily, except Wed, 10a.m.–5p.m.

How Caple Court, How Caple, Hereford HR1 4SX (tel. 01989-740626), must have been cherished by its owners 100 years ago, but less so since. It possesses a Lutyens-style Edwardian garden of stone terraces laid out with herbs and roses, on a handsome wooded hill above the River Wye. Its once lavish water and woodland gardens are undergoing slow restoration after years of neglect, but the terraces and long vista by the house are charming in mid-summer. Open all year, Mon–Fri, 9a.m.–5p.m., Sun, 10a.m.–5p.m., and Sat April–Oct, 9a.m.–5p.m. Entrance £2.50, children £1.25.

Pools, pumps, bog plants and waterlilies are available in huge variety at **Kenchester Water Gardens, Church Road, Lyde, Hereford HR1 3AB (tel. 01432-270981).** There are also extensive display gardens showing different uses of water. Open all year, daily, March–Sept, 9a.m.–6p.m. Oct–Feb, 9a.m.–5.30p.m.

Pembridge is an attractive medieval village and at **Pembridge Terracotta, Pembridge, Leominster, Hereford HR6 9HB (tel. 01544-388696)**, hand-made clay pots are fashioned on the premises, with a wide range of pots for the garden. Open all year, daily, 10a.m.–5.30p.m., but closed Sun in winter.

Rushfields of Ledbury, Ross Road, Ledbury HR8 2LP (tel. 01531-632004), specializes in herbaceous perennials, including euphorbias, hardy geraniums, osteospermums, penstemons and primroses. Open all year, Wed–Sat, 11a.m.–5p.m., or by appointment.

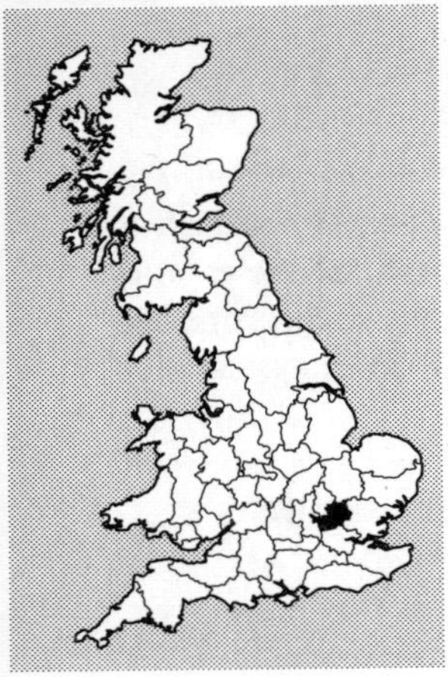

Hertfordshire

MAP NO. 3

Once a rural county of cornfields and respectable, small country houses as immortalised in E.M. Forster's Howards End, *Hertfordshire's close proximity to London has made its land valuable for roads and housing. Its sprawling towns are very much part of the city's commuter belt, and fast trains cut their way through the new towns and suburbs. The chalk ridge of the Chiltern Hills runs along its western and north-western edge, giving way further south to more gentle undulations. Its eastern borders are flatter, however, like neighbouring Cambridgeshire and Essex. The cathedral town of St Albans was know as Verulamium in Roman times, when it was the third largest town in the country. It remains richly historic, with a pleasing blend of the old and new.*

BENINGTON

Benington Lordship

Benington, Stevenage SG2 7BS **TEL.** *01438-869668* **OWNER** *C.H.A. Bott* **HOURS** *April–Sept, Wed and Bank Holiday Mons, 12 noon–5p.m.; also Sun, April–Aug, 2–5p.m., telephone for late winter snowdrop openings* **ENTRANCE** *£2.60, children free* **DIRECTIONS** *In Benington village, off A602 Stevenage–Hertford road*

SPRING | SUMMER | AUTUMN | WINTER

Plant Shop

Barely four miles away from busy Stevenage town centre, Benington Lordship is still enshrouded in a landscape of gentle hills and golden cornfields, and has an atmosphere of times past. Much of its seven acres dates from Victorian and Edwardian designs and plantings, with leafy green shrubberies and winding walks among tall conifers leading to spectacular twin herbaceous borders beside the walled kitchen garden. Grassy slopes lead to a lake of waterlilies, and there is a rock garden fed by a spring, home to bog primulas and sun-loving shrubs. It is a peaceful place for an afternoon's visit, with glorious pastoral views and surprises around each corner. February's snowdrops are spectacular (ring near the time for snowdrop dates, as they depend on the weather). The bulbs run through the ruins of a Norman castle and dry moat, in a part of the garden which is also devoted to winter-flowering shrubs.

HADLEY WOOD

The Beale Arboretum

West Lodge Park, Cockfosters Road, Hadley Wood, Barnet EN4 0PY TEL. *0181-441 5159 × 304* OWNER *The Beale Family* HOURS *April–Oct, Wed, 2–5p.m.* ENTRANCE *£2, children free* DIRECTIONS *Off A111 midway between M25 Jct 24 and Cockfosters station*

SPRING SUMMER AUTUMN WINTER

Access Café

When Ted Beale came to West Lodge Park in 1945, he opened the small mansion house as a quality family-run hotel (which it still is) and developed his passion for trees. The arboretum is now more than 50 years old and contains more than 500 different species and cultivars, making visits particularly rewarding during autumn, when the foliage has multicoloured tints. The hornbeam collection includes nine named varieties of *Carpinus betulus*, including fastigiate and weeping forms. Many plants are grouped together with their relations, as they would be in a botanic garden, so that comparisons can be easily made between varieties. Broad lawns run between them on gently undulating ground. This is filled out here and there with shrubby dells to provide some mystery.

In 1676 the diarist and gardener John Evelyn visited West Lodge Park and reported: 'It is a very pretty place, the house commodious, the garden handsome and our entertainment very free.' He also admired the fact that no 'house, barne, church or building' could be seen, despite the park's proximity to London. Times have changed, and the suburban sprawl tightens its grip around the park, but Mr Beale is planting 18 more acres to complement the existing 10, so even better things can be expected in the future.

CLARENCE ELLIOTT'S CATMINT

The pretty and ubiquitous catmint Nepeta *'Six Hills Giant' is widely available from nurseries and garden centres nationwide, but it has its origins in Hertfordshire. It was brought into cultivation by Clarence Elliott (1907–1969), who had a well-known establishment, the Six Hills Nursery, on the Great North Road at Stevenage. Elliott was a specialist alpine grower and a founder-member of the Alpine Garden Society, but he was also interested in old cottage garden plants. He spotted an unusual form of catmint, with taller stems and larger flowers than were typical, in a local garden in the mid-1930s. The ease with which it could be propagated meant that stocks were soon ready for sale.* Nepeta *'Six Hills Giant' quickly found favour as an accommodating herbaceous plant with soft stems of grey-green, aromatic foliage and lavender-blue flowers, growing up to 3ft tall. It grows well in a sunny position, in well-drained, especially alkaline soil, and makes a good accompaniment to other flowers in the herbaceous border, and pastel-tinted roses. Propagation is by division of the rootstock in spring, or softwood cuttings in summer.*

HATFIELD

Hatfield House

Hatfield AL9 5NQ **TEL.** *01707-262823* **OWNER** *The Marquess of Salisbury* **HOURS** *Late March–Sept: West Gardens – daily, except Good Friday, 11a.m.–6p.m. (last adm. 5p.m.), East Gardens – Mon, except Bank Holidays, 2–5p.m.* **ENTRANCE** *Park and garden £3.10, OAPs £2.90, children £2.30, house, park and garden £5.70, OAPs £4.80, children £3.40* **DIRECTIONS** *In centre of old Hatfield, entrance opposite Hatfield Station; signposted from A1(M) Jct 4*

SPRING SUMMER AUTUMN WINTER

Access | Gift Shop | Café | Plant Shop

DON'T MISS

The 42-acre gardens around Hatfield's famous Jacobean mansion house are laid out formally, with geometrically arranged flowerbeds and much use of yew and box hedging, and yew topiaries. They are largely the inspiration of the present Marchioness of Salisbury, who is one of the country's leading experts on 17th-century gardens. Lady Salisbury has been actively involved in rejuvenating the gardens since she arrived in 1972 and, since that time, they have been run entirely organically. The intention has been to create gardens that are in sympathy with the period of the house, rather than slavishly imitating the period, and the results are superb.

The West Gardens comprise hedge-enclosed flower gardens filled with spring bulbs, herbaceous perennials and shrub roses, planted for a long season of colour. There is also a delightful fragrant garden with seats under bowers of honeysuckle, beside cowslip-scented *Clematis rehderiana*, a herb garden, and a virtuoso Tudor-style knot garden. The East Gardens have further formal flower gardens and topiaries, and lovely woodland walks around the lake.

THE JOHN TRADESCANTS

Gardener, nurseryman and plant collector, John Tradescant the Elder (c.1570–1638) introduced many new plants to Britain, from his travels in Europe and Russia. In 1609 he came to work for Robert Cecil, who was busy building his new house at Hatfield (q.v.). Salomon de Caux, a French expert in fountains, was brought in to create elaborate formal gardens, while Tradescant was sent abroad in search of novelty plants. In 1611 he returned with fine flowers, including martagon lilies and a double hepatica. Later, Tradescant went collecting abroad to stock his own London nursery. His son, also named John, continued to bring in new plants from overseas, especially from the New World. Some of their notes and bills survive in the Hatfield House archives.

ST ALBANS

The Gardens of the Rose

Chiswell Green, St Albans AL2 3NR TEL. *01727-850461*
OWNER *The Royal National Rose Society* HOURS *Mid-June–mid-Oct, daily, 9a.m.–5p.m. (10a.m.–6p.m. Sun and Bank Holidays)* ENTRANCE *£4, disabled £3, children free*

SPRING SUMMER AUTUMN WINTER

Access | Gift Shop | Café | Plant Shop

This is the headquarters and trial ground of the Royal National Rose Society and *the* place to see roses, especially more modern hybrid teas and floribundas. The 25-acre gardens are something of an anachronism, having a formal, old-fashioned air slightly at odds with today's more relaxed views about planting. You will find large beds cut out of the broad lawns to display blocks of single varieties. Nevertheless, it is instructional to see which ones bloom over a long season, which varieties are still putting on a brilliant show in August, into autumn, and to take note of the berries of different species of shrub roses. There are some old roses too, grown in their own area, and some beds feature herbaceous flowers such as delphiniums and catmint. Climbers and ramblers are well represented, forming an avenue walk between the car park and the main house, and they are joined by clematis, to pretty effect, on a long, curving pergola.

And also...

The gloriously colourful world of dahlias can be viewed in September by visiting the trial grounds at **Aylett Nurseries, North Orbital Road, London Colney, St Albans AL2 1DH (tel. 01727-822255)**. This is a large, comprehensively stocked garden centre with dahlias a speciality (free catalogue on request). Open Mon–Sat, 8.30a.m.–5.30p.m, Sun, 10a.m.–5p.m., Bank Holidays, 9a.m.–5p.m.

Crown Topiary, 234 North Road, Hertford SG14 2PW (tel. 01992-501055), covering five acres, specializes in producing and supplying topiary figures made from yew, box and Chinese privet. Architectural shapes predominate but flights of fancy, such as eagles, swans, pitchers, armchairs, etc. are also usually available. Open by appointment only. Price list available on request.

The name **R. Harkness & Co. Ltd, The Rose Gardens, Cambridge Road, Hitchin SG4 0JT (tel. 01462-420402)**, is synonymous with some of the most popular hybrid tea roses bred this century, although the nursery also stocks good ranges of floribunda, patio and climbing roses. One of their most successful recent introductions has been 'Octavia Hill', a glamorous, fragrant, old-fashioned-looking rose that makes a small bush of really delightful pink blooms. Mail orders are dispatched in winter; catalogue free on request. Open daily, 9a.m.–5.30p.m. (10.30a.m.–4p.m. Sun).

Hopleys Plants, High Street, Much Hadham SG10 6BU (tel. 01279-842509), is well worth visiting for its broad range of shrubs, hardy and half-hardy perennials. Many new plants have been raised or introduced to the nursery trade and our gardens by Hopleys, and penstemons, salvias and osteospermums are among their specialities. Mail order is only available in the autumn (send 5 × 1st-class stamps for a catalogue). Open March–Dec, daily, except Tues, 9a.m.–5p.m. (2–5p.m. Sun).

The Van Hage Garden Company, Great Amwell, Ware SG12 9RP (tel. 01920-870811), is an old-established garden centre which offers plenty of interest for gardeners. It carries very broad, well-grown ranges of plants. There are refreshments, display gardens, animal gardens for children, and a miniature steam railway. Open all year, Tues–Sat, 9a.m.–6p.m., Sun, 10.30a.m.–4.30p.m., Mon, 9.30a.m.–6p.m. Entrance free.

Isle of Wight

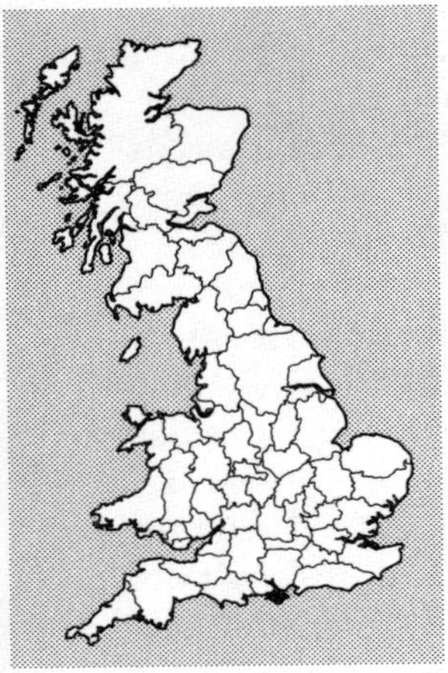

MAP NO. 2

This small island, just 22 miles long and 13 miles at its widest, appeals more to those who enjoy messing about on boats than to gardeners. It is a long-popular holiday destination for families who appreciate the sandy beaches and tailor-made resorts. Since the mild climate provides agreeable conditions for growing a wide range of plants, gardeners have the opportunity to be adventurous. The number of visitors swells dramatically through the summer season, reaching a climax at the start of August when Cowes Week sees the coastline skirted by the triangular handkerchiefs of countless competing sailboats.

GODSHILL

Deacon's Nursery

Godshill PO38 3HW **TEL.** *01983-840750* **OWNER** *B.H.W. and G.D. Deacon* **HOURS** *Daily, except Sun, 8a.m.–4p.m.* **DIRECTIONS** *9m S of Cowes at Godshill, by A3020*

SPRING SUMMER AUTUMN WINTER

Plant Shop | Nursery | Mail Order

This is chiefly a mail order nursery, although you can also call in to buy. Its speciality is fruit, particularly old and rare varieties of apple for dessert, cooking or cider-making. It also sells perry pear, striped Canadian pear, medlar, quince, plum, gage, damson, cherry and other stone-fruit trees. Buying fruit can be a hazardous business if you are not absolutely certain which rootstock (which determines the tree's size and productivity) your trees should be on. Enquire here, however, and you can be sure of getting the right information and advice from these specialist growers.

Trees are lifted and dispatched during the dormant season, from mid-Oct onwards. Send 29p stamp for a catalogue.

VENTNOR

Ventnor Botanic Garden

The Undercliff Drive, Ventnor PO38 1UL **TEL.** *01983-855397* **OWNER** *Isle of Wight Council* **HOURS** *Open all year (temperate house March–Oct)* **ENTRANCE** *Free (50p, children 20p to see temperate house)* **DIRECTIONS** *Signposted from A3055*

SPRING SUMMER AUTUMN WINTER

Access Café Plant Shop

This is not really a botanic garden, although it has a diverse collection of plants. Its position in the Undercliff, a protective, six-mile ledge in the Downs, gives the property good protection from cold north and east winds. Consequently, plants of the southern hemisphere, particularly those of Australasia, grow well. There are cabbage palms and fan palms, silver-leaved astelia and spiky drifts of tall blue echium.

THE 'HOWGATE WONDER' APPLE

Valued for its large, red striped fruit and abundant cropping ability, 'Howgate Wonder' is a local apple, raised in 1915–16 by Mr G. Wratton of Howgate Lane, Bembridge, on the far eastern end of the island. It was subsequently offered commercially from the early 1930s and received the Royal Horticultural Society's Award of Merit in 1949.

As it produces a vigorous growing tree, 'Howgate Wonder' should be grafted onto a dwarfing rootstock if grown in the confined space of a small garden. The substantial size and attractive appearance of this late-keeping cooking apple has made it popular as a show-bench variety, but in cooking its flesh has a tendency to break up. It is often planted in the company of 'Bramley's Seedling' apples as a good pollinator and is hardy enough to be grown successfully in many northern gardens. 'Howgate Wonder' is stocked by many specialist fruit growers, including Deacon's Nursery (q.v.) in the south of the island.

Fine large trees dating from Victorian plantings grace the park, but most of the ornamental planting only started in 1969. In the 1970s Sir Harold Hillier, of the Hillier Nurseries in Hampshire (*q.v.*), provided many of the garden's more obscure shrubs and trees, particularly ones of borderline hardiness which he supplied free provided he could use them as stock plants to provide him with propagating material. There are wafts of Victorian subtropicalness in the choice of plants, and further examples are grown in the temperate house.

And also...

Barton Manor Gardens and Vineyards, Whippingham, East Cowes PO32 6LB (tel. 01983-292835), were once part of the Osborne estate and Prince Albert planted some of its trees, including a cork grove. There are herbaceous borders, a maze of roses and a woodland garden, covering 10 acres. Open June–Aug, weekdays, 10a.m–5p.m. Entrance £3.75, OAPs and groups of 20 or more £3.20, children under 15 (accompanied) free.

Mottistone is a delightful stone village with a well on the green, and a lovely bluebell wood opposite the church to enchant visitors in May. **Mottistone Manor Garden, Mottistone PO30 4ED (tel. 01983-740012)**, has rose gardens, fruit trees and herbaceous borders. Open April–Sept, Wed and Bank Holiday Mons, 2–5p.m., and July–Aug, Sun, 2–5p.m. Entrance £2, children £1.

Osborne House, East Cowes PO32 6JY (tel. 01983-200022), was built by Queen Victoria as a quiet retreat from the pressures of court and empire. She and Prince Albert designed the formal, Italianate gardens which are currently being restored; there are grand terraces and stairways, broad lawns and fine sea views. A Swiss chalet/cottage full of curios can be reached by Victorian carriage. Open April–Oct, daily, house: 10a.m–5p.m. (last adm. 4.p.m.); grounds: 10a.m.–6p.m. (last adm. 5p.m.). Oct, daily, house and grounds 10a.m.–5p.m. or dusk (last adm. 4p.m.). Entrance £6, OAPs £4.50, children £3; grounds-only tickets £3.50, £2.60, £1.80.

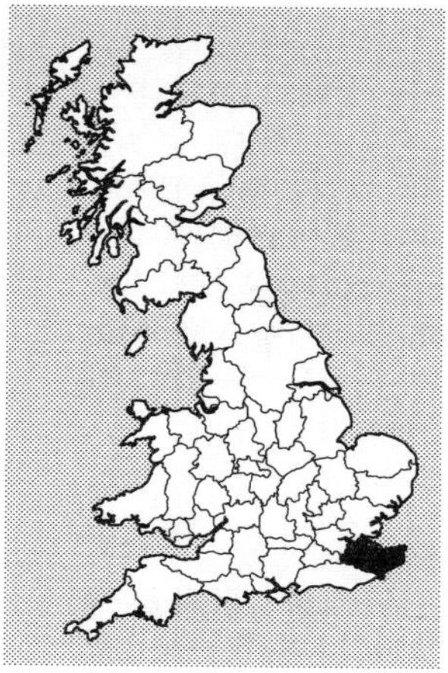

Kent

MAP NO. 3

Crowded and urban in the north-west, forested and wealden at its centre, flat and open towards its chalk-edge coast, Kent is a region of variations and variegations, known since time immemorial as the Garden of England. Its apple and cobnut orchards, hop fields and vineyards testify to a bounteous county; the wealden villages among oak woods display pretty half-timbered houses, coveted by London's commuters. There are castles galore here, a legacy of less settled times, but today Kent looks more benignly on its continental neighbours. Its proximity to the coastline of France has left the county scarred by fast roads and rail, leading to several ferry ports and the cross-channel tunnel.

CANTERBURY

Goodnestone Park

Nr Wingham, Canterbury CT3 1PL **TEL.** *01304-840107* **OWNER** *The Lord and Lady FitzWalter* **HOURS** *Late March–late Oct, Mon–Wed, Thurs–Fri, 11a.m.–5p.m.; Sun, 12 noon–6p.m.* **ENTRANCE** *£2.50, OAPs £2.20, children (under 12) 20p* **DIRECTIONS** *5m E of Canterbury on A257, turn S on to B2046, signposted*

SPRING | SUMMER | AUTUMN | WINTER

Café | Plant Shop

Goodnestone (pronounced Gunston) is a lovely 18th-century park, on undulating ground speckled with oak trees, cedars and chestnuts. Its six-acre garden surrounds an elegant mansion, where Jane Austen often visited and danced, as her sister-in-law belonged to the family which owned it. In front of the house, a broad, lawned terrace is planted with informal groups of shrub roses, and there are many more roses within the lovely walled garden which is filled with summer flowers. The gardens offer many delightful walks, and there is a beautiful woodland garden on an outcrop of acid soil, where camellias, rhododendrons, azaleas and magnolias flourish and provide shelter for woodland herbaceous plants – especially lovely in spring, and for autumnal foliage tints.

SPECIALIST PLANTS AT COPTON ASH

It is easy to drive straight past Tim Ingram's ***Copton Ash Gardens and Nursery, 105 Ashford Road, Faversham ME13 8XW (tel. 01795-535919), 1m S of Faversham, leave M2 at Jct 6: on A251 Faversham–Ashford road (north of M2) opposite eastbound slipway for M2.*** *The garden is hidden away behind a row of ordinary houses, and you park in the limited space of the drive. The garden covers around one and a half acres and is packed with around 3000 different plant species. The specialist nursery has developed from the garden, and its unusual plants, particularly those suited to the relatively warm, dry climate of the south-east, are a speciality. There are, for example, five different species of bupleurum offered, 11 eryngium, and many different helianthemums, penstemons, Australasian and South American plants. Open March–Oct, daily, except Mon and Fri, 2–6p.m.*

CHARING HEATH

Church Hill Cottage Gardens

Charing Heath, Ashford TN27 0BU **TEL.** *01233-712522*
OWNER *Mr and Mrs Metianu* **OPEN** *Feb–Oct, Tues–Sun and Bank Holiday Mons, 10a.m.–5p.m.* **ENTRANCE** *£1.50*
DIRECTIONS *Take Charing Heath road from A20 (Maidstone side of Charing). Turn right at Red Lion, right again after 100yds towards church. Garden is 300yds on right*

SPRING SUMMER AUTUMN WINTER

Plant Shop | Nursery | DON'T MISS

Over the last 17 years Margaret and Michael Metianu have turned one and a half acres of rough, sheep-grazed heathland into one of the most enchanting and plant-packed gardens in the county. Informal, wavy-edged beds and borders were made each year, adding a bit at a time, and Margaret simultaneously began building up a nursery specializing in the cottage garden plants she was growing in the garden. Now their son has joined them in running the nursery, and the garden has become renowned as a place of great beauty and tranquillity.

Hardly any annuals are used, and just a few half-hardy perennials; the emphasis is on really good hardy perennials, among choice shrubs and scattered trees. The soil throughout most of the garden is, says Margaret, 'fairly neutral, of poor fertility and very free-draining – marvellous to work, because it's very light, but certain things, such as roses, do not grow well in most parts'. There are hardy geraniums in great profusion, campanulas, eryngiums, sultry 'Arabian Night' dahlias, verbenas and much else. A relaxed feeling is achieved by allowing self-sown flowers plenty of leeway to do their own thing. It is a garden to tempt me back to Kent at any time of year, to enjoy the garden, poke about the nursery, and while away time in the most pleasant way – talking plants – with the enthusiastic Metianus.

EDENBRIDGE

Hever Castle

Edenbridge TN8 7NG **TEL.** *01732-865224* **OWNER** *Broadlands Properties Ltd* **HOURS** *March–Nov, daily, 11a.m.–5p.m.* **ENTRANCE** *£4.40, OAPs £3.90, children £2.60* **DIRECTIONS** *3m SE of Edenbridge, signposted*

SPRING SUMMER AUTUMN WINTER

Access · Gift Shop · Café · Plant Shop · DON'T MISS

Several times I have had the opportunity to enjoy Hever's magical evenings at mid-summer, for the 70-odd acres of grounds are host to a season of theatre each year, when performances can be preceded by picnics at the lakeside. And what a lake it is. In the early years of the 20th century the American newspaper tycoon William Waldorf Astor employed 1000 men to transform the landscape; 800 of them excavated the 35-acre stretch of water, which provides a serene counterpoint to the more formal areas. At one end of the lake Astor made a four-acre Italian garden, with a confection of steps, colonnades and a loggia, in opulent classical style. The Italian garden houses Roman artefacts along one side, and a spectacular pergola along the other, draped in all manner of vines and climbers. There are also rose gardens, a rock garden, a very good yew maze, lots of topiary, beds of rhododendrons and a traditional dahlia border. And then there is, not least, the double-moated castle itself, which dates from the 13th century. Henry VIII courted his second wife, Anne Boleyn, here, for it was her childhood home. It sits in island splendour, linked by a bridge to a veritable village of outbuildings that have served the estate for centuries.

FAVERSHAM

The Brogdale Horticultural Trust

Brogdale Road, Faversham ME13 8XZ **TEL.** *01795-535286* **OWNER** *Brogdale Horticultural Trust* **HOURS** *Open all year, daily, 9.30a.m.–5.30p.m. (telephone to check opening times for Dec–Feb).* **ENTRANCE** *Free, guided tours £2.50, concessions £2, children £1.50* **DIRECTIONS** *1m SW of Faversham*

SPRING SUMMER AUTUMN WINTER

Access | Gift Shop | Café | Plant Shop | NPC

Brogdale's 150 acres provide a fascinating living museum of fruit. It has national collections of cherries, apples (around 2300 different kinds), pears (around 400 different varieties), plums, hazelnuts, grape vines and currants. Its function was, and is, as a research station, testing new cultivars and conserving the old.

Brogdale has an instructional and institutional layout, and is worth visiting if you have a special interest in fruit or are just inquisitive to know more. Its Apple Day events in October offer entertainment, question-and-answer sessions and all manner of advice on fruit, including identifying unlabelled fruit from your garden. The shop is a marvellous source of fruit for sale when in season, and the huge collections here provide the chance to sample rare and unusual varieties that you won't find in other shops.

GOUDHURST

Bedgebury National Pinetum And Forest Gardens

Nr Goudhurst, Cranbrook TN17 2SL TEL. *01580-211044* HOURS *Open all year, daily, 10a.m.–dusk* ENTRANCE *£2.20, OAPs £1.50, children £1.20, family ticket £6* DIRECTIONS *On B2079 Goudhurst–Flimwell road, 10m SE of Tunbridge Wells*

SPRING SUMMER AUTUMN **WINTER**

Gift Shop · Café

This is an extraordinary place, ideal for crisp winter walks or misty autumn days and so I have highlighted its interest for the tail-end of the year. Yet winter visitors are not here purely for the trees, although they are reason enough. Within Bedgebury's 300 acres you may well come across mushroomers foraging for fungi, botanists botanising in the bogs and undergrowth, and you may even catch sight of flocks of birdwatchers, twitching away behind long-lenses that are trained on the visiting crossbills, which gorge on various pine cones and kernels.

There was already a comprehensive collection of conifers on the Bedgebury Estate when the Royal Botanic Gardens, Kew (*q.v.*), and the Forestry Commission pooled resources to maintain it in 1925. These days it is administered solely by the Forestry Commission and it remains one of the finest collections of conifers in Europe.

Here you can see conifers in all their variety, from dainty dwarf kinds to fully mature hemlocks, cedars and pines.

The tallest tree here is a grand fir, 150 years old and as many feet tall. Close to it and very nearly as tall are several Leyland cypresses, a reminder of the potentially massive size of these popular hedging trees. It's good to see conifers in a setting that can match their own majesty. The undulating, rugged landscape suits them well and incense cedars stand as tall pillars on the hillside like isolated ruins of classical temples. There are also deciduous trees scattered through the pinetum and a broad range of rhododendrons thrives in the acidic soil conditions, bringing some floral colour to the slopes in the first half of the year.

LAMBERHURST

Scotney Castle Garden

Lamberhurst, Tunbridge Wells TN3 8JN **TEL.** *01892-891081* **OWNER** *The National Trust* **HOURS** *April–Oct, Wed–Fri, 11a.m.–6p.m,. Sat–Sun, 2–6p.m., Bank Holiday Suns and Mons, 12 noon–6p.m. (closed Good Friday)* **ENTRANCE** *£3.60, children £1.80* **DIRECTIONS** *On A21, S of Lamberhurst*

SPRING SUMMER AUTUMN WINTER

Access | Gift Shop

The classic view of Scotney is the old, partially ruined castle with its bulging round tower, seen from across the waters of its moat. It seems the perfect setting for the dalliance of lovers: the ruin casually draped with wisteria, vines and roses, and fragrant herbs scenting the partially enclosed courtyard. West and north-west of the castle, the sloping gardens display naturalistic plantings of ornamental trees and shrubs. Thickets of rhododendrons, viburnums and azaleas light up the hillside with kaleidoscopic colours in spring, while the coppiced trees of the woodland are awash with bluebells. Early in the year, snowdrops light up the grassy slopes, followed by primroses and daffodils; autumn sees the foliage tints of parrotia, acers and many other fiery-leaved trees and shrubs. Within its 19 acres there is much to see and enjoy, and always the unfailingly romantic atmosphere, especially late in the day after the bulk of visitors has disappeared.

LYMPNE

Port Lympne

Lympne, nr Hythe CT21 4PD TEL. *01303-264647* OWNER *Mr J. Aspinall* HOURS *Open all year, daily, 10a.m.–5p.m. (or 1hr before dusk in winter)* ENTRANCE *£6.99, OAPs/children £4.99 (includes house, garden, animal park)* DIRECTIONS *3m W of Hythe, on B2067*

SPRING SUMMER AUTUMN WINTER

Gift Shop Café DON'T MISS

Port Lympne provides a fantasial cocktail of zoo, garden and eccentrically decorated house, adding up to a highly enjoyable outing for all ages and inclinations. From the garden visitor's point of view, it is certainly a novelty to walk through 100 yards of hydrangeas to the accompanying sound of baying wolves, or to hear the distant roar of rare Barbary lions while admiring the dahlia borders.

The 15 acres of gardens (within a 300-acre animal park) were originally designed by the wealthy art patron and political host, Sir Philip Sassoon, being laid out from 1919 onwards. From the hydrangea walk you reach the top of the 125-step Trojan stairs, offering wonderful views over the flatlands of Romney Marsh. The stairs lead down to a formal garden of roses, cotton lavender and Hupeh crab apples (which have beautiful spring blossom) and further terraced gardens, divided by walls and hedging. Within the hedged compartments there are bedded-out areas – one in an intriguing chessboard design, another laid out with beds in contrasting stripes. There is a terraced vineyard, a pair of long, mixed borders, a magnolia walk, rose terrace, dahlia terrace and herbaceous border, and surrounding picnic areas.

By the time you have reached the end of the lower terraces, the animals are close at hand – lions, hyaenas, small cats, bison, gibbons and monkeys, etc. It is also well worth looking inside the eccentrically decorated house, which has a delightful Moorish patio with marble floor and five fountains, and a tented room of exotic murals by the celebrated artist Rex Whistler.

PENSHURST

Penshurst Place

Penshurst, Tonbridge TN11 8DG TEL. *01892-870307*
OWNER *Viscount de l'Isle* HOURS *April–Sept, daily, 11a.m.–6p.m.; March and Oct, Sat–Sun only, 11a.m.–6p.m.* ENTRANCE *£5.50, OAPs £5.10, children £3, family ticket £14.50; garden only: £4, £3.50, £2.75*
DIRECTIONS *SW of Tonbridge on B2176, in Penshurst village*

SPRING SUMMER AUTUMN WINTER

Café Plant Shop DON'T MISS

The county of Kent possesses an excessively generous helping of castles and historic houses, many of which are set off by pleasing grounds. Penshurst Place is among the very best of them – an ancient, battlemented house with thick walls of stone and seemingly endless enclosed gardens, formally laid out but displaying a summertime abandonment under a siege of flowers.

The garden covers 10 acres, sub-divided by a mile of yew hedges into mostly formal areas, such as the symmetrically laid out Italian garden of neat box beds and polyantha roses around a central lily-pool. There are avenues of fruit trees and parallel herbaceous borders; a 'Union Jack' garden of red and white roses lined by hedges of blue lavender; a formally laid out cobnut orchard, and smooth lawns pinned down by stout topiary. Flowers, particularly roses, dominate the high season, but spring bulbs and apple blossom make early visits memorable, and autumn sees a magnificent ripening of fruits and foliage. The 100yd-long bed of peonies is spectacular at that expectant moment when spring is retreating in favour of summer.

SISSINGHURST

Sissinghurst Castle Garden

Sissinghurst, nr Cranbrook TN17 2AB **TEL.** *01580-715330* **OWNER** *The National Trust* **HOURS** *Easter–mid-Oct, Tues–Fri, 1–6.30p.m. (last adm. 6p.m.), Sat–Sun, 10a.m.–5.30p.m. (last adm. 5p.m.); timed ticket system means that at busy times visitors may need to wait to enter the garden* **ENTRANCE** *£5.50, children £2.75* **DIRECTIONS** *From M25 Jct 5 take A21 S to Hastings. Before Lamberhurst, turn left onto A262 to Ashford. Signposted once in Sissinghurst*

SPRING SUMMER AUTUMN WINTER

Gift Shop · Café · Plant Shop · DON'T MISS

This world-famous garden was made by the influential gardener and writer Vita Sackville-West and her husband, Harold Nicolson, from 1930 onwards. Its appeal lies in the disciplined framework of walls and hedges (chiefly Harold's department), filled out by wonderfully exuberant plantings of old roses, perennials and cottage garden flowers (Vita's inspiration). The setting itself is wildly romantic: the Nicolsons took on the remains of an Elizabethan mansion with twin towers and rambling, low outbuildings, crumbly, red-brick walls and open courtyards.

Harold's restrained classicism produced a design of bold vistas and allées, complementary to the period of the house, but not slavishly emulating a Tudor layout. By sectioning off the six acres into variously themed areas, the Nicolsons were able to experiment with contrasting atmospheres in different parts of the garden. Vita's innovative White Garden is a poetic composition of white and off-white flowers, set off by green, grey and blue-tinted foliage plants, such as ferns, artemisias, sea kale and grasses. It is soothing, cool, restrained. By contrast, the cottage garden makes the heart beat faster with hot, strong colours – vivid yellow, orange and scarlet poppies, arctotis, cannas and red-hot pokers, against the dark greenery of yew. The rose garden is heady with old-fashioned blooms, sweetly scented and chiefly in shades of pink, joined by complementary blue, mauve and white flowers. Harold's spring garden features massed bulbs in variety, beneath an avenue of pleached limes.

Although the Nicolsons departed a long time ago, their inspiration lives on, through the talents and skills of succeeding head gardeners. There is so much to see and enjoy here that any time of year will be rewarding; visits early or late in the day are usually less crowded however; due to the narrow and uneven paths, wheelchairs are restricted to two at one time, and prams and pushchairs are not admitted.

TUNBRIDGE WELLS

Groombridge Place

Groombridge, Tunbridge Wells TN3 9QG TEL. *01892-863999* OWNER *Andrew de Candole* HOURS *April–late Oct, daily, 10a.m.–6p.m.* ENTRANCE *£5, OAPs £4.50, children £3.50* DIRECTIONS *On B2110, 4m SW of Tunbridge Wells*

SPRING SUMMER AUTUMN WINTER

Access · Gift Shop · Café · Plant Shop

The pretty, moated house (not open) at Groombridge is set beside several delightful, terraced formal gardens rising up a gently sloping hill. Near the house lie formal lawns, a knot garden, a sculpture, and oriental garden, featuring ancient Japanese acers. The 'Drunken' garden displays tipsy topiaries, leaning at odd angles; there is a rose garden, a white garden and a walled kitchen garden. An exciting development in this 164-acre site is the Enchanted Forest woodland garden, where wiggly paths and water gardens ramble through mature woodland. There are bridges crossing the stream at intervals, and new plantings of moisture-loving plants, at their most colourful in spring. As well as being an interesting garden in its own right, Groombridge Place caters for family interests as a whole, with falconry displays from one of England's largest birds-of-prey sanctuaries, canal boat rides and an award-winning children's garden.

YALDING

Yalding Organic Gardens

Benover Road, Yalding, Maidstone ME18 6EX TEL. *01622-814650* OWNER *The Henry Doubleday Research Association* HOURS *May–Sept, Wed–Sun and Bank Holiday Mons; also Oct, Sat–Sun only; all 10a.m.–5p.m.* ENTRANCE *£2, OAPs £1.50, children £1* DIRECTIONS *6m SW of Maidstone, ½m S of Yalding on B2162*

SPRING SUMMER AUTUMN WINTER

Access · Gift Shop · Café · Plant Shop

This five-acre garden is a southern offshoot of the Henry Doubleday Research Association's gardens at Ryton (*q.v.*), in Warwickshire. It is laid out in a series of attractive demonstration gardens, all cultivated entirely organically, and offers both interesting insights into garden making in earlier centuries and a great deal of practical information.

There is a woodland and wildflower walk, a medieval physick garden of culinary and medicinal herbs, a Tudor-style knot garden of interwoven low hedging, a 19th-century cottager's garden of mixed flowers, fruit and vegetables, and another Victorian garden in a more suburban style. There are sumptuous double herbaceous borders in the spirit of Gertrude Jekyll (*q.v.*), allotment gardens, organic vegetable and fruit displays, etc. Yalding shows how everyone can make a really beautiful garden in an ecologically friendly way, working in harmony with nature and not against it.

And also...

J. Bradshaw & Son, Busheyfields Nursery, Herne, Herne Bay CT6 7LJ (tel. 01227-375415), is an old-established family nursery, specializing in a wide range of climbing plants, particularly honeysuckles (around 100 species and cultivars) and clematis, both of which are held here as National Collections. Open March–Oct, Tues–Sat, and Bank Holiday Mons, 10a.m.–5p.m.

Dr Simon Charlesworth, of **Downderry Nursery, 649 London Road, Ditton, Aylesford ME20 6DJ (tel. 01732-840710)**, specializes in producing lavenders, and has more than 60 different species and cultivars. Send 2 × 1st-class stamps for a catalogue. Many plants are sold as rooted cuttings and liners. Visitors only by appointment.

Herbs, wildflowers, cottage garden and aromatic plants are on sale and displayed in the show gardens at **Iden Croft Herbs, Frittenden Road, Staplehurst TN12 0DH (tel. 01580-891432)**. Open all year, Mon–Sat, 9a.m.–5p.m.; also Sun and Bank Holidays March–Sept, 11a.m.–5p.m. Entrance to gardens £1.

For the largest range of fruit trees in the country, contact **Keepers Nursery, Gallants Court, East Farleigh, Maidstone ME15 0LE (tel. 01622-726465)**. Offering over 600 different varieties, they include large ranges of apples, pears, quinces, medlars, walnuts, cobnuts and stone fruits (including damsons and nectarines). They also offer a propagation service if, for example, you want to duplicate a special tree in your garden (most propagation is carried out by budding from late July–August, with young trees usually ready for delivery 18 months later). Open by appointment. Send 2 × 1st-class stamps for a mail order catalogue.

Madrona Nursery, Pluckley Road, Bethersden TN26 3DD (tel. 01233-820100), has a wonderful selection of plants across a selective range of shrubs and trees, hardy perennials, conifers, grasses, bamboos and ferns. The emphasis is on the interesting and unusual, well grown and reasonably priced. Also plants by mail (catalogue £1). Open late March–late Oct, Sat–Tues, 10a.m.–5p.m.

Rayment Wirework, Unit 10, Laundry Road, Minster, Thanet CT12 4HL (tel. 01843-821628), manufactures elegant hand-painted wirework structures for gardens and conservatories. Their range includes plant holders and fancy hanging baskets, intricate gazebos and ornate furniture, in styles inspired by 19th-century French designs. Mail order catalogue on request.

The fortress of **Walmer Castle, Kingsdown Road, Deal CT14 7LJ (tel. 01304-364288)**, was built by Henry VIII as part of his coastal defences against threat of invasion by France or Spain. For the past 300 years its use has been primarily as a domestic residence, however, and it is currently one of the homes of Queen Elizabeth the Queen Mother. The 40-acre gardens are partly walled and include abundant herbaceous borders backed by yew hedging, a traditional kitchen garden with rows of flowers for cutting, and fruit trees, shrubberies, wildflower areas and a new, formal garden. Open April–Oct, daily, 10a.m.–6p.m., Nov–March, Wed–Sun, 10a.m.–4p.m. (closed 24–26 Dec, Jan, Feb and when Lord Warden is in residence). Entrance £4, concessions £3, children £2.

Washfield Nursery, Horns Road, Hawkhurst TN18 4QU (tel. 01580-752522). I chanced upon the nursery by accident, but what a lovely surprise. Its sloping site, surrounded by shrubberies and trees, is well cared for and the quality of plants is high. The nursery specializes in hardy herbaceous perennials – particularly hellebores – and is well worth visiting when looking for the unusual. There is a catalogue (send 4 × 1st-class stamps), but no mail order. The owners suggest anyone making a special journey should always telephone first to ensure the nursery is open. Open Jan–Nov, Wed–Sat, 10a.m.–5p.m.

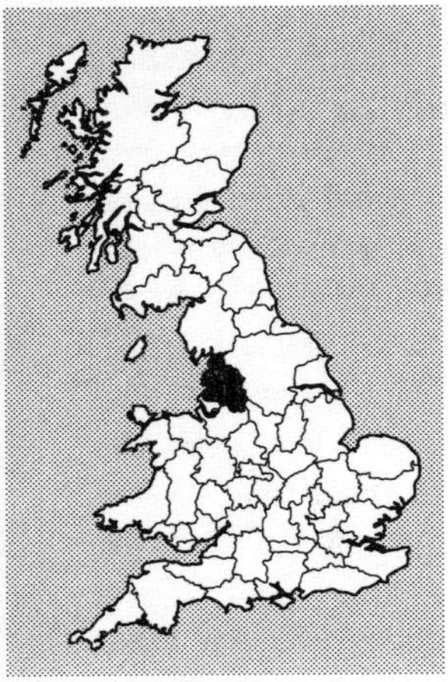

Lancashire

MAP NO. 7

Here is a land of contrasts, renowned for its central role in the Industrial Revolution, with a roll call of hard-working cotton towns – Bolton, Blackburn, Oldham and Manchester – and hard-playing seaside resorts, such as Blackpool, Southport, Lytham St Anne's and Morecambe (famous for its shrimps). The north of the region is a land of high fells, while the spine of the Pennines runs down the eastern boundary. The Forest of Bowland is not really a forest, but a former royal hunting ground and an area of wild beauty and subtle heathland colours among high moors. Its fertile valleys provide good grazing for cattle – the name Bowland deriving from the Celtic buland, meaning cattle pasture.

BARROWFORD

Pendle Heritage Centre

Park Hill, Barrowford, Nelson BB9 6JQ TEL. *01282-695366* OWNER *Lancashire Heritage Trust* HOURS *Garden open all year, daily, except 25 Dec, 10a.m.–5p.m.* ENTRANCE *£2.75 (incl. museum), concessions £1.50, family ticket £6* DIRECTIONS *Come off M65 at Jct 13, 1m from roundabout at junction, then signposted*

SPRING SUMMER AUTUMN WINTER

Gift Shop Café

This six-acre local history centre with old stone buildings, a small farm and country trails has a brick-walled garden, restored to look as it would have done in the late 18th century, using only plants that were then available. Its triangular-shape beds are planted with herbs and salad flowers. Two large, box-edge beds contain assorted flowers and standard gooseberry bushes, with *Rosa gallica officinalis*, the Red Rose of Lancaster. Two further beds contain vegetables and fruit, with espalier pear trees trained on wires beside the path. All plants are organically grown.

There is a steep woodland walk among wildflowers offering views of the beautiful local countryside. The farm buildings include a fine cruck barn, dating from the 16th century, its frame formed from a single oak tree split in half, then roughly shaped to form the inverted V that provides the basic structure of the building. Gawthorpe Hall (*q.v.*) is nearby.

MANCHESTER

Fletcher Moss Botanical Gardens

Millgate Lane, Didsbury, Manchester M20 1AA TEL. *0161-434 1877* OWNER *Manchester City Council* HOURS *Open all year, daily, 9a.m.–dusk* ENTRANCE *Free* DIRECTIONS *5m S of Manchester city centre, S of A5145 close to village of Didsbury, on Millgate Lane*

SPRING SUMMER AUTUMN WINTER

Access Café

This unusual rock garden of 21 acres is over 100 years old and is still one of the finest in the north of England. It was begun in 1889 by Robert Wood Williamson, a solicitor and keen alpine gardener, whose extensive knowledge of these plants was due to the fact that he joined his father (a professor of natural history and botany) on geological expeditions to the mountainous regions of Europe.

You descend the steeply sloping, south-facing garden by narrow, informal paths that wind along and down a series of rocky terraces. They are home to many spring flowers and bulbs, such as cyclamen, crocuses and dwarf narcissi, and small shrubs. There are gentians, saxifrages, phloxes and other typical rock garden flowers crammed into the rockwork, and a small stream feeds several pools on its descent to a larger pond at the bottom.

A LOST LANDSCAPE FOR BOLTON WANDERERS

Up on the western, heather-clad moors of Rivington Pike is ***Rivington Terraced Gardens, Rivington, nr Bolton (tel. 01204-691549), 7m NW of Bolton, 1m NW of Horwich; signs from A673 in Rivington or Grimeford, walk from Rivington Hall and Hall Barn****. The Edwardian landscape architect Thomas Mawson laid out a public park and a private garden at Roynton Cottage for the soap industrialist, William Lever (who became Lord Leverhulme). Mawson resisted any thoughts of stamping a formal garden onto the landscape; instead he laid out the 45 acres of grounds with lawns and winding paths among plantations of exotic and native trees and ericaceous shrubs, sympathetically following the contours of the hillside. Although he was famous for creating grander gardens in the Arts and Crafts style, Mawson declared 'of all the gardens which have administered to my professional enjoyment, none comes into competition with Roynton'.*

Decades of neglect have taken their toll on the gardens and their abandoned buildings, but the naturalistic rockwork is impressive, with ornamental pools and miniature waterfalls, and the views are outstanding. Open all year, daily. Entrance free.

The house and garden were sold early this century to a wealthy neighbour, Fletcher Moss, who gave the property and gardens to the city of Manchester in 1920. Parts of the grounds were developed for leisure facilities, but the rock garden has survived. In 1958 part of the garden was dedicated to the intrepid plant hunter Frank Kingdon-Ward, who was born just two miles away in the village of Withington. Interestingly, his father, Marshall Ward, was a pupil of, and later assistant to, Robert Williamson's father.

And also...

Over 150 different models of vintage garden machinery are displayed at **The British Lawnmower Museum, 106–114 Shakespeare Street, Southport PR8 5AJ (tel. 01704-501336).** The museum workshop restores vintage mowers belonging to enthusiasts, as well as the machinery in its own collection. Open all year, Mon–Sat, 9a.m.–5.30p.m. (closed Bank Holidays). Entrance £1, children 50p.

Ten years ago, next-door neighbours Christine Moore and Judith Bradshaw combined their horticultural interests to open **Catforth Gardens, Roots Lane, Catforth, Preston PR4 0JB (tel. 01772-690561/690269).** Their nursery specializes in hardy herbaceous perennials, and the gardens of their respective houses, and a third in the paddock are also open. The style is informal, abundant planting. Open mid-March–mid-Sept, daily, 10.30a.m.–5p.m. Entrance £2, OAPs £1.50 and children 50p. No mail order.

Gawthorpe Hall, Burnley Road, Padiham, nr Burnley BB12 8UA (tel. 01282-771004), is an early 17th-century stone house on 12 acres of sloping ground above the River Calder. It has Victorian gardens designed by Sir Charles Barry, with a formal parterre of sunburst pattern and gravel paths, and a small formal rose garden. Rhododendrons and bright-foliage shrubs bring spring colour to the woodland walks. Open, house only, Easter–Oct, daily, except Mon and Fri, but open Bank Holiday Mons and Good Friday, 1–5p.m. (last adm. 4.15p.m.), garden open all year, daily, 10a.m.–6p.m. Entrance free; house £2.90, concessions £1.45, children £1.30.

Holden Clough Nursery, Holden, Bolton-by-Bowland, Clitheroe BB7 4PF (tel. 01200-447615), specializes in raising choice, really hardy plants suited to northern gardens. It is a long-established traditional nursery, with a large range of interesting plants, including alpines, grasses, heathers, perennials and shrubs; mail order is available from Oct–March (catalogue £1.40). Open all year, Tues–Sat and Bank Holiday Mons, 9a.m.–5p.m. Last adm. on all days 4.30p.m.

Silverdale is in beautiful limestone country overlooking Morecambe Bay, where you will find **Reginald Kaye Ltd, Waithman Nurseries, Silverdale, Carnforth LA5 0TY (tel. 01524-701252).** There are many rare alpines and rock plants, dwarf trees and conifers, hardy ferns, bog and woodland plants (catalogue 60p, but no mail order). Open Wed–Sat, 10a.m.–5p.m., Sun 2.30–5p.m.

Vegetables are larger than life when grown from seed supplied by **W. Robinson & Sons Ltd, Sunny Bank, Forton, Preston PR3 0BN (tel. 01524-791210).** This is the home of the 'Mammoth' strain of seeds, a speciality which grew out of an earlier family business in market gardening. Robinson's 'Mammoth' onions, leeks, tomatoes and beans (such as the 30in-long 'Liberty' runner beans) are favourites with exhibition growers. Catalogue on request. Open June–Feb, Mon–Fri, and March– May, daily, 9a.m. to 5p.m.

Acid, sandy soil at the National Trust's **Rufford Old Hall, Rufford, nr Ormskirk L40 1SG (tel. 01704-821254)**, provides ideal conditions for rhododendrons in the gardens surrounding a magnificent Tudor hall. There are 14 acres of woodland gardens of shrubs and bulbs, topiaries in the lawns and a small orchard featuring old northern varieties of apple. There is also a tearoom and shop. Hall open April–early Nov, Sat–Wed, 1–5p.m., last adm. 4.30p.m.; garden same days 12 noon–6p.m. Entrance £3.50, children £1.70, family ticket £9.50; gardens only, £1.80, children 90p.

Stydd Nursery, Stonygate Lane, Ribchester, Preston PR3 3YN (tel. 01254-878797), specializes in old-fashioned roses, plus some modern shrub and species roses, climbers and ramblers. Also half-hardy perennials and conservatory plants. Open Tues–Fri, 1.30–5p.m.; Sat 9a.m.–5p.m.; also Sun April–mid-Dec, 2–5p.m. Closed Mon.

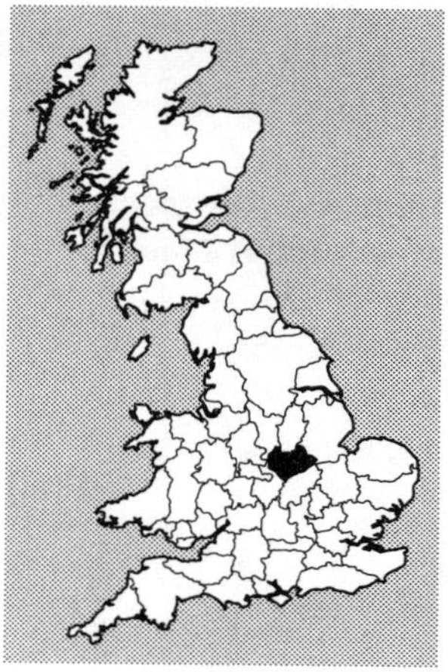

Leicestershire and Rutland

MAP NO. 5

Rutland (originally Rota's Land, owned by Queen Edith, wife of Edward the Confessor, and first recorded in the year 851) is a tiny county, just 15 miles long and 11 miles wide. It had been swallowed up by Leicestershire but recently regained its independent status. Leicestershire engulfs its western boundary, and the entire region is known for its fertile farms, an age-old tradition of hunting, and Melton Mowbray, the home of crusty pork pies, and Stilton cheese. From the gardener's point of view, the region is also the home of Barnsdale, the television gardens of the late and greatly missed Geoff Hamilton.

BELVOIR

Belvoir Castle

Belvoir, nr Grantham, Leicestershire NG32 1PD TEL. *01476-870262* OWNER *The Duke of Rutland* HOURS *April–Sept, Tues–Thurs, Sat–Sun, and Bank Holidays, 11a.m.–5p.m.; Oct, Sun only* ENTRANCE *(Castle and gardens) £5, OAPs £4, children £3; spring garden (by pre-booked appointment for parties only) £3.50* DIRECTIONS *By Belvoir village, 6m W of Grantham (signposted)*

SPRING SUMMER AUTUMN WINTER

Access | Gift Shop | Café

The impressive castle stands in a commanding position above the Vale of Belvoir (pronounced Beaver), its name meaning beautiful view. The castle is packed with notable art treasures and fine furniture; outside, the four-acre Statue Gardens with their 17th-century sculptures descend the hillside below the castle in a sequence of terraces and slopes.

As well as the fine views, there are modern roses, a woodland garden and record trees – the tallest bird cherry and yew tree in Britain.

The Duchess of Rutland's private Spring Garden (open by appointment) has recently been restored, and is a pretty woodland of flowering trees, shrubs and bulbs, set in a natural amphitheatre, hidden away in the woods.

Celebrity Choice

***Adam Pasco, editor of BBC* Gardeners' World Magazine**

'I enjoyed following the development of ***Barnsdale*** *as a television garden since the early 1980s, when Geoff Hamilton moved there. Many of the gardens within it, such as the First Time Garden and the Ornamental Kitchen Garden, were made specifically for Geoff's mini-series on TV. Geoff was a great enthusiast and always aware that you needn't be flush with cash to make a beautiful garden or to make things that work.*

'Now that Barnsdale has been opened to the public, people expect to walk into a pristine garden, with everything just so; but Barnsdale was never like that. Geoff never maintained the whole site in a weed-free state – he didn't have the time or the armies of staff to do that. It was always real gardening, warts and all, and now, since his death, there is a small and enthusiastic team trying to maintain the garden as Geoff would have had it. In this period of transition, from outdoor TV studio into a visitor attraction, the needs of visitors are being taken into account, and I look forward to Barnsdale continuing to be a source of inspiration to millions more gardeners in the future.'

OAKHAM

Barnsdale

The Avenue, Exton, Oakham, Rutland LE15 8AH **TEL.** *01572-813200* **OWNER** *The Hamilton Family* **HOURS** *March–Oct, daily, 10a.m.–5p.m., Nov–Feb, daily, 10a.m.–4p.m. (closed Christmas and New Year)* **ENTRANCE** *£4.50 (£3 in winter)* **DIRECTIONS** *Off A606 between Oakham and Stamford*

SPRING SUMMER AUTUMN WINTER

Access Café Plant Shop

Over a period of 17 years the gardens at Barnsdale became familiar to millions of viewers of the BBC's flagship gardening programme. The home of Geoff Hamilton, Barnsdale covers eight and a half acres of a variety of demonstration gardens, all specially made for *Gardeners' World* and themed series, such as *The Ornamental Kitchen Garden.*

Since 1997 the gardens have been open to the public on a regular basis, and you can wander through 25 different areas, such as the Gentleman's Garden, featuring brick paths and terracing, topiary and trelliswork; the Artisan's Garden, with everything home-made on a tight budget, yet executed with panache; the *Daily Express* garden of herbs and wattle arches; the Elizabethan Kitchen Garden of raised beds and painted finials; and the Paradise Gardens, one with red-brick walls and a conservatory, the other featuring random stepping-stone paths and rustic seating.

Barnsdale Plants Nursery adjoins the gardens, and is run by Geoff Hamilton's son, Nick. It offers a very wide selection of plants propagated from the gardens and specializes in well-grown herbaceous perennials and shrubs, all in peat-free compost. The nursery's own display gardens (separate from the TV gardens) can be visited for £1.50. There is also a mail order service (send 5 × 2nd-class stamps plus A5 envelope for the catalogue).

And also...

Gandy's Roses, North Kilworth, nr Lutterworth, Leicestershire LE17 6HZ (tel. 01858-880398), is an old-established family business, with around 600 varieties of roses available, including a substantial number of climbers. You can buy direct from the nursery which also stocks shrubs, conifers and fruit trees, and by mail for dispatch during the dormant season (free catalogue available on request). Open daily, Mon–Sat, 9a.m.–5p.m., Sun 2–5p.m.

Goscote Nurseries, Syston Road, Cossington, Leicestershire LE7 4UZ (tel. 01509-812121), was begun by Derek Cox in 1964. It is renowned for its extensive stocks of trees – around 210 different varieties – but also sells shrubs, clematis, conifers and rhododendrons, available by mail or direct from the nursery (send 5 × 2nd-class stamps for the catalogue). Open all year, Mon–Fri, 8a.m.–5p.m. (4.30p.m. in winter), Sat 9a.m.–5p.m., Sun 10a.m.–5p.m.

The Herb Nursery, Thistleton, Oakham, Rutland LE15 7RE (tel. 01572-767658), offers herbs, herbaceous plants and wildflowers in variety, with around 500 different plants available. Scented-leaf pelargoniums are a speciality, and there is a display garden featuring plants available from the nursery. There is a catalogue (send an A5 s.a.e.) but no mail order. Open daily, 9a.m.–6p.m. or dusk if sooner.

If you are keen on dahlias or chrysanthemums, it is worth knowing about **Philip Tivey and Sons, 28 Wanlip Road, Syston, Leicestershire LE7 1PA (tel. 01162-692968)**, which has been specializing in these flowers for over 40 years, producing some of its own varieties. The nursery exhibits at the Royal Horticultural Society's shows and others, including the splendid Harrogate Autumn Show, which is always a riot of colourful blooms. (Send s.a.e. and a 1st-class stamp for catalogue.) Open all year, Mon–Fri, 9a.m.–5p.m. (4p.m. in winter), Sat 9a.m.–4p.m.

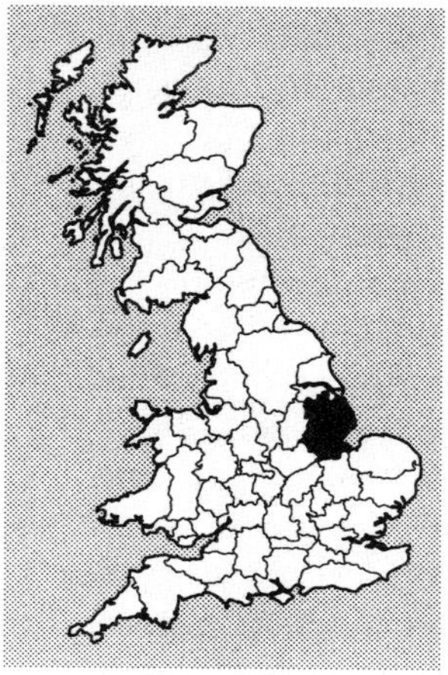

Lincolnshire

MAP NO. 6

Although it is a large county, Lincolnshire is off the beaten track for most tourists; it is completely bypassed by arterial routes linking the north and south of England and its unremarkable landscape – much of it very flat – has proved best suited to arable farms and extensive production of flower bulbs. The broad horizons are punctuated here and there by little more than the odd church tower, under vast skies. The city of Lincoln, perched on a rare hill, was a Celtic settlement before the Romans arrived and named it Lindum Colonia*; its triple-towered cathedral is magnificent. Stamford is an attractive town of stone architecture, brought to fame as television's* Middlemarch.

GRANTHAM

Belton House

Grantham NG32 2LS TEL. *01476-566116* OWNER *The National Trust* HOURS *April–Oct, Wed–Sun and Bank Holiday Mons, 11a.m.–5.30p.m. (closed Good Friday), July–Aug, 10a.m.–5.30p.m. (house open 1–5.30p.m.). Last adm. 5p.m.* ENTRANCE *£4.80, children £2.40* DIRECTIONS *3m NE of Grantham on A607 Grantham–Lincoln road*

SPRING SUMMER AUTUMN WINTER

Access | Gift Shop | Café

Belton House is serene, elegant and surprisingly entertaining. It will be familiar to many as Rosings, the stately home of Lady Catherine de Bourgh, in the BBC's serialisation of *Pride and Prejudice*.

The gardens cover 33 acres within a 1000-acre wooded deer park. When gardening writer J.C. Loudon visited with his wife, in May 1840, he declared: 'We have always understood [Belton] to be one of the best kept places in England, and we certainly found it so, though the family had been absent some months, and were not expected till July.'

There are splendid trees, including a handsome Lebanon cedar, the biggest sugar maple in Britain, and fine avenues of lime and Turkey oak. The Italian garden features urns, a fountain pool and clipped yews, presided over by an exquisite early 19th-century conservatory. The Dutch garden features green and golden yews, and bright seasonal bedding.

The adventure playground and mini-railway will keep children amused. The house is worth seeing, too, for its beautiful carvings. Look out for the 18th-century exercise chair in the library, made for Lord Tyrconnel. Its cushion contains a huge spring, on which his lordship could bounce up and down.

ANTIQUE ALI-BABA JARS

Visitors to the Chelsea Flower Show in 1997 will recall the display of huge antique anforas (oil jars, also known as amphoras) displayed by ***Victoria's Collection, Maltby House, London Road, Louth LN11 9QP (tel. 01507-601221).*** *Anforas date back to ancient Mediterranean lands, where traditionally they were used to ferment wine, or store olive oil. They can be as large as 13ft high, and 6½ft in diameter, weighing as much as 4400lb.*

Such large jars are very rare and expensive, costing from £17,500–£20,000 each, and are usually found in remote locations, buried underground. Victoria's Collection specializes in unearthing and giving them a new lease of life as spectacular ornaments for larger gardens. There is a display garden, but visitors need to make an appointment to view. Open all year, Mon–Fri, 8a.m.–5p.m., closed for 2 weeks at Christmas.

GUNBY

Gunby Hall

Gunby, nr Spilsby PE23 5SS TEL. *01909-486411* OWNER *The National Trust* HOURS *April–Sept, Wed, 2–6p.m. Last adm. 5.30p.m. Closed Bank Holidays. Garden also open Thurs 2–6p.m. (house and garden by prior written appointment to Mr and Mrs J. D. Wrisdale on Tues, Thurs and Fri)* ENTRANCE *(garden only) £2.50, children £1.20 (under 5s free) (house and garden £3.50, children £1.70)* DIRECTIONS *2½m NW of Burgh le Marsh, 7m W of Skegness on S side of A158*

SPRING | SUMMER | AUTUMN | WINTER

Access

Roses are the main event on the seven acres of Gunby Hall in the summer. They clamber up walls, scramble over pergolas, and jostle among traditional herbaceous flowers, and in the kitchen garden provide cut flowers. Even the house, a red-brick mansion built in 1700, is clothed with the stems of fragrant, old-fashioned varieties, such as 'Climbing Lady Hillingdon' (amber) and creamy 'Alister Stella Gray'.

The exuberance of summer flowers is almost overwhelming in the two walled gardens. They contain sumptuous borders beside the straight paths, more roses, a well-stocked large herb garden, greenhouses, and a pretty, blue summerhouse. There are fruit trees, espaliered and pinned to the walls, vegetable beds and cages of soft fruits.

And also...

Baytree Nurseries, High Road, Weston, Spalding PE12 6JU (tel. 01406-370242), is a large, well-stocked and well-run garden centre. It includes demonstration gardens, restaurant and the usual range of garden centre fare. Open daily, 9a.m.–6p.m. in summer (5.30p.m. in winter).

Doddington Hall, Doddington LN6 4RU (tel. 01522-694308), is a red-brick Elizabethan mansion, with five-acre gardens laid out in sympathetically formal style. There are knots and parterres, irises, roses, herbaceous borders and a wild garden with turf maze, stream and fine trees. Open March–April, Sun only; May–Sept, Wed, Sun and Bank Holiday Mons, 2–6p.m. Entrance (gardens only) £2, children £1, (house and gardens) £4, children £2, family ticket £11.

PRIMULA SPECIALISTS

The genus Primula *is a large one, with around 400 species of perennial, mainly alpine, herbaceous plants. They occur in many different habitats, right across the northern hemisphere, and also in the Falkland Islands and the southern tip of South America. British natives include the common pale yellow primrose which ornaments damp woodlands in early spring, and the cowslip of meadow pastures. Popular garden forms include the ubiquitous, jewel-bright bedding polyanthus, and the easy-to-grow candelabra strains that flourish by damp streams. For the enthusiast, there are many challenging alpine species available with exacting requirements, as well as the surreal but enchanting types known as auriculas.*

Mary and Michael Robinson have been growing primulas in huge variety for over 20 years at ***Martin Nest Nurseries, Grange Cottage, Harpswell Lane, Hemswell, Gainsborough DN21 5UP (tel. 01427-668369), 6m E of Gainsborough on A631.*** *You can buy from the nursery which also has a small demonstration garden or by mail (send 3 × 2nd-class stamps for the catalogue). Open daily, 10a.m.–4p.m.*

Hall Farm Nursery, Hall Farm, Harpswell, Gainsborough DN21 5UU (tel. 01427-668412), produces shrubs, perennials and old roses, with the emphasis on interesting and unusual strains. There is also a well-planned one-acre garden with over 100 roses, with lawns and pond. Open all year, daily, 9.30a.m.–5.30p.m.; opening times subject to change in winter (telephone before visiting).

Johnsons Direct, Matmore Gate, Spalding PE11 2PN (tel. 0800-614323), produces two free large, full-colour mail order catalogues each year, offering a wide variety of flower and vegetable seeds, with spring- and summer-flowering bulbs, roses and ornamental shrubs and hardware.

Potterton and Martin, The Cottage Nursery, Moortown Road, Nettleton, Caistor LN7 6HX (tel. 01472-851792), specializes in producing a broad range of alpines and rock plants, also available by mail (send £1 for catalogue). Open daily, 9a.m.–5p.m.

Clive Simms, Woodhurst, Essendine, Stamford PE9 4LQ (tel. 01780-755615), is a mail order fruit nursery, specializing in unusual fruiting plants and uncommon nut trees (send 2 × 1st-class stamps for catalogue). Not open to visitors, except by appointment to collect stock.

Lincolnshire's bulb industry puts on a glorious technicolour display at **Springfields Show Gardens, Spalding PE12 6ET (tel. 01775-724843)**, for the spring season. Plenty of large, swirly beds displaying massed daffodils, tulips, hyacinths and other bulbs, between broad lawns. Open mid-March–mid-May, daily, 10a.m.–6p.m. Entrance £3, OAPs £2.70.

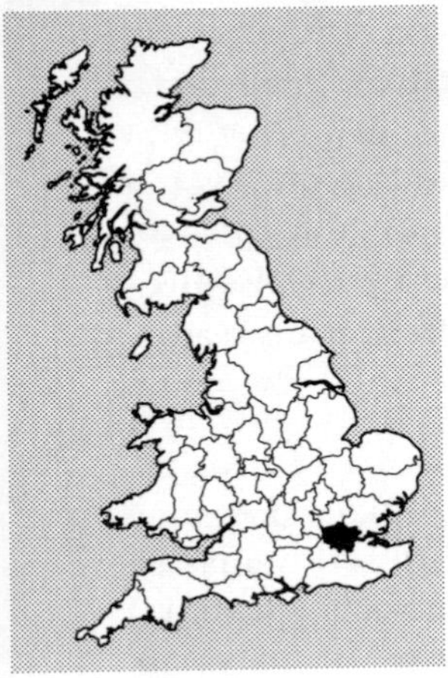

London and Middlesex

MAP NO. 3

England's great capital city is blessed with numerous wonderful parks and squares, its 'green lungs' that help provide all Londoners and visitors with the opportunity for a green walk in a green shade. There are less well-known gardens in London too, such as the rarely opened but richly planted Eccleston Square, and the ancient Physic Garden at Chelsea, started by the Society of Apothecaries in 1673. The internationally important botanic gardens at Kew, and historical grounds of Hampton Court, Ham House and Richmond Park are listed in this Guide *under Surrey, as their postal addresses dictate, although these days they stand on London's south-west perimeter.*

BRENTFORD

Syon Park

Brentford, Middlesex TW8 8JF **TEL.** *0181-560 0881* **OWNER** *The Duke of Northumberland* **HOURS** *House April–end Oct, Wed–Sun and Bank Holiday Mons, 11a.m.–5p.m.; gardens open all year, daily, except 25–26 Dec, 10a.m.–6p.m. (or dusk if earlier)* **ENTRANCE** *Gardens £2.50, children £2; house £5.50, concessions/children £4* **DIRECTIONS** *Between Brentford and Isleworth, on N bank of Thames*

SPRING | SUMMER | AUTUMN | WINTER

Syon Park and Kew Gardens (see Surrey entries) face each other across the River Thames. Syon is the London home of the Duke of Northumberland, and it never ceases to surprise me that most of the views from the house and park are incredibly rural; you might easily be hundreds of miles from the city when you look over the water meadows to Kew.

Capability Brown (*q.v.*) landscaped Syon Park from 1767–1773, adding serpentine lakes and unusual trees. Many of the largest trees here date from his original plantings. It is a delightful park to wander in at any season. In spring, pretty with magnolias and Japanese cherries in bloom, and maples bursting into leaf. In autumn there are the mellow shades of foliage reflected in the lake. Herons fly overhead almost as regularly as the aeroplanes heading for Heathrow, but the peace is more often broken by the shrieking of the resident peacocks. The rose gardens stand beside the house on the site of some early formal gardens that were swept away by Brown.

The park's most impressive architectural feature is the conservatory, which dates from the 1820s and houses tender shrubs, fragrant freesias and carnations. It has a massive glass dome, flanked by curved wings that embrace a formal garden. One wing features a fernery, created among mossy rocks and a fish-pond, while the opposite end goes climatically to the other extreme with a mini-desert, home to weird and wonderful cacti, aloes and aeoniums. Syon Park Garden Centre, also on the estate, is large and comprehensively stocked with plants and sundries.

GARDENING BOOKS IN NOTTING HILL

Garden Books, 11 Blenheim Crescent, London W11 2EE (tel. 0171-792 0777) *close to Ladbroke Grove tube station is, as its name suggests, a bookshop devoted to gardens and gardening. As well as holding a huge range of new and recently published books covering all aspects of plants, flowers, gardens of the world, botany, garden design and garden history, it also holds a range of antiquarian and second-hand books, so you may be lucky and find something here that you had always wanted but found was out of print. They will also post books worldwide on request. Open all year, Mon–Sat, 9a.m.–6p.m.*

ENFIELD

Capel Manor

Bullsmoor Lane, Enfield, Middlesex EN1 4RQ **TEL.** *0181-366 4442 (ask for the Hessian Centre)* **OWNER** *Capel Manor Corporation* **HOURS** *Open March–Oct, daily, 10a.m.–5.30p.m., end Oct–March, Mon–Fri 10a.m.–5.30p.m. (or dusk if sooner)* **ENTRANCE** *£2, concessions £1.50, children £1* **DIRECTIONS** *Off A10 by Jct 25 of M25 (signposted)*

SPRING SUMMER AUTUMN WINTER

Access | Gift Shop | Café | NPC

Capel Manor is a horticultural college which runs a wide range of courses, both vocational and for the interested amateur. The 18th-century former manor house is surrounded by 36 acres of gardens, much of its area divided into plots to demonstrate certain styles, or periods of garden history. They include a Tudor knot garden, a formal 17th-century garden, a Victorian maze, a garden for the disabled, a Japanese garden, and a plantsman's garden. There are alpines, roses, herbaceous borders, flower-arrangers' flowers, woodland gardens, a fragrant Sensory Garden with the sounds of running water, fruit and vegetable plots, greenhouses and conservatories. The college strives to be relevant to modern-day gardeners by the emphasis on small-scale domestic areas, rather than the more scientific, botanical garden approach.

ENFIELD

Myddelton House

Bulls Cross, Enfield, Middlesex EN2 9HG **TEL.** *01992-717711* **OWNER** *Lee Valley Regional Park Authority* **HOURS** *Open all year, Mon–Fri (but not Bank Holidays), 10a.m.–3.30p.m., also last Sun in month Feb–Oct* **ENTRANCE** *£1.50, concessions 75p* **DIRECTIONS** *Off A10 on to Bullsmoor Lane, signposted at Bulls Cross; by train to Turkey Street Station*

THE LONDON PLANE

Stroll through any of London's great parks or historic squares and you will see a sight that is so familiar it will probably pass unnoticed. It is the vast, often buttressed bole and seasonally leafy canopy of the London Plane tree, Platanus × acerifolia *(syn.* Platanus × hispanica*).*

Though as much a part of London as the black cab, the red bus and the Changing of the Guard, this tree is not native to Britain. It is a hybrid of the oriental plane, Platanus orientalis, *and the American buttonwood,* P. occidentalis. P. orientalis *hails from the Levant and is one of the world's biggest and longest-living trees. The Greeks planted it in groves to shade their peripatetic philosophers; Xerxes, King of ancient Persia, stopped his marching army of 1,700,000 to admire a particularly fine specimen.*

The hybrid London plane has been grown here for well over 200 years, and its success in the capital is due to the smoothness of its leaves, which are easily washed clean by rain, and its habit of shedding bark, which also relieves it of suffocating dirt and soot. There are very large specimens in Hyde Park and Berkeley Square, but the biggest London plane in the country is at Mottisfont Abbey (q.v.) *in Hampshire, which stands over 130ft tall, with a 40ft girth and a canopy that covers a third of an acre of ground.*

SPRING SUMMER AUTUMN WINTER

Access NPC

Myddelton House is revered because of its connection with Edward Augustus Bowles (1865–1954), a plantsman of great renown whose classic books, *My Garden in Autumn and Winter*, *My Garden in Spring* and *My Garden in Summer*, were published around the start of the First World War. The third son of a well-to-do Enfield family, Bowles was due to join the Church on graduating from Cambridge University, but he returned to his parents' home after a family bereavement and stayed there for the rest of his life, tending plants instead of a parish. At Myddelton he built up a renowned plant collection, many plants bearing his name or being named by him. Bulbs were one of his specialities, particularly crocuses (*Crocus chrysanthus* 'Siskin', 'Yellowhammer' and 'Snowbunting' were raised by him). Anemones, snowdrops and cyclamen were also favoured, and the National Collection of irises is held here (*Iris reticulata* 'Cantab' is a Bowles introduction).

The Regency house (not open) was refurbished in the mid-19th century, but Bowles never altered it. Professor William Stearn, who knew Bowles, once told me that 'it was a real museum piece, there was no electric light, just candles or incandescent lamps; dining there was a memorable experience. A very big, polished dining table was always adorned with flowers from the garden, and the butler served us in a room where Bowles's ancestors had entertained the essayist, Charles Lamb.'

The garden, which covers four acres, suffered serious neglect for 30 years after Bowles's death, but has undergone gradual restoration in recent years. A visit in any season is rewarding, because of the diverse range of plants. Bowles had a sense of humour, and gathered a collection of 'demented plants', such as the corkscrew hazel with contorted stems, into an area he nicknamed the 'Lunatic Asylum'.

LONDON SW1

Eccleston Square

Pimlico, London SW1 MANAGED BY *Eccleston Square Garden Committee* TEL. *01483-211535 (National Gardens Scheme)* HOURS *Open rarely, in spring and summer for NGS charities (telephone for this year's dates)* ENTRANCE *£1.50, children 75p* DIRECTIONS *In central London, just off Belgrave Road, a few minutes' walk from Victoria Station*

SPRING SUMMER AUTUMN WINTER

Access | Plant Shop | NPC

Eccleston Square is a typical central London square of elegant town houses surrounding their own private, shared green space. The gardens of the square cover four acres and are opened only rarely, but if you happen to be in the area on one of their charity Sundays, it is well worth popping in. The gardens committee (led by well-known plant

THE WESTMINSTER SHOWS

If you are based in London, you do not need to go haring off to far-flung nurseries to find interesting, unusual plants. At the Royal Horticultural Society's Westminster shows, which are held more-or-less monthly throughout the year, the nurseries all come to you. Many of the country's best growers exhibit at these shows, held in the ***Royal Horticultural Halls, Vincent Square and Greycoat Street, London SW1 (tel. 0171-649 1885).*** *Run over two days, these shows also have lively amateur competitions for the best displays of, for example, camellias, daffodils, fruits, dahlias, chrysanthemums, autumn foliage, etc.*

The nursery stands always do brisk trade (regulars among the RHS membership form a polite queue outside, then rush in at the start of the first day). There are also exhibits of botanical art in the January, February and November shows. Small sundries, and gardening books old and new are also sold.

DON'T MISS

photographer Roger Phillips) is very active and has demonstrated by example what can be grown successfully in the dry, dusty and fume-laden conditions of the city centre. Camellias do particularly well, says Roger Phillips, because they show very good tolerance of drought conditions, 'much, much better than rhododendrons in this situation', he advises. The camellia collection in Eccleston Square adds up to aroud 110 different varieties. There is also a National Collection of ceanothus, displaying around 57 varieties, and many different climbing and shrub roses. There are irises and assorted unusual shrubs and perennials and many wildflowers including poppies, marsh-mallows, larkspurs and wild impatiens, which has exploding seed pods.

LONDON SW3

Chelsea Physic Garden

66 Royal Hospital Road, London SW3 4HS TEL. *0171-352 5646* OWNER *Chelsea Physic Garden Company* HOURS *Early April–late Oct, Wed, 12 noon–5p.m., Sun, 2–6p.m., also daily during Chelsea Flower Show week in late May and*

Chelsea Festival week in early June **ENTRANCE** *£3.50, concessions/children £1.80* **DIRECTIONS** *Entrances in Swan Walk and Royal Hospital Road, Chelsea*

SPRING SUMMER AUTUMN WINTER

Access | Gift Shop | Café | Plant Shop | NPC | DON'T MISS

This three-and-a-half-acre walled garden faces onto the Thames Embankment and enjoys an exceptionally mild climate (its ancient olive tree regularly bears fruit in quantity). It was founded in 1673 by the Society of

TOOLS, TRUGS AND TRINKETS

The gardeners of genteel Hampstead and its environs have their own neighbourhood shop of trugs and trinkets and, as you would expect in this area, the emphasis is on genteel decoration along with a little light weeding. ***Judy Green's Garden Store, 11 Flask Walk, London NW3 1HJ (tel. 0171-435 3832),*** *very close to Hampstead tube station, stocks a wonderfully eclectic range of gifts for gardeners, from the practical – tough gloves and steel trowels – to the ornamental, such as painted bird-boxes and Grecian urns. There are wire baskets and willow trugs, clay Provençal melon pots, florists' buckets and galvanised metal watering cans, raffia, labels, antique hand tools and much else besides. Open all year, Mon–Sat, 10a.m.–6p.m., Sun 11a.m.–6p.m.*

Avant Garden, 77 Ledbury Road, London W11 2AG (tel. 0171 229 4408), *nearest tube stations Westbourne Park or Notting Hill Gate, is run by Joan Clifton, who managed the impressive indoor and conservatory plants department at Clifton Nurseries (q.v.) for many years before embarking on her present enterprise. She stocks similarly decorative garden fare, including Avant Garden's own range of wrought-iron garden furniture, armillary spheres, terracotta pots, traditional wirework planters and a selection of galvanised topiary frames. Many items are supplied by mail order. Telephone ahead for opening times.*

Garden bygones, especially old garden tools such as wooden-handled trowels and hand-forks, brass sprayers and chestnut trugs, are regularly stocked by antique dealers ***Tobias and The Angel, 68 White Hart Lane, Barnes, London SW13 0PZ (tel. 0181-878 8902),*** *10 minutes' walk from nearest BR stations Barnes or Barnes Bridge. They also sell besom brooms, reclaimed terracotta pots, wirework baskets and antique items such as old galvanised washtubs, which make unusual plant containers, in an ever-changing stock of goods. Open all year, Mon–Sat, 10a.m.–6p.m.*

Apothecaries, and is the second-oldest botanic garden in England (Oxford University's is the oldest). Formed as a place where the medicinal properties of plants could be studied, it is still involved in botanic and medicinal research, and much of it is laid out in 'order beds' where plants belonging to the same botanical family are grouped together.

A lot of the planting is herbaceous and therefore the garden is at its prettiest and most billowing in summer; there is a National Collection of rock-roses (cistus species) held here and the rock garden is a listed monument. It is one of the earliest rock gardens, made from black basaltic lava-stones brought back from Iceland by Sir Joseph Banks in 1772. Visually, its effect is more currant bun than alpine chasm, but that is how it must stay.

There are many unusual plants here, including Australasian collections under glass, dyers' plants and displays connected to various prominent plant hunters and botanists. Recently the garden's role has extended to educational projects for children. The English Gardening School, which runs courses in gardening, botanical painting and garden design, is based in the main building.

And also...

Jacques Amand Ltd, The Nurseries, Clamp Hill, Stanmore, Middlesex HA7 3JS (tel. 0181-420 7110), is a specialist supplier of bulbs with a very large and interesting stock, well illustrated in their free colour catalogue. The address for catalogues or orders is Jacques Amand Ltd, PO Box 807, Harrow, Middlesex HA1 2YH. Open all year, daily, Mon–Sat, 9a.m.–5p.m., Sun, 10a.m.–4p.m. in April, May, June, Sept, Oct, and 10a.m.–2p.m. in Feb, March, July, Aug, Nov, but closed Sun in Dec and Jan.

Chiswick House, Burlington Lane, Chiswick, London W4 2RP (tel. 0181-742 1225), is a famous Palladian villa, built by Lord Burlington in the 1720s. Its 62 acres of historic grounds, recently substantially restored, include avenues and vistas, a circular pool and a Victorian garden, with formal flowerbeds spectacularly bedded out each spring and summer, beside a fine conservatory. Open all year, daily, 8a.m. to dusk.

Clifton Nurseries, Clifton Villas, Warwick Avenue, London W9 2PH (tel. 0171-289 6851), is a small (one-acre), very stylish urban garden centre packed with a well-chosen range of nursery stock, including topiary plants in variety, and very good ranges of conservatory plants. It also has a good stock of ornamental and terracotta pots, garden furniture and garden antiques. Open all year, Mon–Sat, 8.30a.m.–5.30p.m. (closing 6p.m. in March–Oct); Sun 10.30a.m.–4p.m. (4.30p.m. March–Oct).

Columbia Road Market, Columbia Road, London E2, is a chaotic, noisy street market with many stalls selling garden plants, house plants and cut flowers at bargain prices. A good place to get quantities of summer bedding plants for pots and containers. Open Sun 8a.m.–1p.m.

Fenton House, Windmill Hill, London NW3 6RT (tel. 0171-435 3471), is owned by the National Trust and its delightful one-and-a-half-acre walled garden has been developing in recent years. It is laid out formally, on three levels with lawns, herbaceous borders, an orchard and productive kitchen garden, with naturalised bulbs in the long grass. Open March, Sat–Sun, 2–5p.m.; April–Oct, Sat–Sun and Bank Holiday Mons, 11a.m.–5p.m., Wed–Fri, 2–5p.m.; last adm. 30 mins before closing. Entrance £4.

Holland Park, Kensington, London W8/W11 (tel. 0171-602 9483), is a popular and well-worn urban space with undulating lawns and specimen trees. By far its most interesting feature is a one-acre traditional Kyoto garden composed of carefully placed rocks with a water cascade and pool, and oriental plants. It was designed by Japanese garden designers and laid out in 1991 as a permanent reminder of the Japanese Festival that year. Tranquil and reflective. Open all year, daily, 7.30a.m.–sunset. Entrance free.

Kenwood, Hampstead Lane, London NW3 7JR (tel. 0181-348 1286), is a fabulous, neo-classical house redesigned by Robert Adam in the 1860s. Its 112 acres of landscaped grounds are equally splendid, with meadow walks and ornamental lakes, landscaped by Humphry Repton (*q.v.*). Its popular, evening, open-air concerts at the lakeside are one of the pleasures of London life in summer. Park open all year, daily: summer, 8a.m.–8.30p.m.; winter closes at 4.30p.m. Entrance free.

A former church houses **The Museum of Garden History, Lambeth Palace Road, London SE1 7LB (tel. 0171-261 1891)**. It has fascinating permanent displays of antique gardening tools and old lawn mowers, and an area devoted to the life and work of Edwardian gardener/writer Gertrude Jekyll (*q.v.*). Outdoors is a knot garden of low box hedging laid out to a 17th-century pattern. It was designed by the Marchioness of Salisbury, of Hatfield House (*q.v.*) and celebrates the work of the two John Tradescants (*q.v.*) who are buried on this site. Plants used in the gardens are those known in the 17th century, particularly species discovered by the Tradescants. Open March–2nd Sun in Dec, Sun–Fri, 10.30a.m.–4p.m. (5p.m. Sun). Entrance to museum and garden by donation.

Queen Mary's Rose Garden, Inner Circle, Regent's Park, London NW1 (tel. 0171-486 7905), occupies a purpose-designed, enclosed space with formal beds displaying around 60,000 roses, a breathtaking sight in summer. They are chiefly hybrid teas and floribundas, with a long flowering season, and climbers are trained on posts and swags. There are also herbaceous borders and an ornamental lake with rock garden cascade. A popular lunchtime venue for local office workers with sandwiches. Open all year, daily, from 7a.m. Closing times vary: Jan 5p.m., Feb 6p.m., March 7–8p.m., April 9p.m., May–July 9.30p.m., Aug 9p.m., Sept 8p.m., Oct 5.30–7p.m., Nov–Dec 4.30p.m. Entrance free.

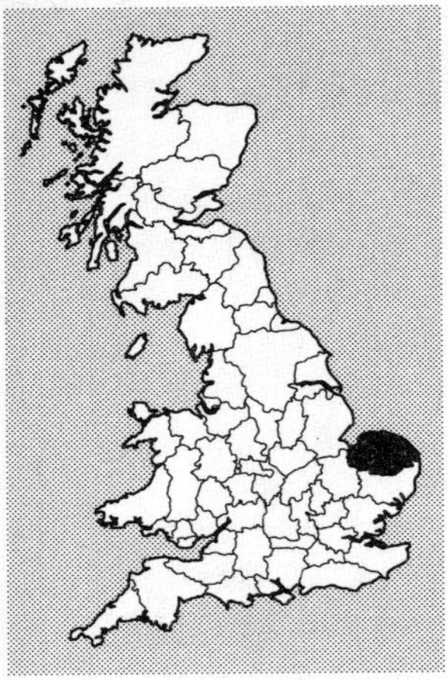

Norfolk

MAP NO. 6

An important textile industry based on woollen goods contributed to the wealth of Norfolk in earlier centuries. As a result, the county's beautiful countryside is dotted with fine flint churches, built in thanksgiving for the prosperity the land brought, but now more often seen in splendid isolation, far from any human habitation. 'Very flat, Norfolk,' remarked one of Noël Coward's characters in Private Lives. *Much of it is, especially around the reed-fringed waters of the Broads, making this a county popular with cyclists. Other parts enjoy a very gently contoured landscape, and the fertile soil nurtures many gardens and nurseries.*

BLICKLING

Blickling Hall

Blickling, Norwich NR11 6NF TEL. *01263-733084* OWNER *The National Trust* HOURS *April–June, Thurs–Sun and Bank Holiday Mons; July–mid-Sept, Tues–Sun and Bank Holiday Mons; Mid-Sept–Oct, Thurs–Sun; all 10a.m.–5.30p.m. (last adm. 4.30p.m., gates close at 6p.m.). House open 1–4.30p.m. Park and woods, daily all year, dawn–dusk* ENTRANCE *£3.20 (Sun and Bank Holiday Mons, £3.50); house and garden £5.50 (£6.50 Sun and Bank Holiday Mons)* DIRECTIONS *On N side of B1354, 1½m NW of Aylsham on A140*

SPRING SUMMER AUTUMN WINTER

Access | Gift Shop | Café | Plant Shop | DON'T MISS

Blickling Hall provides the quintessential National Trust day out. The spectacular house, a 17th-century stately pile, is surrounded by 43 acres of sumptuously planted traditional gardens, and enchanting woods. The east front

THE PERENNIAL BLOOMS OF BRESSINGHAM

You cannot be interested in plants for long without coming into contact with the Blooms' nursery, in the village of Bressingham. Its founder, Alan Bloom (born 1906) grew up in the company of distinguished plant collectors and hybridists such as Amos Perry, E.A. Bowles and Walter Ingwersen, and he was inspired to look out for new plants that showed improvements on existing cultivars.

*At **Bressingham Gardens, Bressingham, Diss IP22 2AB (tel. 01379-687386), on the A1066,** Alan Bloom also developed the concept of informally shaped island beds cut out of the lawn (as opposed to long borders backed by a wall or hedge) for growing herbaceous perennials. The method produced sturdier plants and drastically reduced the need for staking. You can see Alan Bloom's perennial beds (and around 5000 different plant varieties) in the six-acre Dell Garden, open April–Oct, daily, 10.30a.m.–5.30p.m., entrance £3.80.*

Alan Bloom considers that Achillea *'Moonshine',* Agapanthus *'Bressingham Blue',* Aconitum *'Bressingham Spire' and* Crocosmia *'Lucifer' are among his personal favourites of the 170 new plants he has introduced to horticulture during his long life. His son, Adrian, opens **Foggy Bottom Garden** (next door) from April–Nov, Mon and Thurs, and 1st Sun in each month, where ornamental conifers are displayed in great variety, among grasses, heathers and perennial flowers.*

DON'T MISS

of the house looks onto a parterre of four square beds, each fringed with roses and catmint, with yew topiaries in each corner. The beds nearest the house are filled with herbaceous perennials in pink, white, blue and violet hues (especially lovely around mid-summer), while further beds display rich yellows, glowing orange and scarlet tones, brilliant in the later weeks of summer.

There are gravel walks through smooth lawns, shrubberies with azaleas, hydrangeas and dogwoods, classical ornaments and lovely trees in the park, and great lumpy bolsters of ancient yew hedging the entrance.

HEACHAM

Norfolk Lavender

Caley Mill, Heacham, King's Lynn PE31 7JE TEL. *01485-570384* OWNER *Norfolk Lavender Ltd* HOURS *Shop and gardens open all year, daily, 9.30a.m.–5p.m.; tearoom open Nov–Easter, daily, 10a.m.–4.30p.m., Easter–late Oct, 10a.m.–5p.m.* ENTRANCE *Free* DIRECTIONS *13m N of King's Lynn on A149*

SPRING SUMMER AUTUMN WINTER

Gift Shop · Café · Plant Shop · Nursery · NPC

It is as though a little piece of sunbaked hillside has been plucked from the Provençal landscape and transported to this lowland farming area beside The Wash. The 100 acres of lavender fields are at their most beautiful in summer, when they turn into ripples of dusky-mauve, while the bushes are in bloom.

This is the largest lavender farm in Britain where the cut flowers are distilled for lavender oil; many associated products are sold on the premises. The National Collection of lavender is held here, and there are also herb gardens and rose gardens to visit. Harvesting usually begins in mid-July and lasts five to six weeks. The rows are cut mechanically, usually four acres per day. It is worth joining one of the instructive tours of the farm (run daily from Spring Bank Holiday to September); you can even sample lavender in the café, for example, in their lavender and lemon scones.

LODDON

Reads Nursery

Hales Hall, Loddon NR14 6QW TEL. *01508-548395* OWNER *T. and J. Read* HOURS *Easter–Oct, Tues–Sat, 12 noon–5p.m.; also Sun and Bank Holiday Mons, May–Oct, 2–5p.m.* ENTRANCE *Gardens free (barn £1.50)* DIRECTIONS *From Norwich, take A146. Bypass Loddon and continue on A146 past Hales for 1m. Turn right at sign Kirby Cane 1¼/Hales Hall. After 150 yds go right (signposted Hales Hall)*

SPRING SUMMER AUTUMN WINTER

Plant Shop · Nursery · NPC · Mail Order

DON'T MISS

CONTROLLING PESTS NATURE'S WAY

Biological control of garden and greenhouse pests uses natural predators, instead of chemicals, to deal with a wide range of problems. ***Green Gardener, 41 Strumpshaw Road, Brundall NR13 5PG (tel. 01603-715096),*** *produces an informative catalogue of natural pest controls available by mail order, and offers expert advice on how to use predators for maximum effect in the right seasons. There are controls to counter aphids, whitefly, red spider-mite, mealybugs, scale insects, slugs and vine weevils, as well as Enviromesh fabrics for effective barrier protection against carrot fly, cabbage root fly and other creatures.*

There are three reasons to visit this nursery: fruit, interesting conservatory plants, and the barn. Reads has been going for well over 100 years and it offers unrivalled selections of fruit, especially traditional varieties, available by mail as well as on-site (send 4 × 1st-class stamps for the catalogue). There are quinces and kiwi fruit, pineapple-guava and olives. There is also an extensive array of figs with 34 different varieties, constituting the National Collection of these exquisite fruits.

Reads also specializes in citrus, with oranges and lemons in variety, and limes, grapefruit, kumquats, limequats and tangelos (a cross between the grapefruit and mandarin, sometimes known as ugli fruit). The conservatory plants account for half of the catalogue (with more than 70 different varieties of bougainvillea), and the fragrant glasshouses are as thrilling as any you will see in a botanic garden, with the added piquancy that most of what you see is for sale.

Lastly, there is Hales Hall Barn. At 184ft long, with stepped gables and a wonderful ribcage of timbers supporting its newly thatched roof, it is one of the largest and most spectacular barns in the country, dating from around 1480. The one-and-a-quarter-acre nursery also offers topiary and hedging plants in box and yew.

NORWICH

The Plantation Garden

4 Earlham Road, Norwich NR2 3DB **TEL.** *01603-611669* **OWNER** *The Plantation Garden Preservation Trust* **HOURS** *Mid-April–mid-Oct, Sun, 1–5p.m.* **ENTRANCE** *£1, accompanied children free; groups by arrangement* **DIRECTIONS** *On Earlham Road, between Crofters and Beeches Hotels, near St John's Roman Catholic Cathedral*

SPRING SUMMER AUTUMN WINTER

Access

This extraordinary garden is a rare survivor of the Victorian age, bearing many of the hallmarks of late 19th-century style. It was the creation of successful Norwich cabinet maker and upholsterer, Henry Trevor, and in its heyday boasted fine Italianate terraces, formal bedding areas and a magnificent tropical palm house within its 2½ acres. The garden was then a frequent venue for public occasions, as Trevor's obituary of May 1897 reveals: 'His beautiful and well kept grounds he put to the most generous uses. For purposes of flower shows, bazaars and charitable gatherings of any kind and another, the Plantation was continually in demand.'

After Trevor's death, the garden disappeared from public view and for several decades in the 20th century became all but lost in a dense undergrowth of brambles and self-sown sycamores, revealing only tantalising glimpses of masonry beneath smothering curtains of ivy.

In 1980 a group of local enthusiasts formed a Trust and assembled volunteers to unearth the lost garden, which they have very largely succeeded in doing over the last two decades. Now, it is possible once again to enjoy the fascinating mosaic walls of mixed flints and assorted masonry (such as ornate chimney mouldings) and the cast concrete balustrades that Henry Trevor assembled in his lifetime. The palm house was demolished long ago, but the garden retains a magnificent tiered gothic fountain, nearly 30ft tall, and a Victorian rockery with masonry. Its neat lawns have returned and formal flowerbeds have been cut into them once more, following the pattern shown in some rare photographs of the garden. Although it is in the centre of Norwich city, The Plantation Garden is a haven of tranquillity, surrounded by mature trees and shrubberies and exuding much of the atmosphere of its bygone age. Don't expect pristine tidiness if you visit, for it is managed on a shoestring budget by volunteers, but it is well worth seeing this garden for the extraordinary way it has survived and undergone a new lease of life.

Celebrity Choice

***Nigel Colborn, author, novelist and panellist on BBC Radio 4's* Gardeners' Question Time**

'I was really bowled over when I visited **The Old Vicarage** (q.v.), *at East Ruston. It's a magnificent garden – the owners have obviously invested a lot of money in it. I love the way that it combines traditional garden statements – such as classical vistas and the "borrowed landscape" of the distant church – with really quirky, crazy ideas. It all works so well; it's done with boldness and courage, and nothing has been done by half. You can see the freshness of approach in the planting, too. They have used grasses wonderfully well in the borders, and there is a great tropical border with cannas and dahlias and eucomis. The containers have some really original planting in them, too, with bronze-leaved aeoniums, and I noticed a wonderful, rusty-brown rudbeckia which apparently they had selected from some they have grown from seed. It is the most inspiring garden I have seen in ages.'*

SANDRINGHAM

Sandringham House

Sandringham, King's Lynn PE35 6EN TEL. *01553-772675* OWNER *H.M. The Queen* HOURS *Early April–early Oct, daily (but closed late July–early Aug). Also weekends in Oct, all 11a.m.–4.45p.m.* ENTRANCE *£4.50, OAPs £3.50, children £2.50, family ticket £11.50* DIRECTIONS *9m NE of King's Lynn on B1440*

SPRING SUMMER AUTUMN WINTER

Access | Gift Shop | Café | Plant Shop

King Edward VII is said to have remarked that if he had not been King, he would like to have been a gardener. As Prince of Wales he spent the winters at Sandringham, with Princess Alexandra, herself a keen gardener.

During their time, thousands of new trees, shrubs and flowers were imported to ornament the woodlands, watery dells and flower gardens. Pansies in particular were a great favourite of the Princess who devoted a garden to them. Today's visitor will see a simplified version of the original 60-acre gardens, made to be more labour-saving, but still reflecting the Edwardian age. There are lakes, a grotto and a large rock garden, a woodland with decorative flowering shrubs, fine trees and broad lawns.

Sandringham has long been open to the public, and its popularity as a tourist attraction caused King George VI to commission a private garden area, designed by Sir Geoffrey Jellicoe. Here, behind tall hedges and elegant avenues of pleached lime, lies a series of formal garden rooms with box-edged beds of flowering plants.

SAXTHORPE

Mannington Hall

Nr Saxthorpe, Norwich NR11 7BB TEL. *01263-584175* OWNER *Lord Walpole* HOURS *May, Sun, 12 noon–5p.m.; June–Aug, Wed–Fri, Sun, 12 noon–5p.m.* ENTRANCE *£3, OAPs £2.50, children (under 16) free* DIRECTIONS *18m NW of Norwich, 3m NE of Saxthorpe off B1149 via minor roads (signposted)*

SPRING SUMMER AUTUMN WINTER

Access | Gift Shop | Café | Plant Shop

If you are into roses, you will love Mannington Hall and its 10 acres of gardens. Ramblers cascade over post-and-rail enclosures, climbers cling to the flinty walls, shrub roses colonise a large area devoted to their kind, while more disciplined bushes behave themselves in neat beds close to the house. The Hall itself is gloriously romantic, with flint elevations, stone mullioned windows, gothic arches and a crenellated roofline. If that is not enough, there is a moat surrounding it, packed with waterlilies, and wildflowers do their thing in outlying parts of the grounds. There are also rhododendrons in the woods and a relaxed wilderness to set off the ruins of a Saxon church. The walled garden is devoted to a collection of Heritage roses, all wild species and old-fashioned varieties.

SOUTH WALSHAM

Fairhaven Gardens

South Walsham, Norwich NR13 6EA TEL. *01603-270449* OWNER *Fairhaven Garden Trust* HOURS *April–late Oct, Tues–Sun, 11a.m.–5.30p.m. (Sat 2–5.30p.m.), and Bank Holidays* ENTRANCE *£3, OAPs £2.70, children £1* DIRECTIONS *9m NE of Norwich on B1140*

SPRING SUMMER AUTUMN WINTER

Access · Gift Shop · Café · Plant Shop

The Norfolk Broads are unique; they are mainly freshwater lakes, quite shallow, linked by rivers, streams and dykes to form around 200 miles of navigable waterways between Norwich and the north-east coast of Norfolk. They were created by peat extraction in late medieval times, and are part of the man-made landscape. It is unusual to find a garden in this region, which is more widely associated with reedbeds and marshland, but the 180-acre Fairhaven is one of the strangest and most appealing water gardens in the country, best visited in spring. It is a blissfully quiet woodland, wrapped around the large stretch of water known as South Walsham Inner Broad, where the odd sailboat may go scudding by.

A network of water channels runs through the wood with its thousands of primulas, and astilbes, ligularias and skunk cabbages lining the banks. Simple timber bridges cross the waters here and there, and masses of primroses and bluebells colonise the woodland floor. There is a splendid oak tree, believed to be 900 years old, encrusted with self-sown ferns.

And also...

The famous nursery of **Peter Beales Roses, London Road, Attleborough NR17 1AY (tel. 01953-454707)**, produces an extensive range of classic and old-fashioned roses (around 1000 species and varieties), many of which are illustrated in their excellent catalogue (free on request). You can also visit their rose fields (free), or buy from the nursery itself. Open all year, Mon–Fri, 9a.m.–5p.m.; Sat 9a.m.–4.30p.m.; Sun (except Jan) 10a.m.–4p.m.

Bradenham Hall, Bradenham, Thetford IP25 7QF (tel. 01362–687243), was the family home of the Victorian author H. Rider Haggard who wrote *King Solomon's Mines* (1885) and *She* (1887). The 20-acre gardens feature glorious daffodil displays in spring, a comprehensive arboretum and large, old-fashioned rose gardens, marvellous herbaceous borders and a kitchen garden. Open (gardens only) April–Sept, 2nd, 4th and 5th Sundays in each month, 2–5.30p.m. Entrance £3, children free.

Linda Laxton runs **British Wild Flower Plants, 23 Yarmouth Road, Ormesby St Margaret, Great Yarmouth NR29 3QE (tel. 01493-730244).** The nursery specializes in wildflowers grown as plugs or in pots; species include cowslips, scabious, ox-eye daisies, harebells, cuckoo flowers, teasels, bedstraws and vetches. Plants are not gathered in the wild, but are grown from seed, with details of the original seed source (send 4 × 1st-class stamps for the catalogue). Open only by appointment.

Chris Bowers & Son, Whispering Trees Nursery, Wimbotsham PE34 8QB (tel. 01366-388752), is a specialist fruit nursery. There are tree fruits and nuts in variety, with extensive ranges of soft fruit including raspberries, strawberries, currants, gooseberries and blueberries and much more (mail order catalogue £1.50). Open all year, daily, 9a.m.–5p.m.; closed 1–2p.m. at weekends.

Congham Hall Hotel, Grimston, King's Lynn PE32 1AH (tel. 01485-600250), is a country house hotel in 40 acres of park and gardens, with a fine herb garden, featuring around 500 different varieties. Many herbs are for sale. Open April–Sept, Sun–Fri, 2–4p.m. (closed Sat). Entrance free.

Elsing Hall, Elsing, nr East Dereham NR20 3DX (tel. 01362–637224), is a romantic, moated manor house (not open) dating from the mid-15th century, with stone mullioned windows and knapped flint walls. It provides the central focus for lovely gardens, fragrant with roses that drape the walls and fill out the borders. There are wildflower meadows, relaxed plantings and many decorative trees. Open June–Sept, Sun only, 2–6p.m. Entrance £3, children £1.

Four Seasons Nursery, Forncett St Mary, Norwich NR16 1JT (tel. 01508-488344), is never open to visitors but it produces a catalogue (£1) of exceptionally interesting and attractive hardy herbaceous plants. John Metcalf, the joint proprietor, has an artistic eye for plant associations, and knows a good plant when he sees one. Plants are dispatched in autumn and spring.

Holkham Hall, Holkham, Wells-next-the-Sea NR23 1AB (tel. 01328-710227/710374), is a vast stately home set in a 3000-acre deer park that was worked on by William Kent in the mid-18th century, followed by Capability Brown (*q.v.*) and then Humphry Repton (*q.v.*). It is a place where you can really stretch your legs and enjoy the undulating, sheep-grazed park, its fine, huge trees and great lake. There is an 18th-century, six-acre walled garden, richly planted with herbaceous flowers, shrubs and climbers, where there is also a well-stocked garden centre. Open late May–late Sept, Sun–Thurs, 1–5p.m. Park open all year, daily. Garden centre and walled garden, all year, Mon–Sat, 10a.m.–1p.m., 2–5p.m., Sun 2–5p.m. Entrance park and garden centre, free; Hall and bygones museum £6, children £3.

Gardening broadcaster Geoff Amos, of Great Yarmouth, alerted me to the delights of **The Old Vicarage, East Ruston NR12 9HN (tel. 01603-632350**). The 12-acre gardens are laid out formally, with tall hedges helping to filter the wind off the North Sea, which is only 1½ miles away. There are wonderful flower borders and topiaries, sub-tropical plants in profusion (which grow happily here, due to the sea's proximity). There are also banana trees and box parterres, cabbage palms, autumnal blooms and wildflowers in profusion, all in an outstanding setting. Open Easter Sun–late Oct, Sun, Wed and Bank Holiday Mons, 2–5p.m. Entrance £3, children £1.

Raveningham Hall, Raveningham NR14 6NS (tel. 01508-548222), sits in splendid parkland, with lawns near the house flanked by borders of shrubs and herbaceous perennials. Unusual and half-hardy plants feature in the gardens and in the excellent nursery, which is located in the walled kitchen garden and its large greenhouses (send 4 × 1st-class stamps for the catalogue). Open May–July, Wed, 1–4p.m., Sun, 2–5p.m. Entrance £2.

The Romantic Garden Nursery, Swannington, Norwich NR9 5NW (tel. 01603-261488), specializes in box topiary and ornamental standard (mop-headed) trees and shrubs, particularly half-hardy subjects suitable for mild gardens and conservatories, available by mail (send 4 × 1st-class stamps for the catalogue). Open all year, Wed, Fri, Sat and Bank Holiday Mons, 10a.m.–5p.m.

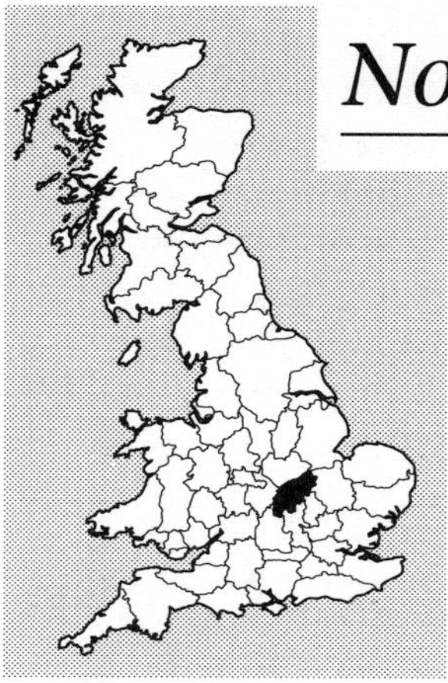

Northamptonshire

MAP NO. 5

This small county in the East Midlands is famous for its bootmakers, and it is worth using up a bit of shoe leather in treading some of its lovely gardens. Featuring low-lying land to the east, the ground sweeps up into chalk and limestone country to the west, taking in the northern fringes of the Cotswolds. The area has a beauty comparable with the neighbouring limestone areas of Oxfordshire and Gloucestershire, but is quiet and sparsely populated. In the 1720s Daniel Defoe considered Northampton to be 'the handsomest and best built town in all this part of England', after it had been rebuilt following the ravaging fires 50 years previously.

CANONS ASHBY

Canons Ashby House

Canons Ashby, Daventry NN11 3SD **TEL.** *01327-860044* **OWNER** *The National Trust* **HOURS** *April–Oct, Sat–Wed incl. Bank Holiday Mons (closed Good Friday), 1–5.30p.m. (or dusk if earlier), last adm. 5p.m.* **ENTRANCE** *£3.60, children £1.80, family ticket £9* **DIRECTIONS** *8m S of Daventry; 5m E of Byfield, by local roads off A361 Daventry–Banbury road (signposted)*

SPRING SUMMER AUTUMN WINTER

Access | Gift Shop | Café

DON'T MISS

The House sits so cosily in its rural setting, with the medieval priory church to one side and nine-acre walled gardens to the other, that it conveys a timelessness and serenity seldom matched in other properties. Its gardens are in a restrained, early 18th-century style, with lawned terraces, straight, formal paths, some topiaries and a collection of old fruit varieties. Wildflowers colonise areas of long grass, and the house itself is worth seeing – an exquisite, well-proportioned 16th-century manor, with later alterations, in the local, ochre-coloured limestone.

SWEET PEAS OF ALTHORP

Fragrant and dainty, with old-fashioned cottage garden appeal, sweet peas are among Britain's most popular flowers. The famous Spencer strain of sweet peas originated in Northamptonshire in the gardens of Althorp (ancestral home of the late Diana, Princess of Wales). Mr Silas Cole was head gardener to Earl Spencer at the turn of the 20th century, running the 50 acres of gardens at Althorp, with their 14-acre kitchen garden. He noticed an exceptional plant arising out of his stocks of sweet peas (some of which had the pink-flowered 'Prima Donna' as a parent), and named it 'Countess Spencer'. The flowers were particularly large and wavy, and Spencer sweet peas were soon in great demand.

COTTESBROOKE

Cottesbrooke Hall

Cottesbrooke, Northampton NN6 8PF **TEL.** *01604-505808*
OWNER *Capt and Mrs J. Macdonald-Buchanan* **HOURS** *Easter–Sept, Wed–Fri and Bank Holiday Mons (gardens only Tues, Wed, Fri), Sun in Sept, 2–5.30p.m. (last adm. 5p.m.)*
ENTRANCE *£2.50, children £1.25 (house and gardens £4, £2)*
DIRECTIONS *10m N of Northampton near A50 (signposted)*

SPRING SUMMER AUTUMN WINTER

Café Plant Shop DON'T MISS

Prepare to be impressed by Cottesbrooke Hall. Its driveway sweeps through the park for two miles, sweeping over an elegant stone bridge that crosses a stretch of water. Around the stately house there are 25 acres of gardens within the vast park; they are variously divided by walls and hedges into several intimate areas, some featuring exuberant herbaceous plantings, others with contrasting greenery of trees and lawns. There is a Dutch garden with formal box parterres enclosing seasonal bedding; a relaxing pool garden, with distant views along a lime avenue; a long terrace walk, flanked by herbaceous borders containing some interesting plants; a rose garden, a garden of statues, and a lovely wild garden washed by a stream, with spring-flowering shrubs and bulbs, and a Japanese bridge.

GUILSBOROUGH

Coton Manor

Nr Guilsborough NN6 8RQ TEL. *01604-740219* OWNER *Mr and Mrs I. Pasley-Tyler* HOURS *Easter–Sept, Wed–Sun, and Bank Holiday Mons, 12 noon–5.30p.m.* ENTRANCE *£3, OAPs £2.50, children £1* DIRECTIONS *10m NW of Northampton, between A428 and A50 (signposted)*

SPRING SUMMER AUTUMN WINTER

Access · Gift Shop · Café · Plant Shop

DON'T MISS

Coton Manor is a friendly farmhouse of local honey-coloured stone, with mullioned windows and a steeply pitched roof. The 10-acre gardens that frame it on two sides are among the most pleasing you will see anywhere, with exceptional ranges of plants and a high standard of upkeep. I bumped into Susie Pasley-Tyler while she was immersed in a small sea of sisyrinchiums, her wheelbarrow on the turf path alongside rapidly filling up with prunings and tidyings from one of the herbaceous borders. This is a hands-on family garden, as it has been for three generations.

Upon her mother-in-law's death in 1990, Susie and her husband, Ian, took over the manor and began some regenerative work in the garden, and the results are impressive. Roses and summer flowers billow around the footings of the manor and lady's mantle fills cracks in the stone paving. More roses, and flower borders near the house are contained by yew hedges, with woodland and water gardens beyond. There are further borders in the lower gardens, and grassy slopes leading to a five-acre bluebell wood – captivating in May. Beyond the recently made herb garden is a nursery worth browsing in for interesting plants, while more are for sale beside the stable yard café, where excellent home-made food is served.

HORTON

The Menagerie

Horton, Northampton NN7 2BX **TEL.** *01604-870957*
OWNER *The Executors of the late Gervase Jackson-Stops*
HOURS *April–Sept, Thurs, 10a.m.–4p.m.* **ENTRANCE** *£3, children £1.50* **DIRECTIONS** *5m SE of Northampton off B526, turn left 1m S of Horton through gate in field (watch out for small sign)*

SPRING SUMMER AUTUMN WINTER

Plant Shop

DON'T MISS

The late Gervase Jackson-Stops, architectural adviser to the National Trust, rescued and restored The Menagerie, a former folly with enchanting rooms and plasterwork, and laid out the three-acre garden with talented Kew graduate, Ian Kirby. Alas, neither of them lived long enough to enjoy this exquisite property for long, but the garden is now open on a regular basis and is worth travelling some distance to see. It commands a hilltop position, with avenues radiating out from the house; the central one of limes leads to a spiral mount, with one on each side in hornbeam terminating in fountain pools. There are two unusual garden buildings, one with a classical front, the other gothic, which, on their far sides, turn into rustic hovels in 18th-century Picturesque style. The planting is exuberant, with choice perennials, abundant roses and flowering shrubs. There is a wetland garden of local native plants, and the Vernal Garden features massed spring bulbs and hellebores under spring-flowering trees and shrubs.

The Menagerie was originally the private zoo of Lord Halifax whose Horton Hall (now demolished) had stood on the opposite hill. Jackson-Stops installed a fantasy grotto of rock and shellwork beneath the building, but it is only possible to see it (and the house) by written appointment.

And also...

Castle Ashby, Northampton NN7 1LQ (tel. 01604-696696), is a handsome Elizabethan mansion, now used as an all-purpose centre for functions, etc. It has a wonderful 200-acre park landscaped by Capability Brown (*q.v.*) with lakes and temple, a Victorian terrace with unusual, carved lettering in the balustrade, a fine orangery and an Italian garden. Open daily, 10a.m.–dusk, with occasional closures during events. Terrace garden by appointment only. Entrance £2.50, OAPs/children £1.

Hill Farm Herbs, Park Walk, Brigstock, Kettering NN14 3HH (tel. 01536-373694), specializes in herbs and cottage garden plants in an attractive setting. There is a herb shop, farm pantry/tearoom (summer) and dried flower room, with display garden. Open Easter–Sept, daily, 10.30a.m.–5.30p.m. Phone for details of winter opening. Entrance free.

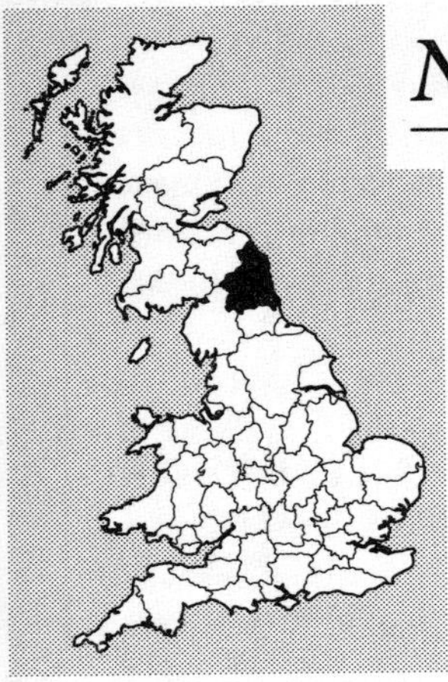

Northumberland

MAP NO. 8

Great rivers, tumbling burns, moorland hills and enchanting stretches of coastline characterise this large county. Abundant stone castles and Hadrian's great wall bear witness to many centuries of border disputes. Something that may surprise visitors new to Northumberland is its sheer size, not to mention the grand panoramas and bracing, clean air. Even at mid-summer it is possible to drive along roads that, more often than not, are traffic-free.

It isn't an easy part of the country for gardeners, however. There can be frosts until June, which often return as early as September. Summer is a glorious, fleeting moment which is celebrated in a galaxy of outstanding gardens.

CAMBO

Herterton House

Hartington, Cambo, Morpeth NE61 4BN TEL. *01670-774278* OWNER *F. and M. Lawley* HOURS *April–Sept, daily except Tues and Thurs, 1.30–5.30p.m.* ENTRANCE *£1.80* DIRECTIONS *2m N of Cambo, just off B6342*

SPRING SUMMER AUTUMN WINTER

Access | Plant Shop | Nursery | DON'T MISS

It would be difficult to leave Herterton House without a boxful of souvenir plants (quaintly wrapped in newsprint) from the Lawleys' small but intriguing nursery, but there is more; the adjoining gardens, covering one acre around their farmhouse, are among the best to be seen in the country.

Facing the lane, in front of the low, Elizabethan farmhouse, the Lawleys (both of whom are artists) have planted a formal topiary garden of English evergreens – ivy, box, yew and holly, enlivened with golden-leaved and variegated forms. To one side, a fascinating cloistered herb garden displays plants valued by medieval physicians and dyers; there is clary – a time-honoured eye remedy – betony – a cure-all since the days of antiquity – and periwinkle, sweet rocket, heartsease, gromwell and woad.

Behind the house, full rein is given to colourful summer flowers, planted in graduated schemes of complementary tones. According to Frank the scheme symbolises the passing of time, from 'pale colours in the morning (near the house), through the richest, brightest colours at mid-day (in mid-garden), to the deep reds and purples at the far end, signifying dusk and night-time'. The effect is captivating, and the Lawleys are currently making another enclosed garden beyond – a box parterre, filled with bright annuals.

CAMBO

Wallington Hall

Cambo, Morpeth NE61 4AR TEL. *01670-774283* OWNER *The National Trust* HOURS *Walled garden April–Sept, daily 10a.m.–7p.m., Oct 10a.m.–6p.m., Nov– March 10a.m.–4p.m. (or dusk if earlier), grounds, all year during daylight hours* ENTRANCE *£2.80, children (over 5) £1.40, house and grounds £4.80 and £2.40* DIRECTIONS *From A1 take A696 past Newcastle Airport, Ponteland and Belsay; Wallington signposted 6m after Belsay*

SPRING SUMMER AUTUMN WINTER

Access | Gift Shop | Café

It is Wallington's magnificent walled garden, hidden away in the woods, that leaves a lasting impression. Its flower gardens drop down a gentle slope in a series of differently planned areas.

A long terrace to one side skirts the famous conservatory, built in 1908 as an indoor garden to provide interest through the chilly Northumbrian winter. Now it is beautiful all year, with summer displays of abutilons, vast fuchsias (including a splendid specimen planted when the conservatory was new) and a wonderful scarlet 'Duke of Buckingham' pelargonium, which clambers up the wall. Below the terrace lie mixed borders of shrubs and flowering perennials, and a naturalistic pool surrounded by moisture-loving plants.

Wallington's great house (open to the public) in its 100-acre park dates from 1688, and is famous for its murals depicting scenes of Northumbrian history and for a charming collection of dolls' houses. Among summer's outdoor events are popular theatrical productions performed in the spacious grounds.

HAND-MADE TERRACOTTA

The Potting Shed, 1–3 Broadgates NE46 1QN (tel. 01434-606811), is in the centre of Hexham, close to the bus station. *It offers an array of traditional terracotta pots, including parsley pots and strawberry jars, all hand-made on the premises and fired to a high temperature for frost resistance. A tiny but bright sales area has been squeezed in beside the workshop.*

FORD

Northumbria Nurseries

Castle Gardens, Ford, Berwick-upon-Tweed TD15 2PZ TEL. *01890-820379* FAX *01890-820594* CONTACT *Hazel Huddleston* HOURS *Open all year, Mon–Fri, 9a.m.–6p.m., March–Oct, weekends, 9a.m.–6p.m., Bank Holidays 10a.m.–6p.m., or by appointment* DIRECTIONS *10m N of Wooler, off A697*

SPRING SUMMER AUTUMN WINTER

Access Nursery Mail Order

Over 1600 different plants are raised within the walled former kitchen garden of historic Ford Castle (open to the public). Few nurseries are as handsomely situated, with the castle as a backdrop and views of the Cheviot Hills. Hardy geraniums, hebes (over 50 hardy varieties), alpines and penstemons are some of the specialities raised by Hazel Huddleston and her partner, who propagate on-site everything they sell.

THOMAS BEWICK

Trees, plants and birds are among the miniature subjects delicately carved onto boxwood blocks by Northumberland's greatest artist, the naturalist Thomas Bewick (1753–1828). His exquisite engravings, vignettes of rural life, are displayed in his birthplace at ***Cherryburn, Station Bank, Mickley, Stocksfield NE43 7DB (tel. 01661-843276), in the Tyne valley, 11m W of Newcastle upon Tyne, 400yds off A695 (signposted). Open Easter–Oct, daily, except Tues and Wed, 1–5.30p.m. (last adm. 5p.m.). Entrance £2.80, children £1.40.***

HEXHAM

Hexham Herbs

The Chesters Walled Garden, Chollerford, nr Hexham NE46 4BQ TEL. *01434-681483* CONTACT *Kevin and Susie White* HOURS *Late March/April–Oct, daily, 10a.m.–5p.m., phone for winter openings* ENTRANCE *£1.20, children (under 10) free* DIRECTIONS *4m NW of Hexham, ½m W of Chollerford, on B6318*

SPRING SUMMER AUTUMN WINTER

Access | Gift Shop | Nursery | NPC

DON'T MISS

One of the oldest and most picturesque towns in the north of England, Hexham is popular with tourists because of its famous 12th-century abbey and proximity to Hadrian's Wall. Mary Russell Mitford, visiting in 1806, described the town as a 'shocking, gloomy place', but few visitors today would agree, as they potter among its antique shops and stone houses perched above the River Tyne.

Hexham's allure for gardeners is chiefly due to the eponymous herb nursery at nearby Chollerford, up the beautiful North Tyne valley. Kevin White (an ex-policeman) and his wife, Susie, have been running Hexham Herbs nursery and garden since 1986.

As well as housing the National Collection of thyme, with more than 120 species and cultivars, this fragrant garden, humming with bees in summer, also boasts one of the largest ranges of culinary and medicinal herbs in the country (900 in all), 300 of which are potted up for sale. Note the clipped box and billowing lavender hedges which line the crunchy gravel paths, and do not miss the hidden-away gardens within the walled framework.

The site of a Roman road crosses the nursery and inspired the Whites to create an enclosed Roman garden featuring edible, sacred and curative herbs grown in Britain by the occupying legions. Common houseleeks were believed to have been a gift from Jupiter, to protect homes from lightning and fire. No doubt there were also plenty of aromatic poultices prepared for chilled and footsore soldiers, in addition to bay leaves for garlanding conquering heroes.

HOWICK

Howick Hall

Howick, nr Alnwick NE66 3LB TEL. *01665-577285* OWNER *Howick Trustees Ltd* HOURS *April–Oct, 1–6p.m.* ENTRANCE *£2, OAPs/children £1* DIRECTIONS *6m NE of Alnwick, off B1339*

SPRING SUMMER AUTUMN WINTER

Access

The elegant mansion was once the home of the 19th-century Prime Minister and social reformer Earl Grey, after whom the tea is named. Commanding a low-lying position close to the sea and sheltered by woods, the Hall has a microclimate quite unexpected in this region. Consequently, the 25-acre gardens boast many tender plants more likely to be seen on the milder coasts of west Scotland or Cornwall.

There are fine displays of rhododendrons, glorious terraced gardens and floral borders near the house, and unusual plants recently collected in the Far East. The wave of agapanthus, a brilliant blue spectacle on the terraces in high summer, has special significance, comprising many of the original plants that were bred to make the popular Headbourne hybrids.

ROTHBURY

Cragside House

Rothbury, Morpeth NE65 7PX TEL. *01669-620333/620266* OWNER *The National Trust* HOURS *Garden April–Oct, daily, except Mon (but open Bank Holiday Mons), 10.30a.m.–6.30p.m., house open same days, 1–5.30p.m. (last adm. 4.45p.m.)* ENTRANCE *House, garden and grounds £5.80; garden and grounds £3.80; family ticket (2 adults, 2 children) £15* DIRECTIONS *1m NE of Rothbury, off B6341*

SPRING SUMMER AUTUMN WINTER

Access | Gift Shop | Café

Rothbury endears itself with a splendid walk along ancient tracks through pink heather above the town, with distant views of the Cheviots on the outward journey and the Simonside Hills on the return, followed by a hearty lunch at the Sun Kitchen teashop in the main street. After that I was prepared to tackle Cragside, a vast 1000-acre estate cloaked in a dark mantle of Wagnerian coniferous forest.

A monument to Victorian invention and wealth, Cragside boasts an extraordinary hilltop mansion designed by the architect Richard Norman Shaw. (Don't miss the awesome, gothic interior.) Built for Lord Armstrong, one of the great pioneers and industrial inventors of the 19th century, it was the first house in the world to be lit by hydro-electricity, one of Armstrong's own inventions.

A rock garden, recently replanted with heathers and alpines, tumbles down the hillside below the house, and the forested gardens are cut by a deep gorge. On the opposite hill is the walled garden, recently restored. Its glasshouses feature extraordinary rotating pots which help exotic fruits evenly ripen, while a slope above the lawns displays an impressive example of Victorian carpet bedding, closely planted with succulents for decorative effect.

CAPABILITY BROWN

Lancelot Capability Brown, the great landscape gardener of the 18th century, was born in 1716 at Kirkharle, a picturesque hamlet in the beautiful Wansbeck valley, and went to school at nearby Cambo. It is easy to see how those early years influenced his taste in garden design; the Brown landscape is visible all around, with its natural hills and gentle folds, dotted by copses of fine trees and watered by gentle burns.

Brown worked on Sir William Loraine's estate at **Kirkharle** *for six years, enhancing the grounds with plantations of oak, beech and chestnut, before moving south to work for William Kent at* **Stowe** (q.v.)*, in Buckinghamshire.*

As he gained renown, his landscaping advice was widely sought by country house owners who engaged him to sweep away the old formal gardens, replacing them with more fashionable rolling turf and naturalistic 'landskip'. **Blenheim** (q.v.), **Chatsworth** (q.v.), **Petworth** (q.v.) *and many other great parks were remodelled by Brown (around 120 in all). His works in Northumberland include improvements to the park at* **Wallington** (q.v.) *and, most importantly, for the Duke of Northumberland at* **Alnwick Castle***, Alnwick NE66 1NQ (tel. 01665-510777). Open Easter Sun–Sept, daily, except Fri, 11a.m.–5p.m., main house 12 noon–5p.m. (last adm. 4.15p.m.).*

STANTON

Bide-a-Wee Cottage

Stanton, nr Netherwitton, Morpeth NE65 8PR TEL. 01670-772262 OWNER *Mark Robson* HOURS *Early May–Aug, Sats only, 1.30–5p.m., parties by arrangement* ENTRANCE *£1.75* DIRECTIONS *3m SSW of Longhorsley on edge of Stanton hamlet*

SPRING SUMMER AUTUMN WINTER

Nursery

DON'T MISS

Mark Robson was 15 when he began making the quarry garden beside his parents' cottage near Morpeth. Now in his late twenties, he regularly opens the two-acre garden, due to popular demand; the gardening grapevine doesn't allow such horticultural treasures to remain hidden for long.

Mark began by gardening in a natural style among the bare rock faces of the quarry, and at the lowest level he made an informal pool, fed by a natural spring. Its edges are planted with large-leaved gunneras and peltiphyllum, astilbes and yellow loosestrife; ferns and foxgloves clasp the rocky crevices.

A note of formality is introduced where a broad turf path runs between a short avenue of 'Scotch Bridget' apple trees. This is an old but rare variety, particularly suitable for northern gardens. Mark grew his trees from cuttings, on their own roots, and says 'Scotch Bridget' is 'a good cooker and eater'.

Under the fruit trees two glorious summer borders are ablaze with red-hot pokers, scarlet campions, shasta daisies and puffs of fine-leaved dill, with a froth of lady's mantle tumbling onto the path. A sunny terrace beside the house supports statuesque cardoons and cotton-thistle, threaded with shimmering pink sidalcea. The garden's structure is underpinned by Mark's exceptionally well-laid stone walls.

Wildflowers are very much a part of Mark's planting philosophy. Everywhere, he has woven them into this extraordinary garden with more exotic choices. Almost everything has been grown by Mark from seed, and some of his most unusual plants are potted up for sale during open days.

And also...

Belsay Hall, Belsay NE20 0DX (tel. 01661-881636), is an austerely neo-classical mansion, with 30 acres of far-flung, unusual gardens. From terraced formal gardens near the house, there are views over a beautiful rhododendron dell. But the most extraordinary area is the great quarry garden with its fern-clad rock faces, towering rhododendrons and surprising fan palms, leading to the picturesque ruins of 14th-century Belsay Castle. Open April–Sept, daily,

10a.m.–6p.m.; Oct–March, daily, 10a.m.–4p.m. (closed 24–26 Dec). Entrance £3.60, OAPs £2.80, children £1.80.

Chillingham Castle, Chillingham NE66 5NJ (tel. 01668-215359/215390), has a fine parterre and long herbaceous border beside the castle, with pleasant woodland walks for springtime. There are also rooms to rent in the castle, ideal for touring the locality. Open Easter weekend, May–Sept, daily, except Tues (open daily during July and Aug), 12 noon–5p.m. Entrance £3.75, OAPs £3, children free.

Kirkley Hall, Ponteland NE20 0AQ (tel. 01661-860808), is a horticultural college with demonstration gardens of well-labelled plants, and a three-acre walled garden of herbaceous perennials and climbers in great variety. There is also a wide range of greenhouse plants under commercial production. Open daily, all year, 10a.m.–5p.m. Entrance free, guided tours of 10 or more £5 per person.

Romantic and lonely **Lindisfarne Castle, Holy Island, Berwick-upon-Tweed TD15 2SH (tel. 01289-389244)**, is accessible at low tide, when the great causeway reappears. Sir Edwin Lutyens remodelled the castle and its walled garden. Gertrude Jekyll provided two sets of planting plans which have recently been the basis for renewed planting. Irises, stachys, hollyhocks and sweet peas thrive here among the persistent winds and shrill cries of gulls. Open April or Good Friday (whichever is first)–Oct, daily, except Fri (garden open Fri only), 1–5.30p.m. (castle), 9.30a.m.–4.30p.m.(garden). Entrance (castle) £3.80, children £1.90, family ticket £10, (garden) free.

Meldon Park, Morpeth NE61 3SW (tel. 01670-772661), is set in an idyllic location, facing south above pastures leading to the wooded valley of Hartburn Dene. Beside the house are formal rose beds and a handsome orangery. A woodland walk through camellias and rhododendrons leads to the attractive four-acre walled kitchen garden with its central herbaceous borders. Open last weekend in May–weekend of 3rd week in June and Aug Bank Holiday, 2–5p.m. Entrance £3, OAPs £2, children 50p.

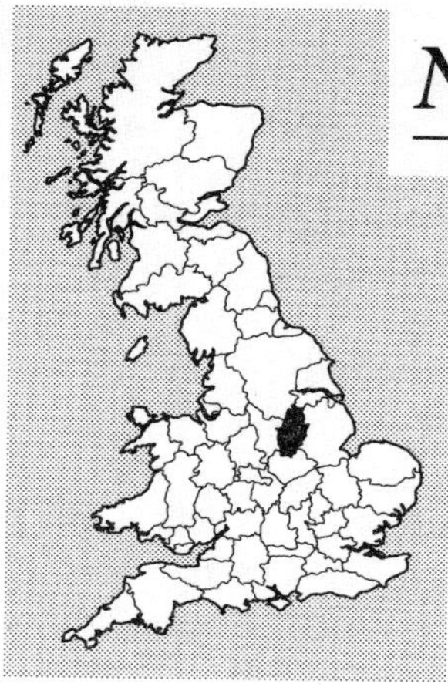

Nottinghamshire

MAP NO. 5

Nottinghamshire is famous for its lace, which has been made here for hundreds of years, and for Sherwood Forest, home of Robin Hood. The Forest is greatly reduced in size from what had been a great royal hunting ground stretching north from Nottingham. Picturesque Newstead Abbey was founded in the centre of the old forest, and enjoys a glorious setting on the River Leen. Much of this north Midlands county is industrial, especially north of the River Trent; in contrast, the southern region undulates gently in fertile farmland, which is characterised by large fields and arable farms.

NEWARK

Pureland Relaxation and Meditation Centre

North Clifton, nr Newark NG23 7AT **TEL.** *01777-228567* **OWNER** *Mr Maitreya* **HOURS** *April–Oct, Tues–Fri, 12 noon–5.30p.m.; Sat–Sun and Bank Holidays, 10.30a.m.–5.30p.m.; lantern-lit evening garden, weekends, Sept, 7–9.30p.m.* **ENTRANCE** *£3, concessions £2.50, children £1.50* **DIRECTIONS** *At North Clifton, mid-way between Newark and Gainsborough, off A1133*

SPRING SUMMER AUTUMN WINTER

Café

This is certainly one of the most unusual gardens in this *Guide*. The Centre is run by Mr Maitreya, a former Zen monk, who conducts courses in relaxation, revitalisation and meditation. He began to transform the one-and-a-half-acre flat field beside his home in 1980, gradually converting it into a Japanese-style garden of water, winding paths, clipped trees and little hills. Missing the hilly and mountainous landscape of Japan, his homeland, Mr Maitreya started to create his own, in miniature. Earth excavated for the ponds was used to make 'hills', and large stones were placed in harmonious positions. Japanese traditional garden elements include water, carp, bridges, moss, stepping-stones, bamboo, clipped evergreens, maples, cherry trees and stone lanterns. There is a recently made Zen garden of rocks and chipped marble, and a Japanese-style tea house, for tea ceremonies. The garden radiates tranquillity, aided by the soothing sounds of water and wind chimes, and there are many seats placed at vantage points which are very popular with visitors who, I noticed, end up sitting in them for hours.

NOTTINGHAM

Felley Priory

Underwood, Jacksdale NG16 5FL TEL. *01773-810230* OWNER *The Hon. Mrs Chaworth Musters* HOURS *All year, Tues–Wed, Fri, 9a.m.–12.30p.m.; March–Oct, every 2nd and 4th Wed, 9a.m.–4p.m.* ENTRANCE *£1.50, children free* DIRECTIONS *From Jct 27 of M1, take A608 (direction Eastwood and Heanor) for ½ m, look out for discreet sign to nursery and garden on left*

SPRING SUMMER AUTUMN WINTER

Access Café Plant Shop Nursery DON'T MISS

This is a garden with everything. It has enormous interest for the plantsman, for there are many unusual trees, shrubs, bulbs and perennials throughout the grounds (the owner is a keen, hands-on gardener). Disciplined structure is provided by walls, mature yew hedges (which are attractively topiarised with top-knots at regular intervals) and treillage enclosures; the borders are abundant and thoughtfully planted and the rose garden is spectacular through summer, with late-flowering clematis providing colour once the roses have finished. The garden's layout is in sympathy with the priory house (not open), which has medieval origins, but it has a rewarding vigour and flair. In the depths of the three-acre garden is a delightful lily-pool, with bog irises and shrub roses lighting up the banks.

NOTTINGHAM

Newstead Abbey Park

Nottingham NG15 8GE TEL. *01623-793557* OWNER *Nottingham City Council* HOURS *All year, daily, 10a.m.–dusk, house April–Sept, 12 noon–6p.m.* ENTRANCE *(gardens only) £2, OAPs/children £1.50 (house and gardens £4, OAPs £2, children £1.50)* DIRECTIONS *11m N of Nottingham, by A60*

SPRING SUMMER AUTUMN WINTER

Access Café

This property is famous as the home of the poet Lord Byron, who inherited the title and estates of his great-uncle (the 5th Lord Byron) when he was just 10 years old. Newstead was originally an Augustinian priory in the late 12th century, but came into the possession of Byron's family in 1539, following Henry VIII's dissolution of the monasteries.

The plan of the 25-acre, early 18th-century formal gardens remains, but not the detail, and there is a large walled garden, geometrically arranged with a series of terraces and sloping lawns, enclosing a rectangular sheet of water, 300ft × 100ft. Beside it are smaller walled gardens and a herbaceous border. There is also an enclosed iris garden and a substantial, formal rose garden. The park's great lake is a magnificent feature, visible from the drive. Its waters flow down a cascade into a spectacular Japanese garden, dating from 1907. It was laid out by a Japanese landscape architect and is a masterly composition of winding paths, waterfalls, pools and stone ornaments, engulfed by bamboos and evergreen shrubs, acers and flowering cherry trees.

THE NOTTINGHAM CROCUS

Two species of crocus are associated with Nottingham: Crocus vernus, *the spring crocus, and* C. nudiflorus, *an autumn crocus. Though not indigenous, being natives of southern Europe and the Middle East, their links with the region go back many centuries. They are thought to have been brought back to England by either knights returning from the crusades or by the Cluniac monks of the Lenton Priory, who may well have cultivated* C. nudiflorus *in their herb gardens, as a cheap and available substitute for the saffron crocus.*

The Gardeners' Chronicle *of March 1872 noted that in spring the flood meadows of the River Trent, near Nottingham, were awash with the silver-lilac blooms of* C. vernus*: 'at the present moment enlivening the Nottingham meadows with thousands of its purple blossoms. Hundreds of "young men and maidens, old men and children" may be seen from the Midland Railway picking the flowers for the ornamentation of their homes. Any stranger fond of flowers who visited Nottingham now for the first time would feel surprised to see large handfuls of Crocuses in the windows of the poorer and middle-class inhabitants. Crocuses in mugs, in jugs, in saucers, in broken teapots, plates, dishes, cups – in short, in almost every domestic utensil capable of holding a little fresh water; and very beautiful they look…'*

Since then, intensive use of land for building and agriculture has seen the rapid demise of these harbingers of spring and autumn, although they have survived in isolated areas such as churchyards and golf courses. Nottingham crocuses thrived in the Trent meadows because they were 'Lammas Lands' – hay meadows that were harvested at particular times of year, allowing the flowering and seed-setting of these blooms. The two species thus survived and spread over the area for hundreds of years. Attempts are now being made to reinstate the flowers locally at sites where they may flourish undisturbed.

And also…

Hodsock Priory, Blyth, Worksop S81 0TY (tel. 01909-591204), is famous for its sheets of snowdrops and aconites early in the year. They are joined by other winter bloomers, such as *Iris unguicularis*, hellebores and fragrant winter honeysuckle, in grounds extending over five acres, with a half-mile woodland snowdrop walk. The summer gardens feature herbaceous borders and old roses. Open winter, for 4 weeks in February–March, daily, 10a.m.–4p.m. (dates depend on the weather, so telephone prior to visiting); April–Aug, Tues–Thurs, 1–5p.m. Entrance £2.50, children free.

Mill Hill Plants, Elston Lane, East Stoke, Newark NG23 5QJ (tel. 01636-525460), is a small nursery offering a selection of herbaceous plants – particularly bearded irises – and shrubs. The pretty half-acre garden alongside is open so customers can see how plants will look when mature. There is also a National Collection of berberis, extending to around 80 different forms of this prickly, spring-flowering shrub. Open March–Sept, Wed–Sun, and Oct, Fri–Sun, Bank Holiday Mons, 10a.m.–6p.m. Entrance £1.20, children free.

Anyone interested in wildflowers should beat a path to **Naturescape, Lapwing Meadows, Coachgap Lane, Langar NG13 9HP (tel. 01949-860592)**. Here is a wildflower farm with visitor centre, covering 40 acres of flowers grown for seed available by mail (send £1 in stamps for catalogue). The flower fields are best at mid-summer, and there are demonstration habitats including a wildlife pond with associated water-margin plants, a bee garden, woodland edge habitat, dry-stone wall and wildlife hedge. There is also a nursery stocking plants for these habitats. Open April–Sept, daily, 11a.m.–5.30p.m. Entrance £1.95, OAPs £1.50 (mid-June–mid-Aug, when flowers at their best, at other times free), children free.

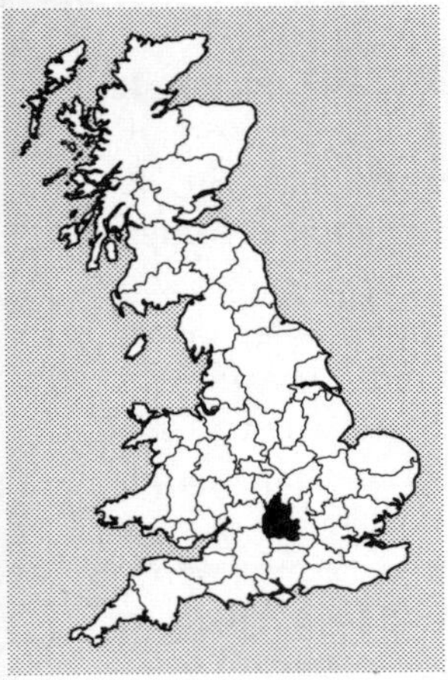

Oxfordshire

MAP NOs. 2, 5

Oxfordshire is a fortunate county with a pleasant, gently undulating landscape, watered by the valleys of the Thames and the Cherwell, both rivers (the Thames is called the Isis at Oxford) running through its fine university city. Oxford began as a frontier town, defending Wessex against the Danes in Saxon times. Its university is the oldest in England, as is its botanic garden. The city of 'dreaming spires' and many of Oxfordshire's fine market towns and villages are built of warm-tinted local stone which adds to their architectural appeal. Much of the wealth of the county was based on a thriving wool trade on the edge of the Cotswolds; Witney, on the River Windrush, 10 miles west of Oxford, is a prime example. A wealthy town in the Middle Ages, it is still famed for its woollen blankets and possesses a fine Blanket Hall built in the early 18th century.

BANBURY

Broughton Castle

Broughton, nr Banbury OX15 5EB TEL. *01295-262624* OWNER *The Lord Saye and Sele* HOURS *Mid-May–mid-Sept, Wed, Sun and Bank Holiday Mons; also Thurs July–Aug; all 2–5p.m.* ENTRANCE *£3.90, OAPs/students £3.40, children £2* DIRECTIONS *2½m SW of Banbury on B4035*

SPRING SUMMER AUTUMN WINTER

Access Café

The 17th-century traveller, Celia Fiennes, was born at Broughton Castle, and I sometimes feel she was a kindred spirit, touring houses and gardens up and down the land and writing them up in her journals. The 14th- to 16th-century fortified manor of soft, brown Hornton stone was certainly a gracious starting point, for it enjoys one of the loveliest settings imaginable, moated by a brook which becomes the River Cherwell downstream.

The entrance gives no hint of the exuberant gardens which lie behind the castle. The walled Ladies' Garden has a formal, central pattern of low box hedging of four fleurs-de-lys, infilled with roses and pointing out to mixed borders which enjoy the shelter of the walls. Beyond are two spectacular colour-themed herbaceous borders, one richly planted in blues, yellows and greens with grey foliage highlights; the other a symphony of deep reds and mauves, tempered by pink and blue hues. The American landscape architect Lanning Roper simplified the gardens, while enriching their planting, nearly 30 years ago, and improvements continue in the range and quality of plants grown here.

BANBURY

Upton House

Nr Banbury OX15 6HT TEL. *01295-670266* OWNER *The National Trust* HOURS *April–Oct, Sat–Wed, 2–6p.m. (last adm. 5.30p.m.)* ENTRANCE *£5, garden only £2.50, family ticket (2 adults, up to 4 children) £12.50* DIRECTIONS *By A422, 7m NW of Banbury, 12m SE of Stratford-upon-Avon*

SPRING SUMMER AUTUMN WINTER

Access | Gift Shop | Café | Plant Shop | NPC

DON'T MISS

Anyone with the remotest interest in art should look inside the house, for it holds an awesome collection, with works by Bosch, Bruegel, Canaletto, Constable and Stubbs. Indeed, from the house it is difficult to know whether there is much of a garden since the view is of a vast lawn, flanked by large yew, pine and cedar trees, with sheep-grazed pastures rising up the hill beyond. Go to the far edge of the lawn, however, and a series of terraced and walled gardens fans out below: part flower gardens, part kitchen garden, all lavishly planted, leading down to a big pond at the bottom.

You can descend the terraces via a steep stairway, or by winding back and forth along the turf paths which run beside the long borders. There is an important National Collection of asters (Michaelmas daisies), adding interest to late-summer/early-autumn visits; there is also a richly planted bog garden to one side, and a pair of herbaceous borders ascending the sloping ground the other side of the kitchen garden. A thrilling 35-acre garden in any season; produce from the kitchen area is occasionally offered for sale.

SULTRY SNAKESHEAD FRITILLARIES

The snakeshead fritillary, Fritillaria meleagris, *is a quietly glamorous wildflower of damp meadows, ideally suited to low-lying ground beside the Windrush and Cherwell rivers in Oxfordshire. Its popular name hints at the slightly sinister ambience of its deep purple, nodding flowers borne on the slenderest of stems. Other vernacular names such as leper's bells, shy widows and sulky ladies also suggest this flower's dark, mysterious qualities.*

Vita Sackville-West wrote in her poem The Land *that the 'snaky flower' was sullen, dangerous and foreign-looking, 'scarfed in dull purple, like Egyptian girls Camping among the furze, staining the waste with foreign colour… An Egyptian girl, with an ancient snaring spell'. Its origins are uncertain, but* F. meleagris *was certainly a well-known and plentiful flower in April and May until 20th-century farming methods with land draining, ploughing and fertilisers severely reduced its numbers.*

The most famous site where this flower survives in profusion is Magdalen College Meadow, Oxford, on the banks of the River Cherwell. Until a few years ago, the banks flooded reliably between November and March, providing ideal conditions for the fritillary to flourish, as it has done here for centuries. Winter flooding has not occurred in recent years of low rainfall, but the meadow is still damp enough for the bulbs to have multiplied in great numbers. Part of their successful management is due to the way the flowers are left to set seed before the hay is cut in July. The meadow is then grazed by fallow deer, the trampling of their hooves providing an ideal seed bed. Fritillaries also have a long association with the Oxfordshire village of Ducklington, beside the Windrush, and Iffley, just south of Oxford, where the flowers are celebrated on Fritillary Sunday, at the height of their flowering season.

FARINGDON

Buscot Park

Faringdon SN7 8BU **TEL.** *01367-240786* **OWNER** *The National Trust* **HOURS** *House and grounds: April–Sept (incl. Easter Sunday but not Bank Holiday Mons), Wed–Fri, 2–6p.m. Also every 2nd and 4th Sat–Sun, 2–6p.m. Grounds only: April–Sept as house, also Mon–Tues (but not Bank Holiday Mons), 2–6p.m.* **ENTRANCE** *House and grounds £4.40, grounds only £3.30, children half-price* **DIRECTIONS** *Between Lechlade and Faringdon on A417*

SPRING SUMMER AUTUMN WINTER

Café Plant Shop

The high point of this 100-acre park is its formal and dramatic water garden, which descends a gentle slope to finish in a great lake. It was designed by Harold Peto (*q.v.*) in 1904, and runs in a series of formal pools and rills, occasionally crossed by little footbridges, all encased by box hedges and fastigiate trees. Other avenues cut through the woodland, offering pleasant walks, although there are one or two fussy areas added more recently which seem out of step with the grandeur of the place. There is also a richly planted walled garden, with mixed borders of shrubs and herbaceous plants; there are also old shrub roses and collections of fruit.

HENLEY-ON-THAMES

Greys Court

Rotherfield Greys, Henley-on-Thames RG9 4PG **TEL.** *01491-628529* **OWNER** *The National Trust* **HOURS** *Garden: April–Sept, daily, except Thurs and Sun, 2–6p.m. (closed Good Friday), last adm. 5.30p.m.; house: Mon, Wed, Fri, 2–6p.m.* **ENTRANCE** *Garden: £3.20; house and garden £4.50, children half-price* **DIRECTIONS** *3m W of Henley-on-Thames, east of B481*

SPRING SUMMER AUTUMN WINTER

Access Café

DON'T MISS

The seven-acre gardens at Greys Court lie a little apart from the main house, filling out and giving coherence to a set of old walls and ruins. Among its pleasures are the fabulous, gnarled wisterias forming a long tunnel showered in pale mauve spring-time blooms; formal box parterres walled in by bricks and flints; a decadent long border devoted to the brief flowering of many scores of peonies; and, my favourite bit, a serene, cobbled walk under the spreading branches of cherry trees that spring from the grass on either side. There are old roses, a kitchen garden, a turf maze and lovely old trees too. It is an idiosyncratic garden that has evolved over recent decades, given enchantment by the fragments of past centuries.

STEEPLE ASTON

Rousham House

Steeple Aston OX6 3QX TEL. *01869-347110* OWNER *C. Cottrell-Dormer* HOURS *Garden all year, daily, 10a.m.–4.30p.m.; house April–Sept, Wed, Sun and Bank Holiday Mons, 2–4.30p.m.* ENTRANCE *£3, no children under 15* DIRECTIONS *2m S of Steeple Aston off A4260 and B4030*

SPRING SUMMER AUTUMN WINTER

Rousham possesses 'the sweetest little groves, streams, glades, porticos, cascades and river imaginable' – Horace Walpole's words, written in 1760, but still apt today. This important, early 18th-century, 25-acre landscape garden has pleasing, pastoral views and was laid out by William Kent in the 1730s, overlying a more formal design laid out a generation before. Its recommended route passes grottoes, cascades and the carved image of a dying gladiator, with waterside walks leading to a handsome stone loggia. There is also a fine walled garden with herbaceous borders, ancient espaliered fruit trees, and an ancient dovecote beside the box-edged rose gardens. 'Rousham is uncommercial and unspoilt with no tea room and no shop', says the leaflet. 'Bring a picnic, wear comfortable shoes and it is yours for the day.' Sound advice for a most enjoyable walk through Arcady. Daffodil time here is lovely, although summer is best for the walled gardens.

WHEATLEY

Waterperry Gardens

Wheatley OX33 1JZ **TEL.** *01844-339226* **OWNER** *School of Economic Science* **HOURS** *March–Oct, daily, 10a.m.–5.30p.m. (6p.m. Sat–Sun), Nov–Feb, 10a.m.–4.30p.m. (closed Christmas and New Year holidays)* **ENTRANCE** *£2.40, OAPs £1.90, children £1.10, Nov–March everyone £1* **DIRECTIONS** *9m E of Oxford, 2½m N of Wheatley; follow signs from M40 Jct 8*

SPRING SUMMER AUTUMN WINTER

Access | Gift Shop | Café | Plant Shop

This was once the Waterperry Horticultural School for Women (now closed) which was opened in 1932 by Miss Beatrix Havergal and her partner, Avice Sanders. Many well-known gardeners (including Valerie Finnis, Mary Spiller and Sissinghurst's former head gardeners, Pamela Schwerdt and Sibylle Kreutzberger) were trained here, and the highest possible standards of horticulture were instilled in its pupils. Parts of Miss Havergal's legacy continue, such as the spectacular 200ft herbaceous border below a south-facing wall – wonderful from early summer well into autumn. There are also shrub and heather borders, herb beds, a rock garden, well-trained fruit trees, many demonstration beds of assorted herbaceous plants, and a knot, and rose garden. The plant centre at the 83-acre garden's entrance has a reasonably wide stock at competitive prices, and there is often produce from the gardens on sale. Any keen gardener will find much of interest and entertainment here.

EUPHORBIAS GALORE

In Evelyn Waugh's Brideshead Revisited, *Lord Sebastian Flyte is overcome by an urge to see the ivies, in all their variety, at* **University of Oxford Botanic Garden, Rose Lane, Oxford OX1 4AX (tel. 01865-276920)***. It is the oldest botanic garden in Britain, and besides ivies there is a National Collection of euphorbia species.*

Apparently, euphorbias were so named by Dioscorides, who had learned of the plant via King Juba of Mauretania; the genus was named after the king's physician, Euphorbus. There are at least 2000 species of euphorbia, and they are extremely diverse in their distribution and hardiness. Some are typical desert succulents, resembling cacti, while others are hardy and valued as ornamental garden plants. Gertrude Jekyll admired E. characias *for its contribution to the herbaceous border in spring, and euphorbias continue to enjoy favour in many people's gardens. It should be remembered, however, that the white latex 'sap' is extremely irritant, liable to blister the skin on contact, and possibly carcinogenic. Wear gloves when pruning. Anyone interested in these unusual plants can see wide ranges of both hardy and greenhouse types in the four-and-a-half-acre University gardens. Open all year, daily, 9a.m.–5p.m. (4.30p.m. Oct–March); greenhouses open 2–4p.m. Closed Good Friday and Christmas Day. Entrance free, except April–Sept, £2.*

WOODSTOCK

Blenheim Palace

Woodstock OX20 1PX TEL. *01993-811091* OWNER *His Grace the Duke of Marlborough* HOURS *House, gardens and attractions: mid-March–Oct, daily, 10.30a.m.–5.30p.m. (last adm. 4.45p.m.). Park: all year, daily, except 25 Dec, from 9.45a.m.–4.45p.m.* ENTRANCE *House and gardens: £7.80, OAPs/children £5.80; garden only, £3, OAPs £1.50; park only, £5 per car, £1 per pedestrian, children 50p, family ticket (2 adults, 2 children) £20* DIRECTIONS *8m N of Oxford on A44; if travelling by motorway (M40) take Jct 9; Blenheim is clearly signposted*

SPRING SUMMER AUTUMN WINTER

Access | Gift Shop | Café | Plant Shop | DON'T MISS

Blenheim Palace is the ultimate stately home – Britain's answer to Versailles and quite breathtaking in its opulence. The birthplace of Sir Winston Churchill, it was built by Sir John Vanbrugh and Nicholas Hawksmoor for the 1st Duke of Marlborough and paid for by the nation, following the Duke's victory at the Battle of Blenheim in 1704.

Outdoors it is spectacular, too, with a 2000-acre park landscaped by Capability Brown (*q.v.*) overlaying a more formal, earlier plan. Some of the formal symmetry was put back in the early 20th century, however, when terraced Italian-style gardens with patterned beds of box were added to the east side of the palace, and elaborate water parterres with fountains were reinstated to the west. There is an impressive eight-acre walled kitchen garden (the sole survivor of the pre-Brown layout) with a recently planted maze, and a rose garden and arboretum. At Blenheim you can see how some of the greatest talents of earlier centuries have interwoven to create a truly great landscape.

And also...

Brook Cottage, Well Lane, Alkerton, nr Banbury OX15 6NL (tel. 01295-670303/670590), is a beautiful, richly planted four-acre hillside garden around a 17th-century house (not open). Features include a water garden, alpine scree, colour-themed borders, over 200 shrubs and climbing roses, many clematis and a range of ornamental trees. Interest is planned for year-round appeal. Open April–Oct, Mon–Fri, 9a.m.–6p.m. Entrance £2.50, OAPs £2.

The Burford Garden Company, Shilton Road, Burford, Oxford OX18 4PA (tel. 01993-823117/823285), is a large, well-stocked garden centre. Its plant displays include around 450 different roses, 75 clematis and 300 varieties of herbaceous plants, with ornamental trees and imported topiaries. Open all year, daily, except 25–26 Dec and Easter Sunday, Mon–Wed 9a.m.–5.30p.m., Thurs–Fri 9a.m.–7p.m., Sat 9a.m.–6p.m., Sun 11a.m.–5p.m.

Clock House, Coleshill, Swindon SN6 7PT (tel. 01793-762476), has an unusual five-acre garden featuring the ground plan of Coleshill House (burnt down in the 1950s) planted in box and lavender, to show where the walls and windows had been. There is also a large greenhouse, a fine lime avenue and wonderful views of the Vale of the White Horse. Open April–Sept, Thurs only, 2–5p.m., also for certain NGS days and by appointment. Entrance £1.50.

Colegrave Seeds, Milton Road, West Adderbury, Banbury OX17 3EY (tel. 01295-810632), is a commercial supplier of seeds to the horticulture industry. Its four-acre trial grounds, rarely open to the public, are well worth seeing on the special open days in August, by anyone with an interest in the latest developments in plant breeding, particularly bedding plants destined for the market. The displays are brash, bright, instructive and well maintained. Open for one NGS day in August. Entrance £2.

Greystone Cottage, Colmore Lane, Kingwood Common, Henley-on-Thames RG9 5NA (tel. 01491-628559), is generously planted for lovely spring displays, with snowdrops and many hellebores in the woods; also note the camellias, azaleas, fritillaries and primulas. Later interest is supplied by old roses and assorted shrubs and perennials. There are also unusual plants for sale. Open for several NGS Suns in spring, and by prior appointment March–June. Entrance £2.

Kelmscott Manor, Kelmscott, Lechlade GL7 3HJ (tel. 01367-252486), is famous for having been the summer home of 19th-century designer William Morris, for 25 years. It will be of interest to anyone with a fascination for the Pre-Raphaelite movement or Arts and Crafts design (Morris's stylised floral designs continue to be influential 100 years on) and the entry ticket includes a tour of the house. The small, enclosed garden was painted in watercolour by Rossetti's model, Maria Spartali Stillman (1844–1927). The standard roses and profusion of plants which she painted (and which inspired Morris) have been reinstated during recent restorations. Open April–Sept, Wed, 11a.m.–1p.m. and 2–5p.m.; 3rd Sat of each month, 2–5p.m. Entrance £6, children £3.

Mattocks Roses, Nuneham Courtenay, Oxford OX44 9PY (tel. 01865-343265), shares premises with a large and well-stocked branch of Notcutts Garden Centre, which is where you should park to visit the Mattocks rose fields which are open late June–Sept for no charge across the road. It is always instructive to see demonstration fields in bloom if you are considering buying some new roses. Their ever-popular County series of roses now includes 'Oxfordshire', bearing pretty, shell-pink blooms over a long season on a low-growing bush. Open all year, Mon–Sat, 9a.m.–5.30p.m. (closing 5p.m. Jan–March), Sun and Bank Holidays, 10.30a.m.–4.30p.m. Catalogue free on request.

The Nursery Further Afield, Evenley Road, Mixbury, Brackley NN13 5YR (tel. 01280-848808 (day), 848539 (eve)), is a small nursery and display garden, surrounded by silvery willows, tucked away on the edge of Mixbury village. It specializes in hardy geraniums and day lilies (*Hemerocallis*), and has a small range of other unusual hardy perennials. Open April–early Oct (Aug by appointment only), Wed–Sat, 10a.m.–5p.m. Entrance free.

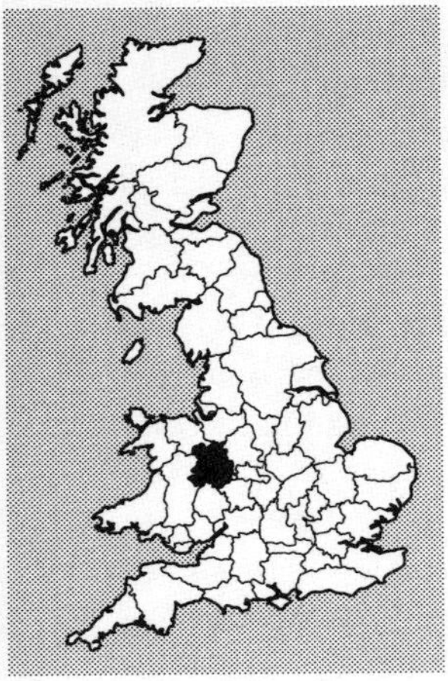

Shropshire

MAP NO. 5

The poet A. E. Housman recalled his homeland as 'the country for easy livers, the quietest under the sun'. This was not always so, however; the county's strategic position on the border with Wales made it the scene of bloody battles for centuries. It is also one of the oldest lived-in regions of Britain; 5000 years ago Stone Age peoples populated the hilly and forested region of Clun, on the westernmost fringes, and to the south a Bronze Age trade route ran across the Clee Hills to join the River Severn. The world's first iron bridge, 196ft long, was built in 1779 to straddle the Severn gorge at Telford, and it remains a potent symbol of the Industrial Revolution which followed.

HODNET

Hodnet Hall

Hodnet, Market Drayton TF9 3NN **TEL.** *01630-685202* **OWNER** *Mr and Mrs A. Heber-Percy* **HOURS** *April–Sept, Tues–Sat, 12 noon–5p.m., Sun and Bank Holiday Mons, 12 noon–5.30p.m.* **ENTRANCE** *£3, OAPs £2.50, children £1.20* **DIRECTIONS** *12m NE of Shrewsbury on A53*

SPRING SUMMER AUTUMN WINTER

Access | Gift Shop | Café | Plant Shop | DON'T MISS

Two things about Hodnet Hall are etched forever on my memory: the fantastic waterscape, created from a chain of big lakes, and the bizarre experience of taking tea with a snarling tiger (albeit a stuffed one), under the glassy gaze of hundreds of severed heads of assorted antelopes, buffalos and rhinoceros. The late-Victorian hall sits on a plateau, looking down into the main pool; half a dozen more lakes ascend the gentle valley to the west. Grassy banks either side are awash with daffodils, rhododendrons and cherry blossom through the spring, followed by astilbes and hydrangeas. There are acers in variety, with Japanese forms elegantly bowing to cast their reflections at the water's edge, and, with a variety of shrubs and trees, they bring a spectacular glow to autumn. It is a really splendid and unusual garden, laid out with imagination in the 1920s and well maintained today. If I lived nearby, its 60 acres would be a regular haunt. Hawkstone Historic Park and Follies (*q.v.*) are nearby (and signposted from Hodnet).

WILLOUGHBRIDGE

The Dorothy Clive Garden

Willoughbridge, Market Drayton TF9 4EU TEL. *01630-647237* OWNER *Willoughbridge Garden Trust* HOURS *April–Oct, daily, 10a.m.–5.30p.m.* ENTRANCE *£2.70, OAPs £2.30, children under 11 free, 11–16-year-olds £1* DIRECTIONS *7m NE of Market Drayton, 1m E of Woore, by A51*

SPRING SUMMER AUTUMN WINTER

Access Café

Much of the tranquillity and appeal of this eight-acre garden is due to its water, whether tumbling down a rocky cascade, or supporting flat plates of lilies, spread out luxuriantly in the still pool. If Claude Monet could visit, he would marvel at the garden's subtle range of textures and colours, and the tremendous variety of plants arranged on its gentle slopes.

The lime-free soil supports festive displays of rhododendrons, a glorious clash of pinks and purples, reds and yellows, followed by a feast of hybrid azaleas in salmon, orange and lemon, with intoxicating fragrance. There is a great deal to satisfy plantsmen here – many unusual bulbs, perennials, camellias and conifers for interest through the seasons. The scree and rock garden above the lake are especially good. The garden was made by Colonel Clive from the 1940s onwards as a tribute to his wife.

HEART OF OAK

Vast forests once covered much of Shropshire, the most significant tree being the oak, because it offered seemingly inexhaustible supplies of stout, hard-wearing timbers for ship- and house-building in medieval and Tudor times. Oaks also provided fodder for the furnaces of the ancient iron industry. Black-and-white oak-framed buildings are still a feature in the region, with one of the most celebrated houses being ***Boscobel, Bishop's Wood, Brewood ST19 9AR (tel. 01902-850244), 8m N of Wolverhampton on an unclassified road between A41 and A5****, on the Staffordshire border. The small two-acre garden is in formal, 17th-century parterre style.*

The property's name derives from the Italian, bosco bello, as it was in the midst of a beautiful wood. King Charles II hid in an oak tree here after the Battle of Worcester in 1651, while Cromwell's men searched the forest. That oak didn't survive in the long term (pieces of it made valuable souvenirs even during the 17th century). Open April–Oct, daily, 10a.m.–6p.m., Nov–March, Wed–Sun, 10a.m.–4p.m. Closed 24–26 Dec, and all Jan. Entrance £3.75, children £1.90, concessions £2.80.

WOLLERTON

Wollerton Old Hall

Wollerton, Hodnet, Market Drayton TF9 3NA **TEL.** *01630-685756* **OWNER** *Mr and Mrs J. Jenkins* **HOURS** *May–Aug, Fri and Sun, 12 noon–5p.m., also Bank Holidays* **ENTRANCE** *£2.50, children 50p* **DIRECTIONS** *11m NE of Shrewsbury, ½m NE of Hodnet, off A53 (follow the brown signs)*

SPRING SUMMER AUTUMN WINTER

Access Café Nursery

This is a formal, three-acre garden, divided into hedged or walled rooms, and inspired by the geometrical garden styles of the 17th century. It has very strong lines of axis, the chief one from the house leading through a symmetrical knot garden enclosed by beech hedges into a sunken rill garden, with a lime allée and further gardens beyond. Its design is appropriate for the house which is the sole remaining wing of what had been an Elizabethan mansion;

it also suits the flat lie of the land, for the subdivisions by hedges help to filter cold Shropshire winds. There are delphinium borders, a garden of 'hot' red and yellow flowers (best in August), a white garden and, beyond the walls, a semi-wild garden of shrubs and trees in grassland sloping down to the valley of the River Tern. Within the formal structure, planting is exuberant and imaginative.

And also...

You can buy roses galore at the famous nurseries of **David Austin Roses, Bowling Green Lane, Albrighton WV7 3HB (tel. 01902-373931).** A group of display gardens for roses has also been laid out over the last 10 years, showing over 900 different roses in ideal conditions. They are mainly old-fashioned and shrub types, together with plenty of David Austin's own-bred English roses. The gardens are surrounded by neat conifer hedges, with borders edged in box and yew. Also worth viewing in summer is the herbaceous garden, featuring many of the plants listed in a separate Hardy Plants catalogue (available free). Open all year, Mon–Fri, 9a.m.–5p.m., Sat–Sun, 10a.m.–6p.m. (closing at dusk mid-Oct–mid-March).

Dolwen, Cefn Coch, Llanrhaeadr-ym-Mochnant, Oswestry SY10 0BLL (tel. 01691-780411), features a delightful four-acre woodland and water garden arranged around Frances Denby's whitewashed, slate-roofed cottage, close to the Berwyn Mountains, with spectacular views. Perched on a rock-peppered hillside, the garden is sympathetically planted with shrubs and perennials, and opens on Fri and the last Sun each month from May–Aug, 2–4.30p.m., and by appointment. Entrance £1. Practical gardening courses and demonstrations are also held in the summer (telephone for details).

The garden of **Erway Farm House, Pentre Coed, nr Ellesmere SY12 9ED (tel. 01691-690479)**, was made in the early 1950s by a keen plantswoman who was influenced by Margery Fish, of East Lambrook Manor Garden (*q.v.*). Its style is relaxed and cottagey, what the owners call 'controlled confusion'. Hellebores are a key feature of early spring, followed by Sprengeri tulips in May and peonies and assorted herbaceous plants in June. Open Feb–May, last Sun of each month, and Easter Saturday–Mon, 2–6p.m. (1–5p.m. in Feb). Entrance £1.50.

Eerie caves, cliffs, castle and concealed grottoes contribute to the thrills of **Hawkstone Historic Park and Follies, Hodnet Road, Weston-under-Redcastle, nr Shrewsbury SY4 5UY (tel. 01939-200611/200300).** Pathways ramble through hilly woods leading to various follies and monuments. In the 18th century, when the romantic landscape was laid out, a hermit with the beard of an old goat dwelt in the caves for 14 years. Open April–Oct, daily, 10a.m.–6p.m. Entrance Mon–Fri £10 per car, Sat–Sun and Bank Holidays £12.

The present six-acre gardens at **Preen Manor, Church Preen, Church Stretton SY6 7LQ (tel. 01694-771207)**, were only begun 20 years ago, but have a growing reputation for their stylish planting and imaginative use of the site. Highlights include a chess garden, gravel garden, fern garden, potager and gallery of pots arranged over brick-and-cobble steps. Teas available. Not suitable for wheelchairs. Open for groups of 15 or more by appointment, and for several days in summer through the National Gardens Scheme. Entrance £2.50, children 50p.

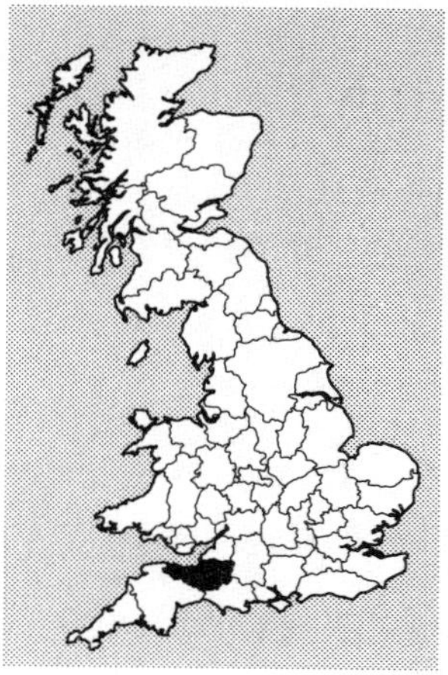

Somerset

MAP NO. 2

Somerset is a county of contrasts, from the flat, watered plains of the Levels to the limestone Mendip Hills, with heather-draped Exmoor in the west. The soft, deep ochre-coloured limestone of Ham Hill has provided building material for countless pretty villages in the south of the county. When I think of Somerset I also picture the small, productive apple orchards that have produced cider for many centuries. A visit to Perry's Cider Mills, Dowlish Wake, near Ilminster, is instructive, but intoxicating, for you can taste a whole range before you buy!

CASTLE CARY

Hadspen Garden and Nursery

Nr Castle Cary BA7 7NG **TEL.** *01749-813707* **OWNER** *N. and S. Pope and N. Hobhouse* **HOURS** *First Thurs in March–Sept, Thurs–Sun and Bank Holidays, 10a.m.–5p.m.* **ENTRANCE** *£2.50, children 50p* **DIRECTIONS** *3½m NW of Wincanton, 2m SE of Castle Cary, by A371*

SPRING SUMMER AUTUMN WINTER

Access Café Plant Shop NPC

DON'T MISS

Sandra Pope and her husband, Nori, had a specialist rose nursery on Vancouver Island, off Canada's Pacific coast, before they packed their bags and came to Hadspen in 1987. The five-acre, old kitchen garden, with its curved wall and south-facing slope, had been partially restored by Penelope Hobhouse in recent years, and presented a great opportunity for laying out a display garden and nursery; it was also an ideal canvas on which to practise their theories on colour harmony.

A large, rectangular lily-pond had formerly been the water cistern for the 18th-century Hadspen House nearby, and the Popes have planted the sunny, terraced walk beside it with plants reminiscent of sun-baked Mediterranean hillsides. The tea-house garden beyond the pool features cool blues and whites in the partial shade of trees, while long, double borders of yellows and creams of varying hue line one of the main paths through the garden.

The two-acre curved wall area (Sandra's domain) is devoted to deep reds and oranges, with darkly toned roses, dahlias and *Helichrysum bracteatum* progressing into delicate half-tones of pastel pinks and pale apricots. This border always gives endless pause for thought; it's cleverly, painstakingly arranged, but appears artless and relaxed.

Two rows of slender beech trees provide shade for Hadspen's famous hosta collection which predates the Popes' arrival; the lower gardens also house a hydrangea border and the National Collection of rodgersia. There is a catalogue of nursery stock sold on site, but no mail order.

CHEDDON FITZPAINE

Hestercombe

Cheddon Fitzpaine, nr Taunton TA2 8LQ TEL. *01823-413923* OWNER *Hestercombe Gardens Project and Somerset County Council* HOURS *Open all year, daily, 10a.m.–6p.m. (last adm. 5p.m.)* ENTRANCE *£3, children (under 15) £1 (under 5s free)* DIRECTIONS *3m NE of Taunton, near Cheddon Fitzpaine (signposted)*

SPRING SUMMER AUTUMN WINTER

Access · Gift Shop · Café · DON'T MISS

On a clear summer's day it is possible to capture wafts of the confident Edwardian age along with the lavender-perfumed air in this famous 50-acre garden; you might expect to bump into Helen Schlegel in *Howards End* in cambric blouse with leg-o-mutton sleeves, poised under a shady parasol. Hestercombe was one of the great success stories of the collaboration of Sir Edwin Lutyens, the designer, and Gertrude Jekyll, who planted it. Here are Lutyens's signature stone walls, circular steps and narrow water rills; there is a long, handsome pergola for climbing roses and beautifully detailed patterning of local stone. Jekyll's plantings (restored in recent years, largely according to her plans) feature generous drifts of herbaceous perennials – irises and delphiniums, grey-leaved lamb's ears and red-hot pokers and, of course, plenty of roses.

The plan for the main gardens is formal and symmetrical, making the most of the southern views of the Taunton Vale and distant Blackdown Hills. A new, interesting development is the restoration of a much older garden on the north side of the house: an 18th-century 35-acre landscape park that was laid out from 1750–1786 by the then owner, the euphoniously named Michael Coplestone Warre Bampfylde. Its great cascade is reminiscent of one that Bampfylde created at Stourhead (*q.v.*) for his great friend, Henry Hoare.

CURRY MALLET

Mallet Court Nursery

Curry Mallet, nr Taunton TA3 6SY **TEL.** *01823-480748* **OWNER** *J.G.S. and P.M.E. Harris* **HOURS** *Open all year, Mon–Fri, 9a.m.–1p.m. and 2–5p.m.; weekends only by appointment* **DIRECTIONS** *5m SE of Taunton, in village of Curry Mallet*

SPRING SUMMER AUTUMN WINTER

Nursery Mail Order

If you like trees you'll love Mallet Court Nursery which sells more than 800 varieties, many of them unobtainable elsewhere. Proprietor James Harris (known as 'Acer' Harris due to his predilection for Japanese maples) is a lawyer and self-confessed collector of stamps, coins and Roman artefacts, and especially of trees. He helps finance botanical expeditions collecting seed in far-flung places in return for a share of the spoils and the results are among the saplings in his densely stocked nursery. Oaks are another speciality as well as broad selections of hollies and magnolias; whatever tree you are searching for, it is probably here. A catalogue (£1 plus s.a.e.) lists trees available by mail order between November and March.

LANGPORT

Kelways Ltd

Barrymore Farm, Langport TA10 9EZ TEL. *01458-250521*
MANAGER *David Root* HOURS *Open all year, except 24 Dec–1 Jan, Mon–Fri 9a.m.–5p.m., Sat–Sun 10a.m.–4p.m.*
DIRECTIONS *In Langport, 10m E of Taunton, on B3153, by A358 and A378*

SPRING SUMMER AUTUMN WINTER

Café | Nursery | Mail Order

This famous old nursery has been operating since 1851 and is now thriving again, under new ownership and management. Astonishingly, around 600 herbaceous peonies are grown here, many being rare Victorian varieties dating from the nursery's glory days, and there is a very large range of bearded irises, too. (Kelways celebrates its fiftieth anniversary of iris growing during 1998.) May and June are the best months for seeing the peony and iris fields awash with pastel hues; the once-famous four-acre Peony Valley has recently been re-sited in a weed-free valley, and is building up steam to become *the* early summer sight of Somerset. It will be opened formally in 1999, featuring around 500 different varieties.

The Kelways colour catalogue features a range of these choice plants, plus an interesting selection of day lilies. The plant centre stocks around 100 each of irises and peonies at any one time, but others can be ordered for dispatch during the lifting seasons – August and September for irises, and November to February for peonies. Send a s.a.e. for catalogue.

LOCAL WILLOW CRAFTS

The flat, wet lowlands of the Somerset Levels provide fertile grazing for cattle and a rich habitat for marshland birds. Willow trees flourish here, too, in sodden fields that yield forests of canes (withies) for the thriving local industry of basket-making. Gardeners will find it well worth exploring this ancient and mysterious fenland to seek out the village of Stoke St Gregory, about 7m W of Langport, in the heart of 'withy country'.

The ***English Hurdle Company, Curload, Stoke St Gregory, Taunton TA3 6JD (tel. 01823-698418), 1¾m from East Lyng off the Taunton–Glastonbury road (A361),*** *specializes in willow hurdles, plant climbers, arches and arbours, hand-made on the premises. They also sell by mail (catalogue free on request). Open Mon–Fri, 9a.m.–5p.m., and Sat, 9a.m.–1p.m. At* ***P.H. Coate and Son, Meare Green Court, Stoke St Gregory, Taunton TA3 6HY (tel. 01823-490249), signposted to the Willows and Wetland Visitor Centre from Durston on the Taunton–Glastonbury road (A361),*** *you can buy flattish, trug-like baskets, intended for cut flowers, but even more useful for carting about secateurs, twine, trowels, hand-forks, tough gloves, etc. Mon–Fri you can watch the skilled basket-makers at work; there is also an interesting visitor centre showing the history of this local rural craft. Open all year, Mon–Sat, 9a.m.–5p.m.*

PORLOCK

Greencombe

Porlock TA24 8NU TEL. *01643-862363* OWNER *Greencombe Garden Trust* HOURS *April–July and Oct–Nov, Sat–Tues, 2–6p.m. or by appointment* ENTRANCE *£3, children 50p. No dogs* DIRECTIONS *On minor road to Porlock Weir, ½m W of Porlock*

SPRING SUMMER AUTUMN WINTER

Café | Plant Shop | NPC

The three-and-a-half-acre garden at Greencombe clings snugly to a wooded hillside on the northern edge of Exmoor, gazing out over the Severn sea. On a clear day, you can see the coast of South Wales on the horizon and the undulating shadow of the Brecon Beacons beyond, formed of the same ancient red sandstone on which Greencombe itself is built.

There has been a garden here for over 50 years, the first 20 of which were due to one Horace Stroud, a keen plantsman. He was followed by the present owner, Joan Loraine, who retired from a globe-trotting career as a schoolteacher in the colonies to tend more diminutive charges, her National Collection of erythroniums, or dog-tooth violets. They peak in April, while other springtime features include drifts of snowflakes, hellebores and primulas that complement the glorious woodland scenes of magnolias, rhododendrons and Japanese acers.

According to Joan Loraine, it is 'a lunatic place in which to garden', facing directly north, in the shadow of a steep hill with little soil overlaying the sandstone. Fortunately, that does not stop her from tending the garden, or the rest of us enjoying its special atmosphere and tranquillity.

SOUTH PETHERTON

Avon Bulbs

Burnt House Farm, Mid-Lambrook, South Petherton TA13 5HE **TEL.** *01460-242177* **OWNER** *C. Ireland-Jones* **HOURS** *Mail order only*

SPRING SUMMER AUTUMN WINTER

Nursery | Mail Order

'Raising plants is in the blood,' says Chris Ireland-Jones who grew up in Zimbabwe, where his parents farmed tobacco. After training in agriculture and a brief spell in printing Chris bought the nursery (then based at Bradford-on-Avon) and moved it here in 1990 where it goes from strength to strength, and frequently wins gold medals from the Royal Horticultural Society.

Bulbs make perfect mail order plants, being easy to pack and post while dormant. The colour catalogue (send 4 × 2nd-class stamps) lists many tempting varieties, including around 20 different fritillaries, 25 cyclamen and 25 alliums.

(I have some spectacular *Lilium regale* bought from Chris, which dependably produce whopping 6ft stems packed with fragrant flowers.)

Twenty different snowdrop species are offered 'in the green' (i.e. while in leaf) in springtime, when they have a better replanting success rate. Look out, too, for some wonderful exotics, such as *Arum palestinum*, surely Cruella de Ville's own flower, bearing deeply sinister maroon-black cowled blooms with a velvety texture. Unusual tulip species are another speciality. If you intend to visit, though, it's essential to phone before travelling any distance due to the seasonality of the stock.

SOUTH PETHERTON

East Lambrook Manor Garden

East Lambrook, nr South Petherton TA13 5HL TEL. *01460-240328* OWNER *Mr and Mrs A. Norton* HOURS *March–Oct, Mon–Sat, 10a.m.–5p.m.* ENTRANCE *£2.50, OAPs £2, children and students 50p* DIRECTIONS *7m E of Ilminster, 2m N of South Petherton, signposted*

SPRING SUMMER AUTUMN WINTER

Gift Shop | Café | Nursery | NPC

This is one of the most famous cottage gardens in the country, surrounding a substantial 15th-century farmhouse of the local ochre Ham stone. It became the home of Margery and Walter Fish in the late 1930s and *We Made a Garden*, Margery's pithy and endearing account of the garden's development, was published in 1956; it quickly became a classic and is still in print (and on sale at East Lambrook, so if you haven't already read it buy a copy; you won't be disappointed).

Margery was passionate about cottage garden plants and keen to save old varieties that could become extinct. She wanted the garden to be 'as modest and unpretentious as the house, a cottage garden in fact, with crooked paths and unexpected corners'. This she achieved, in spite of Walter's insistence on neat lawns, good wide paths and formal, trim hedges.

Today's two-acre garden, in the care of the Norton family, continues the spirit of Margery Fish's cottage garden style, with formidable collections of herbaceous plants including many rarities, and the National Collection of hardy geraniums, the cranesbills loved by Margery. Allow yourself to be seduced by the narrow, come-hither paths that lead into different parts of the garden, but don't miss the adjoining Margery Fish Nursery with its exceptional range of well-grown plants (open same times as garden).

TINTINHULL

Tintinhull House Garden

Farm Street, Tintinhull, nr Yeovil BA22 9PZ **TEL.** *01935-822545* **OWNER** *The National Trust* **HOURS** *Late March–late Sept, Wed–Sun, 12 noon–6p.m., also Bank Holiday Mons, 12a.m.–6p.m.* **ENTRANCE** *£3.50, children £1.80* **DIRECTIONS** *½m south of A303 on edge of Tintinhull village*

SPRING SUMMER AUTUMN WINTER

Café DON'T MISS

This intimate garden, attached to a substantial, beautiful house in the local honey-coloured limestone, covers little more than one acre but packs in a great deal, being divided into separate rooms in early 20th-century style. It was laid out in the 1930s by Phyllis Reiss, a keen amateur gardener, but became especially famous during the tenure of Penelope Hobhouse, the gardening writer and designer, who lived here from 1979–1994.

Penelope says it appeals because it is 'a marvellous, educational garden. Each of its parts can be closely related to the size of many modern gardens, and any one of them can be looked at as though it is a single garden'.

There are hot borders of yellow and red flowers blended with purple foliage, a white garden arranged around a circular fountain, and lawned areas bordered by artistically arranged shrubs, perennials and spring bulbs. A long, flagstone path running straight from the main door of the house to the end of the garden is a bold, inspired creation, and is tremendously effective. But for me, the most engaging area is the kitchen garden. It is thoroughly traditional and workmanlike, with neat rows of vegetables and salads set off by big clumps of euphorbia, with sweet peas garlanding the bean-poles, and scarlet and orange daylilies complementing the bright yellow flowers of courgettes.

Celebrity Choice

Fred Whitsey, gardening correspondent for
The Daily Telegraph

'I have always very much admired the garden at ***Tintinhull****. It is, in my opinion, one of the most important gardens in the country and was made, like so many other really good gardens, by an amateur, Mrs Phyllis Reiss, whom I knew.*

'Tintinhull combines three essential elements for a good garden: firstly, it has a very coherent design; it is divided into "rooms" and their proportions seem exactly right to me. Secondly, it has very well-considered use of colour schemes. And thirdly, it is full of good plantsmanship; there is, within its comparatively small space, a very large collection of plants and they are so cleverly arranged. It only came into prominence in the 1950s, when it was handed over to the National Trust by Mrs Reiss, but we have her to thank for its inspired arrangement and planting.'

And also...

Kim Woodward and Rupert Ashmore make and sell **Ashmore Trugs** from their workshop at **Higher Farmhouse, Shepton Montague, Wincanton BA9 8JJ (tel. 01749-812998).** Rupert makes a variety of high- and low-sided styles in solid pine and Kim paints them in pale blue, yellow, turquoise or antique/distressed finish (the most popular), but the range is also available unpainted. Kim paints special commissions to order. Trugs are also available by mail, for which there is a free colour catalogue.

The National Trust's **Barrington Court, Barrington, nr Ilminster TA19 0NQ (tel. 01460-241938)**, offers a pleasing afternoon's ramble through excellently maintained Edwardian flower gardens influenced by Gertrude Jekyll. Barrington features a white and an iris garden, shrub roses, a lily garden and a magnificent working kitchen garden, plus pleasant tree-lined walks. Open late March–late Oct, daily except Fri, 11a.m.–5.30p.m. (last adm. 5p.m.). Entrance £4, children £2.

Broadleigh Gardens, Bishops Hull, Taunton TA4 1AE, sells bulbs by mail order only (send 2 × 1st-class stamps for a catalogue). The January catalogue features bulbs in growth, such as galanthus, cyclamen and some herbaceous plants; June's catalogue concentrates on dwarf and unusual bulbs. You can also visit the bulb fields in season.

Lower Severalls Nursery, Crewkerne TA18 7NX (tel. 01460-73234), is a handsome stone farmhouse draped with fremontodendron and clematis, and is surrounded by cottage-garden borders. Herbs fill out the display areas beyond, and scented geraniums, culinary herbs and salvias are among the specialities in this appealing nursery. Open daily, except Thurs, 10a.m.–5p.m., Sun 2–5p.m. Entrance £1.50.

Scotts Nurseries at Merriott TA16 5PL (tel. 01460-72306) grows a vast range of stock, especially apples. Since apples have been a speciality for well over a century, local and ancient varieties are well represented. They also grow extensive ranges of roses, shrubs, trees and climbers, available at the garden centre and also through their mail order catalogue (price £1.50). Scotts' jewel-bright rose fields are a local tourist attraction in summer (ask at the garden centre for directions). Open Mon–Sat, 9a.m.–5p.m., and Sun, 10.30a.m.–4.30p.m.

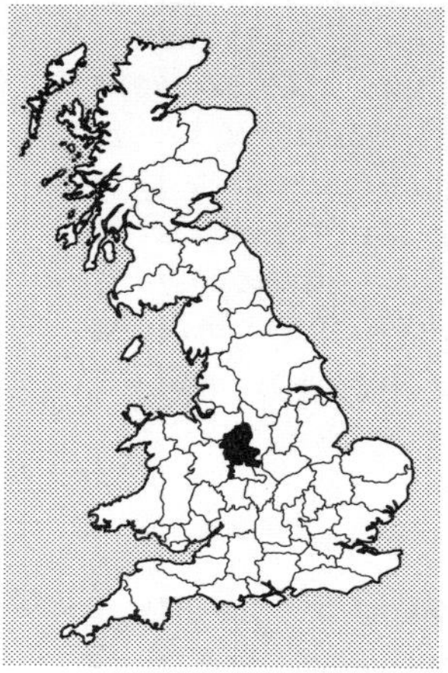

Staffordshire

MAP NO. 5

The M6 motorway slices straight through Staffordshire, linking the industrial conurbations of Birmingham and the Black Country to Liverpool and Manchester. Away from the urban and industrial areas, the 17,000 acres of Cannock Chase embrace miles of beautiful countryside, heath and woodland, threaded with streams and dotted with the remains of Iron Age hill forts. It was once a medieval hunting forest, but these days people are only out hunting for picnic spots, or a bit of peace and quiet.

ALTON

Alton Towers

Alton, Stoke-on-Trent ST10 4DB TEL. *0990-204060* OWNER *Tussauds Group* HOURS MID-*March–early Nov, daily, 9.30a.m.–5p.m. (some later closings in summer)* ENTRANCE *£19, OAPs £6.50, children £15* DIRECTIONS *18m E of Stoke-on-Trent, Jct 15 or 16 of M6 (signposted everywhere)*

SPRING SUMMER AUTUMN WINTER

Gift Shop Café

'The work of a morbid imagination joined to the command of unlimited resources', was gardening pundit J.C. Loudon's summary of Alton Towers in 1822, but then he had an axe to grind because his own proposals for the garden had been rejected. Today, mention of Alton Towers is most likely to conjure images of funfairs and dare-devil rides, but the gardens around the fairground are spectacular, too, set against the gothic backdrop of the ruined hall.

The park covers 500 acres, with a large rock garden cascading down a valley, out of which rise spires of assorted conifers, with sprinklings of golden- and crimson-leaved trees lighting up the landscape. It is an eccentric and romantic place, with delightful garden features, including ornamental pools and a Chinese pagoda fountain, a long walk through a succession of arches fashioned out of sculpted yew, and a very splendid conservatory with beautiful detailing in its curved, domed roof. Do not miss the chance of a cable-car ride from the theme park, gaining an unusual aerial view of the grounds.

LORD ANSON'S BLUE PEA

When Admiral Lord Anson (of Shugborough, q.v.*) returned from his four-year voyage round the world, he inadvertently brought with him horticultural treasure, as well as great material riches. Green food was scarce during the long voyages, but the sailors found an edible pea at Port San Julian, Patagonia, and the ship's cook brought home a few seeds. The plant's bloom was a gem, with sweetly scented, warm blue flowers on a climbing stem with grey-green, slightly fleshy foliage. Lord Anson's pea,* Lathyrus nervosus, *is a perennial of borderline hardiness, and grows best in rich, well-drained soil in a sunny, sheltered position.*

BIDDULPH

Biddulph Grange

Biddulph, Stoke-on-Trent ST8 7SD TEL. *01782-517999*
OWNER *The National Trust* HOURS *April–Oct, Wed–Fri, 12 noon–6p.m., Sat–Sun and Bank Holiday Mons, 11a.m.–6p.m. Last adm. 5.30p.m. or dusk if sooner. Also Sat–Sun in Nov and early Dec, 12 noon–4p.m. or dusk*
ENTRANCE *£4 (Nov–Dec £2), children £2 (Nov–Dec £1)*
DIRECTIONS *½m N of Biddulph, 3½m SE of Congleton, 7m N of Stoke-on-Trent, access from A527 Tunstall–Congleton road*

SPRING SUMMER AUTUMN WINTER

Gift Shop Café

DON'T MISS

Occasionally I come across an old garden that is so extraordinary I wish its maker was still around, so that I could find out more about his or her inspirations and intentions in making it. Biddulph Grange is such a garden; it was made in the mid-19th century, at a time when Britain was rich: from industry at home, and exploiting its Empire abroad. With explorations opening up distant corners of the world, new plants were coming to Britain by the shipload, and new images of culture in other lands caused equal excitement.

At Biddulph Grange you can thus take a mini-world tour. You may go through a Chinese water garden via a Scottish glen; enter a half-timbered cottage, but find the exit is an Egyptian tomb guarded by sphinxes; you may stroll down a stepped pathway lined with hundreds of dahlias from Mexico, or wander among a grove of rhododendrons from Nepal and Sikkim. The house was built with Italian villas in mind, and there are monkey puzzles from Chile, all the rage in Victorian gardens after their rediscovery in 1844.

This is certainly a garden for all seasons, and all tastes. The area called China is especially thrilling. It has a willow-pattern bridge and an ornate temple lined with tiny brass bells, both brightly painted, and nearby a fabulous, gilded water buffalo, gazing out from the shade of a painted canopy. For sheer drama, this 15-acre garden is not to be missed, and is hugely enjoyable in every season.

MILFORD

Shugborough

Milford, nr Stafford ST17 0XB TEL. *01889-881388* OWNER *The National Trust* HOURS *End March–late Sept, daily, 11a.m.–5p.m., and Sun only in Oct* ENTRANCE *£1.50 per vehicle for park (inc. NT members); house £3.50, concessions £2.50* DIRECTIONS *6m E of Stafford on A513, entrance at Milford. Signposted from M6 Jct 13*

SPRING SUMMER AUTUMN WINTER

Access | Gift Shop | Café

This is the ancestral home of the 5th Earl of Lichfield, more widely known as Patrick Lichfield, photographer of society debutantes and Pirelli calendar babes. The 900-acre property is now owned by the National Trust and administered by the local council, but its creation has romantic origins.

Much of its redesign in the 18th century was due to an injection of money, resulting from Admiral Anson's capture of a Spanish treasure ship. The local village, with its cottages, fields, mills and roads, was removed for the benefit of the park, while the old village mill-pond was elevated to the status of a grand lake. Chinese and classical buildings were dotted about the landscape (even on land which did not belong to the Ansons), and scenes were created throughout the grounds to invoke 18th-century ideals of 'delicious melancholy' in their beholder.

Forming suitably grand surroundings around a very palatial mansion, it is a garden of level, open spaces, magnificent old trees and water, retaining some 18th-century 'melancholy', overlaid with Victorian terraces and attractive flower gardens.

And also...

Cottage Garden Roses, Woodlands House, Stretton, nr Stafford ST19 9LG (tel. 01785-840217), is run by John and Teresa Scarman, whose nursery specializes in old-fashioned roses. (There are now branches of the nursery in Europe, where it is known as Roses du Temps Passé.) John Scarman was apprenticed to designer-plantswoman Rosemary Verey and later worked with David Austin Roses, but he and Teresa are now devoted to rescuing and reintroducing worthy but forgotten rose varieties. There is an excellent colour catalogue (£1.50) for buying roses by mail. Open daily, 9a.m.–6p.m.

The 20-acre **Eccleshall Castle Gardens, Eccleshall ST21 6LS (tel. 01785-850151)**, surround a William and Mary mansion house among romantic castle ruins. An ancient lime avenue sets the scene from the entrance, and there are massed rhododendrons followed by roses, herbaceous border and formally planted espalier pears. Open whole of Easter week and mid-May–mid-Aug, Wed and Sun, 1–5.30p.m. Entrance by donation.

Moseley Old Hall, Moseley Old Hall Lane, Fordhouses, Wolverhampton WV10 7HY (tel. 01902-782808), features a reconstruction of a small, 17th-century garden. It is very formal, with a vine-covered tunnel, and a box parterre, the design of which was taken from Thomas Hill's influential book, *The Gardener's Labyrinth*, of 1577. There are old-variety fruit trees, musk roses and naturalised wildflowers in this disciplined but engaging garden. Open late March–May, Sat–Sun, June–Oct, Sat–Sun, Wed (also Tues, July–Aug), 1.30–5.30p.m., Nov–mid-Dec, Sun, 1.30–4p.m., also Bank Holiday Mons, 11a.m.–5p.m. and Tues following 1.30–5.30p.m. Entrance (house and garden) £3.60, children £1.80, family ticket £9.

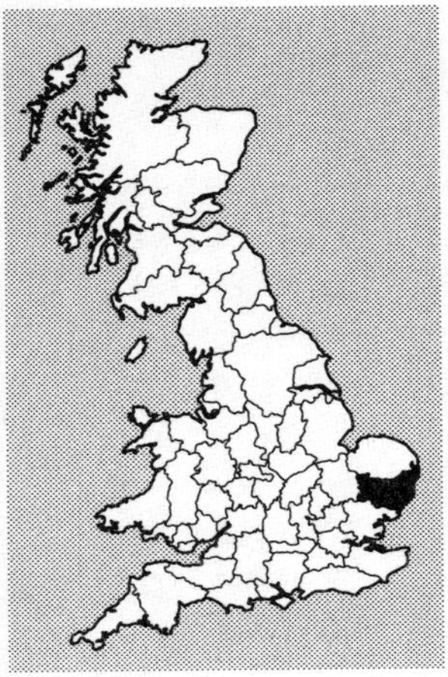

Suffolk

MAP NOs 3, 6

Since Anglo-Saxon times, this has been known as the county of 'southern folk', the 'north folk' living in Norfolk. At the time of the Domesday Book *(in 1086) this was the most densely populated region in England; its fens were drained and forests cleared to make way for arable farming and the raising of sheep. The wool industry brought wealth to Suffolk; its merchants built their timbered houses and fine churches in countless villages and towns, with especially lovely examples at Lavenham and Long Melford. The pounding North Sea continually erodes the sandy beaches and low cliffs of the coast, while further inland the atmosphere is quietly pastoral, much as it was in John Constable's day.*

CODDENHAM

Shrubland Hall Gardens

Coddenham, nr Ipswich IP6 9QH **TEL.** *01473-830449 (for booking in to the health clinic only: 01473-830404)* **OWNER** *Lord de Saumarez* **HOURS** *April–early Sept, Sun only, 2–5p.m.; also Bank Holiday Mons, 2–5p.m.* **ENTRANCE** *£2.50, OAPs/children £1.50* **DIRECTIONS** *4m N of Ipswich, turn off A14 to B1113 at Claydon*

SPRING SUMMER AUTUMN WINTER

Access

There are two ways you can get fit at Shrubland Hall; you can check in as a patient at its health clinic and spend a few days following a regime of raw-food diets and remedial treatments or you can spend an afternoon pacing its grand gardens, running up and down the 100-step Italianate staircase. (The Hall is not open to the visiting public.)

The gardens were laid out by Sir Charles Barry, after he completed the Houses of Parliament in 1860. The owners, inspired by their visits to the great Italian gardens, commissioned Barry to create a series of terraces and stairways to descend from their hilltop house. In its heyday, Shrubland was renowned for its gaudy bedding schemes laid out in endless elaborate parterres. Most of them were swept away by the influential gardener William Robinson (*q.v.*) in the 1880s. Robinson abhorred formal, unnatural bedding and he endeavoured to soften the stonework of the terraces in a mantle of roses and vines.

Hidden in the 50-acre grounds are several notable features, including an Algerian summerhouse of larch poles and bamboo, and a large rock garden built in the 1930s by Walter Ingwersen, of the eponymous alpine nursery in Sussex. The conservatory is fine, too, and there is a programme of restoration under way to rescue the scroll-design box maze and dell garden. Among the park's fine trees are several sweet chestnuts planted by monks about 700 years ago, now stooping, venerable specimens with portly girths. Helmingham Hall (*q.v.*) is nearby. (Wheelchair access around the gardens is limited.)

LOCAL HERO: HUMPHRY REPTON

Born at Bury St Edmunds in 1752, Humphry Repton was the son of an excise officer and educated locally, before being sent to Holland, aged 12. Partially adopted by a wealthy and influential family, he grew up in luxurious surroundings and acquired the manners of a cosmopolitan gentleman. Later, unsuccessful business attempts led him to try out his artistic talents as a landscape gardener, and here he found his métier.

Repton's style favoured balustraded terraces and flowerbeds, rather than the pure grass-and-trees approach of his predecessor, Capability Brown (q.v.)*; his famous Red Books illustrated clients' existing gardens, with flap pages that could be overlaid to demonstrate how the grounds could be improved. Handsome, charming and intelligent, he became greatly sought after. Examples of his work can be seen at Holkham Hall* (q.v.)*, Tatton Park* (q.v.)*, Sheringham and Sheffield Park* (q.v.).

LOWESTOFT

Somerleyton Hall

Somerleyton, nr Lowestoft NR32 5QQ TEL. *01502-730224* OWNER *Lord and Lady Somerleyton* HOURS *Grounds and tearooms April–June, Sept, Sun, Thurs and Bank Holidays, 12.30–5.30p.m.; July–Aug, Sun, Tues–Thurs and Bank Holiday Mons, 12.30–5.30p.m.; Hall 1.30–5.30p.m. Hall and grounds close at 5p.m. in winter* ENTRANCE *£4.20, OAPs £3.80, children aged 5–16 £1.95, family ticket (2 adults, 2 children) £11.70* DIRECTIONS *5m NW of Lowestoft on B1074, 7m SW of Yarmouth on A143*

SPRING SUMMER AUTUMN WINTER

Access | Gift Shop | Café | Plant Shop

Somerleyton Hall has 12 acres of dignified gardens, fragrant in spring when the azaleas and bluebells are in bloom, and pleasantly colourful in summer. The walled garden, at the entrance, has interesting glasshouses with ridge-and-furrow patterned roofs, designed by Sir Joseph Paxton. There are also unusual 'wall-cases' by Paxton along the outer wall, made for growing wall-trained peaches under glass, but now displaying broader ranges of greenhouse plants.

In the grounds beyond there are Victorian shrubberies and fine specimen trees which bring height and shade to the level site. There is a formal rose garden and terrace on the west front, a sunk garden with bedding plant displays by the conservatory tearoom, and a long iron tunnel of roses and wisteria. The yew maze, by Victorian garden designer W.A. Nesfield, has a grassy mount topped by a pagoda at its centre, very popular with visitors.

STANTON

Wyken Hall

Stanton, Bury St Edmunds IP31 2DW TEL. *01359-250287* OWNER *K.M. Carlisle* HOURS *Feb–24 Dec, Thurs–Fri, Sun and Bank Holiday Mons, 10a.m.–6p.m. (Thurs–Sat, from 7p.m.*

the Leaping Hare Vineyard Restaurant is open) ENTRANCE *£2, OAPs £1.50, children under 16 free* DIRECTIONS *9m NE of Bury St Edmunds off A143. Follow brown tourist signs to Wyken Vineyards*

SPRING SUMMER AUTUMN WINTER

Access | Gift Shop | Café | Plant Shop | DON'T MISS

Wyken Hall is an exquisite Elizabethan manor house, plastered and pargeted in the local vernacular style, and painted the colour of raw salmon, a shade or two more daring than the average Suffolk pink. At the front, several rocking chairs, brought from Mississippi, peer between espaliered apple trees growing on very tall stems, in the manner more usually used for pleached limes. You know the garden will be interesting, for it has twists of originality, while maintaining traditional form. Also at the front is a quincunx pattern of brick-and-flint circles with low box hedging, and seasonal infills of flowers.

Beyond, there is a small garden of edibles beside the house, leading to a border of hot colours – scarlet roses, geums and salvias among bronze-leaved impatiens and dahlias, for example. There are three small, linked gardens of traditional, formal design with box and yew hedging, herbs and a dining terrace, a rose garden with central fountain, a kitchen garden and orchard. A nuttery and dell features mown walks through long grasses and wildflowers leading to a young maze of copper-beech hedging. There are also fine old oaks in the grounds. From the wilder areas there are lovely views back to the house, which squats low and content in its wood-enshrouded gardens, while its ornate chimneys attempt to pierce the skyline.

STOWMARKET

Helmingham Hall

Stowmarket IP14 6EF TEL. *01473-890363* OWNER *Lord and Lady Tollemache* HOURS *End April–early Sept, Sun only, 2–6p.m. Also pre-booked parties or individuals on Wed,*

2–5p.m. ENTRANCE *£3.50, concessions £3, children £2*
DIRECTIONS *9m N of Ipswich on B1077*

SPRING SUMMER AUTUMN WINTER

Access | Gift Shop | Cafe | Plant Shop | DON'T MISS

East Anglia possesses more than its fair share of moated properties. Moats were frequently dug in the Middle Ages to protect crops and livestock, or give a house added security. Helmingham Hall is a house of finely patterned brickwork, built in the 15th century. It sits in its own deep water moat, while another, rectangular moat to one side contains its walled garden. The garden moat is thought to have been made in Saxon times as a secure cattle enclosure, its boundary fence having been replaced by a wall in 1745.

Within those walls lies a garden of outstanding quality, with exuberant herbaceous borders framing kitchen-garden beds of fruit and vegetables; fruit trees are also fanned against the walls. Tunnels over the paths are engagingly garlanded with sweet peas, runner beans and gourds, and the turf paths bring a note of calm order to anchor the abundance of summer colour.

A herb and knot garden on the opposite side of the house features fragrant masses of old roses, lavender, violas and herbs, and there is a skilfully laid-out knot garden in low box hedging. The banks of the moats are awash with daffodils and cowslips in spring, followed by pink clover and ox-eye daisies in the long grass. It is a peaceful, timeless place, utterly in tune with its surroundings. Shrubland Hall (*q.v.*) is nearby.

And also...

Goldbrook Plants, Hoxne, Eye IP21 5AN (tel. 01379-668770), specializes in hostas (over 400 varieties), hemerocallis and shade-loving perennials. Mail order (send 4 × 1st-class stamps for catalogue). Open Feb–Dec, Thurs–Sun, 10.30a.m.–6p.m. Closed Jan, Chelsea and Hampton Court Flower Show periods.

Hintlesham Hall, George Street, Hintlesham, Ipswich IP8 3NS (tel. 01473-652334), is of Tudor origins (built by the grandson of the 3rd Duke of Norfolk), overlaid with an elegant Georgian façade. Nowadays it is a splendid luxurious hotel, with a herb garden designed by Beth Chatto for Robert Carrier (a former owner) supplying the kitchen. The gardens are open only to guests staying at the hotel.

Perforated seep-hoses are available by mail order from **Leaky Pipe Garden Systems, Whitehouse Farm, Grundisburgh, Woodbridge IP13 6RR (tel. 01473-738280).** They gently leak water into the soil and are a good way to put irrigation exactly where you need it, at the plants' roots (especially effective when used in conjunction with a digital timer).

Mill Farm Plants and Gardens, Norwich Road, Mendlesham IP14 5NQ (tel. 01449-766425), specializes in garden pinks, with extensive collections of rare old pinks and some of the best modern hybrids – fringed, laced and sweetly scented. Send 5 × 2nd-class stamps for mail order catalogue. Open Feb–Dec, Wed–Mon, 9a.m.–5.30p.m.

Pearl Sulman, 54 Kingsway, Mildenhall, Bury St Edmunds IP28 7HR (tel. 01638-712297), specializes in growing miniature and dwarf pelargoniums, by mail order only. Also at this address, Brian Sulman (separate business) offers regal pelargoniums by mail.

Plants of Distinction, Abacus House, Station Yard, Needham Market IP6 8AS (tel. 01449-721720), offers rarely available seeds (e.g. unusual tropaeolums and many meconopsis species) and choice plants (e.g. *Thunbergia grandiflora* for conservatories and assorted perennial foxgloves) by mail.

Sun House, Hall Street, Long Melford CO10 9HZ (tel. 01787-378252), has richly planted, intimate walled gardens with roses, shrubs, herbaceous plants and over

100 clematis. It is lovingly tended by Maureen and John Thompson, who offer bed-and-breakfast (from around £25 per person) in their studio cottage in the garden, an ideal base for touring the region. The garden is otherwise open only on selective dates – ring first to check. Entrance £2 (given to charity), school-age children free.

Over 2500 different flower and vegetable seeds are available in the full-colour mail order catalogue of **Thompson & Morgan Seeds, Poplar Lane, Ipswich IP8 3BU (tel. 01473-601090).** Notable recent introductions include *Agrostemma* 'Ocean Pearl', *Sphaeralcea* 'Los Brisas' and the flavourful main crop pea 'Rondo'. Their catalogue is also worth combing for interesting species plants.

Michael Loftus ran the well-known Neals Yard Wholefoods in London before leaving to start **Woottens Plants, Wenhaston, Blackheath, Halesworth IP19 9HD (tel. 01502-478258)**, in the early 1990s. The nursery offers hardy and half-hardy perennial plants, including pelargoniums, salvias, penstemons, violas, aquilegias, polemoniums and much more. There is an illustrated catalogue costing £2.50 containing 2000 plants, but no mail order service is available, so you must visit to buy. Open daily, except Christmas period, 9.30a.m.–5p.m.

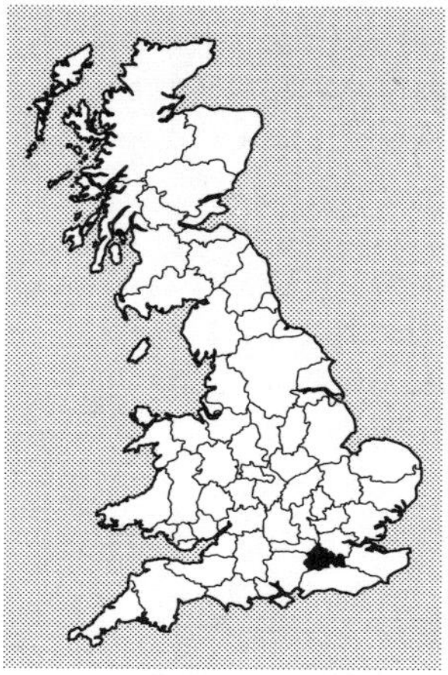

Surrey

MAP NO. 3

London spreads its urban tentacles into the northern reaches of Surrey, and this county is very much commuter-land with frequent rail services into the City. Substantial areas are still rural, however, and little has changed in parts of the wooded Old West Surrey that Gertrude Jekyll wrote about 100 years ago. Wealden Surrey fared much as Wealden Sussex in earlier centuries, where forests were felled for iron smelting. The chalk ridges of the North Downs provide good walking country, including wooded Ranmore Common and the steep escarpment of Box Hill, which was familiar to Jane Austen and her heroine Emma.

DORKING

Polesden Lacey

Great Bookham, nr Dorking RH5 6BD **TEL.** *01372-458203/452048* **OWNER** *The National Trust* **HOURS** *Grounds open daily all year, 11a.m.–6p.m. (or dusk if sooner)* **ENTRANCE** *£3, house and grounds £6* **DIRECTIONS** *5m NW of Dorking, 2m S of Great Bookham, off A246*

SPRING SUMMER AUTUMN WINTER

Gift Shop Café

There are renowned flower gardens at Polesden Lacey, but at any time of year, my favourite part of the 30-acre garden is the Long Walk. It is a broad turf path that runs for quarter of a mile along the hillside, offering panoramic views of the opposite hill and the wooded valley between. It dates from 1761, but Richard Brinsley Sheridan, the playwright, had it considerably lengthened after he bought the property in 1797.

The flower gardens include a walled rose garden, dissected by lavender and box-edged paths, over which run pergolas of climbing roses. There are clematis here too, and an ancient Chinese wisteria. There are lavenders and irises in profusion, and further flower borders including a grand herbaceous border running for 450ft beneath a sunny wall. The winter garden is small but amazingly cheering and fragrant in the bleakest season, with winter-flowering shrubs, hellebores and carpets of early bulbs.

THE SHIRLEY POPPY

*Shirley, a village now engulfed by urban Croydon, lends its name to an exquisite bloom, bred by local vicar Revd William Wilks 100 years ago from a stray field poppy (*Papaver rhoeas*) found in his garden.*

Instead of the usual plain scarlet, this rogue's petals had a halo of white – providing a host of breeding possibilities. From its seeds the Revd Wilks bred generations of poppies, selecting only the best until he achieved an enhanced race bearing white, pastel pinks and double flowers as well as red, all with pale centres. Shirley poppies are still widely sold by seed merchants, although they are not always as true to type as Revd Wilks would have wished.

ESHER

Claremont Landscape Garden

Portsmouth Road, Esher KT10 9JG **TEL.** *01372-469421*
OWNER *The National Trust* **HOURS** *Open all year, Nov–March, daily, except Mons and 25 Dec, 10a.m.–5p.m. (or dusk); April–Oct, Mon–Fri, 10a.m.-6p.m., Sat–Sun and Bank Holidays, 10a.m.–7p.m. (closes 2p.m. in mid-July during concert festival); last adm. 30 minutes before closing*
ENTRANCE *£3, family ticket £8* **DIRECTIONS** *on S side of Esher, on E side of A307*

SPRING SUMMER AUTUMN WINTER

Access | Gift Shop | Café

THE LUTYENS AND JEKYLL PARTNERSHIP

The partnership of the architect Sir Edwin Lutyens (1869–1944) and plantswoman/writer Gertrude Jekyll (1843–1932) was a fruitful one, and their influence on 20th-century garden design has been profound. They collaborated on the planning of 120 gardens prior to the First World War; Jekyll's contribution was usually in providing planting plans (especially of colour-themed herbaceous borders) to embellish the hard landscaping that Lutyens designed. But there was also an energetic exchange of ideas between these two like-minded people, although they were a generation apart in age.

Both favoured using natural, indigenous materials such as local stone and timbers, and they sympathized with the aims of the Arts and Crafts movement. Both were also highly talented artists in their own fields and were fascinated and charmed by the formal gardens of the Italian Renaissance. Their work still survives to a greater or lesser degree at numerous properties around the country, including Lindisfarne Castle (q.v.) in Northumberland, Hestercombe (q.v.) in Somerset and here in Surrey, where it all began.

Lutyens designed Miss Jekyll's own house (not open) at ***Munstead Wood, Heath Lane, Busbridge, Godalming GU7 1UN (tel. 01483-417867)****, where her garden has been undergoing magnificent restoration work in recent years. It is open several days each year, for the National Gardens Scheme (tel. 01483-211535 for this year's dates). Entrance £2, OAPs £1, children free.*

Claremont is a wonderful venue for a picnic or a lakeside stroll, and has been since the 18th century (bring a hamper, a bottle of wine and good company for a matchless afternoon of tranquillity under its fine trees). Now it is revered by historians as one of the most important examples of the transitional stages between the formal gardens of the very early 18th century, and the more naturalistic landscapes that followed in succeeding generations.

Within the 49 acres that survive, it has a spectacular three-acre turf amphitheatre, which the National Trust puts to good use every July as an outdoor auditorium for evening picnics and musical entertainment, and there are numerous woodland paths among camellias and rhododendrons.

Sir John Vanbrugh, Charles Bridgeman and William Kent, the great trio of influential English designers in the early part of the 18th century, each left their mark on the garden. Vanbrugh designed the Belvedere, a hilltop viewing pavilion; the great turf amphitheatre was Bridgeman's work, while we have Kent to thank for the serenely contoured lake and woods. Lord Clive of India bought the estate in 1768 and employed Capability Brown (q.v.) to expand and further soften the contours of the garden. Brown brought in some of the fine cedars that thrive in this great garden today.

KINGSTON-UPON-THAMES

Hampton Court Palace

Hampton Court KT8 9AU **TEL.** *0181-7819500* **OWNER** *Historic Royal Palaces Agency* **HOURS** *Park: all year, daily, dawn–dusk. King's Privy Garden: April–mid-Oct (except 24–26 Dec), daily, 9.30a.m.–5.30p.m.; mid-Oct–March: 9.30a.m.–4p.m. (Mon opens 10.15a.m.)* **ENTRANCE** *Parking £2, garden: £1.70, children £1 (extra to see palace); maze £2, children £1.20; Privy Garden £2, children £1.20; all-inclusive ticket £8.50, OAPs £6.40, children (5–15) £5.60 (under 5s free)* **DIRECTIONS** *On A308 at junction of A309 on N side of bridge over Thames*

SPRING SUMMER AUTUMN WINTER

Access | Gift Shop | Café

This is the famous Thames-side palace of Tudor, Stuart and later kings and queens. Its long canal and avenues of trees radiating out from the palace in a *patte d'oie* (goose-foot) design were laid out in the formal French style by Charles II in 1662. They are reminiscent of the fabulous gardens Charles had seen being made at Versailles.

Today, Charles II's creation is overlaid by the splendour that was added by William III and Queen Mary, who came from Holland in 1689. The massive yew pyramids arranged in neat lines in front of the palace were originally small topiary obelisks, but 300 years of growth have thickened them into giant umbrellas in the lawns. Capability Brown (*q.v.*) worked here in 1768, and he is responsible for planting one of Hampton Court's most renowned features, the massive 'Black Hamburgh' grape vine. This gnarled, monster vine in its own glasshouse is said to have roots that reach the Thames. It produces plenty of grapes which are sometimes sold to the public during the months of August and September.

The maze, now slightly bare in places, is being restored over a five-year period, but visitors can still puzzle their way to its heart. The palace's most colourful areas are the enclosed sunken garden, lavishly bedded out for spring and summer; William III's Privy Garden, recently reopened after a massive restoration programme, which is a fabulous baroque garden of swirling parterres, box hedging, yew topiaries and period flowers, with a massive hornbeam tunnel trained over oak trelliswork, along one side. Hampton Court is the annual venue of Britain's largest outdoor horticultural show, which is spread over several days in mid-July.

OLD GARDENING BOOKS GALORE

Surrey is well served for reading matter when it comes to gardening, particularly where older books are concerned. ***Mike Park, 351 Sutton Common Road, Sutton SM3 9HZ (tel. 0181-641 7796),*** *is a Kew-trained horticulturist who exchanges his trowel (for some of the time) to run a business dealing in second-hand and antiquarian gardening books. Gardens, botany, flower arranging and general gardening come within his compass. He regularly sets up a sales stand at the Royal Horticultural Society's monthly Westminster shows, but also buys and sells by mail order.* ***Ivelet Books, 18 Fairlawn Drive, Redhill RH1 6JP (tel. 01737-764520),*** *also buys and sells gardening, botany, landscape architecture and natural history books by mail, and stocks many of the classic 20th-century works that are now out of print. They send out three or four catalogues each year (available on request).* ***Lloyds of Kew, 9 Mortlake Terrace, Kew, Richmond TW9 3DT (tel. 0181-940 2512),*** *faces more or less on to Kew Green, diagonally opposite the main gate of Kew Gardens. This shop also stocks a range of second-hand and antiquarian garden-related books, particularly botanical ones.*

PIRBRIGHT

Four Aces

Chapel Lane, Pirbright, nr Guildford GU24 0JY **TEL.** *01483-476226* **OWNER** *Mr and Mrs R. St John Wright* **HOURS** *Open several days end of June–early July for National Gardens Scheme, also pre-booked private visits welcome, May–July. Guide dogs only* **ENTRANCE** *£1.50, children 50p* **DIRECTIONS** *5m NW of Guildford on A322 Bagshot Road. Just before Brookwood arch, directly opposite West Hill Golf Club, turn left into Cemetery Pales. After just under 1m, turn sharp left after village sign into Chapel Lane. Four Aces is the 5th house on the right*

SPRING SUMMER AUTUMN WINTER

Access

DON'T MISS

Jane St John Wright is passionate about roses and her extremely pretty ⅔-acre garden is packed with them, draped over pergolas and arches, filling out borders and mixing them with pastel-coloured herbaceous perennials. The style is relaxed and cottagey, with a recently made formal herb garden, two ponds, and terraces studded with pots overflowing with summer flowers. It is a lovely, personal, romantic garden that brings many visitors pleasure every year, and has earned Jane requests from friends and neighbours to redesign their gardens.

RICHMOND

Ham House

Ham TW10 7RS **TEL.** *0181-940 1950* **OWNER** *The National Trust* **HOURS** *House: April–Oct, Sat–Wed, 1–5p.m. (last adm. 4.30p.m.). Garden open all year, daily, except Thurs–Fri, 10.30a.m.–6p.m. (or dusk if sooner). Closed 25–26 Dec and 1 Jan* **ENTRANCE** *House £5, children £2.50, family ticket £12.50; garden £1.50, children 75p* **DIRECTIONS** *On S bank of River Thames, W of A307 at*

Petersham. House is walkable from Richmond via Thames towpath (1½m)

SPRING | SUMMER | AUTUMN | WINTER

Access | Gift Shop | Café | Plant Shop

The splendid house (which is worth seeing – the room stewards are very informative) dates from the 17th century, and its 20-acre gardens are suitably formal to reflect the period style. The Cherry Garden, to one side, is a geometrical parterre of box-edged beds infilled with lavender and santolina (buzzing with bees through the summer), bound by hornbeam tunnels above yew hedging. There are spacious lawns on the south side of the house leading to a 'wilderness' in 17th-century style, with formal hedged enclosures and wildflowers in spring. The terrace beside the house has been recently restored with formal planting, too. The walled garden has a handsome orangery (where refreshments are served); also some fine old trees, a long border of flowers for cutting, and rose beds (of modern varieties) for summer colour.

It is a deservedly popular riverside venue for south-west Londoners, with spacious, well-kept grounds that are pleasant to stroll in at any season.

THE HILEYS' COLOURFUL EXOTICS

*Visitors to the Royal Horticultural Society's shows in London and around the country will be familiar with exotic displays by **Brian and Heather Hiley, 25 Little Woodcote Estate, Telegraph Track, off Woodmansterne Lane, Wallington SM5 4AU (tel. 0181-647 9679).** But the show displays are only a taster; visit the nursery in summer and you are treated to fabulous potted displays of aeoniums and agapanthus, cannas and clivias, pelargoniums and fuchsias, and much else. All are clustered around the old bicycles, well-pumps and other bygones that contribute to the character of this marvellous nursery. There is a mail order catalogue (send 3 × 1st-class stamps) listing their specialist range of tender perennials and grasses. Open all year, Wed–Sat, 9a.m.–5p.m., but phone before visiting between Oct and Easter.*

DON'T MISS

RICHMOND

The Royal Botanic Gardens, Kew

Kew, Richmond TW9 3AB TEL. *0181-940 1171 (recorded information)/0181-332 5000* OWNER *Ministry of Agriculture, Fisheries and Food* HOURS *Open all year, daily, except 25 Dec and 1 Jan, 9.30a.m.–4p.m. (winter), closing later in summer (up to 7p.m., depending on season)* ENTRANCE *£4.50, OAPs/students £3, children (5–16) £2.50, family ticket £12* DIRECTIONS *Main gate on Kew Green, S of Kew Bridge; Kew Gardens underground station is nearby*

SPRING SUMMER AUTUMN WINTER

Access | Gift Shop | Café | DON'T MISS

Whether you arrive at the main gate on Kew Green, or the Victoria Gate (with its shop and visitor centre) which is convenient for Kew Gardens station, you will not be far from the chief attractions, Kew's great glasshouses. The Princess of Wales Conservatory has carefully controlled micro-climates ideal for plants from bone-dry deserts as well as those from humid tropical rainforest (do not miss the huge *Victoria amazonica* waterlilies with leaves up to 8ft across). The famous Victorian Palm House is home to yet more weird and wonderful plants from other lands, as is the even prettier Temperate House. Both were designed by Decimus Burton, the gifted Victorian architect.

Yet Kew's 300 acres encompass a great deal more. They were originally two 18th-century royal estates and, although the gardens are steeped in history, they are renowned worldwide for scientific research and their important botanical collections. Kew Palace is a pretty brick house in the Dutch style, with small formal gardens attached and a laburnum arched walkway, lovely in May. There are long walks through the arboretum to the pagoda, and several pretty stone temples are dotted about the grounds. The Marianne North Gallery, some distance from the main attractions, is one of Kew's most fascinating but least-known assets. It is crammed with the astonishing flower and landscape paintings of Miss North, an intrepid woman who travelled through remote parts of the world, usually alone, in the mid-19th century.

WOKING

RHS Wisley Gardens

Wisley, nr Woking GU23 6QB TEL. *01483-224234* OWNER *The Royal Horticultural Society* HOURS *Open all year, Mon–Sat, 10a.m.–7p.m. (or dusk if sooner); 10a.m.–4.30p.m. in winter; also Sundays, for RHS members only* ENTRANCE *£5, children £1.75 (RHS members free)* DIRECTIONS *7m NE of Guildford, by A3; signposted from A3 and Jct 10 of M25*

SPRING SUMMER AUTUMN WINTER

Access · Gift Shop · Café · Plant Shop · DON'T MISS

Wisley is the gardeners' Mecca, in all sorts of ways. As the flagship garden of the Royal Horticultural Society, its 240 acres demonstrate every conceivable method of gardening and its huge popularity (over 700,000 visitors per year) has led to recent revisions and replanning which will be undertaken over a period of years. Some people (myself included) come to saunter through the gardens in all seasons, for there are always new plants to admire.

The grounds, occupying an undulating site of sandy soil, are graced by many mature trees, among which are areas devoted to mixed flower borders, bedding plant displays, heathers, conifers, rhododendrons and associated plants, Mediterranean plants, fruit trees, vegetable gardens, small model gardens, hedging plants, wonderful glasshouses, and much more. The early 20th-century rock garden, on a hillside, is one of the best of its kind, and there are lovely water gardens below it. There are also scientific trial grounds which are always interesting, where different varieties of certain plants are grown together and compared. Another reason to visit is the extremely well-stocked horticultural and botanical bookshop, and the plant centre is renowned for its well-grown and well-cared-for plants, selected with a discerning eye.

And also...

There is nothing extraordinary about **Chessington Nurseries, Leatherhead Road, Chessington KT9 2NG (tel. 01372-744490)**, nothing, that is, until you stroll into the glasshouses at the rear of this suburban garden centre. This is what makes a visit worthwhile, for there are indoor plant displays that almost rival those of a major botanical garden. Citrus trees and passiflora are specialities, but the whole range of conservatory plants is tremendous. Open all year, Mon–Sat, 9a.m.–6p.m., Sun, 10a.m.–4p.m.

Drummonds of Bramley, Birtley Farm, Horsham Road, Bramley GU5 0LA (tel. 01483-898766), is a two-and-a-half-acre site strewn with an ever-changing selection of architectural antiques and salvage, including old garden ornaments and statuary, iron gates, garden seats, Victorian glass cloches, etc. Great for a rummage around to find something unusual or with a period ambience. Open daily (except 25–26 Dec, 1 Jan and Good Friday), weekdays, 9a.m.–6p.m., weekends, 10a.m.–5p.m.

Green Farm Plants, Bury Court, Bentley GU10 5LZ (tel. 01420-23202), has an enviable reputation for producing an interesting selection of well-grown hardy perennials. The new premises at Bury Court includes a display garden by Dutch plantsman Piet Oudolf. There is no mail order, but the catalogue (send 3 × 1st-class stamps) gives you an idea of the stock grown. Open mid-March–late Oct, Wed–Sat, 10a.m.–6p.m.

The Hannah Peschar Gallery and Sculpture Garden, Black and White Cottage, Standon Lane, Ockley RH5 5QR (tel. 01306-627269), is a tranquil, beautifully planted woodland garden with springs and pools, laid out by garden designer Anthony Paul. Its stock of contemporary sculpture changes, as pieces are sold, and the gardens themselves are inspiring. Open May–Oct, Fri–Sat, 11a.m.–6p.m.; Sun and Bank Holidays, 2–5p.m. Other days (but not Mons) by appointment only. Entrance £7, OAPs/students £5, children £4.

The Isabella Plantation, Richmond Park, Richmond TW10 5HS (tel. 0181-948 3209), is an enclosed woodland garden within the 3500-acre ancient deer park. A richly planted and tranquil oasis within this popular 'green lung' of south-west London, it is a brilliant spectacle at rhododendron and azalea time, from April to June. Streams run through it to fill ponds, usually the haunt of assorted wildfowl, especially unusual ducks; winter sees the blooming of witch hazels and early camellias. Open all year, daily, during daylight hours. Entrance free.

Painshill Park, Portsmouth Road, Cobham KT11 1JE (tel. 01932-868113/864674), is a 150-acre, 18th-century landscape garden, contemporary with Stourhead (*q.v.*) in Wiltshire. Its wonders include a 14-acre serpentine lake, a fabulous island grotto of stalactites and tufa, gothic ruins and temples among woodlands and grassy glades. Lovely at all times of year. Open April–Oct, daily, except Mon (but open on Bank Holidays), 10.30a.m.–4.30p.m.; Nov–March, daily, except Mon and Fri, 11a.m.–4p.m. (or dusk if earlier). Closed 25–26 Dec. Entrance £3.80, concessions £3.30, children £1.50.

Pantiles Nursery, Almners Road, Lyne, Chertsey KT16 0BJ (tel. 01932-872195), specializes in selling really large container-grown trees and shrubs, including unusual and rather exotic varieties, such as dicksonia tree ferns, from Tasmania, and sculptural, weeping cedars. Also bedding plants in profusion. Send s.a.e. for a catalogue. Open all year, Mon–Sat, 8.30a.m.–5.30p.m.; Sun, 9a.m.–5p.m.

Simpson's Seeds, 27 Meadowbrook, Old Oxted RH8 9LT (tel. 01883-715242), is a one-off. 'We are a small "kitchen-table" business; until now, we have grown, prepared, counted, and packed the seed, sundries and plants by hand,' says proprietor Colin Simpson. Tomatoes are their speciality, offering seeds of around 270 different varieties. They also sell all manner of unusual, historical, and just plain weird vegetables, such as tomatillos – a type of physalis used in Mexican cooking. Mail order only. Catalogue free on request.

Vann, Vann Lane, Hambledon GU8 4EE (tel. 01428-683413), has four and a quarter acres of idyllic woodland and flower gardens around a Tudor house with later additions. Gertrude Jekyll (*q.v.*) designed its water garden, with a brook flowing through oak woods underplanted with carpets of spring bulbs. There are roses and herbaceous flowers, topiaries, azaleas and a fine pergola walk. Open for 3–4 individual weeks Easter–July, 10a.m.–6p.m.; also pre-booked private visits welcome. Entrance £2.50, children 50p.

Vernon Geranium Nursery, Cuddington Way, Cheam, Sutton SM2 7JB (tel. 0181-393 7616), is a specialist grower of pelargoniums (around 1100 varieties) and fuchsias. Plants are dispatched as rooted cuttings, or you can buy pot-grown plants at the nursery. Mail order catalogue £2. Open March–July, Mon–Sat, 9.30a.m.–5.30p.m., Sun 10a.m.–4p.m.

Winkworth Arboretum, Hascombe Road, Godalming GU8 4AD (tel. 01483-208477), is a hillside woodland with two lakes. It is wonderful in spring when the azaleas and bluebells are in bloom, and spectacular in autumn, with tints of maples, Katsura trees (cercidiphyllum), and mountain ash in great variety. Open all year, dawn to dusk. Entrance £2.70, children £1.35, family ticket £6.75.

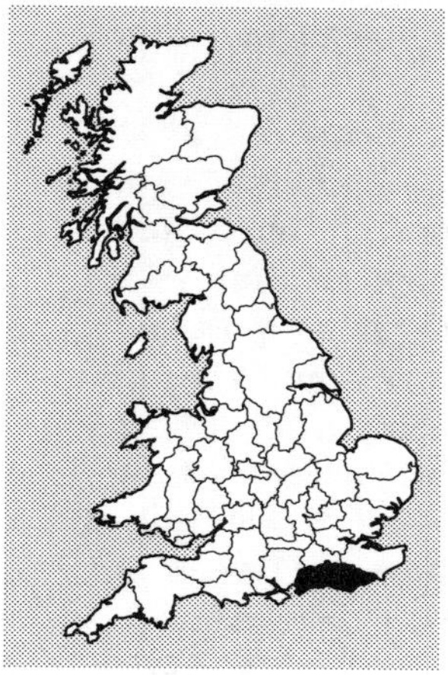

Sussex

MAP NO. 3

Forming a slender lozenge-shape along England's south-eastern coast, Sussex enjoys the contrasts of a wonderful coastline, the chalky spine of the South Downs and the fertile inland sweeps of the Weald, an area once covered with ancient oak forests. Farmland now, the Wealden area is still dotted with tiny hamlets and speckled with ancient ponds. These pools sometimes appear in the middle of nowhere, but are relics of a medieval iron industry where anvils once caused a clamour along the valleys, while the great oaks made prime timbers for warships and fodder for furnaces.

ARDINGLY

Wakehurst Place

Ardingly, nr Haywards Heath, West Sussex RH17 6TN **TEL.** *01444-894066* **OWNER** *The National Trust, maintained by the Royal Botanic Gardens, Kew* **HOURS** *All year, daily (except 25 Dec and 1 Jan), Nov–Jan: 10a.m.–4p.m.; Feb and Oct: 10a.m.–5p.m.; March: 10a.m.–6p.m.; April–Sept: 10a.m.–7p.m. Last adm. ½hr before closing* **ENTRANCE** *£4.50, OAPs £3, children £2.50* **DIRECTIONS** *1½m NW of Ardingly, on B2028*

SPRING SUMMER AUTUMN WINTER

Access | Gift Shop | Café | NPC

This is a great garden for seeing plants, for its collections – especially of trees and shrubs – are vast. However, to me it lacks soul, or at least I find it rather unmoving as a garden. It is run by Kew's Royal Botanic Gardens as their second home and, with all its prominent signposting directing you this way and that, you do get the sense that it is more about function than aesthetics.

Beside the house is a walled garden of herbaceous flowers and pretty climbers, and beyond it a very formal garden enclosed by yews. Follow the signs to the Water Garden, and things start to get better. There are sumptuous magnolias on the slopes and, if you're here in spring, look out for colonies of *Lathraea clandestina*, an unusual parasitic plant, with flowers the colour of amethyst carpeting the grass at the streamside. The water gardens have recently been revamped (wonderful plants but, alas, what happened to the attractive old bridge?). Around and beyond are woodland walks into the valley and Himalayan glade. Rhododendrons feature strongly and the gardens contain National Collections of betula (birches), hypericum, nothofagus (southern beech) and skimmia. Anyone wanting to keep honey-bees happy should plant *Skimmia* × *confusa* 'Kew Green' which has wonderful, sweet perfume carrying in the air for yards; at Wakehurst I noted it seems to be the bee banquet in spring.

EAST GRINSTEAD

Standen

East Grinstead, West Sussex RH19 4NE TEL. *01342-323029* OWNER *The National Trust* HOURS *March–Oct, Wed–Sun and Bank Holiday Mons. Garden: 12.30–6p.m.; house: 12.30–4p.m. Nov–mid-Dec, garden only: Fri–Sun, 1–4p.m.* ENTRANCE *House and garden £5; garden only £3 (£2 Nov–Dec)* DIRECTIONS *2m S of East Grinstead, signposted from B2110*

SPRING | SUMMER | AUTUMN | WINTER

Gift Shop | Café

Standen is the archetypal small country house in the Arts and Crafts style prevailing in the late 19th and early 20th centuries. It was designed by the architect Philip Webb, a lifelong friend of William Morris, and much of its interior is decorated with Morris's distinctive floral wallpapers and fabrics. The 12-acre gardens around it were made in the same period, and are the perfect foil to this appealing house. A broad terrace on the south side nestles the house into its hillside surroundings. From here there are winding paths to explore the shrubberies westwards up the hillside, and more formal areas to the east; a big slab of lawn directly in front is a light and airy breathing space between the two.

It is a garden of great Wealden views, with intriguing walks among fragrant azaleas, contorted Japanese acers, magnolias and other woodland planting. The formal gardens feature rugosa roses, nepeta and irises enclosed by stepped yew hedging. Notable in this area are the huge 'Annie Elizabeth' and 'Bismarck' apple espaliers, planted 100 years ago.

FONTWELL

Denmans

Fontwell, nr Arundel, West Sussex BN18 0SU **TEL.** *01243-542808* **OWNER** *John Brookes Ltd* **HOURS** *March–Oct, daily, 9a.m.–5p.m. (or by appointment)* **ENTRANCE** *£2.80, OAPs £2.50, children (4–16) £1.50* **DIRECTIONS** *Turn S off A27, W of Fontwell racecourse (signposted)*

SPRING SUMMER AUTUMN WINTER

Access · Gift Shop · Café · Plant Shop · DON'T MISS

Denmans was begun by the late Joyce Robinson, a great character who could often be met in her later years zooming about the garden in her powered wheelchair. She and her husband acquired the site in 1946 with 32 acres and a large house which they later sold, whereupon they moved into a cottage in the garden. The current three-and-a-half-acre garden is remarkable for Mrs Robinson's innovative design, with a 'dry river' of gravel running sinuously through it. Its inspiration was a visit to the Greek island of Delos, in 1969, where Mrs Robinson saw that 'everything grew in hot, gravelly soil'. The style is relaxed, with mixed trees and shrubs providing year-round colour and vertical interest, while many perennials and biennials are allowed to self-sow here and there, to enhance its informality.

Garden designer John Brookes arrived in 1980 (he lives in The Clock House on the edge of the garden, and runs design courses from there), and his style has blended well with the Robinsons'. The superb herb garden he made within the walled former kitchen garden is well known and much photographed. There is also a good nursery here offering many of the wonderful plants you see in the gardens, and the restaurant/tearoom serves good, home-made fare in pleasant surroundings.

CROFTWAY NURSERY IRISES

For a brief couple of weeks in late May and early June, two acres of fields near the seaside resort of Bognor Regis are transformed into a Van Gogh landscape of pale blues and mauves, dusky browns, deep reds, mutable pinks, yellows and golds. These are the iris fields of ***Croftway Nursery, Yapton Road, Barnham, Bognor Regis, West Sussex PO22 0BH (tel. 01243-552121), between Yapton and Barnham on B2233****, well worth visiting at this time. There is something about irises – the richness of their colours, the delicacy of individual petals, the rigid nobility of their stems, their sweet fragrance and the sheer ephemerality of their flowers – that I find completely intoxicating. Croftway sells over 150 different varieties, including tall bearded, intermediate bearded and dwarf bearded types, and a good range of* Iris sibirica *cultivars. Their Iris Picnic Weekend at the height of flowering time is now an annual event, when over 26,000 plants are in bloom in the fields. (Proprietor Graham Spencer recommends a telephone call near the time, to check bloom status before travelling.) Irises are also sold by mail (dispatched in August and September only). Send 4 × 1st-class stamps for the catalogue. Nursery open Feb–late Nov, daily, 9a.m.–5.30p.m.*

HAYWARDS HEATH

Nymans Garden

Handcrosss, nr Haywards Heath, West Sussex RH17 6EB
TEL. *01444-400321* **OWNER** *The National Trust* **HOURS** *March–Oct, daily, except Mon and Tues (but open Bank*

Holiday Mons), 11a.m.–6p.m. or dusk if earlier (last adm. 5.30p.m.); Nov–Feb, weekends only, weather permitting (telephone for details) **ENTRANCE** *(house and garden) £5, children £2.50, family ticket £12.50* **DIRECTIONS** *Signposted off M23/A23, SE of Handcross*

SPRING SUMMER AUTUMN WINTER

Access | Gift Shop | Café | Plant Shop | DON'T MISS

Nymans is one of the great gardens of the south-east and another personal favourite of mine. When spring has been mild, the sight of its magnolias can bring tears to the eyes and there is much else to see early on, with its woods flooded by bluebells, extensive use of bulbs – both naturalised and bedded out – and terrific ranges of early-blooming shrubs.

Early summer sees the long grass of the hillside pinetum awash with wildflowers, and in June the small, formal rose garden is at its height of splendour. There are good herbaceous borders in the Top Garden with flowers chiefly

WILLIAM ROBINSON AT GRAVETYE

Gravetye Manor, Vowels Lane, nr East Grinstead, West Sussex RH19 4LJ (tel. 01342-810567), 5m SW of East Grinstead off B2110 at the West Hoathly sign, *is now an extremely luxurious country house hotel and restaurant, but it also has first-class horticultural credentials, as the former home of William Robinson (1838–1935).*

Robinson was the most influential and widely read gardening writer of his day – a sort of Geoff Hamilton of the Victorian and Edwardian age – whose seminal work, The English Flower Garden, *ran to 15 editions during his own lifetime and several more later. He was a prolific writer and publisher of various gardening journals and his approach to wild gardening – using 'perfectly hardy exotic plants under conditions where they will thrive without further care' pre-empted the current vogue for naturalistic and ecological planting styles by a century.*

Born in Ireland and trained at Glasnevin, then Regent's Park, Robinson invested his new-found wealth from publishing in the Elizabethan mansion of Gravetye Manor. He developed its 360-acre gardens with a certain amount of formality near the house and extensive woodland plantings beyond. His gardens have been extensively restored in recent years, but are only open to hotel guests.

in yellow and blue and, at high summer, do not miss the Walled Garden, with its central path ablaze on either side with cosmos, dahlias, salvias, heliotrope and other firework-coloured flowers continuing the splendour until autumn. And there is so much else; a heather and rock garden, Japanese features, a wisteria-drenched pergola, an avenue of majestic limes, sturdy topiary around the romantic ruins of the house. All in all, a garden for all seasons, and one I never tire of visiting.

HORSHAM

Leonardslee Gardens

Lower Beeding, nr Horsham, West Sussex RH13 6PP TEL. *01403-891212* OWNER *The Loder Family* HOURS *April–Oct, daily, 10a.m.–6p.m.* ENTRANCE *£3.50 (£4.50 in May), children £2* DIRECTIONS *4m SW of Handcross at Jct of A279 and A281*

SPRING SUMMER AUTUMN WINTER

Gift Shop · Café · Plant Shop

See Leonardslee's great trees and famous rhododendrons reflected in its tranquil lakes, and it is hard to imagine the scene that would have greeted you 400 years ago. But just think: in the 1580s it was noted that Sussex 'is full of iron mines all over it; for the casting of which there are furnaces ... and an abundance of wood is yearly spent; many streams are drawn into one channel, and a great deal of meadow ground is turned into ponds and pools for driving mills by the flashes, which, beating with hammers upon the iron, fill the neighbourhood round about it, night and day with continual noise'.

Today, it is those hammer ponds that furnish the garden so exquisitely with water. The woods grew again and much planting of rhododendrons and other flowering shrubs began in the first half of the 19th century. From 1889 onwards, Sir Edmund Loder, scion of a famous Sussex gardening family, introduced more exotic plants to

Leonardslee, and also a herd of Tasmanian wallabies, whose descendants continue to hop about the grounds. Sir Edmund's superb 'Loderi' hybrid rhododendrons were bred here in 1901 and make substantial trees today, bearing huge trumpet flowers, pastel-tinted and sweetly scented. The 240-acre grounds include a fine rock garden, an alpine house, a collection of bonsai trees and a temperate glasshouse, but the real attraction is the chance to stride along its miles of woodland paths and gasp in wonder that heavy industry can leave such a captivating legacy.

NORTHIAM

Great Dixter

Dixter Lane, Northiam, nr Rye, East Sussex TN316PH TEL. *01797-252878* OWNER *Christopher Lloyd* HOURS *April–mid-Oct, daily, except Mon (but open on Bank Holidays), 2–5p.m.* ENTRANCE *£3, children 25p (house and garden £4)* DIRECTIONS *½m N of Northiam, turn off A28 at Northiam post office*

SPRING SUMMER AUTUMN WINTER

Plant Shop · Nursery · DON'T MISS

This garden is famous, partly because it is the lifelong home of plantsman and gardening writer Christopher Lloyd; also because it has been loved, nurtured and developed for nearly a century, or at any rate since Sir Edwin Lutyens (*q.v.*) laid his crisp design on it before the First World War.

Part of its magic is that it seems in a time-capsule, protected by its own grounds and stout hedges from suburban encroachment of the rude world beyond. Even the motor car cannot get near the 15th-century house, for the gardens envelope it and access is only via long and narrow paths.

A network of yew hedging and flagstone paths divides Dixter's seven acres into spaces of different character and purpose, demonstrating Lutyens's genius for design, but also his sensitivity to the vernacular buildings of this ancient manor farm. Within the different areas, planting is dynamic and bold. The most famous view is down the Long Border, a richly planted sunny border filled with mixed annuals, perennials, bulbs, shrubs, small trees and climbing plants (particularly clematis) that perform with brilliant colour over a long season. There are experimental beds of perennial plantings, a kitchen garden, large areas of flower-filled meadow dotted with trees, lots of Edwardian topiaries, informal ponds and a thrilling garden of exotic foliage, with colourful cannas and dahlias. The discreet sunk garden, in a corner between barns and oasts, was designed by Mr Lloyd's father and has yet more lively planting, around a formal pool. There is also an excellent nursery of reasonably priced plants also available by mail (catalogue £1).

TRADITIONAL SUSSEX TRUGS

Sussex is the home of the trug, a curved, shallow basket ideal for carting hand-tools, vegetables, fruits or cut flowers through the garden. The word trug derives from the Anglo-Saxon 'trog', meaning boat-shaped, and they are made by steaming and bending slender strips of chestnut and willow. The strips are then riveted firmly to a piece of wood that forms the rim, and another strip wraps around the middle to make a handle. The first Sussex trugs were made in the 1820s by Thomas Smith & Co of Herstmonceux. They are still made there and marketed as ***Sussex Trugs Ltd, Thomas Smith's Trug Shop, Hailsham Road, Herstmonceux, East Sussex BN27 4LH (tel. 01323-832137) on A271 in centre of village****. You can buy them by mail (prices from around £20–£60 incl. postage), or call at the shop, open all year, except Christmas–New Year period, Mon–Fri, 8a.m.–5p.m.; Sat 9a.m.–4p.m.*

PULBOROUGH

Champs Hill

Coldwaltham, Pulborough, West Sussex RH20 1LY TEL. *01798-831868* OWNER *Mr and Mrs D. Bowerman* HOURS *Open for several days each March, May and Aug, for the National Gardens Scheme and for pre-booked parties of 10+* ENTRANCE *£2, children free* DIRECTIONS *From A29 at*

Coldwaltham turn N towards Fittleworth. Champs Hill is 300yds on right

SPRING SUMMER AUTUMN WINTER

Plant Shop

DON'T MISS

This is a really unusual heather garden, planted with great conviction – very pretty in spring and spectacular in August. From various seats on its south-facing slope there are panoramic views of the South Downs, with the meanders of the River Arun winding through the valley below. It covers 27 acres on a sandy hilltop, much of the garden being birch, pine and oak woodland, thinned out here and there for plantings of rhododendrons and naturalised bulbs. Around the house there is a significant collection of heathers, about 300 different varieties, most of them being forms of the summer-flowering bell heather (*Erica cinerea*) and ling (*Calluna vulgaris*). Planting is in bold drifts, following the gentle contours of the ground to make large island beds, with turf paths winding through.

PULBOROUGH

Parham House

Pulborough, West Sussex RH20 4HS TEL. *01903-742021* OWNER *Parham Park Trust* HOURS *April–Oct, Wed–Thurs, Sun and Bank Holiday Mons, 12 noon–6p.m.* ENTRANCE *(Garden only) £3, children 50p; house and garden £5, OAPs £4, children £1, family ticket £10* DIRECTIONS *4m SE of Pulborough on A283*

SPRING SUMMER AUTUMN WINTER

Access Gift Shop Café Plant Shop

DON'T MISS

A long drive runs through the ancient deer park at Parham, and you immediately know you are somewhere special. The high ridge of the South Downs frowns from a distance and the Elizabethan stone house, with its courtyards and outbuildings, sits like a little village in its fortunate setting. (The house is worth seeing, especially during the mid-July garden festival weekend, when there are flower-arranging demonstrations.)

The seven-acre pleasure grounds behind the house include a brick maze set into the turf (always popular with children) and rambling walks to the lake. The walled gardens are the chief attraction, however. There are sumptuously planted, colour-themed double herbaceous borders of blues, purples and greys in one area; yellows and golds in another; deep purples, pinks and golds in yet another. There are walls garlanded in roses and clematis, an orchard, a kitchen garden, flower-filled greenhouses, and further herbaceous borders around the perimeter. Somewhere special indeed.

UCKFIELD

Sheffield Park Gardens

Nr Uckfield, East Sussex TN22 3QX TEL. *01825-790231* OWNER *The National Trust* HOURS *March, Sat–Sun only, 11a.m.–6p.m.; April–mid-Nov, Tues–Sun and Bank Holiday Mons, 11a.m.–6p.m. (or dusk if earlier); mid-Nov–mid-Dec, Wed–Sun, 11a.m.–4p.m.* ENTRANCE *£4.20, children £2.10, parties of 15 or more (not at weekends or Bank Holidays) £3.20 each* DIRECTIONS *5m NW of Uckfield, on E side of A275 (between A272 and A22)*

SPRING SUMMER AUTUMN WINTER

Access | Gift Shop | Café | NPC

The first and only time I have seen a wild mink is when one scampered across the grass and dipped into one of the lakes at Sheffield Park, one autumn. And autumn (particularly mid-October) is the classic time to visit, when the rich scarlets, russets, brilliant golds and deep greens of the surrounding trees are mirrored in its broad waters, their varied silhouettes casting shimmery patterns on a reflected sky. Spring is lovely here too, as rhododendrons and Ghent azaleas (there is a National Collection here) are added to the mix, and the woodland glades are awash with bluebells.

The park covers 120 acres and both Capability Brown (*q.v.*) and Humphry Repton (*q.v.*) contributed to its landscaping. Much planting was carried out early this century, however, and the fantastic collection of exotic trees which bring so much colour and shape in every season is largely due to these later plantings. You can take any one of several marked routes, depending on time and energy available, to circuit one or more of the four large lakes. Among the autumn highlights are the scarlet tupelo trees (*Nyssa sylvatica*), equally vivid liquidambars, and the rusty gold swamp cypress and dawn redwood, both of which, unlike most conifers, are deciduous.

Celebrity Choice

Stephen Anderton, presenter of BBC Radio 4's* Growing Places *and* The Times *gardening correspondent

'I love **Great Dixter** (q.v.). *The garden hangs around the house so well and, wherever you are in the garden, you are always aware of the house. It's a place that is lived in. The garden's Edwardian layout is formal but also incredibly flexible: things are always changing in the planting. Very few gardens work as hard as this one does at being good in all seasons. There is complicated, hard-working herbaceous detail throughout the year, and in high summer, at a time when many southern gardens are looking worn out, Great Dixter's borders are just starting to get going. Also the planting is very selective; nothing gets past an uncritical eye and the garden has lots of personality stamped on it.'*

And also...

Apuldram Roses, Apuldram Lane, Dell Quay, Chichester, West Sussex PO20 7EF (tel. 01243-785769), is a specialist rose grower, with the emphasis on modern varieties. Their rose fields and garden are open during the summer months and there is a mail order catalogue available on request. Nursery open all year, Mon–Sat, 9a.m.–5p.m.; Sun and Bank Holidays, 10.30a.m.–4.30p.m.

Architectural Plants, Cooks Farm, Nuthurst, Horsham, West Sussex RH13 6LH (tel. 01403-891772), is a thoroughly entertaining nursery. It specializes in foliage effects, from plants such as fan palms, banana trees, bamboos, eucalyptus, puyas, pines, agaves and aralias. Its exotic ambience is enhanced by the colonial-style office (complete with corrugated iron roof and spacious verandahs). Nurseryman Angus White's catalogue (dispatched on request) is also a great read. Open all year, Mon–Sat, 9a.m.–5p.m.

Axletree Nursery and Garden, Starvecrow Lane, Peasmarsh, Rye, East Sussex TN31 6XL (tel. 01797-230470), is on a sloping site, hidden-away in the remote, wooded lanes near Peasmarsh. My first visit coincided with the blooming of *Magnolia* 'Wada's Memory', which was a breathtaking sight in the display gardens by the nursery. The proprietors specialize in hardy geraniums, but there are also very many other interesting and well-grown herbaceous plants on sale to personal callers. Send 4 × 1st-class stamps for a catalogue. Mail order available. Great Dixter (*q.v.*) is quite nearby. Open mid-March–late Sept, Wed–Sat, 10a.m.–5p.m.

Highdown, Littlehampton Road, Goring-by-Sea, West Sussex BN12 6PE (tel. 01903-239999), is a remarkable garden, made in a chalk-pit. The creation of Sir Frederick Stern (1884–1967), it became his experimental ground in seeing which plants could thrive on relentlessly chalky soil. It is well known for its peonies, irises and hellebores, and Stern's book, *The Chalk Garden* (out of print but available from some libraries), is still instructive for anyone gardening on similar ground. Open all year, daily, Dec–Jan, 10a.m.–4p.m.; Feb–Mar, 10a.m.–4.30p.m.; April–Sept, 10a.m.–6p.m.; Oct–Nov, 10a.m.–4.30p.m. Entrance free, donations welcome.

Holly Gate Cactus Nursery, Billingshurst Road, Ashington, West Sussex RH20 3BB (tel. 01903-892930), is utterly fascinating. It holds one of the largest collections of cacti and succulents in the country, with ravishing display gardens under glass. Cacti and their seeds are available by mail (send 2 × 1st-class stamps for a catalogue). Open daily, except 25–26 Dec, 9a.m.–5p.m.

Damian Grounds at **Hortus Ornamenti, Saltham Barns, Saltham Lane, Runcton, Chichester, West Sussex PO20 6PU (tel. 01243-782467)**, designs and produces very high-quality hand-made garden tools and accessories, such as trowels, weeding forks and hoes, in stainless steel with smooth, comfortably shaped handles in beech-wood or walnut, from around £25 per item, plus postage. They make luxurious, special presents for keen gardeners; catalogue on request. Primarily mail order but showroom also available to visit by arrangement.

W. E. Th. Ingwersen Ltd, Birch Farm Nursery, Gravetye, East Grinstead, West Sussex RH19 4LE (tel. 01342-810236), is a very traditional and long-established alpine nursery, with plants attractively displayed in cold frames and pans. Bulbs, conifers and some half-hardy plants are also sold. It is a fascinating nursery to browse in and, with its traditional glasshouses, is redolent of times past. Send 2 × 1st-class stamps for a plant list. Open March–Sept, daily, 9a.m.–1p.m., 1.30–4p.m., Oct–Feb, weekdays, 9a.m.–1p.m., 1.30–4p.m.

Lime Cross Nursery, Herstmonceux, Hailsham, East Sussex BN27 4RS (tel. 01323-833229) is *the* place to go to for conifers – they sell around 300 different kinds, from dwarf species to potentially large trees, and hedging plants in variety. Also a general stock of trees, shrubs and climbers. Open all year, daily, 8.30a.m.–5p.m.

Merriments Gardens, Hawkhurst Road, Hurst Green, East Sussex TN19 7RA (tel. 01580-860666), is a well established garden centre with an adjoining 4-acre display garden (plus restaurant). The nursery stocks a broad general range of plants and sundries. In the garden there are colourful flower borders, a rock and scree garden, a foliage border and an arched walkway inspired by Claude Monet's at Giverny. Open all year, daily, 10a.m.–5.30p.m.; garden April–Sept, daily, 10a.m.–5p.m. Entrance £2.50, children £1.

Pashley Manor, Ticehurst, Wadhurst, East Sussex TN5 7HE (tel. 01580-200692), is a handsome Tudor house with Jacobean and Queen Anne additions (not open), in a lovely parkland setting. There are shrubberies of rhododendrons and camellias, walled flower gardens, natural springs feeding a series of ponds, and fine views of the Sussex countryside. Tulip time is celebrated with a festival in April and old-fashioned roses (of which there are many here) feature in a mid-summer rose festival each year. Open mid-Apr–late Sept, Tues–Thurs, Sat, and Bank Holiday Mons, 11a.m.–5p.m. Entrance £4.50, OAPs £4, children (6–12) £4 (under 6s free).

Perryhill Nurseries, Hartfield, East Sussex TN7 4JP (tel. 01892-770377), always has lots of interesting plants among its broad range of stock. As well as offering good selections of hardy and half-hardy perennials and fruit, it keeps a well-chosen range of roses, including wild species, hybrid musk and unusual shrub roses. Open March–Oct, 9a.m.–5p.m.; Nov–Feb, 9a.m.–4.30p.m.

A five-mile-long stone wall runs around the park of **Petworth House, Petworth, West Sussex GU28 0AE (tel. 01798-342207)** a National Trust property. The park was landscaped by Capability Brown (*q.v.*) and covers 700 acres of undulating grassland peppered with clumps of trees and grazed by deer. It is a great place to come for a long walk and a picnic, at any time of year. The gardens, or pleasure grounds, near the house cover 30 acres and are magical through the spring, with grassy walks enlivened by narcissi, primroses, bluebells and fritillaries. Rhododendrons and azaleas bloom among unfurling leaves of Japanese acers and many ornamental trees. Park open all year, daily, 8a.m.–9p.m. (or dusk if earlier); house and gardens, late March–Nov, Sat–Wed, 1–5.30p.m. Entrance house and gardens £5, children (over 5) £2.50, family ticket (2 adults and 2 children) £12.50, pre-booked parties of 15 or more £4.50 per person; free entry to park.

Pots and Pithoi, The Barns, East Street, Turners Hill, West Sussex RH10 4QQ (tel. 01342-714793), sells hand-made, pale-terracotta pots imported from Crete. They have the typical Mediterranean oil-jar shape, some with handles, some delicately patterned; most would make distinctive eye-catchers when well placed in the garden. There is a free leaflet and price list available on request. Open all year except the Christmas–New Year period, daily, 10a.m.–5p.m. (closing 4p.m. in winter).

West Dean Gardens, West Dean, Chichester, West Sussex PO18 0QZ (tel. 01243-818210), has a deeply impressive 2½-acre Victorian walled kitchen garden, restored in recent years. With its astounding ranges of flowers, fruits and vegetables and restored working greenhouses, this is now the best part of the garden, especially if you're into chillies and peppers, for they grow more than 90 different varieties. In the 35 acres of pleasant ornamental grounds there is a remarkable 100yd-long pergola of stone piers and stout timber cross-beams designed by Harold Peto (*q.v.*) in 1910, also recently restored. It focuses on a pavilion at one end and a formal sunken garden at the other. Open March–late Oct, daily, 11a.m.–5p.m. (last adm. 4.30p.m.). Entrance £3.50, OAPs £3, children (over 5) £1.50, family ticket £9.

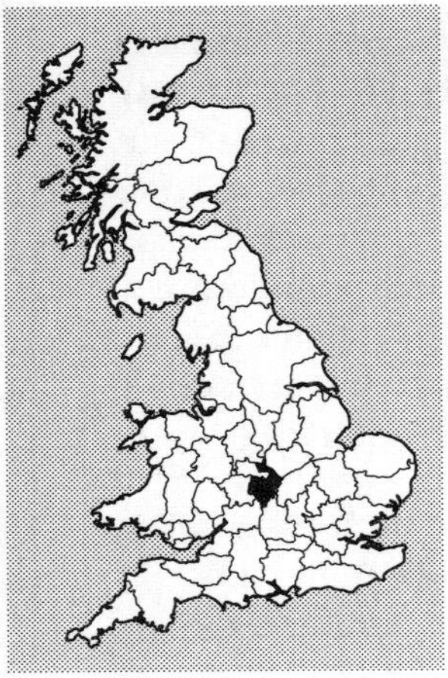

Warwickshire

MAP NO. 5

The industrial heartland of Birmingham and the Black Country lies on the north-western edge of this county, yet the gently undulating landscape around Stratford and Warwick seems a world apart. This is a land of fertile pastures, where agriculture still plays a prominent role, and timber-framed houses of earlier centuries survive as testament to the great oak forests which once covered the area. The oaks are no longer plentiful, but fine specimens in the roadside hedgerows are occasional reminders that this region was once heavily wooded.

CHARLECOTE

Charlecote Park

Charlecote, Wellesbourne CV35 9ER **TEL.** *01789-470277* **OWNER** *The National Trust* **HOURS** *Early April or Easter if earlier–late Oct, Fri–Tues, 11a.m.–6p.m., last adm. 5.15p.m. (house closed from 1–2p.m.)* **ENTRANCE** *£4.80, children £2.40 (inclusive ticket, house and garden)* **DIRECTIONS** *On N side of B4086, 1m W of Wellesbourne, 5m E of Stratford-upon-Avon, use A46, then B4086; from M40 use Jct 15, then A46 and B4086*

SPRING SUMMER AUTUMN WINTER

Access | Gift Shop | Café

The house at Charlecote was built in the 1550s, but now little remains of its 17th-century garden with its straight canals and elaborate parterre designs. Capability Brown (*q.v.*) made sweeping alterations to the 30-acre park in the 18th century, but was refused permission to fell the famous avenue of trees.

A century ago, 20,000 bedding plants were produced yearly at Charlecote, used in a series of display beds in the garden forecourt where today there are low-maintenance lawns. Colourful beds and containers are sited near the house, however, and a handsome deer park with trees lies beyond, through which the River Avon flows. Legend has it that the young William Shakespeare was caught poaching deer here in 1558. Outside the park gates is the **Charlecote Fruit and Flowers Nursery**, offering well-grown and well-displayed perennials, bulbs and alpines.

LAPWORTH

Packwood House Gardens

Lapworth, Solihull B94 6AT TEL. *01564-782024* OWNER *The National Trust* HOURS *Late March–Sept, Wed–Sun and Bank Holiday Mons (closed Good Friday), 1.30–6p.m., Oct, Wed–Sun, 12 noon–4.30p.m. (last adm. ½hr before closing)* ENTRANCE *£2.10, children £1.05 (house and garden £4.20, children £2.10)* DIRECTIONS *Off A3400 (2m away, signposted), 2m E of Hockley Heath, 11m SE of central Birmingham*

SPRING SUMMER AUTUMN WINTER

Access Gift Shop Café Plant Shop DON'T MISS

From the entrance driveway, you get a tantalising glimpse of Packwood's famous yew topiary, beyond the wall of the 10-acre garden. The yews are trimmed into tall, comfortingly rounded cone shapes of varying heights, set in plain lawns, giving the effect of a crowd of people. Beyond, a spiral path leads up a mount thickly planted with box hedging, the top of which is crowned with a mushroom of yew. This area is known as the Sermon on the Mount.

There are remnants of a formal early 18th-century garden beside the Elizabethan house, with a walled area including bee boles at the foot of the southern wall, and attractive brick gazebos built into each of the four corners. Exceptionally well-grown herbaceous flower borders bring dazzling colour to this garden in the summer. Packwood also possesses an unusually large collection of sundials arranged around the house and garden, presumably because an occupant from an earlier century had an obsession with the passing of time.

LEAMINGTON SPA

Jephson Gardens

The Parade, Leamington Spa TEL. *01926-450000* OWNER *Warwick District Council* HOURS *Open all year, daily, 8a.m.–dusk* ENTRANCE *Free* DIRECTIONS *In town centre, main entrance off the Parade beside the tourist info. office, opposite Royal Pump Rooms*

SPRING SUMMER AUTUMN WINTER

Access Café

Royal Leamington Spa has elegant Regency streets and is renowned for its summer floral displays. In its heyday, the rich and famous (including the Duke of Wellington and the actress, Sarah Bernhardt) came to Leamington to take the waters. The Royal Pump Rooms are close to the entrance of the beautiful Jephson Gardens where 13 acres of grounds are laid out with interesting specimen trees, colourful bedding displays, and waterside walks beside the broad River Leam.

RYTON-ON-DUNSMORE

Ryton Organic Gardens

Ryton-on-Dunsmore, Coventry CV8 3LG TEL. *01203-303517* OWNER *The Henry Doubleday Research Association* HOURS *Open all year (except Christmas period), daily, 9a.m.–5p.m.* ENTRANCE *£2.50, concessions £2, children £1.25* DIRECTIONS *5m SE of Coventry, by A45 (signposted)*

SPRING SUMMER AUTUMN WINTER

Access Gift Shop Café Plant Shop

This is the national home of organic gardening, with a series of small demonstration plots on a level 10-acre site. The aim is to educate and encourage people to take a chemical-free, eco-friendly approach to gardening, and the results are certainly impressive.

The essence of organic gardening lies in creating a fertile, humus-rich soil environment to provide plants with nourishment, enabling them to build up some resistance to pests and diseases. Composting and mulching have a big role to play in the gardens, and organic methods using barrier pest controls and natural predators are also demonstrated.

Features include a rose garden, an ornamental kitchen garden, herb gardens, rare vegetables, alpine banks, colourful flowerbeds, and a forest garden.

HAND-MADE TERRACOTTA POTS

Whichford Pottery, at Whichford, nr Shipston-on-Stour CV36 5PG (tel. 01608-684416), 23m from Oxford, take A3400, turn right after Long Compton, *has become famous in recent years for its tough, hand-thrown terracotta pots, which are annually turned into magnificent displays at Chelsea and other flower shows. The pottery was founded by Jim Keeling, who now employs more than 20 local people in the business.*

Each pot is made by throwing or hand-moulding the blended local clays, then the pots are decorated with swags, basketweave designs, or specially ordered patterns such as family crests, before firing. The Whichford designs have a characteristically flared rim, which allows for greater tolerance of soil expansion during frosty weather; traditional Long-Toms are also very popular. If you cannot get to the pottery (open Mon–Fri, 9a.m.–5p.m., and Sat and Bank Holidays, 10a.m.–4p.m.) there is an excellent mail order catalogue (send 6 × 1st-class stamps), pots being delivered nationwide by carrier.

DON'T MISS

WARWICK

The Mill Garden

Mill Street, Warwick CV34 4HB TEL. *01926-492877* OWNER *Arthur Measures* HOURS *Easter–mid-Oct, daily, 9a.m.–dusk; parties preferably by appointment* ENTRANCE *£1, children free (must be accompanied)*

SPRING | SUMMER | AUTUMN | WINTER

Access · Plant Shop

This one-acre garden beneath the walls of Warwick's famous castle is reached from Mill Street. It is a haven of tranquillity beside the River Avon and includes the old castle mill, complete with water wheel, and views of the ruins of the old town bridge. There are mixed shrub and flower borders, a herb garden, raised beds and colour-themed areas, while roses and clematis clamber through the trees. Arthur Measures, the owner, is an octogenarian and keen gardener who regularly opens the garden in order to raise money for charities, including the National Gardens Scheme.

WARWICK

Warwick Castle

Warwick CV34 4QU TEL. *01926-406600* OWNER *The Tussauds Group* HOURS *Grounds open all year, daily (except 25 Dec), April–Oct, 10a.m.–6p.m., Nov–March, 10a.m.–5p.m.* ENTRANCE *£8.95, OAPs £6.40, children £5.40, family ticket £25, for castle and grounds* DIRECTIONS *In the centre of Warwick, signposted, but clearly visible, 2m from M40 Jct 15*

SPRING | SUMMER | AUTUMN | WINTER

Gift Shop · Café

Warwick is a handsome town of generously proportioned streets and houses, its castle generally reckoned the finest medieval example in the country. Perched picturesquely on a bank above the River Avon, its grounds were landscaped by Capability Brown (*q.v.*) in the 18th century. Within the 60-acre gardens, a fine conservatory dating from 1786 houses a model of the famous Warwick Vase – a huge, beautifully decorated Roman urn. The peacock gardens feature both real ones and yew topiary imitation, and sumptuous flowers in the parterre. But the rose garden (made in 1986 from an original Victorian design of 1868) is exceptional. There are pillars, arches and rope swags garlanded by climbers and ramblers, with formally arranged beds of scented shrub roses.

While here, it is worth seeing the amusing waxworks exhibition displayed through 12 rooms of the castle. It features, in a remarkably lifelike way, a weekend house party of 1898, but is best seen without crowds early or late in the day.

And also...

Arbury Hall, nr Nuneaton CV10 7PT (tel. 01203-382804), is a gothicised Tudor/Elizabethan mansion set in pleasing 10 acres of parkland, with fine trees and woods awash with spring bluebells. Rhododendrons, azaleas and a large wisteria provide colour in the same season, and are followed by displays of roses. The novelist George Eliot was born on the estate which featured in her *Scenes From Clerical Life*. Open Easter–late Sept, Sun and Bank Holiday Mons, 2–5.30p.m. (last adm. 5p.m.). Entrance £4.50, children £2.50.

Baddesley Clinton, Lapworth, Knowle, Solihull B93 0DQ (tel. 01564-783294), is an atmospheric, moated manor house, now owned by the National Trust and little changed since 1634. A modestly planted walled flower and fruit garden lies to one side. The grounds include gentle woodland walks around the moat and small lake; a pleasant walk up to St Michael's church is lined with daffodils in spring, being densely carpeted with bluebells shortly afterwards. Open early March–Oct, Wed–Sun, and Bank Holiday Mons (closed Good Friday), 12 noon–5.30p.m. (house opens 1.30p.m.). Entrance £4.60, children £2.30; garden only £2.30, children £1.15.

The **Shakespeare Birthplace Trust, Henley Street, Stratford-upon-Avon CV37 6QW (tel. 01789-204016)**, runs several properties in and around Stratford-upon-Avon, including **New Place/Nash's House** in the town centre (well signposted). This is the site and grounds of Shakespeare's home from 1597 until his death. The Elizabethan-style garden is a reconstruction, with a well-planted and gloriously colourful (although not very authentic) knot garden, surrounded by tunnel walks in Tudor-style trellis work, and further ornamental flower gardens beyond. Open mid-March–mid-Oct, Mon–Sat, 9.30a.m.–5.30p.m. (last adm. 5p.m.), Sun, 10a.m.–5.30p.m. (last adm. 5p.m.); mid-Oct–mid-March, Mon–Sat, 10a.m.–4.30p.m. (last adm. 4p.m.), Sun, 10.30a.m.–4.30p.m. (last adm. 4p.m.). Entrance £3, children £1.50. **Anne Hathaway's Cottage** is a drive away at Shottery, on the western side of town, and features a pleasant country cottage garden of box bushes and annual flowers, surrounding the thatched cottage where Shakespeare's wife lived before her marriage. Open mid-March–mid-Oct, Mon–Sat, 9a.m.–6p.m. (last adm. 5p.m.), Sun 9.30a.m.–6p.m. (last adm. 5p.m.); mid-Oct–mid-March, Mon–Sat, 9.30a.m.–4.30p.m. (last adm. 4p.m.), Sun, 10a.m.–4.30p.m. (last adm. 4p.m.). Entrance £3.50, children £1.50, family ticket £9.

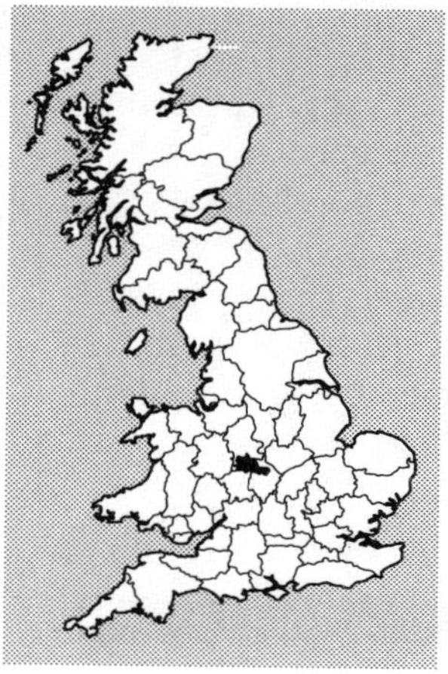

West Midlands

MAP NO. 5

This strongly urban region encompasses the conurbations of Birmingham, West Bromwich, Walsall and Wolverhampton, areas which expanded very quickly during two centuries of industrialisation. Consequently, the region is surrounded and dissected by busy arterial roads, but beyond the urban sprawl, tranquillity returns suddenly in rural, hidden-away villages. Even the commercial heart of Birmingham becomes a floral feast for a week in mid-June, during the Gardeners' World Live Show, at the National Exhibition Centre.

BIRMINGHAM

Birmingham Botanical Gardens and Glasshouses

Westbourne Road, Edgbaston, Birmingham B15 3TR **TEL.** *0121-454 1860* **OWNER** *Birmingham Botanical Gardens and Horticultural Society Ltd* **HOURS** *Open daily all year (except 25 Dec), 9a.m.–7p.m. (Sun, 10a.m.–7p.m.), or dusk if sooner* **DIRECTIONS** *1m SW of city centre, signposted locally in Edgbaston; from M5 (3m away) use Jct 3, then take Halley Road, garden on right*

SPRING SUMMER AUTUMN WINTER

Access | Gift Shop | Café | Plant Shop

This wonderful, 15-acre Victorian park is still imbued with its atmosphere of an earlier age, especially when the brass bands play on a Sunday afternoon in the elegant bandstand.

Unlike many other botanic gardens, this was laid out on its creation in the early 1930s as a public amenity and pleasure garden. Its emphasis is on display, which it does magnificently (complete with exotic birds). The steamy glasshouses include a palm house with tree ferns, cycads and orchids; an orangery packed with flowering plants among the citrus trees; a cactus and succulent house; and a fine tropical house, with banana plants, pineapples and a 24ft lily-pool. Outdoors, the tarmac paths gently ramble past shrubberies of rhododendrons, herbaceous borders, roses, marvellous summer bedding displays, fine Victorian rock and scree gardens, and much more.

WOLVERHAMPTON

Wightwick Manor

Wightwick Bank, Wolverhampton WV6 8EE TEL. *01902-761108* OWNER *The National Trust* HOURS *March–Dec, Wed–Thurs, 11a.m.–6p.m.; Sat, Bank Holiday Suns and Bank Holiday Mons, 1–6p.m., and other days by appointment; house: Thurs and Sat, 2.30–4.30p.m. and Bank Holidays* ENTRANCE *£2.25 (house and garden £5)* DIRECTIONS *3m W of Wolverhampton, up Wightwick Bank (off A454 beside the Mermaid Inn)*

SPRING SUMMER AUTUMN WINTER

Gift Shop Café

Birmingham Botanical Gardens (above) are swirly and bright, redolent of the the dawn of the Victorian age, but those at Wightwick Manor, fashioned a couple of generations later, coincide with Victoria's twilight. The 17-acre gardens were laid out from 1887–1906 and convey the formal inclinations of the age, with dark yew hedges and topiary, and a formal stone terrace, with oak balustrade. Interestingly, this garden is an exact contemporary of those made in Surrey and elsewhere during the Lutyens and Jekyll partnership (*q.v.*), but it lacks the architectural flair of the former and the flower-power of the latter.

The interior of the house gives a better clue to the garden; it is heavily decorated in the Pre-Raphaelite manner, with many original furnishings by William Morris and paintings by Dante Gabriel Rossetti, accompanied by dark, carved panelling and stained-glass windows. Outdoors, the yews form complementary dark walling, as a backdrop to brighter incidents of flowers. There are roses and herbaceous borders, an orchard and, beyond it, rhododendrons gathered around two pools.

And also...

Ashwood Nurseries, Greensforge, Kingswinford DY6 0AE (tel. 01384-401996), has a broad range of plants, but specializes in *Lewisia*, hardy cyclamens, show auriculas and hellebores, for which it is renowned. As well as selling plants, they have an extensive seed list. The colour mail order seed list (4 × 1st-class stamps) is well presented and instructive. Open daily (except 25–26 Dec), Mon–Sat, 9a.m.–6p.m., Sun, 9.30a.m.–6p.m.

Garden Images, Highfield House, Wawensmere Road, Solihull B95 6BN (tel. 01564-794035), produces a free mail order catalogue of gifts for gardeners. It also includes classic tools, dome cloches, plain gardeners' aprons and soft cowhide gloves.

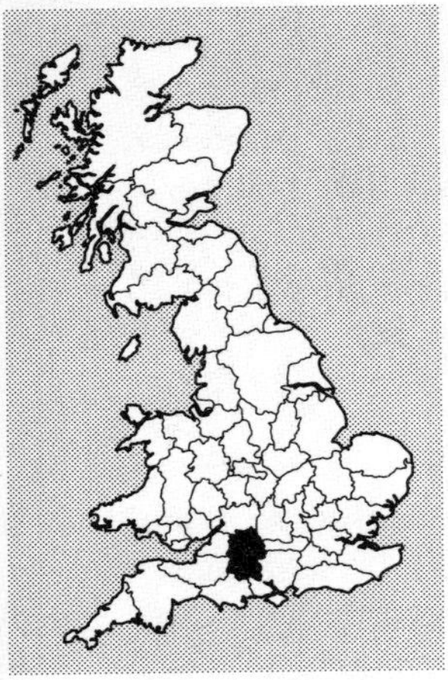

Wiltshire

MAP NO. 2

Farmland dominates Wiltshire; farmland and the great stretch of almost treeless chalk upland that is Salisbury Plain. The rolling Plain is the occasional haunt of Druids (Stonehenge stands proudly upon it) and a vast exercise-ground for the army. Its windswept turf lies as a green mantle over the ancient settlements and tombs of Britain's earliest known inhabitants. From around 5000–2500 years ago this region was the most densely populated in Britain, crossed by the ancient track known as the Ridgeway, which provided a thread of communication from East Anglia to Devon, as they are now known, and the south-west. Today there are infinitely faster road and rail routes linking east and west, but to pause awhile in Wiltshire, especially in its lovely gardens, is worthwhile.

BRADFORD-ON-AVON

The Courts

Holt, nr Trowbridge, Bradford-on-Avon BA14 6RR **TEL.** *01225-782340* **OWNER** *The National Trust* **HOURS** *Late March–Oct, daily, except Sat, 1.30–5.30p.m.* **ENTRANCE** *£3, children £1.50* **DIRECTIONS** *3m SW of Melksham, 3m N of Trowbridge, 2½m E of Bradford-on-Avon, on S side of B3107*

SPRING SUMMER AUTUMN WINTER

From its discreet, narrow entrance, you would not know there is such a large (seven-acre) and varied garden at The Courts. The elegant house (not open) was once a law court for the village, where local cloth weavers could bring their disputes for settlement. Around it, the gardens offer a maze of contrasting open, lawned areas and hedge-enclosed mini-gardens of differing moods and colours. Much of the present layout dates from the 1920s and thirties, under the influence of the Gertrude Jekyll style, with colour-themed borders and lavish use of herbaceous plants contrasted by dark yews. The formal gardens form an L-shape beside the house and beyond is a wilder, unstructured area, which has been planted as an arboretum since the 1950s.

HAROLD PETO: WILTSHIRE'S CELEBRATED GARDEN MAKER

Harold Ainsworth Peto (1854–1933) was the fifth son of Sir Samuel Morton Peto, one of the great Victorian railway contractors, whose estate, Somerleyton Hall (q.v.), in Suffolk, had formal gardens (by Nesfield) in the Italianate style. Harold Peto became a renowned architect and garden designer whose own work, in turn, was strongly influenced by Italian form. In the 1880s his London architectural practice (in partnership with Ernest George) was one of the most fashionable, and the young Edwin Lutyens (q.v.) worked as their assistant for a short while.

Peto's work is noted for its sensitive use of architectural elements, such as terraces, balustrades and stairways, in the broader landscape. His work can be seen here in Wiltshire at Heale Gardens (q.v.) and his own home, Iford Manor (q.v.); and further afield in the partially restored grounds of Easton Lodge (q.v.), Essex, at Buscot Park (q.v.) in Oxfordshire and at Wayford Manor, Somerset (the last opens, on rare occasions, for the National Gardens Scheme).

BRADFORD-ON-AVON

Iford Manor

Bradford-on-Avon BA15 2BA TEL. *01225-863146* OWNER *Mr and Mrs Hignett* HOURS *April–Oct, Sun and Easter Mon, 2–5p.m., May–Sept, Tues–Thurs, Sat–Sun and Bank Holiday Mons, 2–5p.m.* ENTRANCE *£2.50, OAPs/children £1.90 (under 11s free)* DIRECTIONS *2m S of Bradford-on-Avon via Westwood, 7m SE of Bath via A36, also signposted from B3109*

SPRING SUMMER AUTUMN WINTER

DON'T MISS

Several elements combine to make this one of the most pleasingly designed gardens in the *Guide*. The ancient Manor itself (not open) is in a fabulous setting, perched above a picturesque meander of the River Frome. A wooded hill rises behind it, bearing traces of Roman settlements. When Harold Peto (*q.v.*) bought the property in 1899, he laid out a series of terraces linked by stone stairways, and added stone loggias and a colonnade to the grounds. Peto was influenced by Italian design (he made frequent excursions to Italy, in search of ancient artefacts and interesting pieces of masonry), and his translation of the idiom into the Wiltshire landscape is deftly and sympathetically executed. A touch of the Riviera (where Peto also made gardens) is added by the planting – which includes wisterias, grape vines, irises, cypress trees and pines.

Peto admired the rigorous approach of Japanese design and added a small Japanese garden to Iford. There are also delightful streamside plantings and small, formal pools on this 15-acre site.

MIDDLE WOODFORD

Heale Gardens

Middle Woodford, nr Salisbury SP4 6NT TEL. *01722-782504* OWNER *Mr G. Rasch* HOURS *Open all year, daily, 10a.m.–5p.m.* ENTRANCE *£2.75, children under 13 free, except in groups of over 20, when entrance is £2.50 per person* DIRECTIONS *4m N of Salisbury, between A360 and A345, signposted locally*

SPRING SUMMER AUTUMN WINTER

Access | Gift Shop | Plant Shop | DON'T MISS

Tucked away down quiet lanes among the broad loops of the Avon, this is an enchanting, eight-acre garden that really seems to encapsulate 'olde Englande'. Its excellent nursery/specialist plant centre beckons you on arrival, but ignore the temptation, and enjoy the gardens first, for there is much to see.

Broad lawns with trees lead to a formal walled garden, its grass paths delightfully tunnelled with apples and pears, and beds filled with assorted vegetables and cut flowers. A rose-drenched pergola runs along the southern side. Below it, across the lawns, lies a spectacular Japanese garden, dating from the early years of the 20th century. Four Japanese landscape gardeners were imported to make it, and they diverted the nearby river to create cross-streams, over which lies a traditional teahouse. There is appropriate stream-side planting of acers and willows, irises, cherry trees and sprinklings of spring bulbs. A stone lantern and dark red Nikko bridge complete the scene. Near the house, shrub roses have full rein, with a spectacular, rampant hedge of hybrid musk roses including 'Penelope', 'Buff Beauty' and 'Felicia'. Local designer Harold Peto (*q.v.*) designed the terraced gardens near the house, where mixed shrub and herbaceous borders – and more roses – bring pleasure through the seasons.

STOURTON

Stourhead

Stourhead Estate Office, Stourton, nr Warminster BA12 6QD **TEL.** *01747-841152* **OWNER** *The National Trust* **HOURS** *Open all year, daily, 9a.m.–7p.m. (or dusk if sooner); closes at 4p.m. for 3 days in late July during concert season* **ENTRANCE** *£4.40, children £2.40, parties of 15 or more £3.80 each, family ticket £10.30* **DIRECTIONS** *at Stourton, 3m NW of Mere, signposted from A303/B3092*

SPRING SUMMER AUTUMN WINTER

Access | Gift Shop | Plant Shop | DON'T MISS

John Sales, gardens adviser to the National Trust, told me he once received a letter from some people who had visited Stourhead. They wanted their money back, as they had been there, walked around the lake, and could not find any garden. If they were in search of rose beds, flower borders or other more obvious garden features, clearly Stourhead was not for them, as it has none. But it is one of the greatest 18th-century landscape gardens ever made and would certainly feature in my top ten gardens of any kind.

People come to Stourhead for all sorts of reasons: to enjoy the snowdrops and carpets of early bulbs; to see the spectacular rhododendrons in bloom in late spring; for shady woodland walks with plenty of places to pause in summer; or to see the spectacular autumn tints, reflected in the broad 17-acre lake. Others enjoy its scattered buildings, the temples and grotto and allegorical references to Virgil and ancient wisdom. With woodland paths descending the hillside, beautifully composed series of views and fine collections of trees, shrubs and bulbs, it is a 100-acre garden that can be enjoyed at any level, and in any season.

STOURTON

Stourton House Garden

Stourton, Zeals, nr Warminster BA12 6QF **TEL.** *01747-840417* **OWNER** *Mrs Elizabeth Bullivant* **HOURS** *April–Nov, Wed–Thurs, Sun and Bank Holiday Mons, 11a.m.–6p.m.* **ENTRANCE** *£2.50, children 50p* **DIRECTIONS** *At Stourton, 3m NW of Mere, signposted from A303/B3092*

SPRING SUMMER AUTUMN WINTER

Access Café Plant Shop

Lying next door to the restrained landscape park of Stourhead (above), this garden, which is full of flowers, could hardly be more different in character. Forming 4½ acres of sub-divided plots around a former Georgian rectory, Stourton House Garden is renowned for its cut-and-dried flowers, which are sold all year round. Many of them are grown in the former Kitchen Garden, which is devoted to good 'driers' such as helichrysum, delphiniums, golden rod, teasels, achilleas and leeks (which, when left to flower, are as lovely as any of the classier alliums, and make terrific seedheads).

Another enclosed area is bound by Leyland cypress hedges, very effectively clipped into a scalloped pattern along the top, with narrow doorways offering enticing views of further gardens beyond. There are lovely poolside plantings (including carnivorous pitcher plants), wilder, woodland gardens, countless hydrangeas, and a spring garden devoted to unusual daffodils.

LIME-LOVING PLANTS FOR SALE

If you have a garden on limy or chalky soil, then a visit to ***The Botanic Nursery, Bath Road, Atworth, Melksham SN12 8NU (tel. 01225-706597), on A365 in Atworth, behind the clock tower,*** *will undoubtedly prove very rewarding. It stocks around 1500 different hardy perennials and shrubs, the vast majority of which will tolerate, or even relish, sinking their roots into alkaline soils. Proprietors Terry and Mary Baker grow much of their stock from seed, with a strong emphasis on wild species, particularly suitable for the more relaxed, ecological styles now in vogue. Some plants on their list you would be unlikely to track down from any other supplier, and the National Collection of* digitalis *(foxgloves) is held here. Open Feb–Dec, daily, except Tues, 10a.m.–12.30p.m., 2–5p.m.*

And also...

Agralan, The Old Brickyard, Ashton Keynes, Swindon SN6 6QR (tel. 01285-860015), stocks a range of useful gardening products available by mail (catalogue on request). Items include seep-hoses, crop protection fleeces and mulches, non-chemical pest control including pheromone moth traps; also plant sprayers and accessories. Open Mon–Fri, 9a.m.–5p.m. Ring beforehand for occasional weekend and Bank Holiday openings.

Bowood, Derry Hill, Calne SN11 0LZ (tel. 01249-812102), is the stately home of the Earl and Countess of Shelburne. Its pleasure grounds cover 200 acres within a huge park laid out by Capability Brown (*q.v.*). It has lovely parkland and lakeside walks among magnificent trees, with a gushing water cascade, temple and hermit's cave within the grounds. The rhododendron walks are open during their season in May and June. The orangery (now a gallery) was designed by Robert Adam, and in front of it lie formal terraces of rose beds (very bright and cheerful in summer) and neatly clipped columns of yew. There is also a plant centre within the grounds. The family attractions include an extensive adventure playground, a costume gallery in the house, and an 18-hole golf course covering 200 acres within the park. Open April–Oct, daily, 11a.m.–6p.m. (or dusk if earlier). Entrance £5.20, OAPs £4.30, children (over 5) £3.

Think of Wiltshire, and chances are you will picture the open landscapes of the chalk Downs. **Home Covert, Roundway, Devizes SN10 2JA (tel. 01380-723407)**, is perched 400ft up in the Downs, but on a ridge of greensand, which gives the 33-acre garden an acidic soil unusual in this region. It is a highly skilfully designed plantsman's garden, packed with unusual shrubs and perennials planted for a succession of colour all year. Always open by appointment, it is worth travelling to see (please phone for details); groups are welcomed by prior appointment. Open occasionally for the National Gardens Scheme (1998 NGS days are between 4 May and 16 August). Entrance £2, children free.

Landford Trees, Landford Lodge, Landford, Salisbury SP5 2EH (tel. 01794-390808), offers a huge range of ornamental broad-leaved trees, hedging plants and conifers (around 600 different species and varieties in all). Many are field-grown (dispatched in winter) but some ranges also grown in containers and are available any time. Mail order (min. £15) catalogue on request. Open all year, Mon–Fri, 8a.m.–5p.m.

Pound Hill House, West Kington, Chippenham SN14 7JG (tel. 01249-782781), is a 15th-century Cotswold-stone house (not open) surrounded by a series of small gardens planted for interest throughout the year with a formidable range of plants. There is an old-fashioned rose garden with clipped box beds, a small Victorian vegetable garden, a water garden, herbaceous borders, a courtyard garden with well-planted pots, containers, and topiary in box and yew. Open all year, except Jan, Tues–Sun and Bank Holiday Mons, 2–5p.m. Entrance £2. **West Kington Nurseries** (*q.v.*, below) is the owner's family-run business, next door.

Romantic and ancient **Sheldon Manor, Chippenham SN14 0RG (tel. 01249-653120)**, dates from the 13th century, the rare survivor of a long-gone medieval village. Its 11-acre gardens feature old-fashioned roses in profusion, very old yew trees and assorted ornamental trees and shrubs in a lovely setting, with home-made lunches and teas. Open Easter–1st Sun in Oct, Thurs, Sun and Bank Holiday Mons, 12.30–6p.m. (house opens 2p.m.). Entrance (incl. house) £3.50, OAPs £3.25, children under 11 free, 11–16 £1, over 16 £3.

Sherston Parva Nursery, Malmesbury Road, Sherston SN16 0NX (tel. 01666-841066), has a broad range of climbing plants and shrubs suitable for training on walls, including around 100 different clematis; also conservatory plants. Also mail order: send 4 × 1st-class stamps for catalogue. Open all year, daily, 10a.m.–5p.m.

Nurserywoman Derry Watkins specializes in raising half-hardy plants such as choice pelargoniums, salvias, streptocarpus, arctotis and choice gazanias at **Special Plants Nursery, Hill Farm Barn, Greenway Lane, Cold Ashton, Chippenham SN14 8LA (tel. 01225-891686)**. She also runs a series of one-day practical gardening courses in the winter season, on topics such as taking cuttings, pruning, conservatory gardening and container-planting. Open most days, but phone first.

Westdale Nurseries, Holt Road, Bradford-on-Avon BA15 1TS (tel. 01225-863258), specializes in bougainvillea (send 2 × 1st-class stamps plus s.a.e. for their list), displayed in a quarter-acre bougainvillea greenhouse. Also pelargoniums in variety and other plants suitable for conservatories. Open all year (closed 25 Dec), daily, 9a.m.–6p.m.

West Kington Nurseries, West Kington, Chippenham SN14 7JG (tel. 01249-782822), specializes in raising alpines, herbaceous perennials, old-fashioned roses and also topiary plants, available from its plant centre (which also supplies coffee and home-made cakes). Plant centre and garden open all year, daily 10a.m.–5p.m.; nursery open 9a.m.–5p.m. Nurserywoman Barbara Stockitt also opens her garden, **Pound Hill** (*q.v.*, above), which is next door.

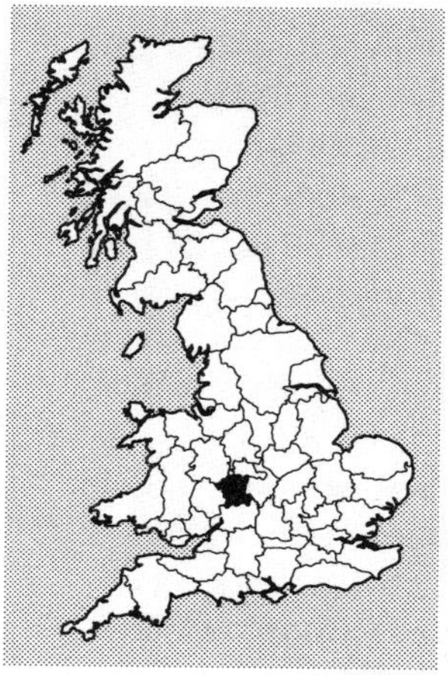

Worcestershire

MAP NO. 5

This is a prime fruit-growing area, with fertile plains watered by the great Severn and Avon rivers, and their tributaries. Market gardening prevails, as roadside farm shops frequently remind you, especially when harvest time arrives for apples and pears. The Georgian town of Pershore derives its name from the quantity of pear orchards that surround it, while the market town of Evesham has medieval buildings and tree-shaded walks beside the Avon. Great Malvern is a handsome spa town, renowned for its bottled water. It lies on the eastern fringes of the Malvern Hills that inspired Edward Elgar, the Victorian composer whose music is so evocative of pastoral Englishness.

GREAT MALVERN

The Picton Garden and Old Court Nurseries

Walwyn Road, Colwall, Great Malvern WR13 6QE **TEL.** *01684-540416* **OWNER** *Mr and Mrs P. Picton* **HOURS** *April–Oct, Wed–Sun, 10a.m.–1p.m., 2.15–5.30p.m.* **ENTRANCE** *£1.50 (nursery free)* **DIRECTIONS** *On B4218 3m SW of Malvern in Colwall village*

SPRING | SUMMER | AUTUMN | WINTER

Access | Plant Shop | Nursery | NPC | Mail Order

Michaelmas daisy borders were popular in late-Victorian and Edwardian gardens of the well-to-do, but are a rare sight now. This two-acre nursery and garden is a tenacious heirloom of that age, however, and holds an important National Collection of these autumnal flowers, displayed in the traditional way.

It was begun by Ernest Ballard, a chemist and hobby gardener who became a nurseryman by default, due to his success in raising exquisite new varieties of *Aster novi-belgii*, also known as New York asters. Ballard's work here spans the first half of the 20th century, and in later years he was joined by Percy Picton, who had gardened at Gravetye Manor for William Robinson (*q.v.*).

New York asters are hard work, needing to be grown from fresh individual shoots, yearly. They are also prone to soil-borne diseases, and are grown best in sterilised soil, followed by regular spraying against mildew. Percy Picton's son, Paul, now runs the nursery and still grows asters in this way, producing glorious firework explosions of pinks, mauves, violets, cerise and white, in a dedicated border best seen in mid-September. He also stocks easy-to-grow species, such as *A. amellus*, *A. frikartii* hybrids, and the tall *A. novaeangliae*.

No yellow asters are available yet, but Ernest Ballard came close by crossing white asters with *Solidaster luteus*, which produced weak, yellow-flowered seedlings during the Second World War. While he was out one day, the War-Ag (responsible for wartime food production) arrived to plough up fields for vegetables; unfortunately, they took the wrong patch, and 30 years' work went under the plough. Ballard never really recovered from the incident.

BOOKS FOR GARDENERS BY MAIL

St Ann's Books, Rectory House, 26 Priory Road, Great Malvern WR14 3DR (tel. 01684-562818), *is a treasure trove of books on botany and gardening, both old and new, listed in their catalogues (two per year on each subject). From the deeply scientific to the downright obscure, if something you want is out of print, or you have not found it elsewhere, you might do so here. (Personal callers only by appointment.) Four catalogues available per year on botany and gardening.*

HERBS IN PARADISE

The Cottage Herbary, Mill House, Boraston Ford, Boraston, nr Tenbury Wells WR15 8LZ (tel. 01584-781575), 2m E of Tenbury Wells, turn off A456 at Peacock Inn. *This true cottage garden (Geoff Hamilton featured it in his* Paradise Gardens *television series) covers one and a quarter acres in an idyllic streamside setting on the Worcestershire/Shropshire border. There are old roses, variegated and wild herbs, dyers' plants and much else, all grown organically. Kim Hurst specializes in producing herbs, aromatics, scented foliage and cottage garden plants. She also gives informative talks on many aspects of herbs, including herb garden designs, wild herbs and their use, growing herbs organically, pot-pourris and preserving,etc. to garden societies and groups by appointment. Open May–July, Sun only, 10a.m.–6p.m.; weekdays by prior arrangement only.*

TENBURY WELLS

Burford House Gardens

Tenbury Wells WR15 8HQ **TEL.** *01584-810777* **OWNER** *Mr C. Chesshire* **HOURS** *Open all year, daily, 10a.m.–5p.m. (or dusk in winter); plant centre 10a.m.–6p.m.* **ENTRANCE** *£2.50, children £1* **DIRECTIONS** *1m W of Tenbury Wells, on A456*

SPRING SUMMER AUTUMN WINTER

Access · Café · Plant Shop · Nursery · NPC · DON'T MISS

This is a tranquil, spacious garden of four acres around a dignified Georgian brick house in a lovely setting, beside the River Teme. It was started (and tended for nearly 40 years) by the late John Treasure, a renowned plantsman with a specialist interest in clematis who ran a large and famous clematis nursery to prove it.

There are curvaceous lawns sweeping around large mixed borders, formal and informal pools, and many fine specimen trees and conifers dotted about the grounds. Ornamental grasses and ferns form splendid drifts on the river bank, and the autumn colours of foliage with the sedums, anemones, echinacea and late-flowering clematis are spectacular. New planting is now invigorating the existing layout. Over 200 different clematis are available from the Treasures of Tenbury plant centre in the grounds, and also by mail order from Oct–April.

TENBURY WELLS

Kyre Park

Tenbury Wells WR15 8RP **TEL.** *01885-410282* **OWNER** *The Rickard and Sellers Families* **HOURS** *Easter–Oct, daily, 11a.m.–6p.m.* **ENTRANCE** *£1.50, children 50p* **DIRECTIONS** *4m S of Tenbury Wells, off B4214*

SPRING SUMMER AUTUMN WINTER

Access | Café | Plant Shop | Nursery | NPC | Mail Order

Kyre Park must have been a very agreeable home in the 18th century. Most of the Georgian house was built onto the shell of a medieval castle. Its park is laid out as a Capability Brown-style landscape garden, overlaying more formal designs. Alas, both house and grounds became badly neglected in recent decades (all the fine fireplaces and fittings in the house were sold) and the park became overgrown. Much clearance and replanting has been carried out more recently under the new owners, and the woods are an ideal habitat for several National Collections of ferns.

The 29-acre park includes pleasant walks around its lakes. Meanwhile, its 18th-century features are gradually being uncovered. Mr Rickard managed to drag me through thickets of brambles and saplings to inspect the remains of a tufa grotto, fed by a spring, which he hopes to restore at some stage.

Most people come here to buy from Rickards Hardy Ferns Nursery, where hundreds of different species and varieties are sold from polytunnels near the car park.

A WALK ON THE WILD SIDE

I have known Kim and Phil Westwood for over 10 years and am full of admiration for their latest project at ***Crown East Heritage Woodland, Crown East Cottage, Crown East, Bromyard Road, Rushwick WR2 5TR (tel. 01905-425645/0421-667093 (mobile)), 3m W of Worcester, off the A44, on Bromyard Road****. Phil is a woodsman and conservationist, and Kim a great cook. Both are good gardeners. Their unspoilt 10-acre wood is a rare remnant of ancient wildwood, with a natural mix of broad-leaved trees and conifers, with coppiced hazel and field maple, and abundant primroses, wood anemones and bluebells.*

To encourage the wild side of gardening and an enhanced awareness of natural habitats, they run a series of one- and two-day courses through the year, on topics including managing hedgerows and wildlife habitats, coppicing, bird identification and guided woodland walks (including one which ends with a cream tea, and a winter walk which is followed by dinner). Visits by appointment.

And also...

Visit **Cotswold Garden Flowers, office at 1 Waterside, Evesham WR11 6BS (tel. 01386-47337/833849); gardens at Sands Lane, Badsey, Evesham WR11 5EZ.** Their speciality is herbaceous perennials, laid out in display gardens and polytunnels in a one-acre field. Open Mon–Sat, 8a.m.–4.30p.m. in summer; Mon–Fri (Sat–Sun by arrangement), daylight hours in winter. Send £1 to the office address for catalogue.

Fibrex Nurseries, Honeybourne Road, Pebworth CV37 8XT (tel. 01789-720788), specializes in pelargoniums and ivies, holding the NCCPG National Collections for both. It is also well known for hardy ferns. Open Jan–March and Sept–Nov, Mon–Fri, 12 noon–5p.m.; April–Aug, Tues–Sun, 12 noon–5p.m. Closed December. Two catalogues available: send 2 × 2nd-class stamps.

Hayloft Plants, Little Court, Rous Lench, Evesham WR11 4UL (tel. 01386-79336), specializes in an interesting range of plug plants, by mail order – useful for anyone lacking the space or time to grow plants from seeds and cuttings. Half-hardy subjects such as argyranthemums, gazanias and arctotis are a speciality, as are a range of penstemons and many other choice species for colourful containers. Mail order only; catalogue free on request.

Madresfield Nursery and Garden Centre, Madresfield, Malvern WR13 5AU (tel. 01684-574066), offers a broad selection of shrubs, trees and herbaceous plants laid out in a Victorian walled garden which still retains its original outbuildings. Open daily, except 25–27 Dec, Mon–Sat, 9a.m.–5.30p.m., Sun, 10a.m.–5p.m.

The one-acre walled garden of **Stone House Cottage, Stone, nr Kidderminster DY10 4BG (tel. 01562-69902)**, artlessly displays a wonderful collection of plants among follies, brick towers and yew hedges. There is also a nursery where you can buy most of the plants you have seen in the gardens. Open March–mid-Oct, Wed–Sat, 10a.m.–5.30p.m. Entrance £2, children free.

Webbs of Wychbold, Wychbold, Droitwich WR9 0DG (tel. 01527-861777), is a huge, well-run garden centre. There are display gardens and a restaurant. Open all year, 9a.m.–6p.m.

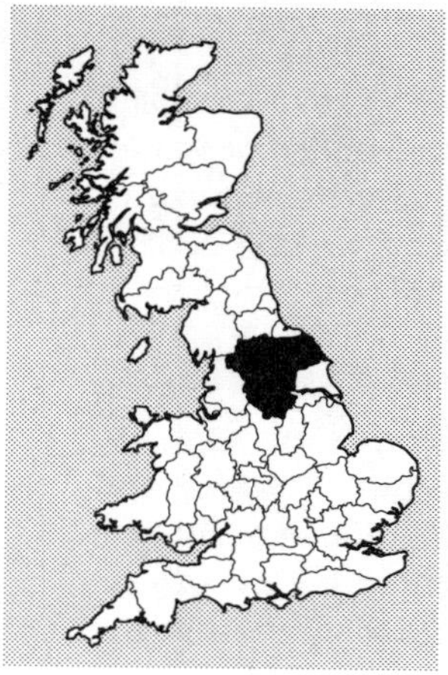

Yorkshire

MAP NO. 7

Yorkshire is the largest county in Britain, with correspondingly broad-ranging, alluring landscapes, from the limestone peaks of the Pennines along the western boundary, to the North York Moors and Cleveland Hills of the east. The Vale of York in the centre is a green, broad plain of rich, alluvial soil, while the south is typified by the hard millstone grit and rich coal seams exploited by industry. Numerous rivers add to the scenic appeal.

Many local writers have brought fame to the region, from the Brontë sisters of the western moors to James Herriott's veterinary adventures among the walled green pastures of the dales. For over 300 years Yorkshire has produced memorable gardens, great and small, and outstanding examples of the 18th-century landscape park. The spa town of Harrogate is a horticultural centre for the region, hosting important spring and autumn flower shows in the Valley Gardens and the North of England Showground, while the Northern Horticultural Society's headquarters are on the outskirts, at Harlow Carr.

APPLETREEWICK

Parcevall Hall

Appletreewick, Skipton BD23 6DE **TEL.** *01756-720311* **OWNER** *Walsingham College (Yorkshire Properties) Ltd* **HOURS** *Good Friday–Oct, daily, 10a.m.–6p.m., winter by appointment* **ENTRANCE** *£2, children 50p* **DIRECTIONS** *1m NE of Appletreewick, off B6265*

SPRING SUMMER AUTUMN WINTER

Access Café Plant Shop DON'T MISS

The 15th-century Hall is hidden away in such a peaceful spot in Upper Wharfedale that it is used as a centre for quiet retreats. The 20-acre site was bought in 1927 by Sir William Milner, a godson of Queen Mary, and both house and garden flourished under his patronage for the next three decades. The garden fell into disrepair after his death in 1960, but recent restoration work has allowed it to flourish once more.

The old orchard, awash with daffodils in spring, has been supplemented by new plantings of historic apple varieties, such as 'Lady Henniker', 'Striped Beefing', 'Cockpit' and 'Gooseberry'. From there, a steep climb provides exquisite views of Middle Wharfedale, washed by stony streams far below. The rock garden was made not by Man but in the Carboniferous era, and is watered by a natural spring that feeds a clear pool. Its margins are surrounded by marsh orchids and scented yellow *Primula florindae*. Rhododendrons flourish, in spite of the limestone, due to overlaying pockets of acid soil, supplemented over the decades by thick dressings of bracken.

The most architectural part of the garden is a series of terraces and lawns by the house, facing south with spectacular views across the dale to the rocky hill of Simon's Seat. There are also herbaceous borders, lily-ponds and a pergola of climbing roses, a soft focus around the buttressed terraces of pink and buff gritstone.

HARROGATE

Harlow Carr Botanical Gardens

Crag Lane, Harrogate HG3 1QB TEL. *01423-565418* OWNER *Northern Horticultural Society* HOURS *All year, daily, 9.30a.m.–6p.m. or dusk if sooner* ENTRANCE *£3.40, OAPs £2.60* DIRECTIONS *1½m W of Harrogate town centre on B6162 Otley road*

SPRING SUMMER AUTUMN WINTER

Gift Shop · Café · Plant Shop · NPC

DON'T MISS

The saying goes, 'If it grows at Harlow Carr, it will grow anywhere' which testifies both to the climate and soil. Now the headquarters of the Northern Horticultural Society, the original garden at Harlow Carr was created on 30 acres of pasture leased from Harrogate Council, together with a dilapidated early-Victorian bath-house, built to take advantage of a sulphurous stream. As you would expect of a large demonstration garden run by an organisation, the emphasis is on horticulture and education, without the personal touch of a private garden.

Since its infancy half a century ago, Harlow Carr has expanded to 68 well-maintained acres supporting an astonishing variety of plants in unenviable acid clay exposed to chilly winds. The stream, with bog plants filling its banks, separates the intensively cultivated gardens from the woodland. There are fine rock gardens, a winter garden, and four different themed areas for displaying particular groups of plants. Besides the important trial and demonstration gardens testing new varieties of vegetables and flowers, there are five National Collections of plants, including calluna, hypericum and rhubarb, as well as dryopteris and polypodium ferns.

CELEBRITY CHOICE

***Geoffrey Smith, panellist of BBC Radio 4's* Gardeners' Question Time**

'I spend many a Sunday afternoon at ***Fountains Abbey*** *(q.v.) because its landscape garden speaks of the tranquillity of centuries.* ***Castle Howard*** *(q.v.) is also magnificent; such an immense landscape. Its sheer extravagance is breathtaking.*

'I also greatly admire the gorgeous herbaceous borders of ***Newby Hall*** *(q.v.) and the way they sweep away from the house, down a gentle slope to the river. But, above all others, the garden I love most is* ***Parcevall*** *(q.v.), 1000 feet up in the Dales. It's a sublime place and not just because of the plants, although it has a fine collection, but also for the landscape around it.* ***York Gate*** *(q.v.), at Adel, is second only to Parcevall; it's an intimate family garden, but full of good plantsmanship.'*

RIPON

Fountains Abbey and Studley Royal

Ripon HG4 3DY TEL. *01765-608888* OWNER *The National Trust* HOURS *Open all year, daily, 10a.m.–5p.m. (7p.m. April–Sept, last adm. 6p.m.), except 24 and 25 Dec and every Fri in Nov–Jan* ENTRANCE *£4.20, children £2, family ticket £10* DIRECTIONS *4m W of Ripon, off B6265*

SPRING SUMMER AUTUMN WINTER

Access Gift Shop Café DON'T MISS

The political career of John Aislabie, Chancellor of the Exchequer, burst with the South Sea Bubble in 1720 and he fled, disgraced, to his Yorkshire estate to create a landscape garden. Studley Royal is a garden of trees, sculpted lawns and, above all, differing moods of water. To enjoy Aislabie's intended sequence of surprises in this 800-acre World Heritage site, begin at the discreet entrance at Studley Roger rather than Fountains Abbey, where all the tourists are directed, which is like starting a meal with the pudding.

At the entrance the River Skell plunges over the cascade into a huge lake. But stand on the bridge and you will see that, before its liberation, the water runs along the orderly confines of a formal canal, beside which smooth lawns form a level, semicircular sward. Cut into the turf, like precise shapes lifted from rolled-out pastry, lie the silent moon ponds: a perfect circle flanked by symmetrical crescents, reflecting the dark woods and temple behind.

More eye-catching temples are placed around the gardens, but the most compelling one long predates the garden, being the ruins of the Cistercian Fountains Abbey. Glimpsed through the trees, its melancholy tower and crumbling gothic arches invite further exploration and you can follow the river upstream to the abbey ruins. Fountains was initially a place of austerity and toil, yet by the 13th century its estates were producing around 30,000lb of wool per year, for a rich and powerful monastic empire. The waters of the Skell skirt its foundations much as the distant generations of Aislabies would have known it.

THE RUSSELL LUPINS

George Russell (the fifth son of a shoemaker, he was born in 1857 at Stillington, around 10 miles north of York) worked for many years as a professional gardener in the York region. His private passion was lupins, and he spent more than 20 years on his allotments breeding a new strain bearing large, tightly packed flower spikes in a new range of colours. Word spread and nurserymen and seedsmen from all over the country came to buy his amazing stock. He resisted all offers until one day he finally capitulated and accepted an offer from Jimmy Baker, of Wolverhampton. The new plants caused a sensation when exhibited at the Royal Horticultural Society in 1937, and immediately became a famous and popular strain.

RIPON

Newby Hall

Nr Ripon HG4 5AE TEL. *01423-322583* OWNER *R.E.J. Compton* HOURS *April–Sept, daily except Mon, but open Bank Holiday Mons, 11a.m.–5.30p.m.* ENTRANCE *£4, OAPs £3.50, children (4 and over) and disabled people £2.70* DIRECTIONS *4m SE of Ripon, off B6265*

SPRING SUMMER AUTUMN WINTER

Access | Gift Shop | Café | Plant Shop | NPC | DON'T MISS

When John Claudius Loudon (the Geoff Hamilton of the early 19th century) visited Newby Hall in 1837, he could find little to praise: 'A mass of flower beds... extremely ill placed [with] nothing to recommend them and it is seen at a glance that they have no business where they are.'

Ninety-odd years later, the 30-year-old Major Edward Compton turned much of the garden's 25 acres into a golf course, an entertaining diversion while his vast plantings of shelter trees were growing (for shelter is needed to fend off the persistent winds hurling across the moors). This accomplished, he began his master plan, which is largely the layout you now see. If Loudon were to come back today he would surely report very differently, for this is one of the most richly planted and thoughtfully laid out gardens in the country.

The double herbaceous borders are famous, running – spectacularly – for 300 yds down a gentle slope to the River Ure, forming the main axis from the house. To either side are intimate, enclosed gardens of varying themes, that were inspired by Lawrence Johnston's garden at Hidcote Manor (*q.v.*) in Gloucestershire. Sylvia's Garden features flowering plants chiefly for spring and early summer, and the rose pergola is draped in assorted climbing varieties, leading to an Edwardian rock garden designed by the indefatigable Ellen Willmott (*q.v.*). From there, a curving pergola suspends springtime tresses of laburnum flowers. There are fine trees, old-fashioned roses and autumn foliage shrubs in great variety, and the richness of planting is largely due to the skills and enthusiasm of the present owners, Robin Compton (Major Edward's son) and his wife, Jane. Newby Hall also holds a National Collection of cornus.

YORK

Castle Howard

Nr York YO6 7DA **TEL.** *01653-648333 (recorded message) or 01653-648444* **OWNER** *Castle Howard Estates Ltd* **HOURS** *Mid-March–Oct, daily, 10a.m.–5.30p.m. (last adm. 4.30p.m.)* **ENTRANCE** *£4, children £2 (house and grounds £6.50, OAPs £5.50, children £3.50)* **DIRECTIONS** *5m SW of Malton, 14m NE of York, by A64*

SPRING SUMMER AUTUMN WINTER

Access · Gift Shop · Café · Plant Shop · DON'T MISS

The creation of three men – the 3rd Earl of Carlisle, the gentleman-architect John Vanbrugh and his brilliant assistant Nicholas Hawksmoor – Castle Howard is a fascinating example of how an owner managed to enjoy and shape a vast landscape in the last days of the 17th century. Horace Walpole captured the essence of it in 1772: 'Nobody told me that I should at one view see a palace, a town, a fortified city, temples on high places, woods worthy of being each a metropolis of the Druids, the noblest lawn on earth fenced by half the horizon and a mausoleum that would tempt one to be buried alive... I have seen gigantic places before but never a sublime one.' It later featured in the television adaptation of *Brideshead Revisited* in the early 1980s.

Wear comfortable shoes and allow plenty of time to explore the Temple of the Four Winds, the Roman bridge and Hawksmoor's mausoleum, the outstanding set pieces in the huge 1000-acre park. Ray Wood, on the east side of the house, is a 20-year-old naturalistic garden of rhododendrons, bluebells and specimen trees planted within an older woodland. Fountains by Nesfield remain in the formal gardens in front of the house, and there is a large collection of old-fashioned and species roses in the old walled kitchen gardens.

APPLES OF THE NORTH

R.V. Roger Ltd, The Nurseries, Pickering YO18 7HG (tel. 01751-472226), 26m N of York, 1m S of Pickering, on A169, *stocks a huge range of plants, including roses, trees, hedging, conifers, heathers, shrubs, climbers, herbaceous plants and fruit, available from the plant centre and also by mail (catalogue £1.50). Fruit is a speciality, particularly apples which grow well in the north, of which they stock over 60 varieties on a range of rootstocks, grown in their own field. Since 'Cox's Orange Pippin' is intolerant of cold conditions, Anthony Roger recommends the self-fertile dessert apple 'Sunset' as a substitute. He also suggests 'Newton Wonder' (also self-fertile), 'Fortune', a mid-season variety for picking in September, and 'Balsam', one of his favourites, which should be picked in November and is ready to eat from February. His other favourites are 'Epicure', 'because it is so delicious', and 'Brownlees Russet', 'the best russet to grow in the north'. As they are field grown, the bulk of the fruit is dispatched between November and March, while dormant. Apple Day (around 21 October) is celebrated at the nursery with fruit tastings, displays, and experts who will identify visitors' own fruit and offer advice on growing. Open daily, 9a.m.–5p.m. (Sun 1–5p.m.); closed during Christmas period between 25 Dec–2 Jan.*

SHEEP SHEARS – FOR TRIM TOPIARY

***Burgon & Ball Ltd, La Plata Works, Holme Lane, Sheffield S6 4JY (tel. 0114-233 8262)**, has been producing agricultural tools since 1730, but its sheep shears are no longer confined to trimming livestock. The sharp blades and single-handed action have proved useful to topiarists for trimming evergreen sculptures in box and yew with precision. The shears come in two sizes, and are available by mail order. The firm also produces the Bay Tree Collection of unusual and decorative garden objects, included in a free full-colour mail order catalogue, from the above address.*

And also...

The 66-acre historic gardens of **Bramham Park, Wetherby LS23 6ND (tel. 01937-844265)**, are famed for being laid out in the French style of Le Nôtre in the very early 18th century. There is a geometric arrangement of straight avenues cut through woodland, flanked by high beech hedges. The park is said to be haunted by riderless horses that fled from the Battle of Bramham Moor in 1408. They were witnessed by the present owner's father, Colonel Francis Lane Fox, during the 1930s; he thought he heard the local hunt riding across the park and held open a gate for them to pass, but nobody came, and when the sound of galloping hooves died away, he realised he had heard the horses. There are miles of walks to stretch your legs, punctuated by statues, temples, obelisks and formal ponds, while the flower gardens are confined to an Edwardian design of formal rose beds in front of the house. Open Easter weekend (but not Good Friday), May and Spring Bank Holiday weekends, and late June–early Sept (closed two weeks in July), Tues–Thurs, Sun, and Bank Holiday Mons, 1.15–5.30p.m. (last adm. 5p.m.). Entrance to grounds only £2.50, OAPs £2, children £1, house and gardens £4, OAPs £3, children £2.

Brodsworth Hall, Brodsworth, Doncaster DN5 7XJ (tel. 01302-722598), is a Victorian stone mansion in classical Italian style, fascinating for its well-preserved interior. It gives a good insight into the Victorian country house life. The 16-acre gardens are landscaped in high

Victoriana with dense shrubberies, symmetrical bedded-out flower gardens, a mystical quarry garden with natural cliffs and artificial rockwork decked with ferns, and a box-edged rose garden, with iron pergola. Open April–Oct, Tues–Sun and Bank Holidays, 1–6p.m. (closes at dusk in Oct); garden open at 12 noon; last adm. to house and gardens 5p.m. Entrance £4.50, OAPs £3.40, children £2.30, garden only £2.50, OAPs £1.90, children £1.

If you like delphiniums, you'll love **8 Dunstarn Lane, Adel, Leeds LS16 8EL**, home of retired Liberal MP, Richard Wainwright. His two-acre garden is famous for its collection of delphiniums, laid out in three 225ft-long herbaceous borders created over 60 years ago by his father. More than 60 different varieties are displayed in the gardens, which open at peak time for a couple of Sunday afternoons in July. For this year's dates consult or telephone the NGS (01483-211535).

Carthusian monks founded **Mount Grace Priory, Staddlebridge, Northallerton DL6 3JG (tel. 01609-883494)**, in 1398, living as hermits in four-roomed cells, each with its own garden. One has been carefully reconstructed with a garden of raised beds featuring herbs. Also on the 11½-acre site is an Arts and Crafts-style house built at the turn of the century, incorporating earlier buildings, and a one-acre Victorian garden of stepped terraces and shrubberies. Open April–Oct, daily, 10a.m.–6p.m. (last adm. 5.30p.m.); Nov–March, Wed–Sun, 10a.m.–4p.m. (closed 1–2p.m. in winter). Entrance £2.70, concessions £2.10, children £1.40.

Norton Conyers, nr Ripon HG4 5EQ (tel. 01765-640333), was visited by Charlotte Brontë in 1839 and provided the inspiration for Thornfield Hall in *Jane Eyre*. Its two-acre 18th-century walled garden contains herbaceous borders, an historic orangery and pick-your-own fruit in season, plus a small plant sales area specializing in unusual hardy plants. The garden is open every Sun and Bank Holiday Mons from Easter Sunday–mid-Sept, 11.30a.m.–5p.m., and Mon–Sat for one week in late July,

2–5p.m.; house open mid-June–mid-Sept, Mons, and Mon–Sat for one week in late July (same as for garden), also Bank Holiday Suns and Mons, 2–5p.m. Entrance (garden) free, (house) £2.95, OAPs £2, children (10–16) £2.50, rates for parties on application.

Tree enthusiasts will enjoy the 85 acres of **Thorp Perrow Arboretum, Bedale DL8 2PR (tel. 01677-425323),** home to over 2000 tree species, including National Collections of ash, oak, walnut and lime. It is a pleasant place for springtime walks, particularly when thousands of daffodils and bluebells are in bloom, and in autumn when tree foliage tints can be spectacular. Open daily all year, dawn to dusk. Entrance £3, children and OAPs £2.

The Valley Gardens, Valley Drive, Harrogate (run by Harrogate Council, tel. 01423-500600), are on a 42-acre site on the south-western side of the town centre, opposite the famous Royal Pump Room. They convey the civic pride of this prosperous spa town, with colourful and precise formal bedding for spring and summer, and a long dahlia border for late summer and autumn, a pleasing place to walk off lunch or tea taken at **Betty's**, the famous tearoom nearby. Gardens open all year, 24 hours a day. Entrance free.

York Gate, Back Church Lane, Adel, Leeds LS16 8DW (tel. 01132-678240), is seldom open since its owner, the enchanting Sybil Spencer, died a few years ago, but when it is, it is definitely worth visiting. Within one acre the Spencer family created a series of themed gardens, including a herb garden, two vegetable gardens, a mini-pinetum, pavement maze, white garden, raised pool and interesting topiary. Mrs Spencer left it to the Gardeners' Royal Benevolent Society, and it is now a home for retired professional gardeners, who continue to maintain its excellence. It is open occasionally for charities such as the NGS, and by appointment, 2–6p.m. Entrance £2.50, children free.

NORTHERN IRELAND

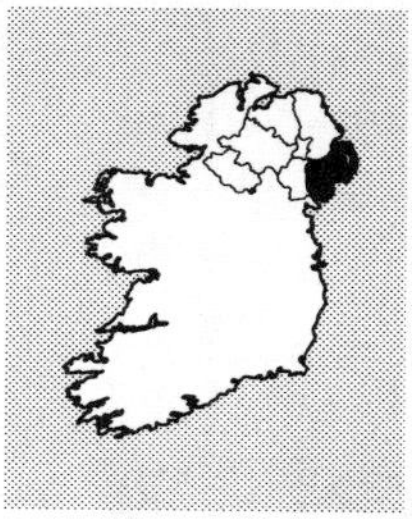

Ards and Down

MAP NO. 8

Speaking as someone used to the crowded south-east of England, I find one of the great joys of visiting gardens in Ards and Down is the tranquillity to see and photograph them at leisure. There is no doubt that the region is under-visited while harbouring some priceless horticultural jewels.

It is a rural region of small hills, stony outcrops and quiet lanes; friendly, relaxing and endlessly rewarding for anyone who takes a pleasure in plants and an undisturbed landscape. Strangford Lough, an inland sea enclosed by the Ards Peninsula, is famous for migrating and nesting birds, seals and other wildlife, but several fine gardens are also positioned on its shores.

CASTLEWELLAN

Castlewellan National Arboretum

The Grange, Castlewellan, Forest Park BT31 9BU **TEL.** *013967-78664* **OWNER** *Dept of Agriculture, N. Ireland* **HOURS** *Open all year, daily, 10a.m.–dusk* **ENTRANCE** *£3 cars, £6 mini-buses* **DIRECTIONS** *25m S of Belfast, 4m NW of Newcastle, by A24*

SPRING SUMMER AUTUMN WINTER

Access Café

Castlewellan Arboretum is famous for raising the eponymous golden-leaved Leyland cypress (which, you cannot help noticing, is extensively used as garden hedging in the region). The Arboretum sits on sloping ground on the northern side of the beautiful Mourne Mountains, four miles inland from the sea. Its tree collection, spread over 108 acres, was begun more than 100 years ago by the Annesley family, and the acidic soil supports a classic cocktail of rhododendrons, camellias, South American and Antipodean trees and shrubs, arranged within the extensive walled gardens and around the lakeside. Walks here at any time of year are rewarding, but spring and autumn are the most spectacular for their floral and foliage bounty respectively, while the many white-flowered eucryphias are a summer speciality.

NEWTOWNARDS

Mount Stewart

Greyabbey, Newtownards BT22 2AD **TEL.** *012477-88387/88487* **OWNER** *The National Trust* **HOURS** *Gardens, April–Sept, daily, 11a.m.–6p.m., Oct, Sat and Sun, 11a.m.–6p.m., March, Sun only, 2–5p.m. (house sometimes opens at different times)* **ENTRANCE** *£3, children £1.50; 50p (children 25p) extra to see house, family ticket (garden only) £7.50, (house and garden) £8.75* **DIRECTIONS** *15m SE of Belfast, 5m SE of Newtownards, on A20 Portaferry road*

SPRING SUMMER AUTUMN WINTER

Access Café DON'T MISS

Some gardens are remarkable for their plant collections, some for their rigorous design, and others are special for the particular atmosphere imbued by their makers. Mount Stewart combines all of these three assets and is among the most memorable of the hundreds that I have visited for this *Guide*.

The 80-acre garden was chiefly laid out during the 1920s by Edith, Marchioness of Londonderry. Edith, known to her close friends as 'Circe, the Sorceress', was a remarkable woman by any standards: an influential political hostess, she founded the Women's Legion in 1915 which provided jobs for women while men were away fighting and greatly improved the status of women in the workplace. Following the First World War, Edith spent much of her time at Mount Stewart and refurbished the house interiors as well as giving ex-servicemen employment in laying out the formal gardens.

The Italian garden on the south front of the house comprises richly planted formal parterres (best in summer) modelled on those of Dunrobin Castle, Sutherland, Edith's childhood home. Beyond is the Spanish garden, with rills and formal pool, surrounded by impressive arcaded hedges of Leyland cypress. The sunk garden on the west side was laid out according to plans sent by post from Gertrude Jekyll (*q.v.*) although its plantings of yellow and orange, blue and purple flowers and foliage is largely to Edith's specification. Mount Stewart's gardens were deeply personal to Edith and are imbued with symbolism; its shamrock garden, enclosed by yew hedges, contains a topiarised Irish harp in yew and a ground pattern featuring the Red Hand of Ulster, planted seasonally with scarlet flowers. The Dodo terrace features cast concrete animals from The Ark, a dining club regularly hosted by Edith in London. All Ark members had amusing or apposite nicknames, often referring to animals: Edith's philandering husband was Charley the Cheetah, Winston Churchill was called Winnie the Warlock, while the financier and journalist William Astor was Billy the Goat.

Mount Stewart's sheltered position, dependable rainfall and lime-free soil have all encouraged rapid growth of rare and sub-tropical plants in the formal gardens and glorious rhododendrons and magnolias in the surrounding woodlands and lakeside. Edith's extravagant spending on their creation hardly dented her husband's vast coal-mining fortune. An interesting, little-known mark of Edith's independent nature is that she had a twining snake tattooed up her left leg while visiting Japan in 1904. It remained a private foible until hemlines were raised in the 1920s and '30s, whereupon its discovery caused a sensation.

SAINTFIELD

Rowallane

Saintfield, Ballynahinch BT24 7LH TEL. *01238-510131*
OWNER *The National Trust* HOURS *early April–end Oct, Mon–Fri, 10.30a.m.–6p.m., weekends, 2p.m.–6p.m. Nov–late March, Mon–Fri, 10.30a.m.–5p.m.; closed 25,*

26 Dec and 1 Jan ENTRANCE *£2.50, children £1.25, reduced rates in winter* DIRECTIONS *11m SE of Belfast, 1m S of Saintfield, on A7*

SPRING SUMMER AUTUMN WINTER

Access Café DON'T MISS

With Rowallane and Mount Stewart (*q.v.*) in reasonably close proximity, you can witness, in one day, two completely opposing forces in garden-making – the formal and naturalistic. Each has its own sense of place, with Mount Stewart's reflecting and responding to the formal house it surrounds, while Rowallane's 52-acre garden moulds itself to the landscape. It could hardly do otherwise, for Rowallane sits firmly in drumlin land, an undulating, rocky landscape formed in the Ice Age, leaving bare rocks and smooth boulders pushing up through pockets of acidic soil.

'My son always calls it eiderdown country, because it looks buttoned-down,' says Rowallane's head gardener, Mike Snowden, and the description is apt. The only formal area at Rowallane is the walled kitchen garden, but even that is now given over to naturalistic plantings of primulas and meconopsis threaded among specimen shrubs and trees, including a towering *Magnolia veitchii*, spectacularly in bloom in spring. The point of Rowallane is its plant collections, of endless fascination to any keen gardener, while its gentle contours and thoughtful planting make it a pleasure for anyone. You can saunter at random through woods and glades, among the flowering shrubberies, or tiptoe between the boulders in the rock garden. Most visitors come to see the fine collection of rhododendrons, between mid-April and mid-June, assembled by the garden's makers, the Revd John Moore in the last half of the 19th century and his nephew, Hugh Armytage Moore, in the first half of the 20th. Rowallane has also produced many of its own distinctive plant varieties, including the hybrid *Hypericum* 'Rowallane', *Chaenomeles* × *superba* 'Rowallane', and a crocosmia, viburnum, primula and meconopsis. The property was farmed before the arrival of the Revd Moore and its small, stone-walled fields and domestic atmosphere add to the garden's friendly character.

STRANGFORD

Castle Ward

Strangford, Downpatrick BT30 7LS TEL. *01396-881204* OWNER *The National Trust* HOURS *House open Good Friday–Sun after Easter, daily, rest of month Sat–Sun only, May–Aug, daily, except Thurs, Sept–Oct, Sat–Sun only, 1–6p.m., grounds open daily all year, dawn–dusk* ENTRANCE *£2.60, children £1.30, family ticket £6.50* DIRECTIONS *On S shore of Strangford Lough, 7m NE of Downpatrick, 1½m W of Strangford village on A25*

SPRING SUMMER AUTUMN WINTER

Access Gift Shop Café

Glorious views of the seawater inlet of Strangford Lough, fine woodland walks and a pleasing, intimate Victorian garden of exotics are some of the pleasures of a visit to the 700-acre estate of Castle Ward. (There is also a three-week opera season in June.) Owing to the mild local climate, the parkland trees grow into magnificent specimens, their feet bathed in seas of bluebells in late spring.

The sunken garden, on the north side of the house, is walled and formal, with sculpted lawns enclosing beds of roses and seasonally bedded-out flowers. Castle Ward's cabbage palms in this area have formed stout-trunk trees that bring a vertical emphasis, while tender exotics such as *Beschorneria yuccoides* and fascicularias take advantage of the sheltering walls and surrounding forest trees.

Visit the extraordinary house; it is an entertainingly schizophrenic mix of classical austerity on its south-western front and a contrasting gothick style on the north-east, due to the opposing tastes of its creators, Bernard Ward (later Lord Bangor) and his wife, Lady Anne. The curious his-'n'-hers arrangement continues indoors, too. 'Mr Ward is building a fine house,' wrote Mrs Delany, while visiting in

1762, 'but... it is a pity it should not be judiciously laid out. He wants taste and... his wife is so whimsical that I doubt her judgement. If they do not do too much they can't spoil the place, for it hath every advantage from nature that can be desired.' From the point of view of sunlight, Lady Anne perhaps drew the short straw in taking the north-east elevation, but she did have, at least, compensating spectacular views of the undulating park and distant Lough.

And also...

Ballyrogan Nurseries, The Grange, Ballyrogan, Newtownards BT23 4SD (tel. 01247-810451), are open by appointment with Gary Dunlop, the proprietor, who holds the National Collections of crocosmia, celmisia and euphorbia in his rugged and rocky three-acre garden. Send 2 × 1st-class stamps for a catalogue of his extensive list of nursery plants, which can be ordered by mail.

Carraig Beag, 1 Cloughey Road, Portaferry, Newtownards BT22 1ND (tel. 012477-28777), covers two-thirds of an acre, at the southern end of Strangford Lough. The home of Mrs D. Wallace, it features extensive planting, including two ponds with associated planting for seasonal interest. Open by appointment only, May–Aug. Entrance £2, children free, reduced rates for parties of 20 or more.

Roses are the speciality at **Dickson Nurseries Ltd, Milecross Road, Newtownards BT23 4SS (tel. 01247-812206)**. This firm was founded in 1836 and many well-known 20th-century roses have been bred here, including 'Grandpa Dickson', a yellow hybrid tea, and the popular patio rose, 'Sunseeker'. The nursery is open Mon–Thurs, 8a.m.–12.30p.m. and 1–5p.m., and Fri, 8a.m.–12.30p.m. A mail order list of roses is free on request.

---

9 Portaferry Road, Greyabbey BP22 2RU (tel. 012477-88351), the first house on the shore side of Portaferry Road, on the shores of Strangford Lough, is near the famous Mount Stewart gardens (*q.v.*). Here is a delightful, private seaside garden divided into richly planted, individual sections by Mrs Betty Brittain, who is pleased to show visitors round, by appointment. Entrance £2, OAPs £1, children free, reduced rates for parties of 20 or more.

Seaforde Gardens and Tropical Butterfly House, Downpatrick BT30 8PG (tel. 01396-811225), boast the National Collection of eucryphia, as well as a hornbeam maze and a large, walled garden (part of which is a commercial nursery raising over 700 different trees and shrubs, and there is a Butterfly House with tropical plants). There is also a tearoom and the gardens are accessible to the disabled. All is set within eight acres of a lovely landscape park with fine mature trees and rhododendrons. Open Easter–end Sept, Mon–Sat, 10a.m.–5p.m., Sun, 2–6p.m. Oct–Mar, Mon–Fri, 10a.m.–5p.m. (closed for Christmas–New Year period). Entrance for garden £2, children £1.20, tropical Butterfly House £2, children £1.20, combined ticket £3.50, children £2.

Belfast and Antrim

MAP NO. 8

It is a deeply ingrained part of Irish hospitality to ensure that everyone is well fed and watered, and I enjoyed a hearty meal and a few beers in good company at the amazing Crown Liquor Saloon (a gas-lit, exotically tiled Victorian pub) in Belfast on my first day here – a good start. Beyond the city, the landscape is undulating, small farmland, with wooded glens and a spectacular coastline, particularly at The Giant's Causeway where some 40,000 steps formed from basalt columns, due to the even cooling of volcanic lava 60 million years ago. Harebells, thrift and sea campions eke a living in the windy headlands, while pyramidal orchids and burnet roses cling to the dunes of Murlough Bay, watching over Scotland's Western Isles, just a few miles away by sea.

BELFAST

Belfast Botanic Garden Park

Stranmillis Road, Belfast BT7 1JP **TEL.** *01232-324902* **OWNER** *Belfast City Council Parks Dept* **HOURS** *Open all year, daily, 7.30a.m.–dusk* **ENTRANCE** *Free* **DIRECTIONS** *In the University area, about a 10-minute walk from Donegall Square, between University and Ulster Museum*

SPRING SUMMER AUTUMN WINTER

Café

The city of Belfast built its wealth on the traditional industries of shipbuilding, rope-making, linen and tobacco, and an enjoyable couple of hours can be spent in its Botanic Gardens, which reflect the boom times of the Victorian age. The gardens were founded in 1828 and cover around 30 acres; they are partly formal, with seasonal bedding set into broad lawns, and contain 5000 different plants with special collections of Irish-raised cultivars and *Bromeliaceae* (the tropical plant family which includes pineapples). There are fine herbaceous borders and a rose garden with around

8000 plants, but the glasshouses are the highlight of a visit. The restored palm house, built in the mid-19th century, is one of the finest and earliest surviving examples of curvilinear glass and cast ironwork with a gracefully domed roof, while the Tropical Ravine House nearby offers views from a balcony into a more steamy jungle of ferns, bananas, waterlilies and vines from the tropics (pull the chain to operate the waterfall!).

Within the Botanic Gardens lies the fascinatingly eclectic Ulster Museum, with exhibits ranging from Irish antiquities to modern art, to treasures from a wreck of the Spanish Armada.

TEMPLEPATRICK

Patterson's Spade Mill

751 Antrim Road, Templepatrick BT39 0AP TEL. *01849-433619* OWNER *The National Trust* HOURS *Easter Bank Holiday, daily, 2–6p.m.; April, May and Sept, Sat, Sun and Bank Holidays only, 2–6p.m.; June–Aug, daily, except Tues, 2–6p.m.* ENTRANCE *£2.50, children £1.25* DIRECTIONS *3m E of Templepatrick on A6 (Belfast–Antrim road)*

SPRING SUMMER AUTUMN WINTER

Gift Shop

Comparatively few people have seen a garden spade being made by hand, but it is fascinating, and a visit to this time-capsule cottage industry is well worthwhile; you can buy a spade to take home or order one tailored to your own measurements. (Ring the mill first, to check demonstration times, if you want to see spade-making in action.)

At least 171 different types of spade have been recorded in Ireland, their shapes having evolved to suit different types of terrain; a winged spade is suitable for cutting out blocks of peat, whereas the Annalong spade is designed with a taper to wedge into stony soils. Six different styles are regularly made at Patterson's now, the typical model having a long, fairly narrow blade, useful for digging in confined spaces, for example in well-stocked flowerbeds where you want to avoid disturbing surrounding plants.

All the spades start as a 4in × 2in × ¾in block of steel, which is heated and hammered into shape before being riveted to an ash shaft. It is hot, noisy, heavy work, with the vast hammer being driven by water from the River Ballygowan and the dusty air in the dimly lit mill filled with the blended smells of oil, metal and wood shavings.

And also...

Redcot, 35 King's Road, Belfast BT5 6JG (tel. 01232-796614), is a two-and-a-half-acre garden with mixed plantings of shrubs and trees, and double herbaceous borders extending 100ft, plus woodland, wild areas and a fernery. Open by appointment with Mr and Mrs Knox Gass, and for local charities during July. Entrance £2.

---

13 Cairnburn Gardens, Cairnburn Road, Belfast BT4 2HY (tel. 01232-763575), is an average-sized suburban garden, 'no lawns', says Mrs Merrick, but 'stuffed full of a very good range of unusual herbaceous plants', which she is pleased to share with visitors, by appointment only, from May to Sept. Entrance £2.

SCOTLAND

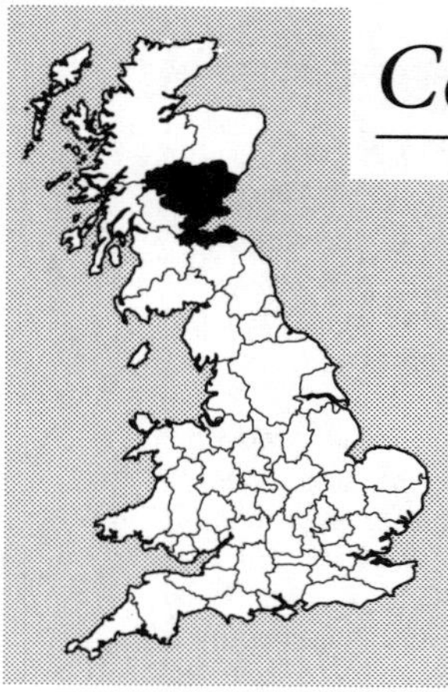

Central Scotland

MAP NO. 8

This region encompasses the areas previously known as Fife, Lothian and Tayside, parts of which are now fragmented into unitary authorities. South of the Firth of Forth lies Edinburgh, the Heart of Midlothian, with its castle perched on a core of ancient volcanic rock. The Lothian region is peppered with castles and battlefields and, like other parts of Scotland, a liberal sprinkling of golf courses. North of the Forth lies the ancient Kingdom of Fife with its pleasantly undulating farming landscape, sandy coastline and attractive fishing villages. Dunfermline was once the seat of the Scottish monarchy but Fife's great claim to fame now is the university town of St Andrews, home of the Royal and Ancient Golf Club. Perthshire and Kinross, with Angus, occupy the former Tayside. It has a lush greenness and a picturesque hardiness with ancient, wind-blasted granite hills and broad, forested glens. There are deep inland lochs fed by countless mountain burns, and tough wildflowers eke a living in moorland and scree. The region is perfect for outdoor pursuits such as hill walking, fishing, seasonal shoots, birdwatching and skiing, while botanists enjoy browsing the hillsides of Glens Clova and Doll.

BALERNO

Malleny Garden

Balerno, nr Edinburgh, Lothian EH14 7AF **TEL.** *0131-449 2283* **OWNER** *National Trust for Scotland* **HOURS** *April–Oct, daily, 9.30a.m.–7p.m., Nov–March daily, 9.30a.m.–4p.m. (house not open)* **ENTRANCE** *£1* **DIRECTIONS** *In Balerno, off A70 Edinburgh–Lanark road*

SPRING SUMMER AUTUMN WINTER

NPC

JAMES GRIEVE AND HIS PLANTS

James Grieve joined Dicksons Nursery in Edinburgh in 1859, where he became involved with plant hybridisation while managing the nursery. His particular interests in plant breeding were concerned with achimenes, carnations, phlox, rhododendrons and violas, but his name is most familiar today for the well-known apple that is named after him.

The apple 'James Grieve' is renowned for its excellent sweet flavour, well-balanced acidity and use as both a dessert apple and a cooker (the latter when used fresh). It arose as a seedling, open pollinated from 'Pott's Seedling' or from 'Cox's Orange Pippin', and was introduced to the trade by Dicksons in 1893. In 1897 it received an Award of Merit from the Royal Horticultural Society, followed by a First Class Certificate in 1906. It is an ideal fruit for northern gardens where summers are cooler and allow the fruits to develop at a steady pace, but is not a good choice in the humid west of the country, where it may develop canker.

Covering just three acres, this is a pretty, summery garden attached to a 17th-century house. Its group of four yew trees, clipped like slender mushrooms on stalks, are 400 years old and dominate the garden, standing in huddled conversation beside smooth lawns. There are fine herbaceous borders, 12ft deep and sumptuously planted, and a large collection of old-fashioned roses. To see this garden at its best, visit around mid- to high summer. The garden also houses an important National Collection of bonsai.

CRIEFF

Drummond Castle

Muthill, nr Crieff, Perth and Kinross, Tayside PH7 2HZ **TEL.** *01764-681257* **OWNER** *Grimsthorpe & Drummond Castle Trust Ltd* **HOURS** *May–Oct, daily, 2–6p.m. (last entry 5p.m.)* **ENTRANCE** *£3, OAPs £2, children (aged 5–16) £1.50* **DIRECTIONS** *2m S of Crieff, off A822*

SPRING SUMMER AUTUMN WINTER

DON'T MISS

The spectacular gardens of Drummond Castle lie in a level valley bottom, made all the more dramatic because you get an aerial view first, from the castle's courtyard, high up on a ridge of rock towering over the valley. The symmetrical parterres are laid out with neat swirls and lines of low, box hedging, partly infilled with gravel and partly with brilliant roses and summer bedding. Topiarised variegated hollies, green and golden columns of yew and cypress, and mop-headed, purple-leaved acers and plums bring vertical accents into the pattern, and all is immaculately maintained.

The garden was laid out in the 1830s, but in the highly wrought style that prevailed in the 17th century. At the heart of the parterre is a celebrated sundial, made by John

DAVID DOUGLAS – OUR MAN IN AMERICA

David Douglas (1798–1834) was one of several intrepid Scottish plant hunters whose pioneering journeys have helped to enrich our gardens. Born at Scone, Perthshire, he was the son of a stonemason. His childhood fascination for natural history led him early into a botanical career, beginning at Scone Palace, in the gardens of Lord Mansfield. Work followed in the botanic garden of Glasgow University, where he caught the attention of W.J. Hooker, the regius professor. Douglas joined Hooker on botanising expeditions through the highlands, which led to trips much further afield for the Royal Horticultural Society. He made three expeditions to America, which was at that time still largely unexplored and inhabited by the indigenous tribes of American Indians. In the tradition of the great plant hunters of the 19th century, his journeys involved great hardship and danger. Tough and resourceful, Douglas survived encounters with grizzly bears, fevers, shortage of food, harsh climates and unfriendly Indians. His explorations led him deep into country which had never encountered a white man, and on one occasion his canoe capsized, leaving him to be spun through a whirlpool before being tossed onto a bank, having lost his irreplaceable journals and 400 plants. Alas, on his third expedition he paused in the Hawaiian islands where his body was found in a pit trap, having been gored by a wild bull.

In his short life Douglas gathered 20,000 plant specimens and introduced around 200 new species which are now widely grown in Britain. They include many American pines, the grand fir Abies grandis, *the Douglas fir* Pseudotsuga menziesii, *the fabulous* Arbutus menziesii *with its cinnamon-coloured peeling bark, and the aromatic Californian 'headache' tree,* Umbellularia californica.

Mylne, master mason to Charles I, dating from around 1630. The vegetable and fruit gardens and glasshouses beyond a beech hedge at the rear are also worth visiting, and the trees in the surrounding woods and park are unusually large and beautiful.

There is partial wheelchair access.

CULROSS

Culross Palace

Culross, Fife KY12 8JH **TEL.** *01383-880359* **OWNER** *National Trust for Scotland* **HOURS** *Good Friday–end Sept, daily, 11a.m.–5p.m. (last adm. 4p.m.)* **ENTRANCE** *£4.20, concessions/children £2.80, family ticket £11.20, organised school parties £1 each* **DIRECTIONS** *On A985, 4m E of Kincardine Bridge, 12m W of Forth Road Bridge*

SPRING **SUMMER** AUTUMN WINTER

Access | Gift Shop | Café

Culross is a well-preserved medieval village with narrow, cobbled streets, picturesquely set on the north shore of the River Forth. Its palace was not a royal residence but home to a wealthy merchant; tour the atmospheric rooms, with beautifully painted timber ceilings, to set the scene before venturing into the garden.

At the rear, the garden rises in steep terraces, covering barely one acre of ground. It is laid out in medieval style, in a series of rectangular raised beds containing culinary, medicinal and dyers' herbs, with some salads and vegetables. Although the planting is not exclusively devoted to plants used in medieval Scotland, the period flavour is preserved with timber boards edging the beds, and woven willow hurdles and a rustic willow tunnel providing part of the framework. I visited on a bright, summer's day when the crunchy paths were quite dazzling; on closer inspection they turned out to be crushed seashells, making a fine contrast to the soft green herbs.

THE SCOTCH THISTLE

Scotland embraces the thistle as its emblem flower, and at Drummond Castle (q.v.) the distinctive outline of this flower has been adapted to wonderful effect in the layout of the garden's great parterre. The emblematic use of the thistle dates from the Middle Ages, when it was adopted by Stuart kings in their heraldic coats of arms. It is thought that the thistle was seen to be a suitable mascot, being tough, durable and defiant, or perhaps because of its prickly aggressiveness.

There is some debate over which particular species of thistle is the appropriate one. Certainly the cotton thistle, Onopordum acanthium, *is decorative enough and makes a fine garden plant where there is room for it. Out of a base rosette of large, silver-grey leaves the leafy flower stem rises to a towering 7–8ft, making this biennial a wonderful spectacle in the flower border. Its neat heads of typical purple thistle flowers are handsome, although small in comparison to the great eruption of foliage. The spear thistle,* 'Cirsium vulgare', *is another candidate for the title of Scotch thistle, bearing classic thistle flowers above fearsomely thorny stems and foliage. It is certainly the more ubiquitous wildflower of the two, and the more likely to have been adopted early on, although for garden purposes its ornamental charms are limited except for use in 'wild' areas of naturalised flowers.*

CUPAR

Hill of Tarvit Mansion House

Cupar, Fife KY15 5PB TEL. *01334-653127* OWNER *National Trust for Scotland* HOURS *Garden: (summer) 9.30a.m.–9.30p.m., (winter) 9.30a.m.–sunset, daily, throughout the year. House: Easter, May–Sept, and Oct, weekends, 1.30–5.30p.m.* ENTRANCE *(House and garden) £3.70, OAPs/children £2.50, (garden) £1 and 50p, by honesty box* DIRECTIONS *2m S of Cupar, on A916*

SPRING | **SUMMER** | AUTUMN | WINTER

Gift Shop | Café

Terraces of broad lawns follow the gentle contours of the site around Hill of Tarvit's Mansion House. The grey-stone, symmetrical house was built during the Edwardian age, in

1906, for one Frederick Sharp, a financial tycoon and art collector, whose ancestors made their fortune turning jute into sackcloth, greatly in demand for sandbags during the American Civil War.

The four-acre garden, like the house, was designed by Sir Robert Lorimer, a prominent local architect, in the contemporary formal style prevailing. The setting is deliberately green, with neat yew hedges and topiaries framing the lawns on the south side, and an interesting series of yew buttresses seemingly 'supporting' a retaining wall beside the lowest terrace, which is reached via a grand stone stairway.

A south-facing wall, enclosing the gardens on the north side of the house, provides shelter for a long herbaceous border in the Edwardian style, punctuated with flowering shrubs such as roses, philadelphus and buddleias. From here you can enter the woodland garden, through a fine gateway, and climb the steep path up to the monument on Tarvit Hill, where you will be rewarded with breath-taking panoramic views.

GEORGE FORREST – OUR MAN IN CHINA

Like David Douglas (q.v.) and Robert Fortune (q.v.), both of whom preceded him, George Forrest (1873–1932) was a tough, lone Scot with an unquenchable thirst for finding plants in far-flung lands. Born in Falkirk, Forrest worked as a chemist's apprentice before going to Australia, where he travelled and worked for 10 years. On his return to Scotland he took employment in the Herbarium of the Royal Botanic Garden, Edinburgh, but within a year he was travelling in the high mountains of Yunnan province, in north-west China.

Chinese explorations occupied his time for the next 28 years, in a total of seven major expeditions which also took him to upper Burma and Tibet. Many popular garden plants were first brought to Britain by Forrest, including Pieris forrestii, *many exquisite rhododendron species, primulas in great variety, camellias, gentians, berberis, buddleias, cotoneasters and mahonias. Today it is hard to imagine the potential perils of looking for plants. Forrest narrowly escaped with his life in 1905 when maurauding Tibetan monks hunted down his collecting party and murdered all but one of them. Hampered by lack of food, an injured and painful foot and travelling under darkness, Forrest spent 10 days retreating back to safety.*

More than 30,000 plant specimens were gathered on his journeys and returned to Edinburgh. George Forrest died in Yunnan province, of heart failure, while out shooting grouse.

EDINBURGH

Royal Botanic Garden

Inverleith Row, Edinburgh, Lothian EH3 5LR **TEL.** *0131-552 7171* **OWNER** *Dept of Agriculture and Fisheries for Scotland* **HOURS** *Daily all year, except 25 Dec and 1 Jan Nov–Feb, 10a.m.–4p.m.; March–April, 10a.m.–6p.m.; May–Aug, 10a.m.–8p.m.; Sept–Oct, 10a.m.–6p.m.* **ENTRANCE** *Free, donations welcome* **DIRECTIONS** *1½m N of city centre, at Inverleith*

SPRING SUMMER AUTUMN WINTER

Access | Gift Shop | Café | Plant Shop | DON'T MISS

This is a centre for botanical research, for which it has a worldwide reputation, but it is also a thrilling garden for visitors. The higher parts of the garden enjoy fabulous views of the city, and its 65 acres include every type of plant imaginable. There is an extensive and beautifully laid out rock garden, a large collection of heathers, a spectacular herbaceous border (backed by very tall beech hedging), excellent demonstration gardens and examples of different types of hedging trees and wonderful glasshouses. These contain large collections of plants from the humid tropics and arid deserts.

The locally acidic soils nurture many rhododendron species and other plants of the Far East, chiefly grown from seed collected in the wild. Look out for the lovely oriental herbaceous flowers such as the Himalayan poppies, variously petalled in bright blues, reds, yellows and white according to their species. Future generations of botanists and horticulturists learn their craft here, and the standard of maintenance is very high.

PERTH

Bell's Cherrybank Gardens

Cherrybank, Perth, Perth and Kinross, Tayside PH2 0NG **TEL.** *01738-452317* **OWNER** *United Distillers UK* **HOURS**

April–early Oct, daily, 9a.m.–5p.m. ENTRANCE *£2, OAPs/children £1*

SPRING SUMMER AUTUMN WINTER

Access | Café | Plant Shop | NPC

These gardens occupy a wedge-shape piece of undulating ground around the headquarters of Arthur Bell & Son, on the south-west side of Perth. They are immaculately maintained and comprise an important collection of heathers (around 1000 different varieties are grown here), planted in generous drifts between snaking paths and neat lawns. A natural burn flows into the garden from the Glasgow Road, providing an ideal source of water for the garden's pools and fountains. The tapestries of colour are particularly good in late summer, the prime flowering period, but there are many spring- and early summer-flowering species here, too.

PERTH

Branklyn Garden

Dundee Road, Perth, Perth and Kinross, Tayside PH2 7BB
TEL. *01738-625535* OWNER *National Trust for Scotland*
HOURS *March–Oct, daily, 9.30a.m.–sunset* ENTRANCE *£2.40, concessions/children £1.50* DIRECTIONS *On E edge of Perth, off Dundee Road, ½m from Queen's Bridge*

SPRING SUMMER AUTUMN WINTER

Access | Gift Shop | Plant Shop | NPC

Covering just under two acres, this richly stocked plantsman's garden on Perth's outskirts was begun in 1922 by plant enthusiasts John and Dorothy Renton, on the site of a former orchard. The garden has a solidly mature but well-kept feel and, despite the fact that it has not been in private ownership since 1967 (when it was passed to the National Trust for Scotland), it is intimate and informal.

Its specialities are rhododendrons, alpines, hardy herbaceous plants of the Far East, and colourful swaths of spring bulbs. Spring and early summer are its greatest months, but autumn sees the brilliant russet and golden tints of numerous acers and azaleas. Look for the National Collection of *Cassiope* – dwarf evergreen shrubs related to rhododendrons and heathers.

PITTENWEEM

Kellie Castle

Pittenweem, Fife KY10 2RF TEL. *01333-720271* OWNER *National Trust for Scotland* HOURS *Daily, 9.30–sunset; castle May–Sept, Easter and weekends, 1.30–5.30p.m.* ENTRANCE *£1, concessions 50p (£3.50 and £2.30 for castle)* DIRECTIONS *3m NW of Pittenweem village, on B9171 (signposted)*

SPRING SUMMER AUTUMN WINTER

Access | Gift Shop | Café

DON'T MISS

A pretty, pleasing, utterly peaceful walled garden of one and a half acres, snuggling under the castle's massive bulk of buff-grey stone. My first impression upon entering through the gate in the garden wall was of a distinctly feminine nature, and it wasn't surprising to discover that the head gardener is a woman, Kathy Sayer, who has maintained it organically since arriving in 1990.

Knee-high box hedges line the gravelled paths which run around the garden's perimeter, dividing it into three main sections, with fruit tree-studded lawns filling the centre. The garden's chief function has always been to produce fruit, vegetables and flowers for the house. There are also many old roses (around 90 different varieties), and a pair of low hedges of the crimson-and-white striped *Rosa gallica* 'Versicolor' (*Rosa Mundi*), reputed to have been here for over 100 years. Poppies and peonies, lupins, lavatera and dame's violet all contribute to the abundant beauty, and self-sown flowers are allowed to stay in situ wherever possible. Kathy Sayer's hens are regularly allowed to roam the garden, assisting the organic slug-control.

A two-storey summerhouse in one corner of the garden was designed by the Arts and Crafts architect, Sir Robert Lorimer – Kellie Castle was his family's summer home in the late 19th and early 20th century.

And also...

Bolfracks, Aberfeldy, Perth and Kinross, Tayside PH15 2EX (tel. 01887-820207), is in a lovely situation overlooking the Tay river valley. Its walled garden features mixed borders of trees, shrubs and perennials and masses of roses, both old and modern, for a long season of blooms. A woodland garden with a natural stream provides the setting for many rhododendrons, azaleas, primulas and meconopsis, and masses of naturalised bulbs. Not suitable for wheelchairs. Open April–Oct, daily, 10a.m.–6p.m. Entrance £2, children under 16 free.

Early spring bulbs entice local visitors to **Cambo Gardens, Kingsbarns, St Andrews, Fife KY16 8QD (tel. 01333-450054).** Created around the Cambo Burn, the Victorian walled garden also sports old roses and a recently laid-out ornamental potager; there are also plants for sale. Open all year, daily, 10a.m.–6p.m. or dusk if earlier. Entrance £2, children free.

Cluny House and Gardens, by Aberfeldy, Perth and Kinross, Tayside PH15 2JT (tel. 01887-820795), has a plantsman's woodland garden specializing in rhododendrons, candelabra primulas, meconopsis and other acid-loving plants from the Far East in a romantically wild setting. Particularly lovely in spring and autumn. Open March–Oct, daily, 10a.m.–6p.m. Entrance £2, children under 16 free.

The original 'Pleasance' gardens at **Edzell Castle, Edzell, nr Brechin, Angus, Tayside DD9 7UE (tel. 01356-648631)**, were laid out in 1604 and, although they fell to rack and ruin, were reinstated in the 1930s in their 17th-century style. There are rose beds, box edging, plus box and yew topiaries contained within walls that are decorated with sculptured stone panels and niches. Open April–Sept, Mon–Sat, 9.30a.m.–6p.m., Sun, 12 noon–6p.m.; Oct–March, Mon, Tues, Wed and Sat, 9.30a.m.–4p.m., Thurs, 9.30a.m.–12.30p.m., Sun, 2–4p.m. Entrance £2.30, OAPs £1.75, children £1.

Falkland Palace, Falkland, Fife KY15 7BU (tel. 01337-857397). Built between 1501 and 1541 by James IV and James V, Falkland Palace was the country residence of Stewart kings and queens (including Mary Queen of Scots) who hunted deer and wild boar in the surrounding forest. The three-acre garden, however, dates from the 1940s and '50s, and is chiefly the work of garden designer Percy Cane, who laid out herbaceous borders around the broad lawns, and planted trees and shrubs to extend interest through the seasons. Roses garland the old garden walls, and summer herbs and delphiniums are a popular spectacle. The royal tennis court, reputedly the world's oldest, is still used. Open April–Oct, Mon–Sat, 11a.m.–4.30p.m.; Sun, 1.30–4.30p.m. Entrance £2.10, children £1.40 (palace and grounds £4.10 and £2.70).

Glamis Castle, Glamis, by Forfar, Angus, Tayside DD8 1RJ (tel. 01307-840242/840393), is a turreted, pink-sandstone palace that was a childhood home of Queen Elizabeth the Queen Mother. An 18th-century landscape park surrounds the castle; its two-acre, Italian-style garden features herbaceous borders contained within stout yew hedges, with a formal fountain and ornamental gazebos. There is also an interesting sundial in the grounds. Open end March–late Oct, daily, 10.30a.m.–5.30p.m. (10a.m.–5.30p.m. July–Aug), last adm. 4.45p.m. Entrance £2.40, OAPs/children £1.30 (extra to see castle).

Glendoick Garden Centre, Glendoick, Perth, Tayside PH2 7NS (tel. 01738-860260), specializes in rhododendrons, azaleas and other ericaceous shrubs (particularly enkianthus and kalmia), with primulas and meconopsis. There is also a comprehensive mail order catalogue (send £1.50 in stamps) for orders exceeding

£30-worth of plants. Open all year, daily, 9a.m.–5p.m. (9a.m.–6p.m. in summer). Entrance free.

House of Pitmuies, Guthrie, by Forfar, Angus, Tayside DO8 2SN (tel. 01241-828245), has beautiful walled gardens leading to an informal riverside walk. Pride of place goes to the semi-formal gardens with a series of long borders of delphiniums and roses. Other fine features include a collection of fruit of special interest, glasshouses and conservatories, an alpine meadow and woodland garden. Open April–Oct, daily, 10a.m.–5p.m. Entrance £2.

Inveresk Lodge, 24 Inveresk Village, Musselburgh, East Lothian EH21 7TE (tel. 01721-722502), has pretty gardens, laid out in informal terraces on a steep slope. As well as many herbaceous plants and grasses, there is a border of shrub roses, a selection of climbing roses and plenty of trees, shrubs and flowers bringing interest through the autumn. The very attractive village of Inveresk, dating from the late 17th to early 18th centuries, is also well gardened. Two walled gardens, Shepherd House and Catherine Lodge, have very fine gardens which are occasionally open to the public for special charity days. Open all year, Mon–Fri, 10a.m.–4.30p.m., Sat–Sun, 2–5p.m. (Oct–March closed Sat). Also open under Scotland's Gardens Scheme – tel. 0131-229 1870 for this year's dates. Entrance £1.

Kinross House, Kinross, Perth and Kinross, Tayside KY13 7ET (tel. 01577-862900), is a late 17th-century mansion surrounded by four acres of beautifully proportioned, formal walled gardens. The walls themselves are decorated with statuary and ornamental gates, and within their enclosure are sumptuous herbaceous borders, some colour-themed, with roses, yew hedges and lovely views over the loch. Open May–Oct, daily, 10a.m.–7p.m. Entrance £2.

St Andrews Botanic Garden, The Canongate, St Andrews, Fife KY16 8RT (tel. 01334-477178/ 476452), on the western side of town, straddles the meandering waters of Kinness Burn. It is part of the historic university, with specialized alpine and rock gardens, a lake and woodland garden, including rhododendrons and azaleas. The interesting glasshouses shelter tropical plants and orchids, cacti and alpines. Open daily, 10a.m.–7p.m. (closes 4p.m. Oct–April). Entrance £1.50, children and OAPs 75p.

The University of Dundee Botanic Garden, Riverside Drive, Dundee, Tayside DD2 1QH (tel. 01382-566939), is a teaching institution, with systematic beds of plants grouped by their families, but is interesting and well prepared for visitors, too. There are areas set aside to demonstrate plant communities for different habitats, drought-resistant plants, carnivorous ones, interesting glasshouses, fine trees and a lake. Open all year, Mon–Sat, 10a.m.–4.30p.m. (closing 3.30p.m. Nov–Feb), and Sun, 11a.m.–4p.m. (closing 3p.m. in winter). Entrance £1.50, OAPs/school-age children 75p.

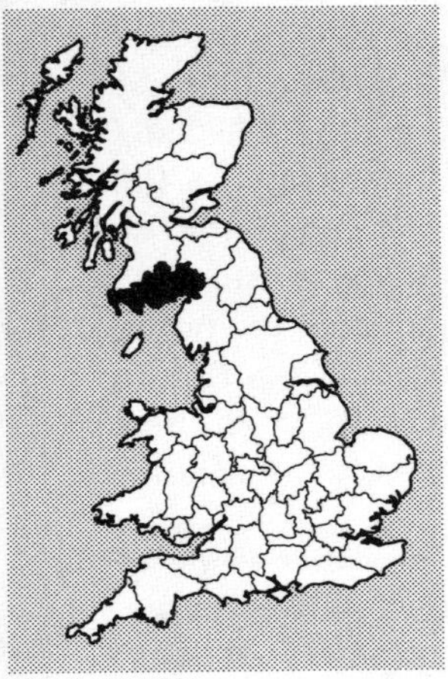

Dumfries and Galloway

MAP NO. 8

A site of varying landscapes – the desolate inland region of the Glenkens, with its mountains, lochs and waterfalls, the hilly pastures of Dumfriesshire, and the low, sea-enveloped terrain of West Galloway, which reaches out to the north-east stretches of Ireland, just a short boat-crossing away. It is more usual for people to pass through the region, en route to Glasgow or Carlisle, but there are some renowned horticultural highlights. The sheltered coastal gardens thrive thanks to the warming influence of the Gulf Stream, which creates a milder, but wetter climate than other parts of Scotland.

CASTLE DOUGLAS

Threave Garden

Castle Douglas DG7 1RX **TEL.** *01556-502575* **OWNER** *National Trust for Scotland* **HOURS** *Open all year, daily, 9.30a.m.–sunset; walled garden and glasshouses 9.30a.m.–5p.m. Visitor Centre and shop open April or Good Friday–Oct, 9.30a.m.–5.30p.m.* **ENTRANCE** *£4, concessions/children £2.70, family ticket £10.70, school party £1* **DIRECTIONS** *Off A75, 1m W of Castle Douglas, 19m W of Dumfries – take A75, then turn off signposted 'Threave'*

SPRING SUMMER AUTUMN WINTER

Access · Gift Shop · Café · Plant Shop

Of the 1200 acres of the Threave estate, 60 are devoted to gardens. There is plenty of labour to keep them up to scratch, for this is the National Trust for Scotland's own training school for full-time gardeners. Threave is particularly famous for its spring displays of daffodils (around 200 different varieties), which carpet the lawns surrounding the Victorian red-sandstone mansion house. However, there is much else to see through the year, in the mixed borders, peat and rock gardens and, especially, the old walled kitchen garden, with its Victorian glasshouses, traditional herbaceous borders, assorted vegetables and trained fruit.

STRANRAER

Castle Kennedy and Lochinch

Stair Estates, Rephad, Stranraer DG9 8BX TEL. *01776-702024* OWNER *Earl of Stair* HOURS *April or Easter if earlier–Sept, daily, 10a.m.–5p.m.* ENTRANCE *£2, OAPs £1.50, children £1, free for disabled* DIRECTIONS *5m E of Stranraer from A75, left at Castle Kennedy village and 1m down private drive (signposted)*

SPRING SUMMER AUTUMN WINTER

Access Café Plant Shop

With its long avenues of dark trees, imposing, pointed turrets and views of the deep waters of the Black Loch, this 75-acre site can be a slightly spooky place in gloomy weather. It is lifted by spectacular spring colour from the rhododendrons, and is interesting on several counts.

The original gardens were laid out by the 2nd Earl of Stair in the early 18th century. He was a Field Marshal and British Ambassador to France, and laid out the gardens with military precision in a series of formal rides and cross-axes, using the man- and horsepower of the Royal Scots Greys and Inniskilling Fusiliers. Several rides meet at the Round Pond, a circular pool packed with lilies in a two-acre site. A monkey puzzle avenue, over 100 years old, leads from the pool towards the castle, thought to be the tallest and finest avenue of its type in Britain. A smooth bowling green and sculpted turf terraces are part of the early gardens landscaped by the soldiers, and the garden boasts many specimen trees of terrific size which flourish in the mild, moist climate. The garden's rhododendron collection enjoys international renown (many hybrids were actually bred here), and some of the oldest were grown from seed brought back by Sir Joseph Hooker from the Himalayas in the mid-19th century. There is also a walled garden of herbaceous flowers beside the ruins of the 15th-century Castle Kennedy, which is also within the grounds.

POPPIES FROM THE FAR EAST

*If there is one time of year when I envy gardeners in the cooler, northern stretches of the UK, it is in late spring–early summer, when the vivid, blue-petalled Himalayan poppies (*Meconopsis *species) are in bloom. They relish the cool climate and moisture-laden atmosphere of the north-west and are a feature of* ***Craigieburn Classic Plants, Craigieburn House, by Moffat DG10 9LF (tel. 01683-221250), from A74 take A708 at Moffat towards Belkirk for 2m, then on left.*** *Woodland and moisture-loving plants are the nursery's speciality and unusual species of meconopsis can be bought from the nursery and admired within the recently developed, adjacent eight-acre show garden beside it. Open Easter–late Oct, Tues–Sun and Bank Holiday Mons, 12.30–8p.m.*

STRANRAER

Logan Botanic Garden

Port Logan, Stranraer DG9 9ND TEL. *01776-860231* OWNER *Royal Botanic Garden, Edinburgh* HOURS *March–Oct, daily, 9.30a.m.–6p.m.* ENTRANCE *£3, concessions £2.50, children £1, family ticket £7* DIRECTIONS *14m S of Stranraer off B7065*

SPRING SUMMER AUTUMN WINTER

Access | Gift Shop | Café | Plant Shop | DON'T MISS

The 14-mile stretch of road south of Stranraer down the Mull of Galloway is dull and featureless, making the arrival at Logan Garden all the more pleasing, for you suddenly step into a three-and-a-half-acre sub-tropical oasis that takes full advantage of the warming Gulf Stream climate. It has much in common with Tresco Abbey Gardens (*q.v.*) on the Isles of Scilly, for it is rich in plants from the southern hemisphere which can be grown outdoors in few other parts of Britain.

There are Chatham Island forget-me-nots from the South Pacific Ocean, bearing clear blue flowerheads and large, pleated leaves, South African daisies in variety, and rare trees from Chile. The cabbage palms are memorable, forming avenues of 40ft-high trees, while tree ferns and huge fan palms add to the tropical scenery. Anyone interested in plants will find it hard to tear themselves away on a fine summer's day; also enjoy its tranquillity, for the remote location ensures that overcrowding from visitors is never a problem. The food in the garden's Salad Bar was also good on my visit.

And also...

Arbigland, Kirkbean DG2 8BQ (tel. 01387-880283), is an enchanting, 15-acre private garden featuring fine specimen trees, and interestingly planted woodland walks down to a secluded beach beside the Solway Firth. One area, featuring Japanese azaleas and acers arranged around a water garden, is aptly called 'Japan', while the foundations of a house pre-dating the present Georgian one are home to a sunken rose garden. Open May–Sept, Tues–Sun, and Bank Holiday Mons, 2–6p.m. Entrance £2, OAPs £1.50, children 50p.

Broughton House, 12 High Street, Kirkcudbright DG6 4GX (tel. 01557-330437), belonged to renowned Scottish artist E.A. Hornel in the early decades of the 20th century. Its one-and-a-half-acre garden is a curious hybrid of Scottish country garden and oriental styles, and leads down to the estuary of the River Dee. Behind the 18th-century town house (in town centre, signposted), there are broad lawns and herbaceous borders joined by Japanese cherry trees and waterlily-pools with stepping-stones. This peaceful artist's home is now a museum of his and other artists' work. Open 1 April or Good

Friday–Oct, daily, 1–5.30p.m. (last adm. 4.45p.m.). Entrance £2.40, concessions £1.60.

The two-and-three-quarter-acre 17th-century walled garden at **Cally Gardens and Nursery, Gatehouse of Fleet, Castle Douglas DG7 2DJ (fax 01557-815029)**, offers many rare and unusual species among the 3500 plants listed in its catalogue (send 3 × 1st-class stamps). Herbaceous perennials, particularly geraniums, agapanthus, crocosmias and grasses are a speciality, and many plants on offer have been grown from seed recently collected on expeditions to far-flung corners of the world. Open Easter–early Oct, Sat–Sun only, 10a.m.–5.30p.m. Entrance free.

Elizabeth MacGregor, Ellenbank, Tongland Road, Kirkcudbright DG6 4UU (tel. 01557-330620), specializes in unusual herbaceous perennials, particularly violas and violettas, of which she offers over 100 different varieties (send 4 × 1st-class stamps for a catalogue). Open to visitors (but please ring first) April–Oct, Fri–Sat only, 10.30a.m.–5.30p.m.

Old and new fruit varieties are the speciality of **J. Tweedie Fruit Trees, Maryfield Road Nursery, Maryfield, nr Terregles, Dumfries DG2 9TH (tel. 01387-720880).** New varieties currently available include 'Pax' gooseberry, 'Canada Red' rhubarb, and dwarf cherry trees on Edabriz rootstocks. Send a s.a.e. for the mail order catalogue. Open Sat, late Oct–March, 9.30a.m.–2p.m.

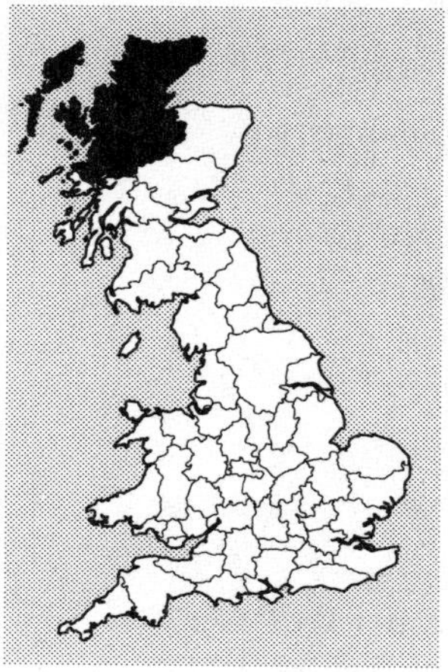

Highland

MAP NO. 8

Nothing impresses itself so much in this region as the overpowering presence of the ancient mountains. It is a landscape of awesome rock faces, smoothed and pared down by distant ice ages, where volcanic remains have left craggy peaks. Rainfall is very high throughout the region and year, while persistent winds prune trees into asymmetrical shapes. It is the domain of hardy sheep which nonchalantly graze the roadsides. But there are splendid gardens here, too, and excellent nurseries, in this sparsely populated area in the far north of Scotland.

THE BRAES

Glamaig Cottage

The Braes, Portree, Isle of Skye IV51 9LL TEL. *01478-650226* OWNER *Mr and Mrs R. Townsend* HOURS *Easter–mid-Sept, daily, dawn to dusk* ENTRANCE *£1, OAPs 50p* DIRECTIONS *8m S of Portree, at end of B883*

SPRING SUMMER AUTUMN WINTER

Access

DON'T MISS

This is one of the most remote gardens I have visited. It is seven miles down a single-track road on Skye in the Western Isles, overlooking Loch Sligachan and the smaller islands of Raasay and Scalpay. It is an interesting two-acre plantsman's garden, made over the last 30 years by Richard and Ursula Townsend, who have fashioned it in a natural style befitting the steeply sloping site, which has a burn and waterfalls in its centre.

Spring and early summer see many rhododendrons in bloom, with waterside plantings of candelabra primulas and the bright crimson lanterns of *Crinodendron hookerianum*, which hails from Chile. There is a mini-pinetum, a wild heather bank, a productive kitchen garden, and a collection of exotic trees and shrubs around the burn. A lawn beside the house is surrounded by rock garden plants and summer-flowering perennials.

PRIMULAS GALORE AT ARDFEARN

Many of the customers who buy from ***Ardfearn Nursery, Bunchrew, Inverness IV3 6RH (tel. 01463-243250), 4m W of Inverness, by A862,*** *select their plants from a mail order catalogue, but this is a nursery worth visiting if you are in the area. This open, breezy site is ideal for raising healthy, extremely hardy plants, and the nursery stocks a broad selection of alpines and rock-garden plants from all over the world. Primulas are a speciality (around 90 different species and varieties are grown here), with gentians, celmisias and assorted small shrubs and conifers that are suited to the acid soils that prevail in this region. Open all year, daily, 9a.m.–5p.m. Mail order Oct–March (send 4 × 2nd-class stamps for the catalogue).*

DURNAMUCK

Sea View Garden Gallery

Durnamuck, Dundonnell, Wester Ross IV23 2QZ TEL. *01854-633317* OWNER *S. and I. Nelson* HOURS *Mid-May–mid-Sept, Tues–Sat, 10a.m.–6p.m.* ENTRANCE *£1, children free* DIRECTIONS *Signposted off A832 Gairloch–Dundonnell road at Badcaul for 1m*

SPRING | **SUMMER** | AUTUMN | WINTER

Access

Sea View is an intimate, half-acre cottage garden, laid out since 1990, surrounding a stone crofter's cottage overlooking Little Loch Broom. Its owners, Simone and Ian Nelson, came from the Lake District to settle here in 1989 and, while Ian paints watercolour landscapes, Simone develops the garden, which was previously virgin heathland, now made fertile with tons of composted manure.

Hedges of griselinia and escallonia help to filter persistent winds. There are also raised beds of alpines and seasonal perennials, a heather bed, pond and bog area, a narrow border of herbaceous plants, and a small kitchen garden with raised vegetable beds and fruit trees. All is well maintained, and the bright day of my visit belied the extreme difficulties of making any sort of garden here, where work is often delayed by weeks of steady rain.

KYLE OF LOCHALSH

Lochalsh Woodland Garden

Lochalsh House, Balmacara, by Kyle of Lochalsh, Ross-shire IV40 8DN TEL. *01599-566325* OWNER *National Trust for Scotland* HOURS *All year, daily, 9a.m.–sunset* ENTRANCE *£1 (honesty box), concessions/children 50p* DIRECTIONS *Off A87, 3m E of Kyle of Lochalsh*

SPRING SUMMER AUTUMN WINTER

Access

Lochalsh Woodland Garden is more woodland than garden, its craggy slopes covered with heather, seedling birches and pines, and bracken. It enjoys a peaceful position overlooking the waters of Loch Alsh, and is a pleasant place for a picnic.

Many of its mature oaks, larches and pines on its 13 acres were planted around 1887, as a shelterbelt to Lochalsh House (not open). There are rhododendrons scattered through the woods, mainly slightly tender varieties planted by E. H. M. Cox of Glendoick (*q.v.*) in the early 1960s, from wild seed collected in the Himalayas. The position is outstanding, warmed by the influence of the Gulf Stream, and enjoys views of the Sound of Sleat and parts of Skye. The National Trust for Scotland calls this 'very much a garden in the making', and they are extending the plantings of hydrangeas, fuchsias, bamboos, ferns and rhododendrons.

PERENNIALS BY THE LOCH

Like Ardfearn Nursery (above), ***Abriachan Nurseries, Loch Ness Side, by Inverness IV3 6LA (tel. 01463-861232), 9m SW of Inverness, on A82, ignoring side roads marked to Abriachan,*** *enjoys a splendid location. It overlooks the deep, dark waters of Loch Ness and offers an extensive nursery, and two acres of gardens to explore within 10 acres of hazel woodland. Margaret and Donald Davidson came here 15 years ago and have built up a solid reputation for producing a wide range of well-grown perennials, both hardy and half-hardy. There are campanulas, a huge selection of primulas (which thrive in the hazel woods), helianthemums, many geraniums, peonies and other old-fashioned border plants. Hardy penstemons thrive (due to the protective influence of the loch), and rosemary does exceptionally well on the free-draining acidic sandy soil. There is also a lively and informative mail order catalogue (send 3 × 1st-class stamps). Open Feb–Nov, daily, 9a.m.–7p.m. (dusk when earlier). Entrance to garden £1, children 20p. (The site is on a hill and is not disabled-friendly.)*

DON'T MISS

NAIRN

Cawdor Castle

Cawdor, by Nairn IV12 5RD **TEL.** *01667-404615* **OWNER** *The Dowager Countess of Cawdor* **HOURS** *May–Oct, daily, 10a.m.–5.30p.m. (last adm. 5p.m.)* **ENTRANCE** *£2.70 (castle and grounds £5, OAPs £4, children £2.70)* **DIRECTIONS** *6m SW of Nairn, on B9090*

SPRING SUMMER AUTUMN WINTER

Access | Gift Shop | Café | DON'T MISS

Cawdor and Inverewe (*q.v.*), the latter way over to the west, are the jewels in the Highlands' horticultural crown. The former is sumptuously filled with herbaceous borders and roses galore, formally laid out in symmetrical patterns on level ground beside the castle. There are lavender-edged beds with roses filling out the centres; long borders packed with traditional seasonal flowers, including peonies, lupins, delphiniums, heleniums, penstemons and campanulas in a glorious explosion of summer colour; broad lawns, beautiful trees and plenty of seats for the weary (easily seen, for they are painted bright red).

Away from the main show gardens is a less-visited secret garden with a holly maze bordered by laburnum tunnels. Beyond is a beautifully made, box-edged herb garden, and a yew-enclosed white garden with modern central fountain. Around these are colour-graded Jekyll-style herbaceous borders leading through cool blues and yellows into warmer reds and plum colouring. Everything is maintained to a very high standard.

ORD

An Acarsaid

Ord, Sleat, Isle of Skye IV44 8QN TEL. *01471-855218*
OWNER *Mrs E. McInnes* HOURS *Open Easter–Oct, daily, 12 noon–5.30p.m.* ENTRANCE *Donations to charity*
DIRECTIONS *On the waterfront at Ord, 5m from A851 along unclassified, single-file track*

SPRING SUMMER AUTUMN WINTER

An Acarsaid (The Anchorage) is a neat, white bungalow, the retirement home of Eileen and the late Ranoull McInnes. It lies in an uncompromisingly exposed position perched on a limestone crag, facing the Atlantic ocean and merciless winds. It is what I would call a plantsman's garden with atmosphere – impossible to avoid the latter, due to its incredible location – and gentle humour thrown in for good measure. The two-acre garden is spread along a steep, rocky hillside and makes creative use of the natural stone to hand, which Ranoull McInnes fashioned into stairways, low walls and cobblestone paths. Near the seaward entrance is a fabulous animal skeleton cemented into the garden wall, bearing the legend Each Uist Earballach (Ranoull McInnes was a Gaelic-speaking native of Skye), and further description reveals the creature as being Hydro Equus Extendus, a rare, long-tailed water horse related to the Loch Ness Monster. (I won't spoil your fun in guessing what the skeleton really is, but the McInneses had me fooled for a long time about this!)

A thoughtfully numbered route leads through the garden past a rock bank of primulas, saxifrages, aquilegias, mountain avens and other alpines to the front garden, which is home to an eclectic collection of roses, spring and summer bulbs, meconopsis, hardy geraniums, ferns and much else. A handsome mountain ash is beautifully garlanded with white-flowered 'Wedding Day' roses and an unnamed scarlet climbing rose. The clifftop woodland garden is a semi-wild area, leading through a shrubbery to a viewpoint of Skye's spectacular Cuillin mountains, which are marked out on a display board for identification, although their peaks are often masked by clouds and tempestuous rain. Tough plants eke a living out of the shallow soil of this weather-blasted garden. It is a place which has an unruly character entirely appropriate to its setting.

POOLEWE

Inverewe Garden

Poolewe, Wester Ross IV22 2LG **TEL.** *01445-781200* **OWNER** *National Trust for Scotland* **HOURS** *Open all year, daily, 9.30a.m.–9p.m. (closes 5p.m. mid-Oct–March)* **ENTRANCE** *£4.80, OAPs and children £3.20* **DIRECTIONS** *On A832 by Poolewe, 6m N of Gairloch*

SPRING SUMMER AUTUMN WINTER

Access | Gift Shop | Café | Plant Shop | NPC | DON'T MISS

On my first visit to Inverewe I arrived at 8p.m., and had this fabulous garden all to myself, just me – and millions of midges. Be sure to arrive liberally doused with repellent; the gardeners wear netted headgear on still days, when midges are a serious problem.

Since a three-mile labyrinth of paths winds through the garden, you can lose yourself in the richly planted woodland featuring large collections of rhododendrons, eucalyptus, olearias and many other plants of the southern hemisphere, which thrive here due to the warming influence of the Gulf Stream. Among them are woodland perennials in variety, lily-pools, bold drifts of candelabra primulas and shuttlecock ferns.

The house front is enlivened by a curved herbaceous border, spectacular from June to August, and below is a rock garden sloping down to the shore. The sunny walled garden also faces the sea, and displays a sumptuous blend of herbaceous and annual flowers, vegetables, fruit and pergolas draped with climbing roses and clematis. The garden was made by Osgood Mackenzie in the latter half of the 19th century. Seeing all its rich variety, it is hard to believe that when Mackenzie arrived the estate was a treeless wasteland. It lies at 57.8°N, closer to the Arctic Circle than St Petersburg and most of Labrador, and on one of the world's most windswept coastlines. It is also exceptionally well maintained. Garden Cottage Nursery (*q.v.*) is nearby, and good meals are served at the Poolewe Hotel, on the opposite shore of the loch.

THE ANCIENT SCOTS PINE

When caught in low-angled sunlight the scaly, buff-orange bark of Pinus sylvestris, *the Scots pine, lights up in a fiery glow, heightening the contrast with its clouds of dark green needle-foliage.*

The ancient Caledonian Pine Forest is said to be the only true native forest in Britain, although only parts of it remain in scattered clumps through the Highland region. The trees, often characterfully mis-shapen, sparsely populate the hillsides here and there, rising out of coarse mats of springy heather.

In medieval times the scene was quite different. The native pines and birches spread in a great forest across the Highlands from Perth to Ullapool. Alas, wholesale felling of trees began in the late 17th century to supply charcoal for a thriving iron industry and timbers for warships and construction purposes.

Scots pines were planted as waymarkers for drovers' routes through England in the 18th century. They were invaluable for signalling where grazing and rest places could be found.

Some replanting of indigenous pines has been carried out in the Highlands in the last two decades but fenced protection from grazing deer and sheep is needed for them to thrive. In unfenced areas there is now little or no natural regeneration of the once great forest and therefore it is dying out.

SLEAT

Clan Donald Visitor Centre

Armadale Castle, Sleat, Isle of Skye IV45 8RS **TEL.** *01471-844305/844227* **OWNER** *Clan Donald Lands Trust* **HOURS** *Gardens open all year; Visitor Centre (which has a good café) April–early Nov, daily, 9.30a.m.–5.30p.m* **ENTRANCE** *£3.40, concessions/children £2.20* **DIRECTIONS** *At S end of Skye on A851 (single-track road), 14m S of Broadford; or by ferry, in summer, from Mallaig on the mainland to Ardvasar*

SPRING SUMMER AUTUMN WINTER

Access · Gift Shop · Café · Plant Shop

This fine garden lies in the Sleat (pronounced slate) peninsula, in the far south of the Isle of Skye. There are 40 acres of gardens and woodland within the vast (20,000-acre) Clan Donald Lands estate. They include new ponds with a rock garden in an informally landscaped area with winding paths in turf and gravel. A long, luxuriantly planted traditional herbaceous border lies in a sheltered position beyond the tree-speckled lawns behind the ruined castle. Above the border is a terraced walk beside a raised bed featuring hypericums and sages, sedum, santolina and phygelius. The trees at Clan Donald are magnificent, especially the mossy beeches, and there are many rhododendrons, including recently planted specimens. Wildflowers are a feature in the many areas of long grass and meadow, with colonies of orchids under the wych-elms.

The property enjoys fabulous easterly views of the mountains of the mainland and the waters of the Sound of Sleat. While you're here, do visit an interesting exhibition in the Study Centre, outlining the work of Martin Martin, a native of Skye in the late 17th–early 18th century. The author of *A Description of the Western Isles* (1703), Martin became a doctor and was well versed in traditional cures of the islanders, who used local plants and products of the sea and coastline to make various remedies.

STRATHCARRON

Attadale Gardens

Strathcarron, Wester Ross IV54 8YX TEL. *01520-722217* OWNER *Mr and Mrs E. Macpherson* HOURS *April–Oct, Mon–Sat, 10a.m.–5.30p.m.* ENTRANCE *£2, children £1* DIRECTIONS *On A890 between Strathcarron and South Strome*

SPRING SUMMER AUTUMN WINTER

Access

The 10-acre gardens are laid around Attadale House, on the edge of a vast Highland estate. Although the gardens are on level ground, steep hills and cliffs rise up sharply along the north-eastern edge, the lowest slopes of which contain a rhododendron walk above a water garden. There are further woodland walks leading to a small, formal sunk garden, a box-edged herb and kitchen garden, and a rhododendron dell. The gardens lie in a spectacular landscape, although visitors may find the persistent sheep flies are a problem in summer.

And also...

Brin Herb Nursery, Brin School Fields, Flichity, by Farr, Inverness IV1 2XD (tel. 01808-521288), stocks over 300 varieties of herbs and wildflowers grown at 700ft above sea level, with bulbs, salads, cut herbs and strawberries in season. There are also well-labelled display gardens, a restaurant specializing in herb-flavoured food and teas, and seeds for sale. Open Mid-March–Oct, Mon–Sat, 9a.m.–6p.m., Sun, 2–5p.m. Entrance free.

The entrance drive to **Dochfour Gardens, Inverness IV3 6JY (tel. 01463-861218)**, winds through a mature wood of larches, firs, birch and beech at the foot of craggy hills overlooking Loch Ness. The 17-acre gardens are set among topiarised yew hedges, with lavender-edged rose beds, a herbaceous border and a kitchen garden (with pick-your-own strawberries in season). But it is the trees here that impress most, particularly a fine deodar near the house (not open). A delightful water garden has spreading parrotias and Japanese acers beside a bank of rhododendrons and meconopsis. Open April–late Oct, Mon–Fri, 10a.m.–5p.m., Sat–Sun, 2–5p.m. Entrance £1.50, OAPs and children £1.

Dunvegan Castle, Dunvegan, Isle of Skye IV55 8WF (tel. 01470-521206), is a fortress stronghold dating from the 13th century that has been continuously inhabited by the chiefs of the Clan MacLeod. There are 10 acres of 18th-century gardens with rhododendron woodlands and impressive natural waterfalls. Some garden walks end at the castle jetty, where boat trips can be taken from spring to autumn to a seal colony in Loch Dunvegan. Gardens open all year; castle, mid-March–Oct, daily, 10a.m.–5.30p.m. (last adm. 5p.m.). Entrance to castle £4.50, children £2.50 (gardens only £3.50 and £1.80 and guidebook to gardens £2.50).

Garden Cottage Nursery, Tournaig, Poolewe, Achnasheen, Wester Ross IV22 2LH (tel. 01445-781339), stocks a wide range of plants in an informal garden setting, surrounded by trees and wild rhododendrons. Shrubs suited to the west coast, with primulas and moisture-loving plants, are their speciality. Many of the plants, seen at Inverewe can be bought here; there is also a mail order catalogue (send 4 × 2nd-class stamps). Nursery only open Easter–Oct, Mon–Sat, 12 noon–7p.m.

The Hydroponicum, Achiltibuie, Ullapool IV26 2YG (tel. 01854-622202), is a purpose-built growing environment where modern, soil-less growing methods are used in conjunction with heat and sunlight. Bananas, grapes, citrus fruits, figs and giant blackberries flourish in the solar-heated, insulated growing houses, and strawberries are picked from April to September. Access is for guided tours only. The fruits are used in the adjacent café. Open Easter–Sept, daily, 10a.m.–6p.m. (last guided tour 5p.m.). Tour £4, concessions £3, children £2, family ticket £10.

Leckmelm Shrubbery and Arboretum, by Ullapool, Wester Ross IV26 2RH, is a tranquil woodland best seen at rhododendron time, although it has some splendid trees too, including a magnificent weeping beech. It was laid out in the 1870s, but from 1940 it lay unattended for 45 years until the present owners began a programme of scrub clearance and restoration. Open April–Sept, daily. Entrance £1.50.

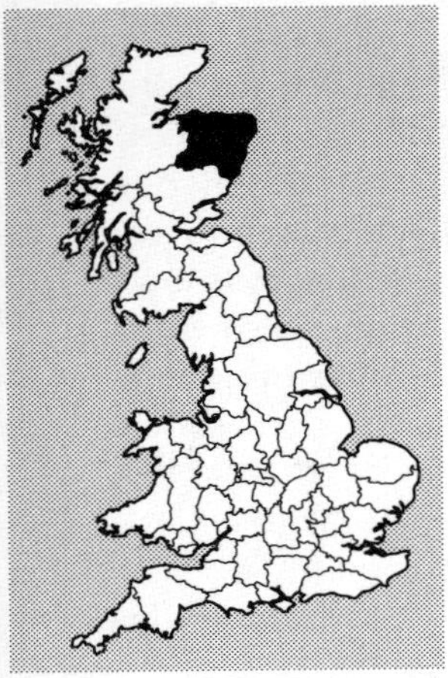

Moray and Aberdeenshire

MAP NO. 8

This area (until recently known as Grampian) encompasses tracts of the spectacular heather-clad Grampian Mountains – snow-capped throughout the winter, and worn by wind and ice – the scenic valley of Royal Deeside, the fishing harbours of the North Sea coast and the handsome, sparkly-granite town of Aberdeen, the 'silver city by the silver sea'. The region is also famous for its culinary heritage: the salmon and trout of its magnificent rivers, the fine Aberdeen Angus cattle and plentiful distilleries of Scotland's most famous export, its whisky. There are also numerous medieval castles, bearing witness to clan wars but, thankfully, some of them are now more pleasingly surrounded by magnificent gardens.

BANCHORY

Crathes Castle

Banchory, Aberdeenshire AB31 3QJ **TEL.** *01330-844525* **OWNER** *National Trust for Scotland* **HOURS** *Castle: 1 April (or Good Friday if sooner)–Oct, daily, 11a.m.–5.30p.m. (last adm. 4.45p.m.); garden and grounds all year, daily, 9.30a.m.–sunset* **ENTRANCE** *£4.80, concessions/children £3.20, family ticket £12.80 (garden £4 and £2.60)* **DIRECTIONS** *On A93, 3m E of Banchory and 15m W of Aberdeen*

SPRING SUMMER AUTUMN WINTER

Since the four-acre walled garden is divided into eight separate, themed areas, unquestionably making it one of Scotland's finest summer gardens, visitors should allow plenty of time to explore it. They are divided partly by old stone walls and partly by magnificent yew hedges dating from 1702, out of which rise bulging topiaries, which greatly add to the garden's appeal.

There are herbaceous borders in variety, and the planting was partly inspired by the writings of Gertrude Jekyll (*q.v.*) and William Robinson (*q.v.*) at the turn of the century, both of whom advocated a looser, freer style of planting than had been seen in rigidly formal Victorian gardens of the late 19th century. Some borders are colour-schemed white and cream, there is a garden of blue flowers, a well-stocked rose garden, and a golden garden featuring golden-foliage and yellow-flowered plants. The traditional herbaceous borders are sumptuously planted in the Edwardian manner. The restored glasshouses contain an important collection of old-fashioned Malmaison carnations with peony-like clove-scented flowers in a spectrum of pastel pink tints.

The grey-walled castle, in the north-west corner, towers over these highlights. Also see the exquisite 16th-century painted ceilings, coloured with natural pigments, featuring heroes of the past. Drum Castle (below) is close by, on the road to Aberdeen.

BANCHORY

Drum Castle

Drumoak, by Banchory, Kincardine and Deeside, Aberdeenshire AB31 3EY **TEL.** *01330-811204* **OWNER** *National Trust for Scotland* **HOURS** *Easter weekend, and May–Sept, daily, 10a.m.–6p.m. (castle opens 1.30–5.30p.m., last adm. 4.45p.m.). Grounds/wood open all year, daily, 10a.m.–6p.m.* **ENTRANCE** *Castle, gardens and grounds £4, OAPs/children £2.70 (gardens/grounds £1.80 and £1.20)* **DIRECTIONS** *Off A93 (signposted), 3m W of Peterculter, 10m W of Aberdeen, 8m E of Banchory*

SPRING | SUMMER | AUTUMN | WINTER

Access | Gift Shop | Café | Plant Shop

Drum Castle's solid, square tower is one of the three oldest tower houses in Scotland, dating from the late 13th century, although it has been added to over succeeding centuries. It is enveloped by green pastures and magnificent specimen trees, but the main interest for gardeners is the distant two-and-a-quarter-acre walled garden which has been recently redesigned to display a comprehensive collection of old roses, within a formal framework, best seen at mid-summer.

Beyond it, the grounds include the Old Wood of Drum, 117 acres of ancient natural oakwood, one of the few remaining relics of a vast forest which once covered the lower slopes of the Dee Valley. The forest, which has existed since the last glaciation (10,000 years ago), was used as royal hunting ground from the mid-13th century onwards. Any time of year is rewarding for following the well-marked woodland walks among its oaks, birches and Scots pines, although bright days in spring and autumn show it in particularly beautiful light.

PITMEDDEN

Pitmedden Garden

Pitmedden, Ellon, Aberdeenshire AB41 0PD **TEL.** *01651-842352* **OWNER** *National Trust for Scotland* **HOURS** *May–Sept, daily, 10a.m.–5.30p.m. (last adm. 5p.m.)* **ENTRANCE** *£3.70, concessions/children £2.50, family ticket £9.90, party of adults (20) £3 each, school party £1* **DIRECTIONS** *On A920, 1m W of Pitmedden village and 14m N of Aberdeen*

SPRING SUMMER AUTUMN WINTER

Access · Gift Shop · Café · Plant Shop · DON'T MISS

Here is a classic four-acre formal garden of green boxwood parterres laid out partly in swirling embroidery patterns, and partly with heraldic designs, in the French-influenced style favoured by wealthy landowners in the 17th century. Although the original garden did not survive in succeeding centuries (it had long been ploughed up in favour of fruit and vegetables), a suitably formal design was reinstated by the National Trust for Scotland in the 1950s.

Between the low hedges, the patterns are filled in each year with 40,000 colourful seasonal bedding plants, in blocks of single colours. They are planted out in May, creating a glorious sight at high summer. There are three miles of box hedging to be clipped each year; besides forming the swirling embroidery patterns, they also spell out mottoes of the Seton family who lived at Pitmedden: 'Sustento Sanguine Signa' (with blood I bear the standard), states one, surrounding the Seton family crest. Also of interest on this 120-acre estate are Pitmedden's sundials, its sturdy pair of garden pavilions, and collections of old varieties of tree fruits.

And also...

Brodie Castle, Forres, Moray IV36 0TE (tel. 01309-641371), has long been famous for its daffodils, for the owner in the late 19th and early 20th century produced over 400 new varieties on the estate, during its heyday. The collection is once more being established at the castle, and presently around 100 Brodie-raised varieties can be seen in the castle's 175 acres of grounds during April and early May. Open Easter weekend–Sept, Mon–Sat, 11a.m.–5.30p.m., and Sun, 1.30–5.30p.m., and Oct weekends. Entrance £4, concessions £2.70.

James Cocker & Sons, Whitemyres, Lang Stracht, Aberdeen AB9 2XH (tel. 01224-313261), is an old-established rose nursery, founded in 1841. Among the classic, top-selling roses bred here are 'Alec's Red', 'Glenfiddich' and 'Silver Jubilee'. Cocker's mail order rose catalogue (updated each May), offering over 300 varieties, is free on request, or call at the nursery and garden centre, open daily, 9a.m.–5.30p.m., closed Christmas.

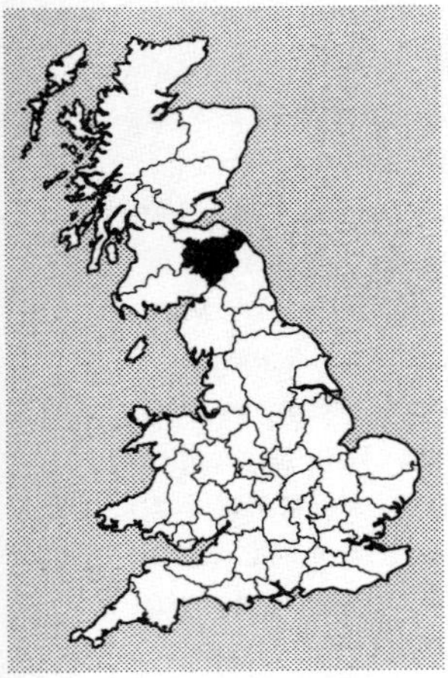

Scottish Borders

MAP NO. 8

The gentle landscape of the Borders features green, undulating hills, broad dales and old drovers' roads which make stimulating walking country. There are two tweeds to note, the famous river washing through the region, and the local cloth fashioned from the wool of countless sheep roaming the surrounding hills. Wool production has been an important industry for many centuries, although these days finer wools are imported for the softest fabrics. Melrose is an unassuming, small town, famous for its sublime ruin, a 12th-century Cistercian abbey, which Sir Walter Scott maintained should be visited in moonlight. Just south of Melrose, the three-peaked volcanic outcrops of the Eildon Hills loom over Tweeddale, offering outstanding views of the now peaceful borderlands.

JEDBURGH

Monteviot

Jedburgh, Roxburghshire TD8 6UQ TEL. *01835-830380* HOURS *April–Oct, Mon–Fri, 12 noon–5p.m.; first weekend of every month, 12 noon–5p.m.* ENTRANCE *£2, OAPs £1, children under 14 free* DIRECTIONS *4m from Jedburgh. Turn off A68 on to B6400 to Nisbet, N of Jedburgh. Entrance second turning on right*

SPRING SUMMER AUTUMN WINTER

Access | Plant Shop

A box-edged parterre filled with culinary herbs lies next to the house (not open), and is the oldest part of the garden, enjoying views of the River Teviot below. At a lower level there is a terraced rose garden where stone walls help contain the heady, rosy fragrances of mid-summer, and this area, too, enjoys marvellous valley views. In the 1960s the garden designer, Percy Cane, designed a formal lawned and stepped area, the River Garden, that runs right down to the water's edge; its encircling beds are well stocked with mixed plantings of shrubs, small trees and perennials for a tapestry of colour through the seasons.

The garden's arboretum and pinetum contain exceptionally good specimen trees, dating from the latter half of the 19th and early 20th century. There is also a delightful water garden, crossed by three linked timber bridges, fed by a natural spring, surrounded by rhododendrons and lush waterside perennials.

MELROSE

Priorwood Garden

Melrose, Roxburghshire TD6 9PX **TEL.** *01896-822493* **OWNER** *National Trust for Scotland* **HOURS** *End March–late Dec, Mon–Sat, 10a.m.–5.30p.m., Sun, 1.30–5.30p.m. (or dusk if sooner)* **ENTRANCE** *£1* **DIRECTIONS** *In Melrose, on A6091, adjacent to the Abbey*

SPRING SUMMER AUTUMN WINTER

Gift Shop Plant Shop

Priorwood has an unusual walled garden, overlooked by Melrose Abbey's 15th-century ruins. Most of the plants are grown for the purpose of cutting, for dried flower arrangements. There are flat-headed achilleas and spiky, metallic blue globes of echinops, poppies and alliums producing attractive seed-pods, and spires of blue delphinium. Several hundred different plants are grown and dried on this three-acre site and are also on sale in the property's shop. Beside it, the extensive orchard contains a collection of historic apple varieties which illustrate the history of the apple in cultivation. This inspired the *Priorwood Orchard Recipe Book* (on sale in the shop), which features suggestions ranging from apple sorbet and toffee apple pudding to jam and cider.

A FORTUNE – FROM ALL THE TEA IN CHINA

Tea drinking is so firmly embedded in British culture that it seems strange that only 150 years have passed since the secrets of tea cultivation were learned from the Chinese. For this we have to thank Robert Fortune (1812–1880), one of several fearless Scottish plant hunters who risked life and limb in search of new plants.

*Fortune was born in Berwickshire and worked at Edinburgh's Royal Botanic Garden before heading south to run the indoor plants section of the Horticultural Society's garden at Chiswick. At the end of the first Opium War, China began to open up to foreign trade and Fortune began an expedition in 1842 in search of peonies, bamboos, 'the plant which produces rice paper' (*Tetrapanax*), kumquats and other exotics. For the salary of £100 per year, plus £500 for expenses, he risked the wrath of the suspicious Chinese nurserymen and resisted attacks from pirates. His second trip to China in 1848 was for the East India Tea Company. As the tea industry was a closely guarded secret by the Chinese, Fortune disguised himself as a Chinaman from a distant province in order to learn the necessary information and acquire tea plants (*Camellia sinensis*). He was then able to supply the Company with 2000 young tea plants, 17,000 germinated seedlings and half a dozen Chinese expert tea-makers.*

Several more expeditions to the Orient proved equally successful. As well as acquiring more tea, Fortune returned with many now familiar garden plants, including Japanese anemones, the winter-flowering honeysuckle Lonicera fragrantissima, *weigela, pompom chrysanthemums, tree peonies, primulas, forsythia and brilliantly coloured azaleas.*

ST BOSWELLS

Mertoun

St Boswells, Melrose, Roxburghshire TD6 0EA **TEL.** *01835-823236* **OWNER** *The Duke of Sutherland* **HOURS** *April–Sept, Sat–Sun and Bank Holiday Mons, 2–6p.m.* **ENTRANCE** *£1, children 50p* **DIRECTIONS** *2m NE of St Boswells on B6404*

SPRING SUMMER AUTUMN WINTER

Access

DON'T MISS

Mertoun provides exceptionally satisfying garden-visiting. The 26-acre grounds are beautiful, framed with magnificent trees, set beside the River Tweed. The sloping, three-acre walled garden is especially good; one path rises through an old orchard and the perimeter paths are lined with crisp box hedging, enclosing vegetables and herbs in neat rows, and abundant bushes of summer fruits. Fan-trained pears, plums and apples make productive use of the attractive stone walls, and less hardy fruits – figs and peaches – are nurtured in the traditional way under glass. There are borders of peonies, irises, delphiniums, lupins and other old-fashioned flowers, and cut-flower beds devoted to gladioli, for which the garden and its gardener are renowned.

Like so many Scottish gardens, spring sees an explosion of colour from rhododendrons and azaleas, and the alpines and waterside plants. The grounds are laid out informally, with a burn running through to join the Tweed that marks the southern boundary. An unusual feature in the garden is a circular dovecote dated 1576, thought to be the first to have been built in Scotland to provide fresh meat through the winter.

STOBO

Dawyck Botanic Garden

Stobo, Peeblesshire EH45 9JX **TEL.** *01721-760254* **OWNER** *Royal Botanic Garden, Edinburgh* **HOURS** *Mid-March–mid-Oct, daily, 10a.m.–6p.m. Other times by appointment* **ENTRANCE** *£2, concessions £1.50, children 50p* **DIRECTIONS** *8m SW of Peebles, on B712*

SPRING SUMMER AUTUMN WINTER

Gift Shop · Plant Shop

This is a lovely woodland site, breathtaking in spring and autumn, run by the Royal Botanic Garden in Edinburgh as one of their satellite gardens – they also run Logan Botanic Garden (*q.v.*) near Stranraer, and the Younger Botanic Garden (*q.v.*) at Benmore, Argyll. Trees are the thing at Dawyck which is famous for the Dawyck beech, *Fagus sylvatica* 'Dawyck' (sometimes listed as 'Fastigiata'), an unusual columnar form of beech which was raised here before 1850.

Some of the oldest larches here date back to plantings around 1725, and many of the assorted conifers have achieved over 100ft in height. Also note the introduction of colourful rhododendrons and other flowering shrubs, and the masses of spring bulbs, especially narcissi. The lovely woodland walks ramble through the steep slopes above a tributary of the River Tweed, accompanied by the music of water gushing down the rocky cascades.

And also...

Abbotsford House, Melrose, Roxburghshire TD6 9BQ (tel. 01896-752043), was the home of Sir Walter Scott. He designed the formal gardens near the house in the 1820s, and planted the woodland garden beyond. There is a walled kitchen garden with attractive orangery, herbacous borders, roses and fruit trees. Open mid-March–Oct, daily, 10a.m.–5p.m. (but 2–5p.m. on Sun, April–May, and Oct). Entrance £3.50, children £1.80.

The Hirsel, Coldstream, Berwickshire PD1 24LP (tel. 01890-882834), is an all-year-round garden. There are snowdrops and aconites followed by massed daffodils in spring. Rhododendrons and azaleas bloom through late May and June, and rose beds and shrub borders bring summer colour, followed by various autumn tints and berries. The grounds are also well known for being a visiting and nesting site for numerous migrant birds. Open all year, daily, during daylight hours. Entrance £2 per car.

Kailzie Gardens, Kailzie, Peebles, Peeblesshire EH45 9HT (tel. 01721-720007), features a substantial walled garden within its 17 acres, with a mixture of kitchen produce, lawns, ornamental plantings and a fine glasshouse. There are roses, double herbaceous borders and flowers for drying. The woodland area features walks among rhododendrons, primulas and Himalayan blue poppies. Open early April–Oct, daily, 11a.m.–5.30p.m. (to dusk in winter). Entrance £2, children 50p.

Manderston, Duns, Berwickshire TD11 3PP (tel. 01361-883450). Here are 56 acres of gardening on the grand scale. There are four richly planted formal terraces overlooking a serpentine lake, with a woodland garden beyond. The gardens feature further richly planted areas for summer colour, with fountains, statuary and a rose pergola. Open mid-May–late Sept, Sun and Thurs, 2–5.30p.m. Entrance £2.50, children 50p.

The gardens of **Mellerstain, Mellerstain House, Gordon TD3 6LG (tel. 01573-410225)**, were laid out in the early 20th century by Reginald Blomfield, proponent of the formal garden style. There are balustraded terraces ornamented with roses and topiary, and fine views of the Cheviot Hills to the south. Beyond the formal gardens is a well-treed landscape park with a lake. Open May–Sept, Sun–Fri (closed Sat), 12.30–5p.m. (last adm. 4.30p.m.). Entrance £2.

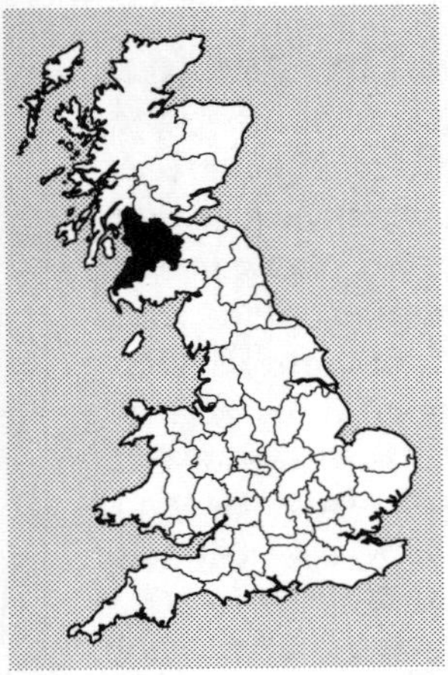

Western Scotland

MAP NO. 8

This large region encompasses Argyll, Ayrshire, Dumbartonshire and the industrial and cultural conurbation of Glasgow and the Clyde. Loch Fyne, a sea loch, is famous for its seafood, particularly smoked kippers, and for the lovely gardens of Crarae. It is a land of clan castles and wonderful landscape, with unpredictable weather. Ayrshire attracts visitors for its links golf courses as much as its seaside resorts, Troon and Turnberry being the most famous. From the latter, and from nearby Culzean Castle, you have good views of Ailsa Craig, the offshore island and seabird sanctuary, whose name is commemorated in popular varieties of onion and tomato.

BRODICK

Brodick Castle

Brodick, Island of Arran KA27 8HY TEL. *01770-302462* OWNER *National Trust for Scotland* HOURS *Garden and country park, all year, daily, 9a.m.–dusk (castle: April–Oct, daily, 11.30a.m.–5p.m.)* ENTRANCE *£2.30, concessions/ children £1.50 (castle and grounds £4.30, children £3)* DIRECTIONS *Car ferry from Ardrossan to Brodick (55 mins), then A481 N for 2m, signposted from Brodick*

SPRING SUMMER AUTUMN WINTER

Access | Gift Shop | Café

Brodick's red-sandstone castle sits above a sheltered bay on the east side of the Island of Arran. It is protected from south-westerly gales by the massif of the Arran mountains, which add considerably to the drama of the 200-acre site. There has been a fortress here for at least 1000 years, although the castle dates from the 13th to 19th centuries. Its walled garden was built in 1710, and today is planted in Victorian style, with carpet bedding, copious roses and summer-flowering perennials and annuals. The woodland gardens are famous for their collection of rhododendrons, which were rapidly accumulated during the 1920s and thirties by Mary Louise, the 6th Duchess of Montrose, who lived in the castle and took a huge interest in its garden until her death in 1957. Rambling paths descend the hillside to the seashore, taking in the beauty of spring-flowering shrubs, pools of cobalt-blue poppies and luscious waterside plantings of primulas and gunnera. There is also a pretty, rustic summerhouse and a restored ice house in the grounds; the gardener gives weekly guided walks during the summer months.

MAYBOLE

Culzean Castle Country Park

Maybole, South Ayrshire KA19 8LE **TEL.** *01655-760274*
OWNER *National Trust for Scotland* **HOURS** *Garden and country park, all year, daily, 9.30a.m.–dusk; castle, Visitor Centre, etc., April–Oct, daily, 10.30a.m.–5.30p.m.*
ENTRANCE *£3.50, concessions/children £2.40, family ticket £9 (castle and grounds £6.50 and £4.40, family ticket £17)*
DIRECTIONS *2m S of Ayr, on A719, 4m W of Maybole*

SPRING SUMMER AUTUMN WINTER

Access | Gift Shop | Café | Plant Shop

Culzean enjoys a majestic site, its castle rising out of the clifftop, with the sea raging on the rocks below. It is the National Trust for Scotland's most visited property (with around 230,000 visitors per year), offering 563 acres of undulating parkland, with lovely lakes and woods. The elegant castle and its home farm were designed by Robert Adam in the late 18th century (worth seeing for the magnificent armoury display and Adam's virtuoso Oval Staircase), and there are pretty features dotted about the grounds, including a beautifully restored camellia house, and a fine fountain of stylised dolphin and oyster-shell design.

The 30-acre gardens include a large, walled area, partly used for plant sales, with a range of glasshouses set beside glorious double herbaceous borders. Also within the walled gardens are wilder, shrubby areas, with specimen trees and broad lawns for picnics. Beside the castle, the formal, terraced gardens feature tender plants that are nurtured by the mild, coastal position and reflected warmth of the stone walls.

MINARD

Crarae Glen Garden

Crarae, Inveraray, Argyll PA32 8YA **TEL.** *01546-886614* **OWNER** *The Crarae Garden Charitable Trust* **HOURS** *All year, dawn–dusk; Visitor Centre 10a.m.–5p.m.* **ENTRANCE** *£2.50, children aged 5–16 £1.50, family ticket (2 adults, 2 children) £7* **DIRECTIONS** *On A83, S of Inveraray, on W side of Loch Fyne*

SPRING SUMMER AUTUMN WINTER

Gift Shop · Café · Plant Shop · DON'T MISS

The natural and exotic come together at Crarae to create a wondrous experience: dramatic Highland landscape mixed with choice plants from the Far East. A burn runs through the steep ravine that is the focus of the 50-acre garden. Informal paths wind around the valley sides and occasionally cross it, by timber bridges.

The garden was made in the first half of the 20th century by Lady Grace Campbell, aunt of the celebrated plant hunter, Reginald Farrer, followed by her son, Sir George Campbell. Farrer introduced many rhododendron species to Britain, and to Crarae, following his journeys to Kansu in 1914 and upper Burma in 1919. Other gardening friends contributed seeds and plants to the garden through the succeeding decades, and Sir George maintained two incontrovertible maxims: 'Never plant too close, but allow room for natural development', and 'Always try to ensure that the plants look natural in their setting.'

Spring is glorious here, not only with the rhododendrons for there are many other acid-loving shrubs and perennials threaded through the gardens; autumn brings spectacular leaf tints from a multitude of trees. The garden also contains a neolithic burial chamber and part of a 4500-year-old cairn.

BILL MACKENZIE AND HIS YELLOW CLEMATIS

I had the honour and pleasure of meeting the late Bill Mackenzie on several occasions thanks to the renowned plantswoman Valerie Finnis, who introduced us. I recall Bill's soft Argyllshire accent and the thrill of seeing his eponymous clematis in bloom, in his own garden.

Bill Mackenzie was truly a link with the past, for he first went to work at Edinburgh's Royal Botanic Garden in 1928, at the tail end of the golden age of plant hunting, when George Forrest and Frank Kingdon-Ward were still sending back hitherto unknown plants from China. 'It was a golden age,' Bill had told me, 'with many thousands of new plants that had never been seen before coming in by the barrowload. We were overwhelmed. It wasn't just an ounce or two of seed of each new plant, but pounds of it in many cases. You sowed what you could, pricked off what you could and the rest went to the tip. Such terrible waste but it was far too much material for us to handle.'

After the Second World War Bill was appointed curator of the Chelsea Physic Garden (q.v.) and became friends with Valerie Finnis, who was in charge of alpine plants at Waterperry Gardens (q.v.) in Oxfordshire. During a visit to Waterperry, Bill spotted a yellow clematis seedling and, he recalled, 'the next thing I knew, Valerie had it up at the Royal Horticultural Society's show and got an award for it'. She named it Bill Mackenzie. The desirable, bright yellow clematis is renowned for its vigour and generous amounts of lantern-like flowers produced from high summer well into autumn, followed (and often accompanied by) silky, silvery seedheads. It is a hardy, easy-to-grow climber, flowering best when planted deeply into rich, well-manured soil, in a bright position.

And also...

An Cala, Isle of Seil, Argyll PA34 4RF (tel: 01852–300237). This garden was designed in the 1930s; set against a stunning backdrop of islands and sea, it nestles into the surrounding cliffs and features a waterfall, burns, ponds and rockery formed from bedrock. Open April–Oct, daily, 10a.m.–6p.m. Entrance £1.

Angus's Garden, Barguillean Farm, Taynuilt, Argyll and Bute PA35 1HY (tel. 01866-822381), enjoys a wonderful setting beside Loch Angus. The oak and birch woods shelter collections of rhododendrons in the nine-acre gardens which are in the process of being made; the nurseries alongside specialize in rhododendrons and other ericaceous plants. Open March–Oct, daily, 9a.m.–dusk. Entrance £1.50.

Ardchattan Priory, Connel, Oban PA37 1RQ (tel. 01631-750274), is thought to be the second oldest inhabited house in Scotland (it was founded in 1230), and the venue of the last Gaelic Parliament. The priory features fine herbaceous borders in summer, and plenty of roses and hebes. Spring sees lovely drifts of daffodils in the woodland, followed by flowering rhododendrons and azaleas. Open April–Oct, daily, 9a.m.–6p.m. Entrance £1.

Ardmaddy Castle Gardens, Balvicar, Oban, Argyll PA34 4QY (tel. 01852-300353), has a working, formal walled garden with dwarf box hedging, unusual vegetables and fruit. There is a water garden, extensive outer shrubberies and woodland in a marvellous situation overlooking the sea and distant islands. Open all year, daily, 9a.m.–sunset. Entrance £2, children 50p.

Arduaine Garden, National Trust for Scotland, Arduaine, by Oban, Argyll PA34 4XQ (tel. 01852-200366), holds an important collection of rhododendron species, sheltered by large trees planted 100 years ago. Its position on the west coast allows it to enjoy the warming influence of the Gulf Stream, allowing a range of slightly tender plants to be grown. There are rambling woodland walks, best seen in spring, and the garden possesses lily-pools fed by natural springs, beside which are lush plantings of ferns, irises and blue poppies. The Loch Melfort Hotel, next door, provides comfortable accommodation. Open all year, daily, 9.30a.m.–sunset. Entrance £2.40, concessions/children under 18 £1.60, family ticket (2 adults, up to 6 children) £6.

Bargany Gardens, Old Dailly, Girvan, South Ayrshire KA26 9QL (tel. 01465-871249), consist of pleasant woodland, best seen at rhododendron time, for the colourful displays among good specimen trees and conifers. There are also good spring bulb displays, a lily-pond and a rock garden. Open March–Oct, daily, 10a.m.–7p.m. (4p.m. early and late in the season). Entrance by donation.

Barwinnock Herbs, Barrhill, by Girvan, Ayrshire KA26 0RB (tel. 01465-821338), specializes in producing culinary, medicinal and fragrant-leaved plants, all organically grown, for collection and by mail. (Send 3 × 1st-class stamps for catalogue.) Open April–Oct, daily, 10a.m.–6p.m.

The extensive woods and 1860s pinetum at **Blairquhan Castle, Straiton, Maybole, Ayrshire KA19 7LZ (tel. 01655-770239)**, can be viewed along its three-mile private drive beside the River Girvan. Its walled kitchen garden has been skilfully redesigned with ornamental plantings replacing vegetable crops. Open mid-July–mid-Aug, daily, except Mon, 1.30–6p.m. Entrance £3.50, OAPs £2.50, children £2 (house and garden).

Finlaystone Country Park, Langbank, Renfrewshire PA14 6TJ (tel. 01475-540285/540505), was designed in 1900 and has been enhanced over the years, with 10 acres of gardens and another 70 of mature woodlands dissected by walks. There are traditional herbaceous borders beside neat lawns, mature shrubberies and fine views of the River Clyde, a garden of fragrance and a bog garden among its delights. Open all year, daily, 10.30a.m.–5p.m. Entrance £2, OAPs/children £1.20.

Glasgow Botanic Garden, 730 Great Western Road, Glasgow G12 0UE (tel. 0141-334 2422), has lovely greenhouses and conservatories with displays of plants from the tropics as well as desert plants and those from the temperate regions. Outdoors there are fine herbaceous borders, good specimen trees, a rock garden, a lake and topiaries. Owned by City of Glasgow Council. Open all year, Mon–Fri, 7a.m.–dusk (glasshouses 10a.m.–4.45p.m., closing 4.15p.m. in winter), Sat–Sun, afternoons only. Entrance free.

Greenbank Garden, Flenders Road, Clarkston, Glasgow G76 8RB (tel. 0141-639 3281), has two and a half acres of walled garden, and 13 of policies surrounding an elegant Georgian house built in 1764 for a Glasgow merchant. The attractive garden demonstrates the wide range of ornamental plants that can be grown in the region; there are annuals, perennials, shrubs, trees and rock garden plants. Open all year, daily, 9.30a.m.–sunset, except 25–26 Dec and 1–2 Jan. Entrance £3, OAPs/disabled/unemployed £2, children aged 5–17 £2, family ticket (2 adults and up to 6 children) £8, National Trust members free.

Younger Botanic Garden, Benmore, Dunoon, Argyll PA23 8QU (tel. 01369-706261), covers over 100 acres and is run by the Royal Botanic Garden, Edinburgh, as a satellite garden, specializing in plants appropriate to the setting. It is famous for its extensive ranges of flowering trees and shrubs, rhododendrons and conifers. Its renowned avenue of tall wellingtonia trees was planted in 1863; there are also good examples of monkey-puzzle trees, which grow well in this region. Open mid-March–Oct, daily, 10a.m.–6p.m. Entrance £2, concessions £1.50, children of school age 50p.

WALES

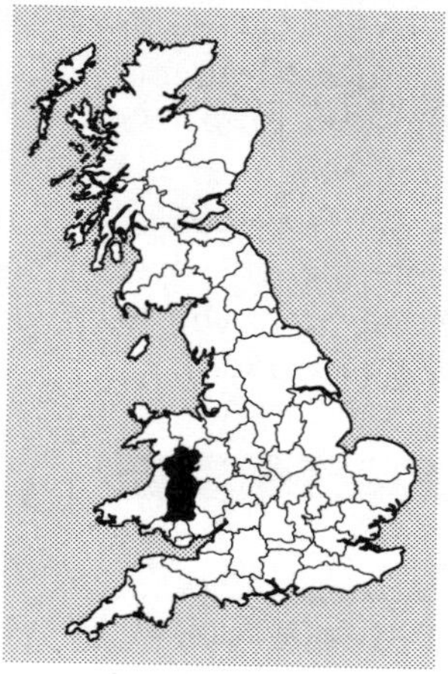

Mid Wales

MAP NO. 4

This region is covered by the large county of Powys. Quiet, gentle hills of green pasture and sheep are a feature of its landscape, dotted with small market towns and villages of Tudor timber and Georgian brick. Reliable breezes blowing in from the south and west power small forests of windmills on some of the higher ground, while the water run off from the Cambrian Mountains in the west helps to fill the deep reservoir of Lake Vyrnwy, supplying water to distant Liverpool. The area is more popular with walkers than gardeners, and the famously scenic Offa's Dyke Path runs along the region's eastern edge.

WELSHPOOL

The Dingle Nurseries and Garden

Welshpool, Powys SY21 9JD **TEL.** *01938-555145* **OWNER** *of the nursery, A. and K. Joseph, of the garden, R. and B. Joseph* **HOURS** *Open all year, Wed–Mon, 9a.m.–5p.m.* **ENTRANCE** *£1.50 (donated to charity) (nursery free)* **DIRECTIONS** *3m N of Welshpool; take A490 (direction Llanfyllin) for 1m, turn left at sign for Dingle Nursery or Frochas, then left again after 1¾m (signposted)*

SPRING SUMMER AUTUMN WINTER

Access Nursery

DON'T MISS

Centuries-old sheep farms and ancient oak woods surround this thriving four-acre garden and nursery, created by Barbara and Roy Joseph. Under the distant gaze of Moel y Golfa, the Bald, or Stony Hill, the Dingle reflects in miniature some of the dramatic features of its surroundings. The garden's paths zig-zag down its rugged slopes, and a small, natural stream fills a big pool at the bottom. An astonishing range of plants is packed into the garden to bring colour and interest in every season, with each bed carefully colour-themed for harmonious juxtaposition of flower and foliage tints. The adjoining nursery is renowned for its range of well-grown plants, especially trees, shrubs and conifers, but there is no catalogue or mail order.

WELSHPOOL

Powis Castle

Welshpool, Powys SY21 8RF TEL. *01938-554338/Infoline 554336* OWNER *The National Trust* HOURS *April–June, Sept–Nov, daily, except Mon–Tues, July–Aug, daily, except Mon, 11a.m.–6p.m. (but open Bank Holiday Mons), last adm. ½hr before closing* ENTRANCE *£5, children £2.50 (under 5s free), family ticket £12.50 (extra to see castle or go on a guided tour)* DIRECTIONS *1m S of Welshpool*

SPRING SUMMER AUTUMN WINTER

Gift Shop · Café · DON'T MISS

My first visit to Powis Castle was on an unseasonally cold and grim day one spring, but it is in the power of the garden to win you over, whatever the weather, with its velvety wraps of yew hedging and warmly tinted red sandstone fortress. A return more recently, in contrast, basked in semi-tropical weather, brought out the richness of the planting for which Powis is so well known.

Powis is one of the treasures in the National Trust's horticultural crown, a garden on the grand scale, but not only impressive by its size – 55 acres; the setting is magnificent, its terraces run in deep, parallel steps down the hillside and are extensively planted, and the garden speaks of centuries of care and development. The retaining walls of the terraces feature clouds of blue ceanothus, late-flowering phygelius, and abutilons; the herbaceous beds are an opulent, Edwardian mix of classic border plants such as monkshoods, asters, crocosmias and red-hot pokers, and there are imaginatively planted containers, too.

Huge, irregular domes of clipped yew dribble over the wall of the top terrace; they began life as small, pointed topiaries lining the stairway in the original 17th-century garden, but now form a soft green cushion around the castle's foundations. Spare some time, too, to see the lower formal gardens with their pyramidal apple trees, vine tunnel and roses, and the grassy slopes ornamented with specimen trees.

Celebrity Choice

***Stephen Lacey, author, journalist and presenter of BBC2's* Gardeners' World**

*'**Powis Castle** (*q.v.*)is practically on my doorstep, so I go there quite a lot at all times of year and all times of day. It's amazingly scenic and I love driving through the park. There is a lushness in the west of Britain, because of the rain, that you don't get in the east; Powis has a fertile feel to it with things growing buxomly. It is a rich source of planting ideas and the planting changes quite a lot from year to year. Colours in the planting are quite intense and the borders have helped me to develop a taste for strong colours, such as the scarlets and oranges of crocosmias. Unlike many gardens, this one gets better and better as the season progresses and is really good in August, not only from the flowers; you get other things, such as the great showers of rose-hips from* Rosa glauca *and* R. *"Highdownensis" and you will often see magnificent sunsets there.'*

And also...

A group of medieval buildings makes up the delightful **Tretower Court, Crickhowell, Powys NP8 1RF (tel. 01874-730279).** A relatively new medieval garden, laid out in 1991, now complements the Court and has been planted as authentically as possible to illustrate the typical garden of a wealthy commoner in the mid-15th century. Visit in summer to enjoy the tunnel arbour and small pavilion draped in vines, roses and honeysuckle; the enclosed gardens feature trelliswork, turf seats, fragrant herbs, irises, lilies, fountains and a chequerboard pattern of flowerbeds. Open late March–late Oct, daily, 10a.m.–6p.m. (closing at 4.30p.m. in Oct and March). Entrance £2.20.

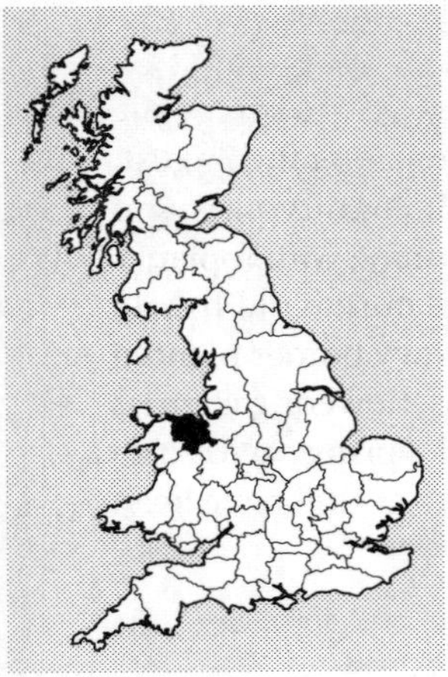

North-east Wales

MAP NO. 4

Waterfalls and lakes, wooded hills and broad pastures characterise this rural region, which embraces Flintshire, Wrexham, Denbighshire and part of Conwy. The Clwydian hills form a long spine from the north coast down to the town of Llangollen, while the Berwyn range heralds the higher mountains of Snowdonia in the west. Llangollen swells with visitors in summer, and is famous for its International Music Eisteddfod in July; it boasts a magnificent 1000ft aqueduct by Thomas Telford, with horse-drawn barges conveying passengers along the calm waters of the former industrial canal.

CHIRK

Chirk Castle

Chirk, Wrexham LL14 5AF **TEL.** *01691-777701* **OWNER** *The National Trust* **HOURS** *April–late Sept, Wed–Sun and Bank Holiday Mons, and weekends in Oct, gardens 11a.m.–6p.m. (last adm. 4.30p.m.), castle 12 noon–5p.m.* **ENTRANCE** *£4.40, children £2.20; garden only £2.20 and £1.10* **DIRECTIONS** *½m W of Chirk village, off A5, 8m S of Wrexham, signposted*

SPRING SUMMER AUTUMN WINTER

Access | Gift Shop | Café

The yew hedges at Chirk are the signature feature of the gardens, for they appear as stout and impenetrable as the castle's walls and have suitably castellated tops to echo the masonry. Forming an enclosure to the terraced lawns, the yews also provide much needed shelter on this staggering, hilltop site.

The castle, finished around 1310, was used to survey the movements of the defeated Welsh tribes along the English border. The surrounding six-acre 18th-century park and gardens speak of more recent, peaceful times, with topiaries and terraced lawns, a sunken garden featuring old hybrid tea and floribunda roses, and a long, wavy border planted with flowering shrubs. Here, the azaleas, flowering cherries and lilacs are a glorious feature of spring, with the magnolias, dogwoods and rhododendrons that have been planted since the last war by Lady Margaret Myddelton.

HILLTOP TREES FROM DOWN UNDER

Everything you have ever wanted to know about eucalyptus, the gum trees of Australasia, is contained in the excellent catalogue from ***Celyn Vale Nurseries, Allt-y-Celyn, Carrog, Corwen, Denbighshire LL21 9LD (tel. 01490-430671).*** *They grow here in six acres on the hillside, 800ft up, and the proprietor, Andrew McConnell, has made extensive studies of the hardiness of different species in recent years. His plants are raised from seed obtained from wild plants growing in very cold, exposed habitats which ensures the hardiness of his stock, comprising some 50 different eucalyptus species, and about 10 acacias from Australia and Tasmania. Plants are generally sold by mail, but you can browse and buy direct from the nursery (open March–Oct, Mon–Fri, 9a.m.–4p.m.), although telephone appointments are appreciated.*

LLANGOLLEN

Plas Newydd

Hill Street, Llangollen, Denbighshire LL20 8AW TEL. *01978-861314* OWNER *Denbighshire County Council* HOURS *April–Oct, daily, 10a.m.–5p.m.* ENTRANCE *£2, children £1, family ticket £5, 15% reduction for parties of 20 or more* DIRECTIONS *From A5 to Llangollen, turn up Hill Street (signposted)*

The Ladies of Llangollen – Eleanor Butler and Sarah Ponsonby – came to Plas Newydd in 1780, having run away from their Irish homes and, over the next 50 years, created one of the most famous and talked about gardens in the Romantic style. (Famous visitors included Wordsworth, Shelley, Sir Walter Scott, Dr Darwin and his son, Charles, and the Duke of Wellington.) According to Prince Pückler-Muskau, who visited them in 1828, they 'took it into their heads to hate men, to love only each other, and to live from that hour in some remote hermitage... neither lady has ever passed a night out of their cottage... [and] no one presentable travels to Wales unprovided with an introduction to them'.

Influenced by the 19th-century writer Sir Uvedale Price, and Rousseau, they transformed the four acres surrounding their lonely cottage by planting shrubberies, glades of white lilacs for romantic, moonlit walks, thickets of 'Lilaks [sic], Laburnums, Seringas [sic], White Broom, Weeping Willow, Apple Trees, poplar'; they assembled gnarled and twisted tree branches into summerhouses, balustrades and naturalistic bridges to cross the River Cuffleymen. Mosses, ferns and salvaged stone remnants from nearby Valle Crucis Abbey add to the Romantic idyll.

The river in its ravine, mature forest trees and sombre, weeping conifers continue to capture some of the spirit of the place, in spite of a good deal of building now occupying the surrounding landscape. Subsequent owners have added flowerbeds around the house, and some marvellous topiaries in green and golden yew.

The Ladies added three ornately carved timber porches to the house front (for which they held a 'Porch Warming Party'), and it is well worth seeing the house interior too, which has further examples of the Ladies' self-confessed 'oak carving mania'. Alas, the house is no longer crammed with curiosities, as it was in their day. Pause, too, to enjoy the views of Castell Dinas Brân, the Trevor rocks and Berwyn Mountains that so enchanted the Ladies, and inspired their gardening.

HOME-GROWN SAFFRON BY MAIL

Once a flourishing industry in 16th-century England, saffron (obtained from Crocus sativus*) is not popularly grown today, but Caroline Riden produces both the corms and the harvested aromatic strands on the farm. The crocuses need a sunny spot and free-draining, manured, slightly alkaline soil, and should be planted from June–Aug, while dormant. For a mail order form and cultivation details, send a s.a.e. to* ***Caroline Riden, Caer Estyn Farm, Rhyddyn Hill, Caergwrle, Flintshire LL12 9EF (tel. 01978-761558).*** *Open by appointment only.*

WREXHAM

Erddig

Nr Wrexham LL13 0YT TEL. *01978-355314* OWNER *The National Trust* HOURS *Late March–end Oct, daily except Thurs and Fri (but open Good Friday), 11a.m.–6p.m., July–Aug, 10a.m.–6p.m., Oct, 11a.m.–5p.m.* ENTRANCE *£3.60, children £1.80 (extra to see house)* DIRECTIONS *2m S of Wrexham, signposted from A525*

SPRING SUMMER AUTUMN WINTER

Access | Gift Shop | Café | NPC

The list of wall fruits originally planted in the formal, early 18th-century gardens of Erddig features such specialities as 'Kanatian Peach', 'Blew Perdrigon Plumb', 'Scarlett Newington Netorn', 'Gross Blanquett Pare' and 'Orange Apricock', to name a few. Fruit continues to be an important theme of the gardens at Erddig, for the National Trust has restored the near-derelict gardens to something approaching their former glory, and searched out old varieties grown in the period.

There are pyramid-shape apple trees, and further fruits in formal plantations and splayed against the extensive walls; Portuguese laurels are clipped into mophead shapes to imitate orange trees in white timber Versailles tubs, and the formality is completed by broad lawns and a central, rectangular canal.

It is a spacious, airy two-and-a-half-acre garden, not especially intimate or atmospheric, but great for long walks in the park, especially when the daffodils are in bloom, while the National Collection of ivy invites closer scrutiny of the shadiest of the garden's walls. The house and outbuildings on this 1700-acre estate feature interesting exhibits of the upstairs/downstairs lifestyle, and there are riding stables, and a timber workshop producing well-made garden furniture for sale.

And also...

Anyone interested in the formal four-acre Victorian gardens of W.A. Nesfield should visit **Bodrhyddan Hall, Rhuddlan, Denbighshire LL18 5SB (tel. 01745-590414).** A magnificent parterre beside the south front of the house is laid out in elegant scrolls and other patterns in low box hedging, seasonally infilled with bedding plants in blocks of single colours. Among the artefacts to be seen indoors is a 3000-year-old Egyptian mummy. Open June–Sept, Tues and Thurs, 2–5.30p.m. Entrance £3, children £1.

Dibley's Nurseries, Llanelidan, Ruthin, Denbighshire LL15 2LG (tel. 01978-790677), specializes in streptocarpus, the tender Cape primrose that comes in glorious shades of violet and blue-mauve, and tints from red to pink to white. A frequent medal winner at the Royal Horticultural Society's shows, the nurseries are open daily from April–Sept, 9a.m.–5p.m., or you can order by mail (send an A4 s.a.e. for the extensive catalogue).

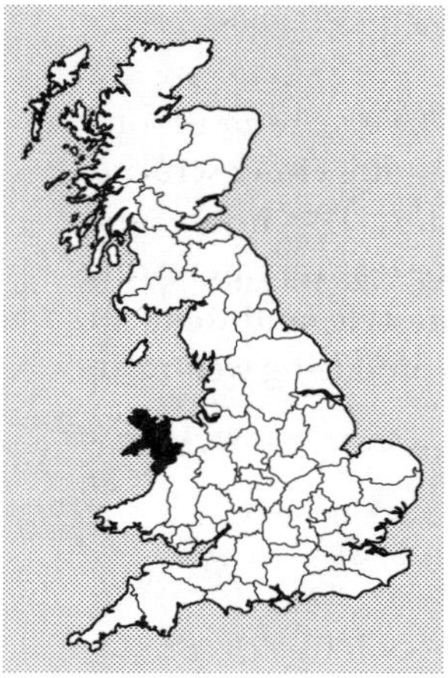

North-west Wales

MAP NO. 4

This is a land steeped in myths and heroes, more frequently trodden by walkers and climbers than by gardeners, for the 845 square miles of the Snowdonia National Park is the region's dominating feature. It is a landscape of pale, moisture-laden air, brooding peaks veiled in mist and shadow, and deep cauldrons filled with chill waters cascading from the glacial highlands. The weather can change from brightness to gloom in an instant, and has the power to inspire similar mood changes in the visitor; at such times the frequent roadside invitations to nearby farms, to take tea, are especially welcoming. Both houses and gardens make use of the local Ffestiniog slate, a stone of mutable beauty and sheen, like a magpie's wing.

COLWYN BAY

Bodnant Garden

Tal-y-Cafn, Colwyn Bay, Conwy LL28 5RE TEL. *01492-650460* OWNER *The National Trust* HOURS *Mid-March–Oct, daily, 10a.m.–5p.m. (last adm. 4.30p.m.)* ENTRANCE *£4.20, children £2.10* DIRECTIONS *8m S of Llandudno and Colwyn Bay, off A470 (signposted)*

SPRING SUMMER AUTUMN WINTER

Gift Shop | Café | Plant Shop | DON'T MISS

Bodnant is largely the combined result of two families, the owner's and the gardener's, working in tandem through the 20th century. (Head gardener Martin Puddle is the third generation of Puddles to take charge of the garden, for his

PLANT HUNTERS' PLANTS

Sue and Bleddyn Wynn-Jones are so smitten with plants from the Far East that they regularly go on expeditions to Taiwan, Korea and the Himalayas to collect wild seed. The results of their travels are among the rarefied list of plants sold in their nursery, ***Crûg Farm Plants at Griffiths Crossing, nr Caernarfon, Gwynedd LL55 1TU (tel. 01248-670232), 2m NE of Caernarfon, ¼m off main A487 Caernarfon–Bangor road.*** *Shade-loving plants are a speciality, and the list of hardy cranesbill geraniums which tops 300 includes many species unavailable elsewhere. If you like to seek out rare plants to fox your friends, a visit here is a must (allow plenty of boot-space for purchases). Much of the stock is also on view in the walled display gardens. Open end Feb–mid-Sept, Thurs–Sun and Bank Holiday Mons 10a.m.–6p.m., or by appointment. There is no mail order but for their extensive plant list send a s.a.e. with 1 × 2nd-class stamp.*

grandfather arrived in 1920, to work for the 2nd Lord Aberconway.)

The story begins with Henry Davis Pochin, an industrial chemist and inventor, who discovered how to turn soap white. He bought the estate in 1874 and planted its famous laburnum walk and the exceptional conifers in the Dell. His grandson, Henry (later, the 2nd Lord Aberconway), invested heavily in the garden during the early part of the 20th century, and we must thank him for the fine terraced upper gardens with lawns around the house, and the great collections of woodland plants. (From the terraces, note the fine views of the Snowdonia mountains to the west.)

While the upper gardens are restrained and formal, with flower and rose borders and neat lawns, by far the most exciting part is the Dell, a steep valley carved by a tributary of the River Conwy, where the sound of rushing torrents adds to the spectacle. The south-west-facing hillside of thin, acidic soil is home to countless rhododendrons and magnolias which flare up in starbursts of white, pink, yellow and red between the bare branches of woodland trees. Many of the old conifers now form skyward pillars reaching up through the valley, while winding paths and timber bridges invite further exploration.

The 80-acre garden's most interesting building is the attractive Pin Mill, at the end of a formal canal in the upper gardens. It was an early 18th-century garden lodge, which became a pin factory and then a tannery, before being brought stone-by-stone all the way from Gloucestershire, to take up its present, more dignified employment.

BUXTON'S BLUE GERANIUM

'A pearl beyond price' is how the influential plantsman, Graham Stuart Thomas, describes Geranium wallichianum *'Buxton's Variety' in his seminal work,* Perennial Garden Plants. *It thus went on to everybody's wish-list and is now widely grown, but its origins lie here, in forested Betws-y-coed on the River Conwy. Edmund Charles Buxton (1838–1925) came from Hendon, but moved to Coed Drew, Betws-y-coed, to plant a hillside garden in the spectacular but uncompromising landscape of Snowdonia. Buxton's clear blue geranium is invaluable for its long season of bright blue button flowers with white eye, prolific in bloom and backed by attractive foliage that takes on blood-red tints as the season progresses. It arose in his garden from the more mauve-tinted Himalayan species of* G. wallichianum. *E.C. Buxton is also remembered in a desirable, pale yellow anthemis.*

PENRHYNDEUDRAETH

Plas Brondanw

Llanfrothen, Gwynedd LL48 6SW **TEL.** *01766-770484/ 770814* **OWNER** *Trustees of the Second Portmeirion Foundation* **HOURS** *Open all year, daily, 9a.m.–5p.m.* **ENTRANCE** *£1.50, children 25p* **DIRECTIONS** *3m N of Penrhyndeudraeth, off A4085, on the Croesor Road*

SPRING SUMMER AUTUMN WINTER

DON'T MISS

Formal gardens do not feature strongly in Wales; the nation's gardeners more usually respond to the mountainous topography and acid soils by taking a naturalistic approach. Not only is Plas Brondanw a notable exception, but it is one of the most enchanting gardens you will see anywhere, although it is little known.

The estate was given to 25-year-old Clough Williams-Ellis in 1908 as a birthday present from his father. 'Nothing, just then, could possibly have been more ecstatically welcomed by me,' he recalled. A young architect with vision, and strongly imbued with the contemporary Arts and Crafts style, Williams-Ellis plotted the garden, a long, narrow strip of about two acres, dividing it into hedged rooms punctuated by slender columns of Italian cypress, which fare surprisingly well here.

This is an intimate, domestic and comfy garden, set against the awesome backdrop of the Snowdonia mountains. Its tiered yew topiaries are exceptionally fine, with deep crowns recalling traditional Welsh hats; the walls of local stone and slate shimmer in metallic mauves and browns in the rain, but transport the garden into Mediterranean mode when the sun shines.

Flowers do not feature strongly, for this is chiefly a garden of green architecture and reflective pools, but with its vistas directing your gaze to the summits of Moel Hebog and Cnicht in the distance, fancy blooms close to hand would seem an irrelevance.

There is a pleasant walk, on the other side of the road, up a steep hill to a folly look-out. Williams-Ellis was in the Welsh Guards when he got married in 1915, but, always an individualist, requested a ruin as a present from his fellow officers, instead of the usual silver salver. After the war he turned the gift of a pile of stones into the present viewing tower.

PENRHYNDEUDRAETH

Portmeirion

Penrhyndeudraeth, Gwynedd LL48 6ET TEL. *01766-770228* OWNER *Portmeirion Ltd* HOURS *Open all year, except 25 Dec, daily, 9.30a.m.–5.30p.m.* ENTRANCE *£3.50, OAPs £3, children £1.75* DIRECTIONS *Off A487 at Minffordd between Penrhyndeudraeth and Porthmadog*

SPRING SUMMER AUTUMN WINTER

Gift Shop | Café | Plant Shop

DON'T MISS

Next time I come here I shall check into the rather splendid Portmeirion Hotel (which runs the village) and spend a little longer in this enchanting and eccentric place. Set into approximately 175 acres of woodland gardens on the sea-shore, Portmeirion is best known as the location for the cult TV series, *The Prisoner*. It was designed by the rich and talented architect Clough Williams-Ellis (see Plas Brondanw, above), to accommodate 'like-minded and highly civilised persons'. He invited an eclectic mix of artists, philosophers, left-wing sympathisers, scientists and writers to take up residence and, during his lifetime, many did.

The village is speckled with fan palms, cabbage palms and Italian cypress trees, all of which flourish because of the warming influence of the Gulf Stream. Rhododendrons, fuchsias and hydrangeas add to the ice-cream hues of the delightful, painted buildings.

Try to see Portmeirion on a sunny day, to capture the essence of Riviera frivolity, so incongruously set between the broad estuary sands of Traeth Bach and the veiled, misty mountains of Snowdonia.

And also....

Bodysgallen Hall, Llandudno, Conwy LL30 1RS (tel. 01492-584466), is a luxurious country-house hotel of pink sandstone, mainly Jacobean, with deeply impressive walled gardens, part of the 214 acres of land, open to residents and diners. There is a symmetrical box parterre filled with fragrant herbs, a rockery with cascade and a walled rose garden featuring white and pale yellow flowers that glow in the fading light of a summer's evening. The productive kitchen garden supplies food for the restaurant, and there are also extensive woodland walks – a fabulous place for a special treat weekend, with Bodnant Garden (*q.v.*) just a few miles up the road. Open all year, daily. Entrance free to patrons of the hotel.

The National Trust's **Plas Newydd, Llanfairpwll, Anglesey LL61 6DQ (tel. 01248-714795)**, is not to be confused with Plas Newydd in Denbighshire (*q.v.*), and the Ladies of Llangollen. This Plas Newydd lies above the narrow, yacht-speckled channel of the Menai Strait and gazes south-east across the water to Snowdonia's handsome peaks. Humphry Repton (*q.v.*) worked here on improving the gardens, followed by the 1st Marquess of Anglesey and his descendants, and the 169-acre gardens offer pleasingly informal walks among an impressive collection of flowering trees and shrubs. Many plants from the southern hemisphere flourish here in the mild microclimate. The far-flung rhododendron garden, nearly a mile's walk from the house, is a naturalistic woodland filled with marvellous specimens, but is only open from April to early June, during the flowering season. Garden open Easter weekend–Oct, Sun–Thurs, 11a.m.–5.30p.m. Entrance £2, children £1, house and garden £4.20, children £2.10, family ticket £10.50.

You need to make an excursion down the slender Lleyn Peninsula to reach the National Trust's **Plas-yn-Rhiw, Pwllheli, Gwynedd LL53 8AB (tel. 01758-780219).** Here is an intimate and rambling cottage garden, just ¾ acre, with stout box hedges and simple topiaries, narrow and bumpy stone paths, and an eclectic mix of flowering and foliage plants with bulbs. Its feminine nature, with the emphasis on fragrance, is due to the three Keating sisters and their mother, who bought the handsome stone farmhouse and surrounding hillside in 1938, with the clear intention of preserving it for later generations to enjoy. Open April–mid-May, daily, except Tues and Wed, mid-May–Sept, daily, except Tues, noon–5p.m. (last adm. 4.30p.m.). Entrance £3.20, children £1.50, family ticket £8.

Sundialman at Cae Gwyn, Capel Curig, Betws-y-coed, Conwy LL24 0DH (tel. 01690-720288), specializes in hand-made garden sundials in engraved brass and slate, and armillary spheres. An illustrated catalogue is available on request (send a s.a.e.), but commissions and restorations are also undertaken. Open by appointment only.

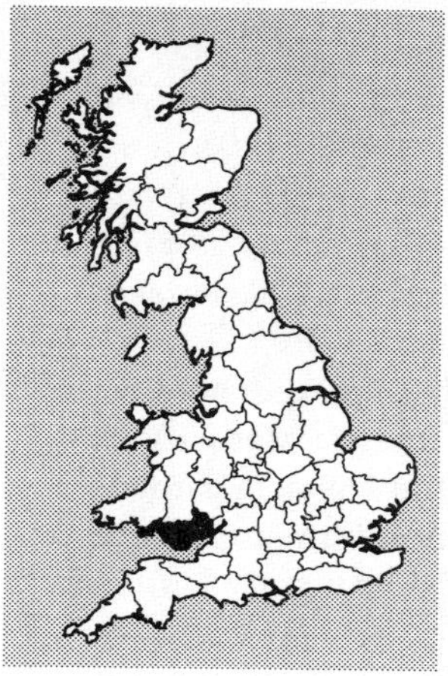

South Wales

MAP NO. 4

This region encompasses the reinstated Monmouthshire, the county of Wales that is south-easternmost (for some years known as Gwent) and the industrial heartland of Glamorgan. With its industrial heritage and strong associations with mining, this is the most densely populated part of Wales. From the 18th century onwards, the famous Rhondda Valleys provided work for thousands in the (now defunct) mines, but at a price, for the beautiful landscape draining the southern edge of the Brecon Beacons rapidly became scarred by industry, as dark and satanic as the mountain waters were sweet and pure. Monmouthshire is garlanded on its eastern boundary by the beautiful meanders of the Wye Valley and the ancient chase of the Forest of Dean. The valley and the ruins of the Cistercian Tintern Abbey inspired William Wordsworth to 'thoughts of more deep seclusion', and they continue to enchant visitors to this day.

CARDIFF

Dyffryn Botanic Garden

St Nicholas, Cardiff CF5 6SU TEL. *01222-593328* OWNER *Vale of Glamorgan Council* HOURS *Open all year, daily, 10a.m.–dusk* ENTRANCE *£2, OAPs/children £1.50, family ticket £6* DIRECTIONS *4m SW of Cardiff on A4232, turn S on A4050 and then W to Dyffryn*

SPRING SUMMER AUTUMN WINTER

Access | Gift Shop | Café | Plant Shop

The renowned Edwardian landscape architect, Thomas Mawson, laid out the 55 acres of gardens around Dyffryn's splendid mansion. Close to the house the formal gardens with symmetrical, seasonal flowerbeds and enclosed garden rooms set to one side, tie the architecture of the mansion seamlessly into its grounds. On the south side, a broad lawn with central water canal and lily-pond creates a grand setting, enhanced by topiary and formal planting. There is a rose garden, a glasshouse of exotic orchids, a herbaceous walk, a classical garden with fountain inspired by those excavated at Pompeii, and a rotunda of yew. The wilder gardens and arboretum beyond the formal areas contain many fine specimen trees and shrubs, dating from the days of the great plant hunters earlier this century. Japanese maples are a feature of the oak woods.

DEVAUDEN

Veddw House

Devauden, Monmouthshire NP6 6PH TEL. *01291-650836*
OWNER *Anne Wareham and Charles Hawes* HOURS *Open Easter–mid-Sept, Sun, 2–5p.m.* ENTRANCE *£2, children 50p Parties welcome by appointment* DIRECTIONS *Devauden is on B4293, almost midway between Chepstow and Monmouth*

SPRING SUMMER AUTUMN WINTER

Access

The four acres of Veddw House gardens are varied and colour-themed. Two acres around the house are divided by formal and informal hedging of box, yew, beech and cotoneaster into a variety of separate gardens and colour borders. In spring the meadow, full of small bulbs, is a major feature. This is bordered on one side by a formal vegetable garden where two flower borders – one full of roses, the other herbaceous – contain the brick and gravel paths, which define beds where cabbages mingle with clipped box and standard 'Iceberg' roses.

The conservatory provides protection for a range of tender and exotic plants and offers a view of the crescent border, filled with flowering perennials and shrubs. On the hillside beyond is a developing garden, featuring grasses and low-growing perennials. The yew walk, with a *trompe l'oeil* urn, leads to a small hazel copse, with a ruined cottage, and then on to two acres of woodland walks.

THE BISHOP'S FAMOUS DAHLIA

Many gardeners value the brilliant scarlet blooms and deep bronze foliage of Dahlia *'Bishop of Llandaff', which originated in this region. Llandaff was an ancient cathedral city perched on the banks of the River Taff, but is now swallowed up in the conurbations of Cardiff. Local nurseryman Fred Treseder, who came from Cornwall, spent 50 years dabbling in breeding new dahlias. When his friend, Bishop Hughes of Llandaff, admired a new red dahlia, the nurseryman promptly named it after him. It was awarded an Award of Merit by the Royal Horticultural Society in 1928, and became widely grown during the following decade. In 1936* The Spectator *declared that it was 'the most popular flower of the moment in many parts of England'. Plant fashions come and go, and 'Bishop of Llandaff' faded into obscurity for many years, but its current vogue is partly due to a revived interest in strongly coloured flowers, and a trend towards creating 'hot' borders, like those at Hidcote* (q.v.).

NEWPORT

Tredegar House

Newport NP1 9YW **TEL.** *01633-815880* **OWNER** *Newport Borough Council* **HOURS** *April–Sept, Wed–Sun, 11.30a.m.–4p.m.* **ENTRANCE** *(house and garden) £3.95, concessions £3, children £2, family ticket £10.50* **DIRECTIONS** *2m from Newport, signposted from M4 Jct 28 and A48*

SPRING SUMMER AUTUMN WINTER

The walled gardens at Tredegar have been undergoing restoration since important archaeological evidence of formal, Tudor gardens was unearthed. A tracing of an early 17th-century plan shows that the house (also open) was surrounded on two sides by a series of walled enclosures roughly following the present ones, with a 'great gate' into 'the great bowling greene', a wilderness or maze with a corner arbour, a garden plot 'contrived in walks and borders for trees and flowers', and three orchards with 550 trees planted 'dyamond wise'.

Part of the old layout was covered for 200 years by a thick layer of soil from the excavated lake (made *c.*1790), and archaeological investigations revealed an intricate layout of paths, beds, a small mount and a pair of parterres in front of the orangery. The main central path was of coal dust, bordered with crushed seashells; the patterns of the parterre were formed with different materials such as crushed lime mortar, seashells, brick and coal dust. These have been reinstated, along with espalier fruit trees and box hedging.

The 90-acre park dates from the late 18th century, and one of its avenues, predating the naturalistic Landscape movement, has managed to survive. Deep 19th-century herbaceous borders line the central cedar garden.

SWANSEA

Clyne Gardens

Mumbles Road, Black Pill, Swansea SA2 9DU TEL. *01792-298637* OWNER *Swansea City Council* HOURS *All year, daily, dawn–dusk* ENTRANCE *Free* DIRECTIONS *3m W of Swansea, on coast road*

SPRING SUMMER AUTUMN WINTER

NPC

This beautiful 50-acre woodland garden is best seen in spring. The local acid soil nurtures many fine rhododendrons, notably the large-leaved Falconera types, of which there is a National Collection here (the gardens also hold National Collections of acid-loving pieris, enkianthus and triflora rhododendrons. There are sumptuous magnolias, gunneras and candelabra primulas at the streamside, and fragrant azaleas creating a delightful place for a springtime stroll. Refreshments are served during the peak season, in May.

And also...

Creta Cotta Pots and Urns, Jubilee Cottage, Penrhos, nr Raglan, Monmouthshire NP5 2LE (tel. 01600-780416), are hand-made to traditional designs in terracotta from Crete. Sizes vary from a few inches to over 4ft in height. Also fuchsias and herbs for sale. Open weekends, 10a.m.–6p.m., at other times by appointment. Telephone for price list.

Penpergwm Lodge, Abergavenny, Monmouthshire NP7 9AS (tel. 01873-840208). This is a lovely, three-acre formal garden with mature trees, hedges and lawns, a potager of unusual plants and vegetables, an apple and pear pergola and south-facing terraces featuring sun-loving plants. There is also a nursery alongside, specializing in unusual hardy perennial plants. Catriona Boyle's School of Gardening, now in its 12th year, is run from here. Open April–Sept, Thurs–Sat, 2–6p.m. Entrance £1.50, children free. Private visits and parties welcome.

Plantasia, Parc Tawe, Swansea, West Glamorgan SA1 2AL (tel. 01792-474555), is a tropical oasis covering 1600 sq m laid out under a glass pyramid in a modern shopping centre in the middle of Swansea. Its steamy environment contains one of the finest collections of tropical plants in Britain (excluding the larger botanical gardens), holding around 1400 different species and cultivars. There is also a tropical butterfly house, a wildlife room with snakes, lizards, tarantulas and scorpions and a large colony of leaf-cutting ants, and an aquarium. Open all year, Tues–Sun and Bank Holidays, 10a.m.–5p.m. (closed 25–26 Dec and 1 Jan). Entrance £1.70, concessions £1.

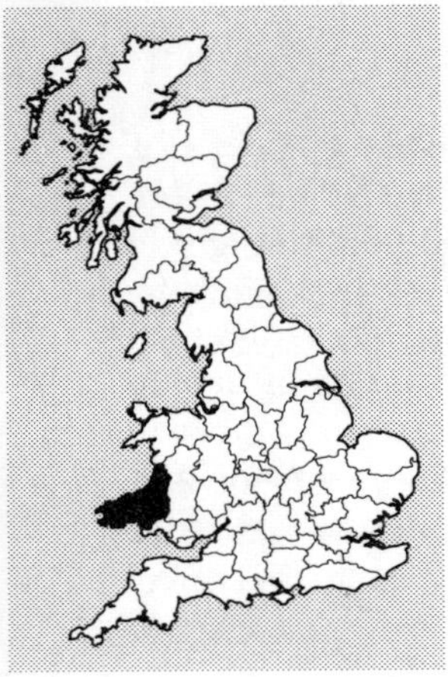

West Wales

MAP NO. 4

Britain's smallest national park is situated here, along the Pembrokeshire coast, and the area encompasses dramatically beautiful stretches of coastline, with steep cliffs and tiny, offshore islets. Prehistoric monuments scattered through the region provide evidence of thousands of years of human occupation, and the area is steeped in myths and Arthurian legend. Fishing continues to be an important source of livelihood around the coast, with seafood a local speciality (try the Carew oysters, or crabs and lobsters brought in at Milford Haven). Further inland, gardeners are already building up steam in anticipation of the new National Botanic Garden for Wales at Middleton Hall, Llandeilo, due to open in May 2000, following a £21 million grant from the Millennium Fund and a huge landscaping project. I can't wait to see it.

CWMBACH

Post House Gardens

Cwmbach, Whitland, Carmarthenshire SA34 0DR **TEL.** *01994-484213* **OWNER** *Mrs J. Kenaghan* **HOURS** *All year, daily, 10a.m–dusk, open by appointment only* **ENTRANCE** *£1.50, OAPs £1, children 50p* **DIRECTIONS** *From Carmarthen, go W on A40, then B4298 through Meidrim. Take centre lane signposted Llanboidy, go right at crossroads (direction Blaenwaun), then right at next crossroads to Cwmbach*

SPRING SUMMER AUTUMN WINTER

This 20-year-old garden features extensive plantings of rhododendrons and other acid-loving plants in a pretty waterside setting beside the River Sien. Extending for five acres in a long, lozenge shape (incorporating the site of an old quarry and a former mill) it is chiefly an informal garden of handsome exotic trees, shrubberies and seasonal bulbs, exuberant in spring and early summer. Jo Kenaghan describes the painstaking process of making the garden in detail in her entertaining and informative leaflet that guides you round the garden, and I didn't envy her battles with 60-degree inclines to fell trees and excavation of slate to provide planting holes. Anyone interested in plants will find much to browse over; and there are plants for sale, grown on the premises.

THE TENBY DAFFODIL

*Wales possesses both the daffodil and the leek as its national flowers, the former being worn by many in buttonholes on St David's Day (1 March). The origins of this custom are unclear, but the south-west corner of Wales certainly has a species all of its own, the Tenby daffodil (*Narcissus pseudonarcissus *ssp.* obvallaris*). Bearing clear yellow flowers on short, sturdy stems, the Tenby daffodil was first documented by the Welsh botanist R.A. Salisbury in 1796. It appeared reliably and abundantly in fields and pastures of Carmarthenshire and Pembrokeshire, particularly around Tenby every spring. Once word of its beauty and novelty caught the attention of gardeners and bulb suppliers the wild plants began to be dug up by the cartload.*

The plant was harvested almost to extinction during the 19th century, and in 1894 the Cardiff Naturalists' Society observed that teams of bulb collectors had scoured the greater part of south Pembrokeshire 'for several seasons in a vigorous attempt to meet the phenomenal demand'. Ruthless gathering of bulbs for the retail trade was followed by the ploughing up of grasslands during two world wars and the continued use of land for intensive farming. In its wild state, the Tenby daffodil became very scarce indeed, although it survived in gardens, hedgebanks and churchyards.

Recent years have seen renewed efforts by the local authorities to re-establish their indigenous flower. Now, happily, the area of Tenby is once again bathed in the brilliant gold of its handsome narcissus in springtime. Gardeners wanting to obtain bulbs of N. p. *ssp.* obvallaris *can find them on the lists of a few select bulb specialists, including* ***John Shipton (Bulbs), Y Felin, Henllan Amgoed, Whitland, Carmarthenshire SA34 0SL (Tel. 01994-240125).*** *Open by appointment only. For a mail order catalogue, send a s.a.e.*

HAVERFORDWEST

Hilton Court

Roch, Haverfordwest, Pembrokeshire SA62 6AE TEL. *01437-710262* OWNER *Mr and Mrs P. Lynch* HOURS *Feb, daily, 10.30a.m.–3.30p.m., March, daily, 10.30a.m.–5p.m., April–Aug, daily, 10a.m.–6p.m., Sept, daily, 10.30a.m.–5p.m., Oct, daily, 10.30a.m.–3.30p.m., Nov–Dec, weekends only, 10.30a.m.–3.30p.m., Jan closed* ENTRANCE *Voluntary charity donation* DIRECTIONS *A487 St David's road from Haverfordwest; approx. ¾m beyond Simpson Cross, look for sign to Hilton on left*

SPRING SUMMER AUTUMN WINTER

Access · Gift Shop · Café · Plant Shop · Nursery

This attractive garden and plant centre adjoins an early 18th-century house on an old estate, and is a treat for anyone holidaying on the scenic Pembrokeshire coast. Water features strongly, for the existing stream has been used to fill a chain of lakes, where the mid-summer highlight is a spectacular display of waterlilies and other aquatic plants. These include impressive stands of *Gunnera manicata*, bearing leaves expanding to 8ft or more, on sturdy, thorny stems.

Within Hilton Court's 11 acres of garden (which have only been created over the last 10 years or so), there are pleasant walks among fine flowering trees and shrubs which provide interest over a long season. The property's close proximity to the sea means the garden centre specializes in plants tolerant of strong winds and a salt-laden atmosphere.

MAPS

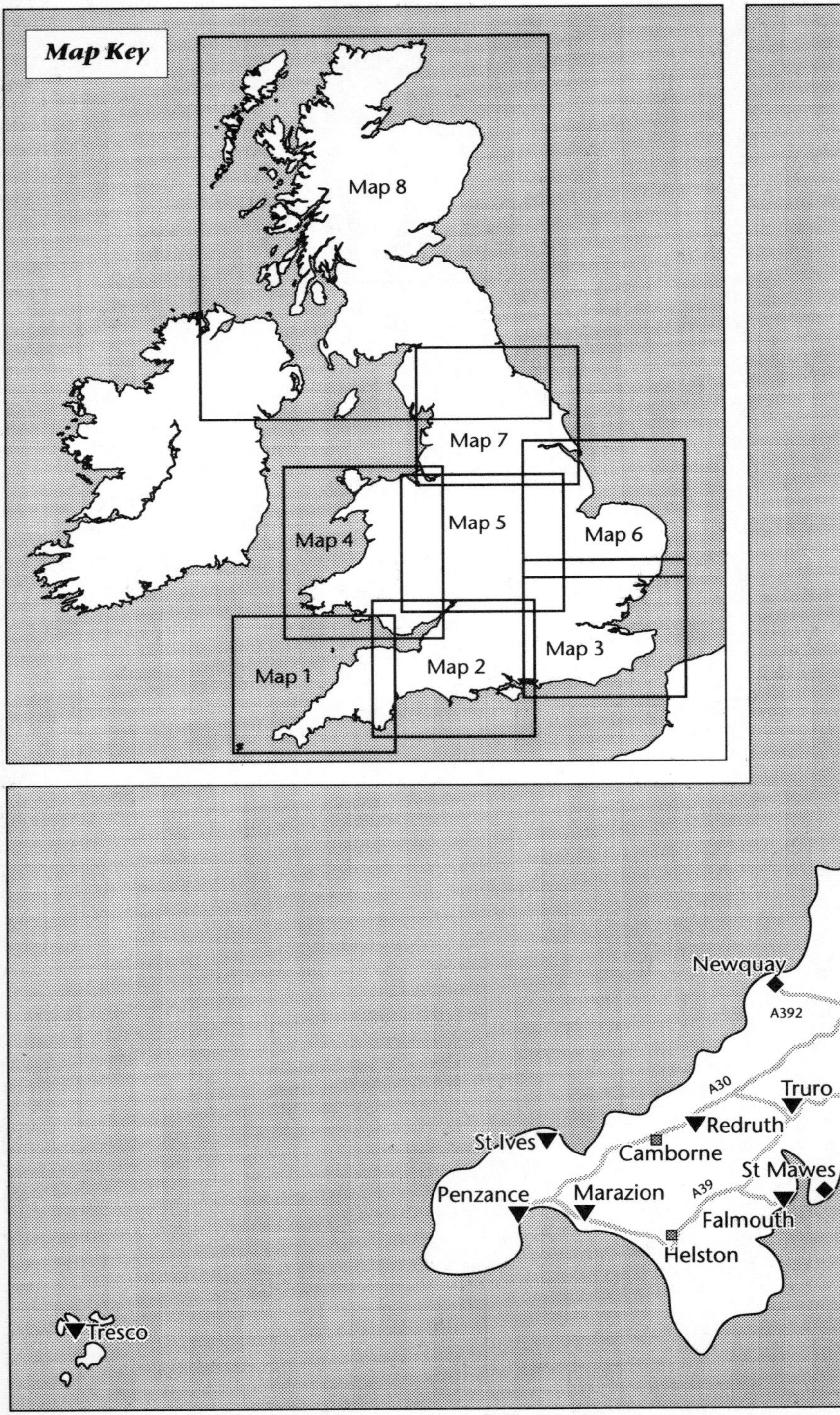
Map Key
Map 8
Map 7
Map 5
Map 4
Map 6
Map 3
Map 2
Map 1
Newquay
A392
A30
Truro
Redruth
St Ives
Camborne
St Mawes
Penzance
Marazion
A39
Falmouth
Helston
Tresco

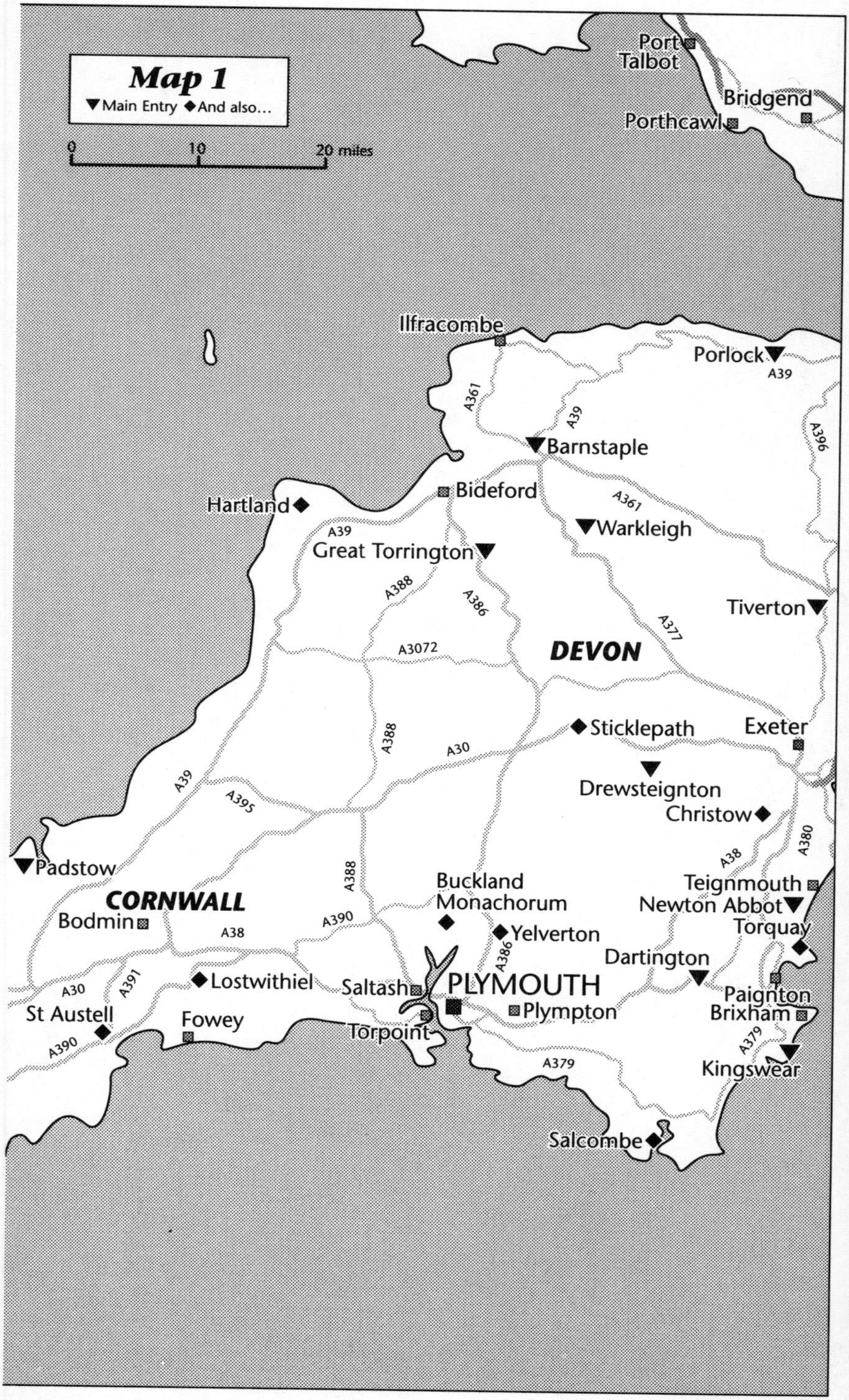
Map 1
▼Main Entry ◆And also...
0
10
20 miles
Port Talbot
Bridgend
Porthcawl
Ilfracombe
Porlock
A39
A361
A39
A396
Barnstaple
Bideford
Hartland
A361
Warkleigh
A39
Great Torrington
A388
A386
Tiverton
A377
A3072
DEVON
Sticklepath
Exeter
A388
A30
Drewsteignton
A39
A395
Christow
A380
A38
Padstow
A388
Buckland Monachorum
Teignmouth
CORNWALL
Newton Abbot
Torquay
Bodmin
A38
A390
Yelverton
A386
Dartington
A30
A391
Lostwithiel
Saltash
PLYMOUTH
Paignton
St Austell
Fowey
Plympton
Brixham
Torpoint
A379
A390
A379
Kingswear
Salcombe

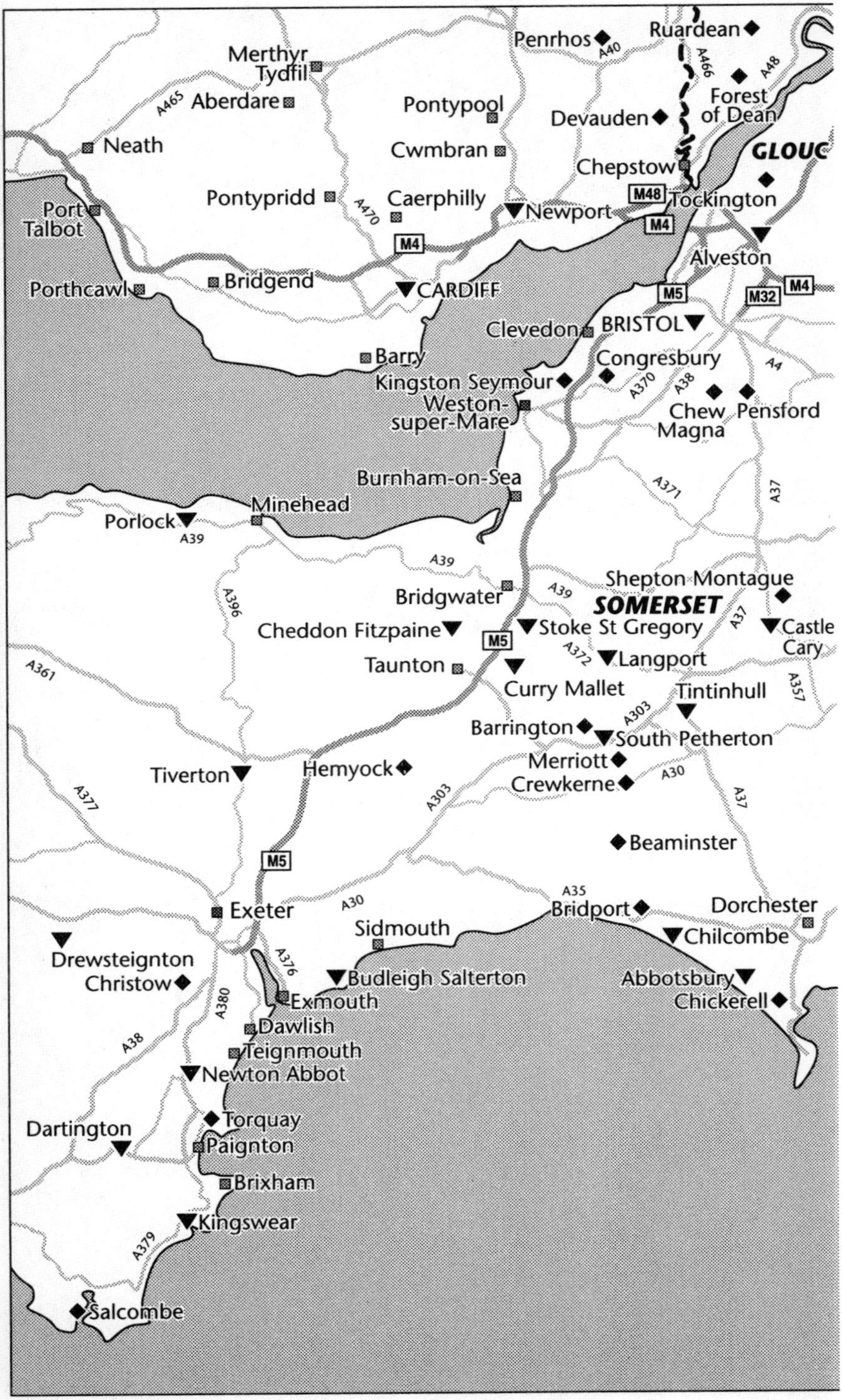

Penrhos
Ruardean
A40
A466
A48
Merthyr Tydfil
Forest of Dean
A465
Aberdare
Pontypool
Devauden
GLOUC
Neath
Cwmbran
Chepstow
M48
Tockington
Pontypridd
Caerphilly
Port Talbot
A470
Newport
M4
Alveston
Porthcawl
Bridgend
CARDIFF
M5
M32
Clevedon
BRISTOL
Barry
Congresbury
A4
Kingston Seymour
A370
A38
Weston-super-Mare
Chew Magna
Pensford
Burnham-on-Sea
A371
A37
Minehead
Porlock
A39
A396
Bridgwater
Shepton Montague
SOMERSET
Cheddon Fitzpaine
Stoke St Gregory
Castle Cary
A372
Langport
Taunton
Curry Mallet
A357
A361
Tintinhull
A303
Barrington
South Petherton
Merriott
Tiverton
Hemyock
Crewkerne
A30
A377
Beaminster
A35
Exeter
Bridport
Dorchester
Sidmouth
Chilcombe
Drewsteignton
A376
Christow
Budleigh Salterton
Abbotsbury
Exmouth
Chickerell
A380
Dawlish
Teignmouth
Newton Abbot
Torquay
Dartington
Paignton
Brixham
Kingswear
A379
Salcombe

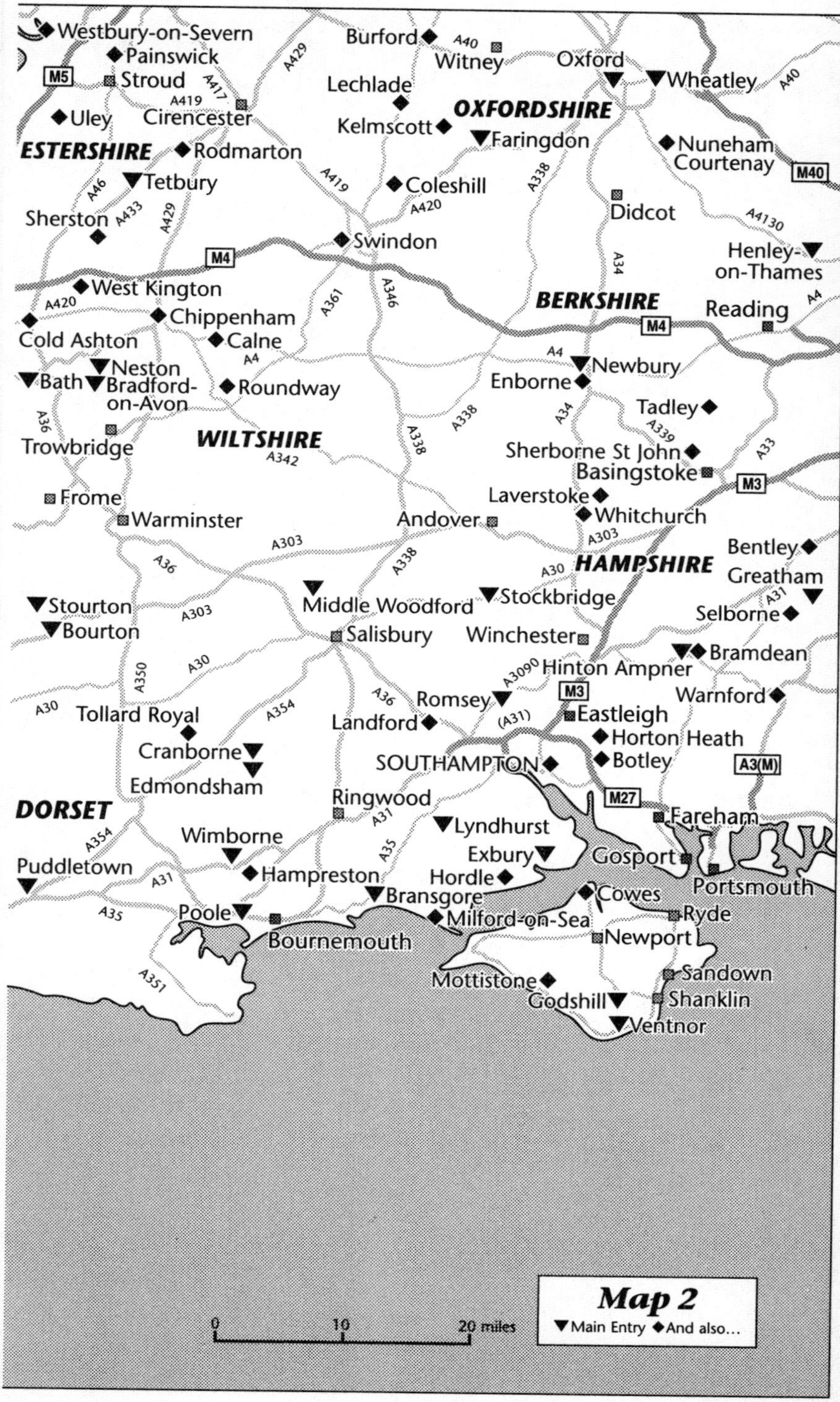
Map 2
▼Main Entry ◆And also...
0
10
20 miles
Westbury-on-Severn
Painswick
Stroud
M5
Uley
Cirencester
A419
A417
A429
ESTERSHIRE
Rodmarton
Tetbury
A46
A433
A429
Sherston
Burford
A40
Witney
Oxford
Wheatley
A40
Lechlade
OXFORDSHIRE
Kelmscott
Faringdon
Nuneham
Courtenay
M40
Coleshill
A419
A420
A338
Didcot
A4130
Henley-
on-Thames
Swindon
M4
West Kington
A420
Cold Ashton
Chippenham
Calne
A361
A346
A34
BERKSHIRE
Reading
A4
M4
A4
Neston
Bath
Bradford-
on-Avon
Roundway
A4
Newbury
Enborne
Tadley
A36
Trowbridge
WILTSHIRE
A342
A338
A338
A34
A339
Sherborne St John
A33
Basingstoke
M3
Laverstoke
Whitchurch
Frome
Warminster
Andover
A303
A303
A36
A338
A30
HAMPSHIRE
Bentley
Greatham
Stourton
Bourton
A303
Middle Woodford
Stockbridge
A31
Selborne
Salisbury
Winchester
Bramdean
A350
A30
A3090
Hinton Ampner
A30
Tollard Royal
A354
A36
Romsey
M3
Warnford
Landford
(A31)
Eastleigh
Horton Heath
Cranborne
SOUTHAMPTON
Botley
A3(M)
Edmondsham
Ringwood
M27
DORSET
A31
Fareham
Lyndhurst
A354
Wimborne
A35
Exbury
Gosport
Puddletown
Hampreston
Hordle
Portsmouth
A31
Bransgore
Cowes
A35
Poole
Milford-on-Sea
Ryde
Bournemouth
Newport
A351
Sandown
Mottistone
Godshill
Shanklin
Ventnor

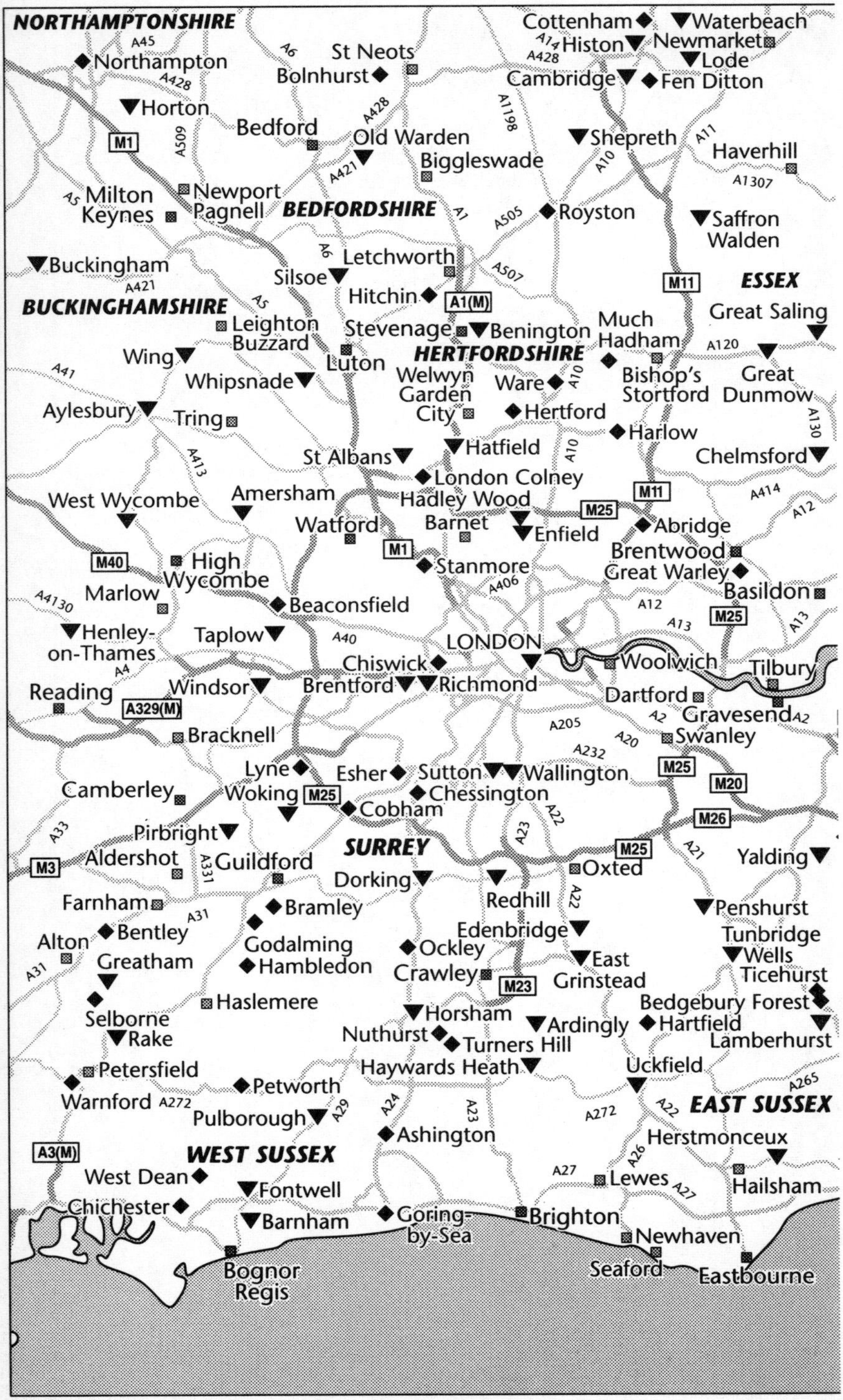
NORTHAMPTONSHIRE
A45
Northampton
A428
A6
St Neots
Bolnhurst
Cottenham
Waterbeach
A14
Histon
Newmarket
A428
Lode
Cambridge
Fen Ditton
Horton
A428
Bedford
A1198
M1
A509
Old Warden
Shepreth
A11
Haverhill
A421
Biggleswade
A10
A1307
A5
Milton
Keynes
Newport
Pagnell
BEDFORDSHIRE
A1
A505
Royston
Saffron
Walden
A6
Letchworth
Buckingham
Silsoe
A507
M11
ESSEX
A421
Hitchin
A1(M)
BUCKINGHAMSHIRE
A5
Leighton
Buzzard
Stevenage
Benington
Much
Hadham
Great Saling
A120
Wing
Luton
HERTFORDSHIRE
A41
Whipsnade
Welwyn
Garden
City
Ware
A10
Bishop's
Stortford
Great
Dunmow
Aylesbury
Tring
Hertford
A130
Harlow
A413
Hatfield
A10
St Albans
Chelmsford
London Colney
Amersham
West Wycombe
Hadley Wood
M11
A414
M25
A12
Watford
Barnet
Abridge
Enfield
M40
M1
High
Wycombe
Stanmore
Brentwood
Marlow
Great Warley
A406
Basildon
A4130
Beaconsfield
A12
A13
M25
A13
Henley-
on-Thames
Taplow
A40
LONDON
A4
Chiswick
Woolwich
Tilbury
Reading
Windsor
Brentford
Richmond
A329(M)
Dartford
A2
Gravesend
A2
A205
A20
Swanley
Bracknell
A232
Lyne
Esher
Sutton
Wallington
M25
Camberley
M20
Woking
M25
Chessington
Cobham
A22
M26
A33
Pirbright
A23
M25
A21
Aldershot
SURREY
M3
A331
Guildford
Yalding
Oxted
Dorking
Farnham
Redhill
A22
Bramley
Penshurst
A31
Bentley
Edenbridge
Tunbridge
Wells
Alton
Godalming
Ockley
A31
East
Grinstead
Greatham
Hambledon
Crawley
Ticehurst
M23
Haslemere
Bedgebury Forest
Horsham
Selborne
Ardingly
Hartfield
Rake
Nuthurst
Turners Hill
Lamberhurst
Petersfield
Haywards Heath
Uckfield
Petworth
A265
Warnford
A272
A29
A24
A23
A272
A22
EAST SUSSEX
Pulborough
Ashington
Herstmonceux
A3(M)
WEST SUSSEX
A26
West Dean
A27
Lewes
Hailsham
Fontwell
A27
Chichester
Goring-
by-Sea
Brighton
Barnham
Newhaven
Bognor
Regis
Seaford
Eastbourne

SUFFOLK
Bury St Edmunds
Mendlesham
Stowmarket
Needham Market
Coddenham
Hintlesham
Grundisburgh
Long Melford
Sudbury
Ipswich
Felixstowe
Harwich
Little Canfield
Colchester
Kelvedon
Fingringhoe
Thorpe-le-Soken
Weeley Heath
Wickham Bishops
Witham
Clacton-on-Sea
Maldon
Rayleigh
Southend-on-Sea
Canvey Island
Sheerness
Rochester
Gillingham
Whitstable
Herne Bay
Margate
Chatham
Sittingbourne
Minster
Ramsgate
Faversham
Ditton
East Farleigh
Canterbury
Deal
Charing Heath
KENT
Staplehurst
Bethersden
Sissinghurst
Dover
Folkestone
Lympne
Hythe
Hawkhurst
Northiam
Hurst Green
Peasmarsh
Hastings
Bexhill-on-Sea
A14
A12
A134
A1017
(A604)
A131
A1124
A120
A133
A130
A127
A2
M2
A299
A28
A253
A257
A256
M20
A229
A2070
A20
A259
A21
A271
Map 3
Main Entry
And also...
0
10
20 miles
© MAPS IN MINUTES™ (1997)

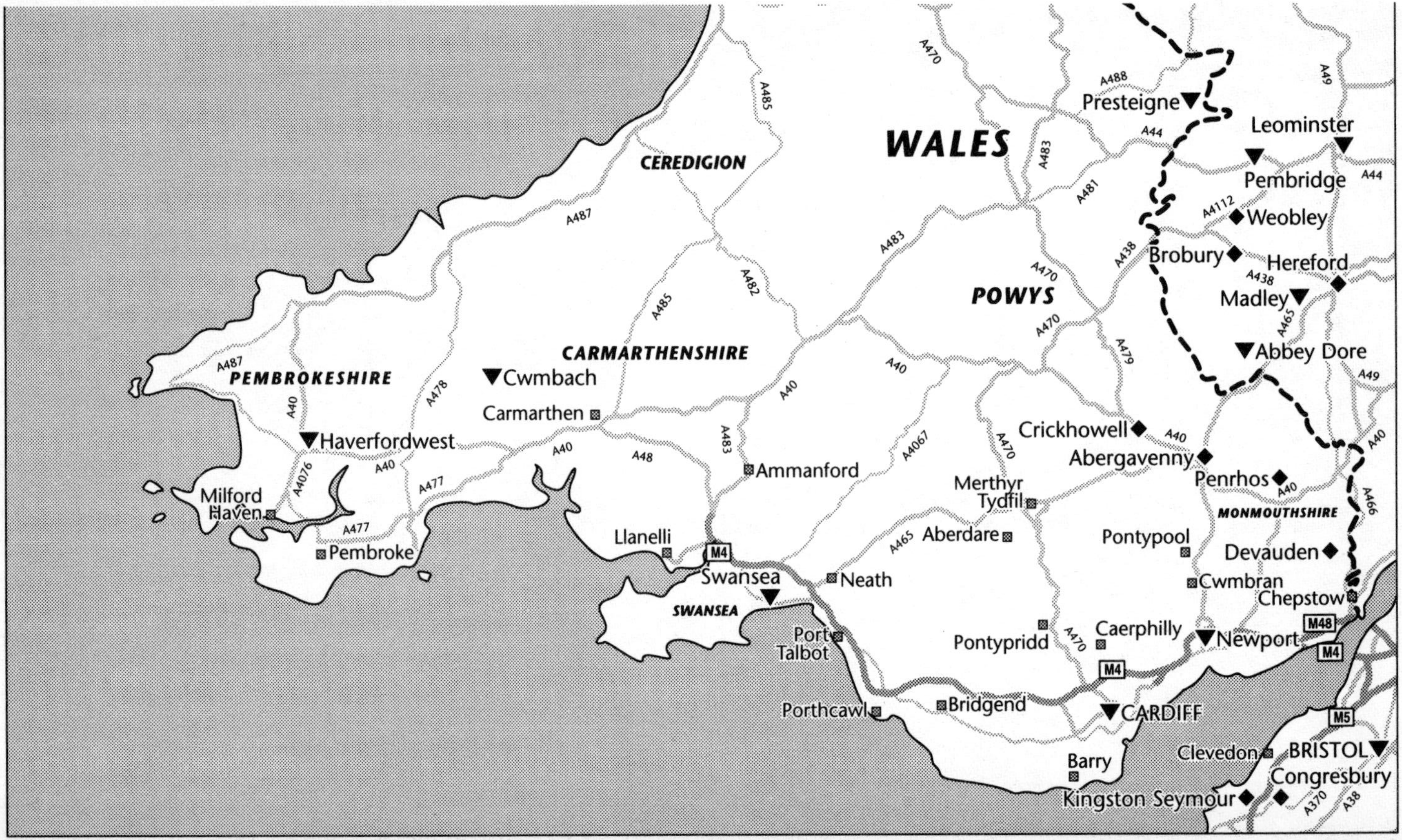
WALES
CEREDIGION
PEMBROKESHIRE
CARMARTHENSHIRE
POWYS
SWANSEA
MONMOUTHSHIRE
Presteigne
Leominster
Pembridge
Weobley
Brobury
Hereford
Madley
Abbey Dore
Cwmbach
Carmarthen
Haverfordwest
Milford Haven
Pembroke
Llanelli
Swansea
Ammanford
Neath
Port Talbot
Porthcawl
Bridgend
Aberdare
Merthyr Tydfil
Crickhowell
Abergavenny
Penrhos
Pontypool
Devauden
Cwmbran
Chepstow
Pontypridd
Caerphilly
Newport
CARDIFF
Barry
Clevedon
BRISTOL
Congresbury
Kingston Seymour

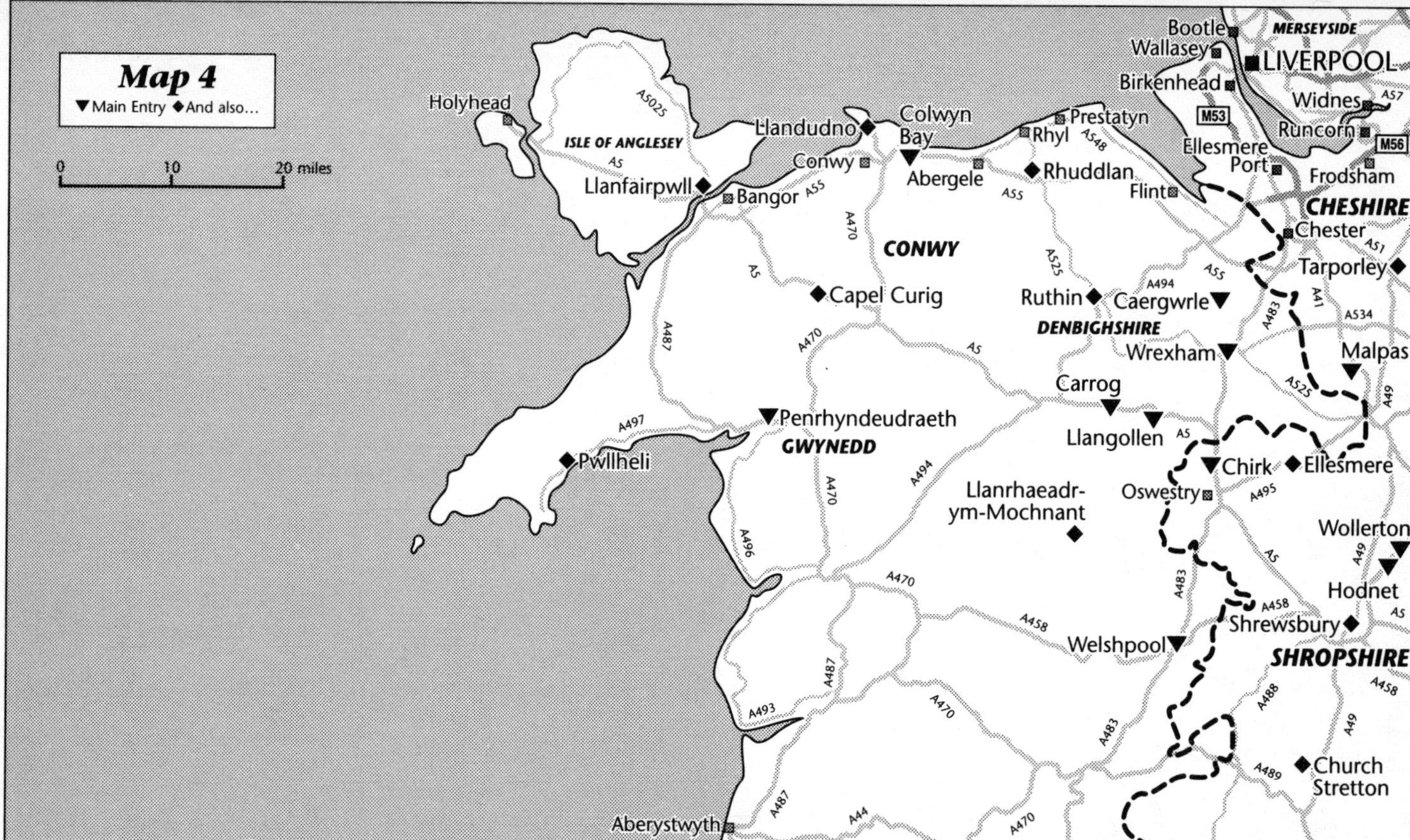
Map 4
▼Main Entry ◆And also…
0
10
20 miles
Holyhead
ISLE OF ANGLESEY
A5025
A5
Llanfairpwll
Bangor
A55
Llandudno
Conwy
Colwyn Bay
Abergele
Rhyl
Prestatyn
A548
Rhuddlan
Flint
A55
A470
CONWY
A5
Capel Curig
A525
Ruthin
DENBIGHSHIRE
A494
Caergwrle
Wrexham
A487
A470
A5
Carrog
Llangollen
A497
Penrhyndeudraeth
GWYNEDD
Pwllheli
A494
A470
Llanrhaeadr-ym-Mochnant
Oswestry
Chirk
Ellesmere
A495
A496
A470
A458
Welshpool
A483
A487
A493
A470
A483
A487
A44
A470
Aberystwyth
Bootle
MERSEYSIDE
Wallasey
LIVERPOOL
Birkenhead
Widnes
A57
M53
Runcorn
M56
Ellesmere Port
Frodsham
CHESHIRE
Chester
A51
Tarporley
A55
A483
A41
A534
Malpas
A525
A49
A5
Wollerton
A49
Hodnet
A5
A458
Shrewsbury
SHROPSHIRE
A458
A488
A49
A489
Church Stretton

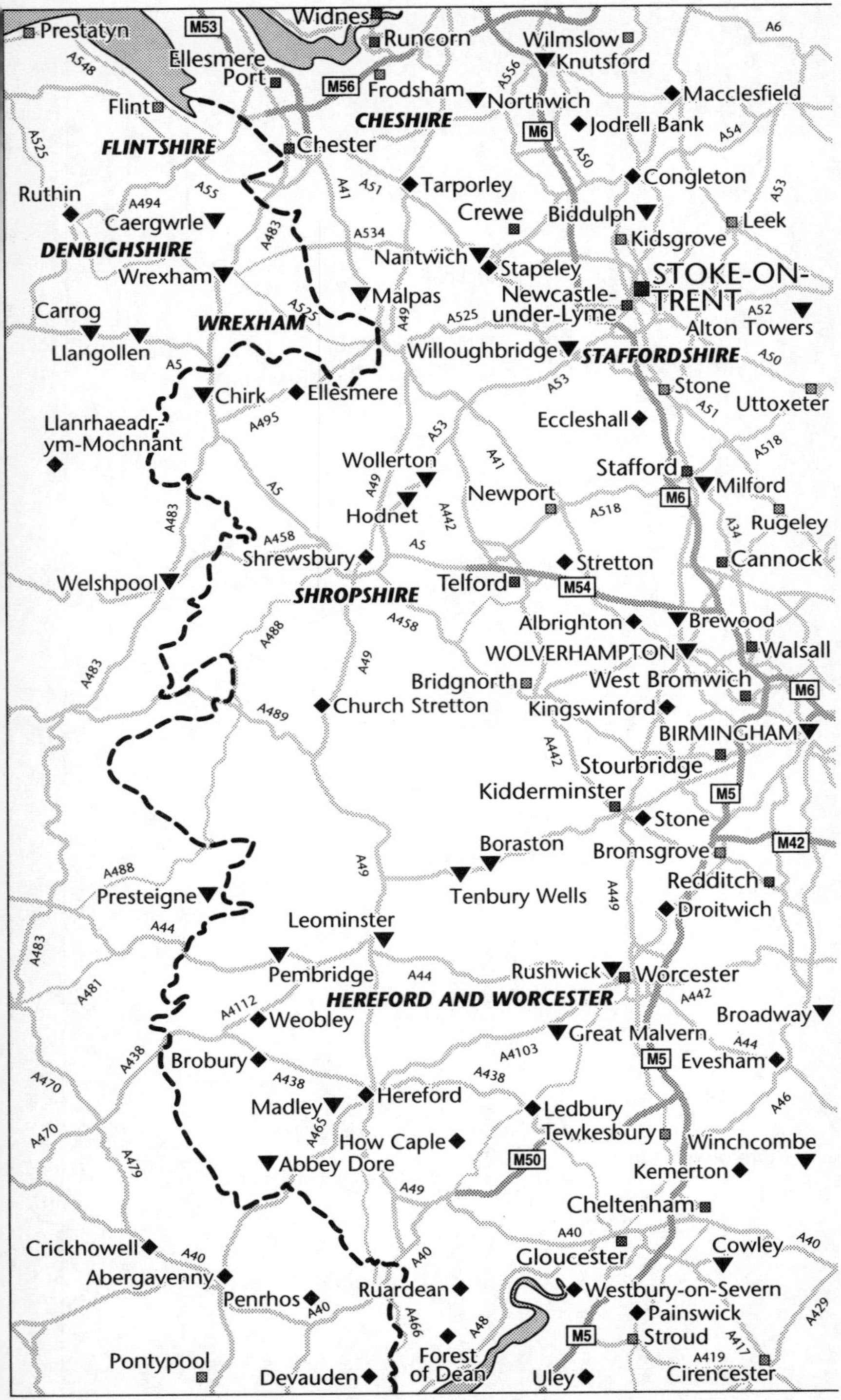
Prestatyn
M53
Widnes
Runcorn
Wilmslow
A6
Knutsford
A548
Ellesmere Port
M56
Frodsham
A556
Macclesfield
Flint
Northwich
CHESHIRE
M6
Jodrell Bank
A54
A525
FLINTSHIRE
Chester
A50
Congleton
Ruthin
A55
A41
A51
Tarporley
A53
A494
Caergwrle
Crewe
Biddulph
Leek
A483
A534
Kidsgrove
DENBIGHSHIRE
Nantwich
Stapeley
Wrexham
STOKE-ON-TRENT
Malpas
Newcastle-under-Lyme
Carrog
A525
A49
A525
A52
Alton Towers
WREXHAM
Llangollen
Willoughbridge
STAFFORDSHIRE
A50
A5
Chirk
Ellesmere
A53
Stone
Uttoxeter
Llanrhaeadr-ym-Mochnant
A495
Eccleshall
A51
A53
A41
A518
Wollerton
Stafford
Milford
A49
Newport
M6
A5
A483
Hodnet
A442
A518
Rugeley
A34
A458
A5
Shrewsbury
Stretton
Cannock
Welshpool
Telford
M54
SHROPSHIRE
A488
A458
Albrighton
Brewood
Walsall
WOLVERHAMPTON
A483
A49
Bridgnorth
West Bromwich
M6
Church Stretton
Kingswinford
A489
BIRMINGHAM
A442
Stourbridge
Kidderminster
M5
Stone
Boraston
Bromsgrove
M42
A488
A49
Redditch
Presteigne
Tenbury Wells
A449
Droitwich
A44
Leominster
A483
Rushwick
Worcester
Pembridge
A44
A481
HEREFORD AND WORCESTER
A4112
A442
Broadway
Weobley
Great Malvern
A44
A438
A4103
M5
Evesham
Brobury
A470
A438
A438
Hereford
A46
Madley
Ledbury
A470
A465
How Caple
Tewkesbury
Winchcombe
A479
M50
Abbey Dore
Kemerton
A49
Cheltenham
A40
Crickhowell
A40
Cowley
A40
Gloucester
A40
Abergavenny
Ruardean
Westbury-on-Severn
Penrhos
A40
A466
Painswick
A429
A48
M5
Stroud
A417
A419
Pontypool
Forest of Dean
Devauden
Uley
Cirencester

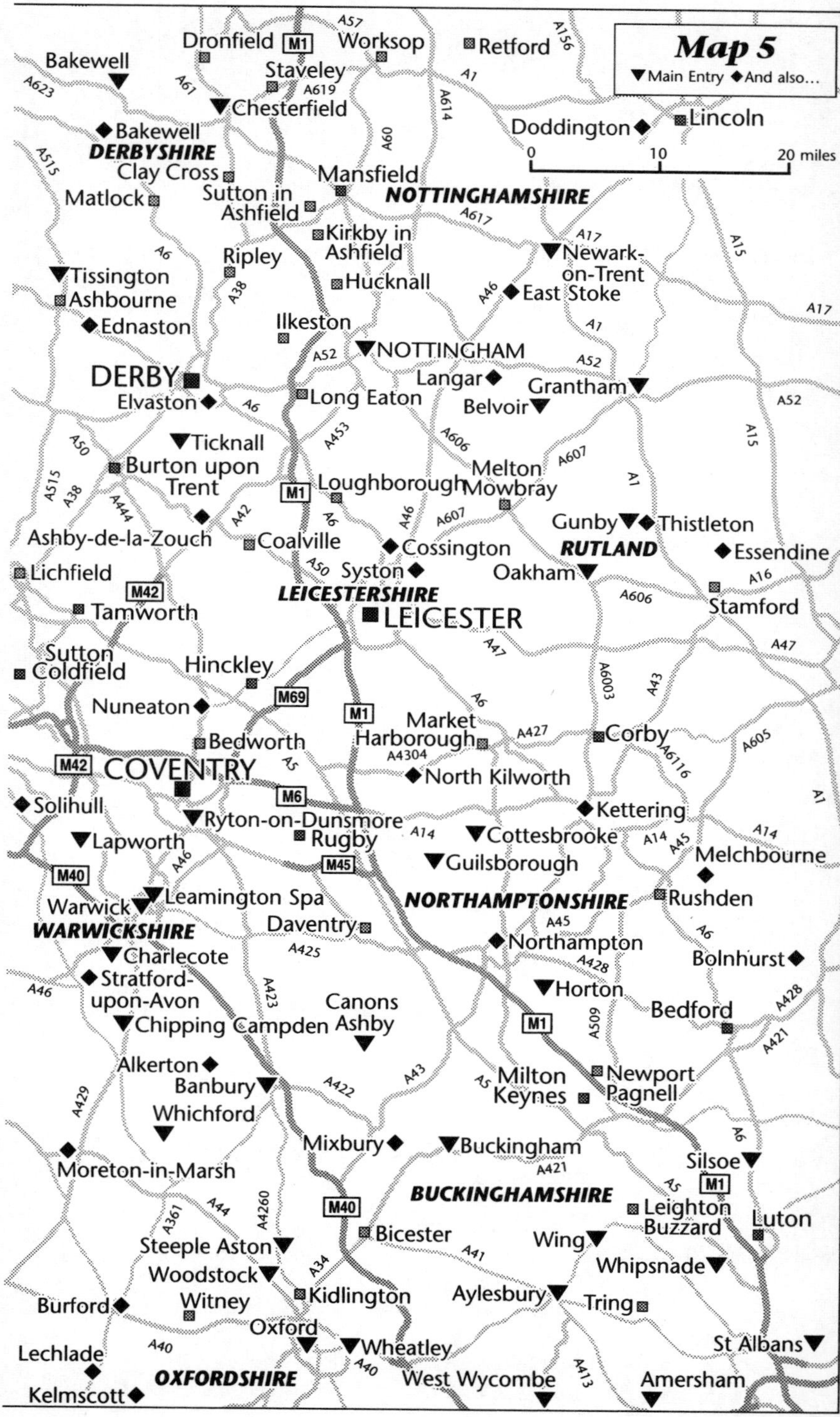
Map 5
▼Main Entry ◆And also…
0
10
20 miles
Dronfield
M1
A57
Worksop
Retford
A156
Bakewell
Staveley
A623
A61
A619
A1
A614
Chesterfield
A60
Doddington
Lincoln
Bakewell
DERBYSHIRE
A515
Clay Cross
Mansfield
Matlock
Sutton in Ashfield
NOTTINGHAMSHIRE
A617
Kirkby in Ashfield
A17
A15
A6
Ripley
Newark-on-Trent
Tissington
A38
Hucknall
A46
East Stoke
Ashbourne
A17
Ednaston
Ilkeston
A1
NOTTINGHAM
A52
A52
DERBY
Langar
Grantham
Elvaston
A6
Long Eaton
Belvoir
A52
A453
A606
A15
A50
Ticknall
Melton Mowbray
A607
Burton upon Trent
A1
A515
A38
M1
Loughborough
A444
A42
A6
A46
A607
Gunby
Thistleton
Ashby-de-la-Zouch
Coalville
Cossington
RUTLAND
Essendine
A50
Syston
Oakham
Lichfield
A16
M42
LEICESTERSHIRE
A606
Stamford
Tamworth
LEICESTER
A47
A47
Sutton Coldfield
Hinckley
A6003
A43
M69
A6
Nuneaton
M1
Market Harborough
A427
Corby
A605
Bedworth
A6116
M42
COVENTRY
A5
A4304
North Kilworth
A1
M6
Solihull
Ryton-on-Dunsmore
Kettering
A14
Cottesbrooke
A14
A45
A14
Lapworth
Rugby
Melchbourne
A46
M45
Guilsborough
M40
Leamington Spa
NORTHAMPTONSHIRE
Rushden
Warwick
WARWICKSHIRE
Daventry
A45
A6
Northampton
A425
A428
Bolnhurst
Charlecote
A46
Stratford-upon-Avon
A423
Horton
A428
Canons Ashby
Bedford
Chipping Campden
M1
A509
A421
Alkerton
A43
A5
Milton Keynes
Newport Pagnell
Banbury
A422
A429
Whichford
A6
Moreton-in-Marsh
Mixbury
Buckingham
Silsoe
A421
A5
M1
BUCKINGHAMSHIRE
A44
A4260
M40
Leighton Buzzard
Luton
A361
Steeple Aston
Bicester
Wing
A41
A34
Woodstock
Whipsnade
Burford
Witney
Kidlington
Aylesbury
Tring
Oxford
A40
St Albans
Lechlade
Wheatley
A413
A40
OXFORDSHIRE
West Wycombe
Amersham
Kelmscott

HULL
Goole
Immingham
Grimsby
Cleethorpes
Thorne
Scunthorpe
Nettleton
Gainsborough
Hemswell
Harpswell
Louth
Retford
Lincoln
Doddington
LINCOLNSHIRE
Newark-on-Trent
East Stoke
Boston
Langar
Grantham
Belvoir
Heacham
Melton Mowbray
Weston
Spalding
Grimston
King's Lynn
Gunby
Thistleton
RUTLAND
Essendine
Oakham
Wisbech
Wimbotsham
Stamford
Downham Market
Peterborough
March
Corby
Market Harborough
Prickwillow
Kettering
CAMBRIDGESHIRE
Ely
Cottesbrooke
Huntingdon
Guilsborough
St Ives
Melchbourne
Hemingford Grey
Burwell
NORTHAMPTONSHIRE
Rushden
Cottenham
Waterbeach
Histon
Northampton
St Neots
Lode
Bolnhurst
Cambridge
Fen Ditton
Horton
Bedford
Old Warden
Shepreth
Haverhill
M62
M18
M180
M181
M11
M1
A63
A15
A18
A46
A159
A631
A16
A1031
A156
A1
A57
A158
A52
A617
A17
A606
A607
A151
A47
A10
A1122
A6003
A43
A6
A427
A605
A141
A1101
A6116
A14
A45
A428
A1198
A509
A11

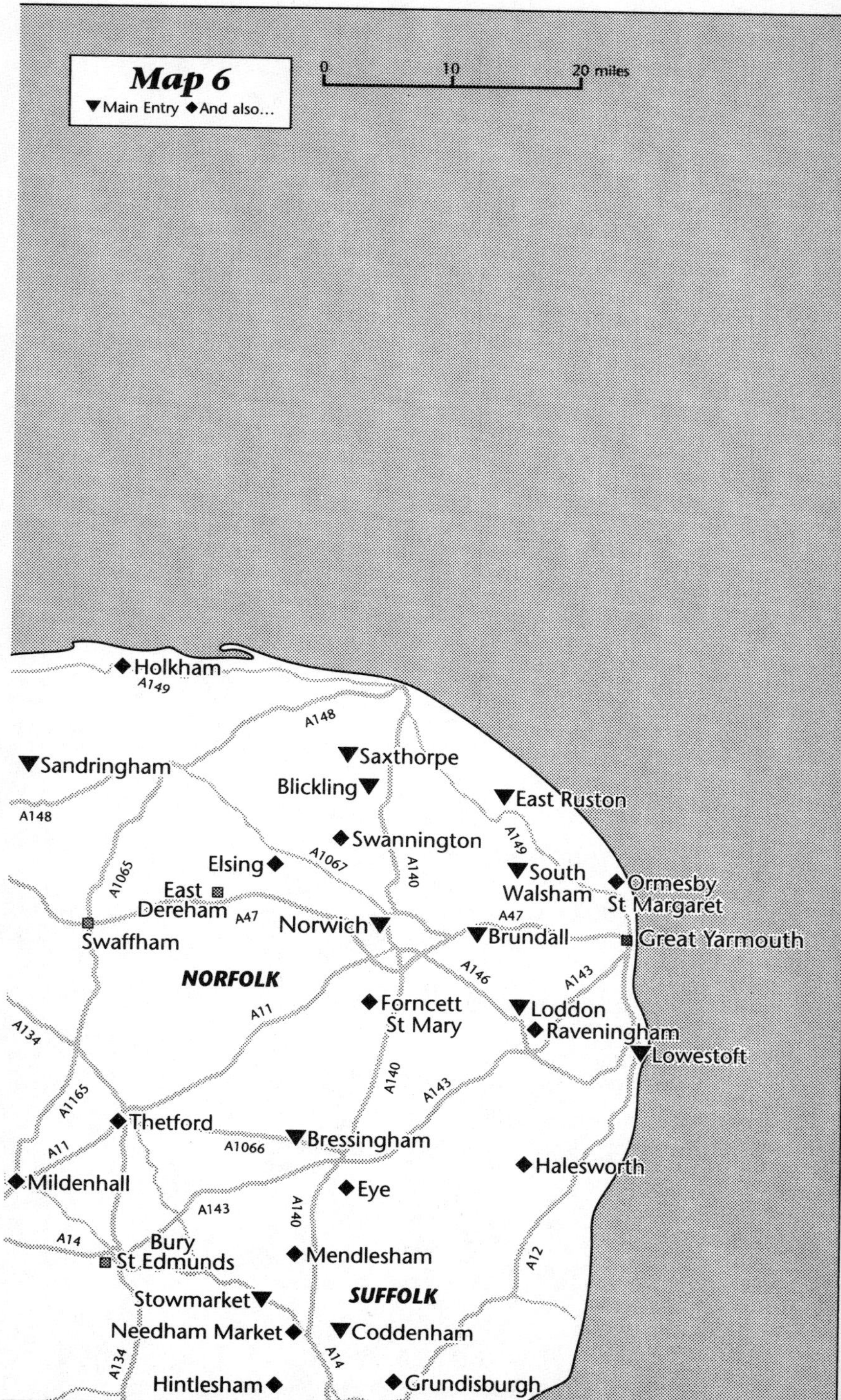
Map 6
▼Main Entry ◆And also...
0
10
20 miles
Holkham
A149
A148
Sandringham
A148
Saxthorpe
Blickling
East Ruston
Swannington
A149
Elsing
A1067
A140
A1065
South
Walsham
Ormesby
St Margaret
East
Dereham
A47
Norwich
A47
Brundall
Great Yarmouth
Swaffham
NORFOLK
A146
A143
Forncett
St Mary
Loddon
A11
Raveningham
A134
Lowestoft
A140
A143
A1165
Thetford
Bressingham
A1066
A11
Halesworth
Mildenhall
Eye
A143
A140
Bury
St Edmunds
A14
Mendlesham
A12
Stowmarket
SUFFOLK
Needham Market
Coddenham
A14
A134
Hintlesham
Grundisburgh

Carlisle
A689
A68
Beamish
Consett
Alston
M6
Durham
A6
A686
A689
Brandon
CUMBRIA
Spennymoor
DURHAM
Bishop Auckland
A66
Penrith
A689
Melkinthorpe
Appleby-in-Westmorland
A1(M)
A66
A591
A688
Darlington
A66
Ambleside
A685
Windermere
Hawkshead
A1
Kendal
Bedale
M6
A684
A590
Grange-over-Sands
NORTH YORKSHIRE
Ulverston
Silverdale
A6
Ripon
A65
A683
A61
Morecambe
Lancaster
Heysham
Appletreewick
M6
A59
Harrogate
Forton
A682
Skipton
Holden
Ilkley
A65
LANCASHIRE
A6068
Keighley
Yeadon
A650
A6
Colne
Barrowford
Catforth
Ribchester
Nelson
Bingley
A59
LEEDS
M55
Padiham
BRADFORD
Preston
Burnley
M621
M65
A646
Halifax
Accrington
Batley
A59
Blackburn
Brighouse
M61
A58
WEST YORKSHIRE
Southport
M6
Rochdale
M62
Huddersfield
A570
A59
Rufford
Rivington
M66
M1
A58
Bury
A62
Ormskirk
Standish
Bolton
A629
Middleton
Skelmersdale
Wigan
Oldham
M58
A628
Stocksbridge
Kirkby
Salford
MANCHESTER
A616
St Helens
M67
LIVERPOOL
M62
Glossop
Sale
M63
M56
Stockport
M62
Warrington
Cheadle
A57
Widnes
A57
Altrincham
M53
A6
Runcorn
Wilmslow
Ellesmere Port
A556
Knutsford
Bakewell
M56
Frodsham
Northwich
Macclesfield
A623

Map 7
Main Entry
And also...
0
10
20 miles
SUNDERLAND
Houghton le Spring
Peterlee
A19
Hartlepool
A689
Redcar
Middlesbrough
A66
A171
Whitby
A172
A684
Northallerton
A169
A171
Scarborough
A19
A170
Pickering
A170
A168
A165
A64
A1(M)
Bridlington
(A166)
Knaresborough
A19
A166
A614
A59
York
Wetherby
A61
A64
A58
Tadcaster
A19
A1035
A165
A163
Beverley
A1079
Garforth
A1
A614
A164
Selby
A63
M62
HULL
Castleford
A63
A63
M62
Pontefract
Goole
Wakefield
M18
A15
Hemsworth
Immingham
A61
Thorne
Scunthorpe
Grimsby
M181
M180
M180
A18
SOUTH YORKSHIRE
Doncaster
Nettleton
A46
A1(M)
A159
A15
A16
Rotherham
Gainsborough
A631
SHEFFIELD
Hemswell
A631
Blyth
Harpswell
Louth
A57
A156
Dronfield
M1
Retford
A46
Staveley
Worksop
A619
A57
A158
A1

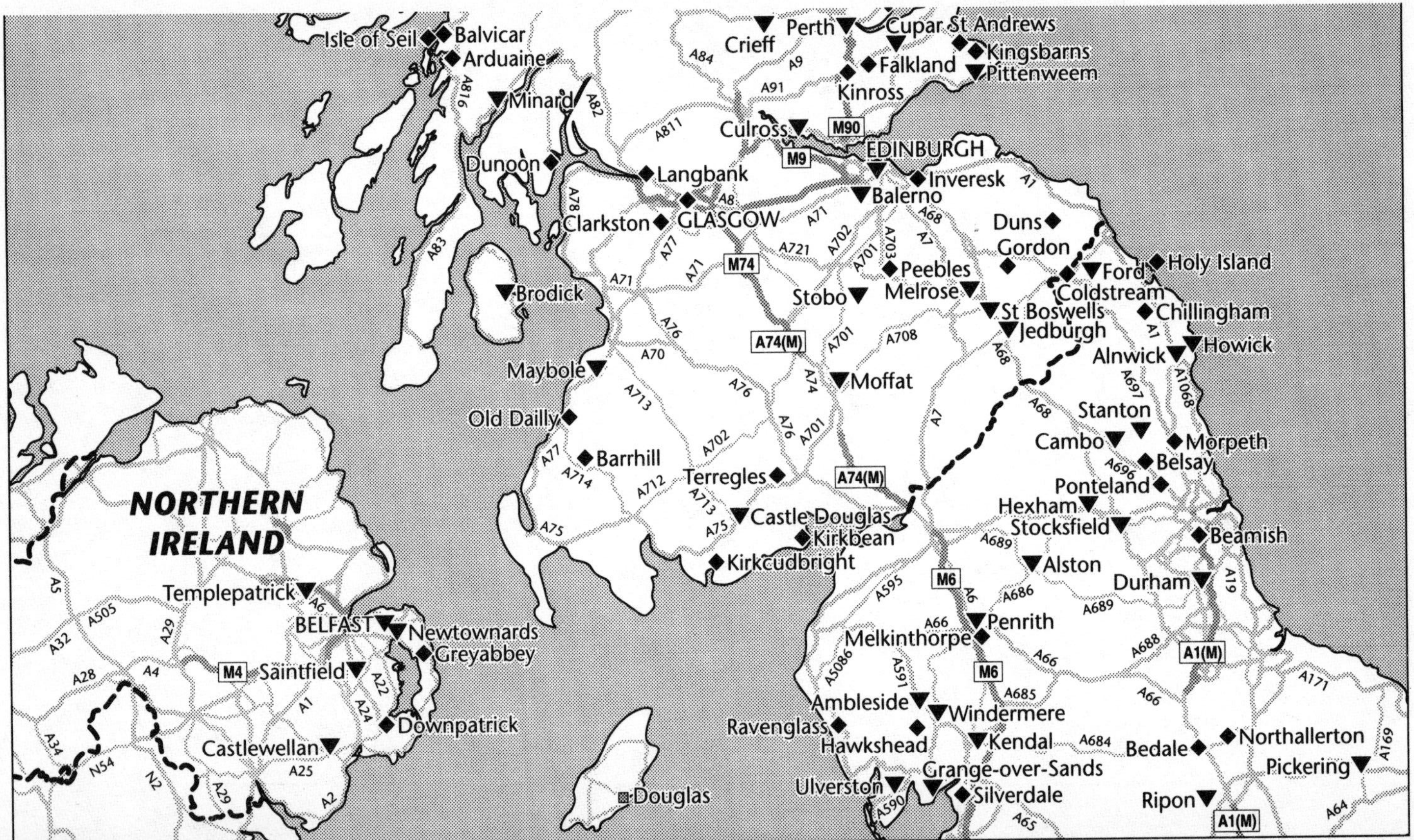
NORTHERN IRELAND
Isle of Seil
Balvicar
Arduaine
Minard
Dunoon
Brodick
Crieff
Perth
Cupar
St Andrews
Kingsbarns
Falkland
Pittenweem
Kinross
Culross
EDINBURGH
Langbank
GLASGOW
Clarkston
Inveresk
Balerno
Duns
Gordon
Peebles
Melrose
Stobo
Holy Island
Ford
Coldstream
Chillingham
St Boswells
Jedburgh
Alnwick
Howick
Maybole
Moffat
Old Dailly
Barrhill
Terregles
Castle Douglas
Kirkbean
Kirkcudbright
Stanton
Cambo
Morpeth
Belsay
Ponteland
Hexham
Stocksfield
Beamish
Alston
Durham
Templepatrick
BELFAST
Newtownards
Greyabbey
Saintfield
Downpatrick
Castlewellan
Douglas
Penrith
Melkinthorpe
Ambleside
Windermere
Ravenglass
Hawkshead
Kendal
Grange-over-Sands
Ulverston
Silverdale
Bedale
Northallerton
Pickering
Ripon
M90
M9
M74
A74(M)
M6
M4
A1(M)
A816
A82
A84
A9
A91
A811
A8
A78
A83
A71
A77
A721
A702
A703
A701
A68
A7
A1
A76
A70
A708
A74
A713
A714
A712
A75
A697
A1068
A696
A689
A19
A595
A686
A66
A688
A5086
A591
A685
A684
A171
A169
A64
A65
A590
A5
A505
A32
A29
A28
A4
A6
A22
A24
A34
N54
N2
A25
A2

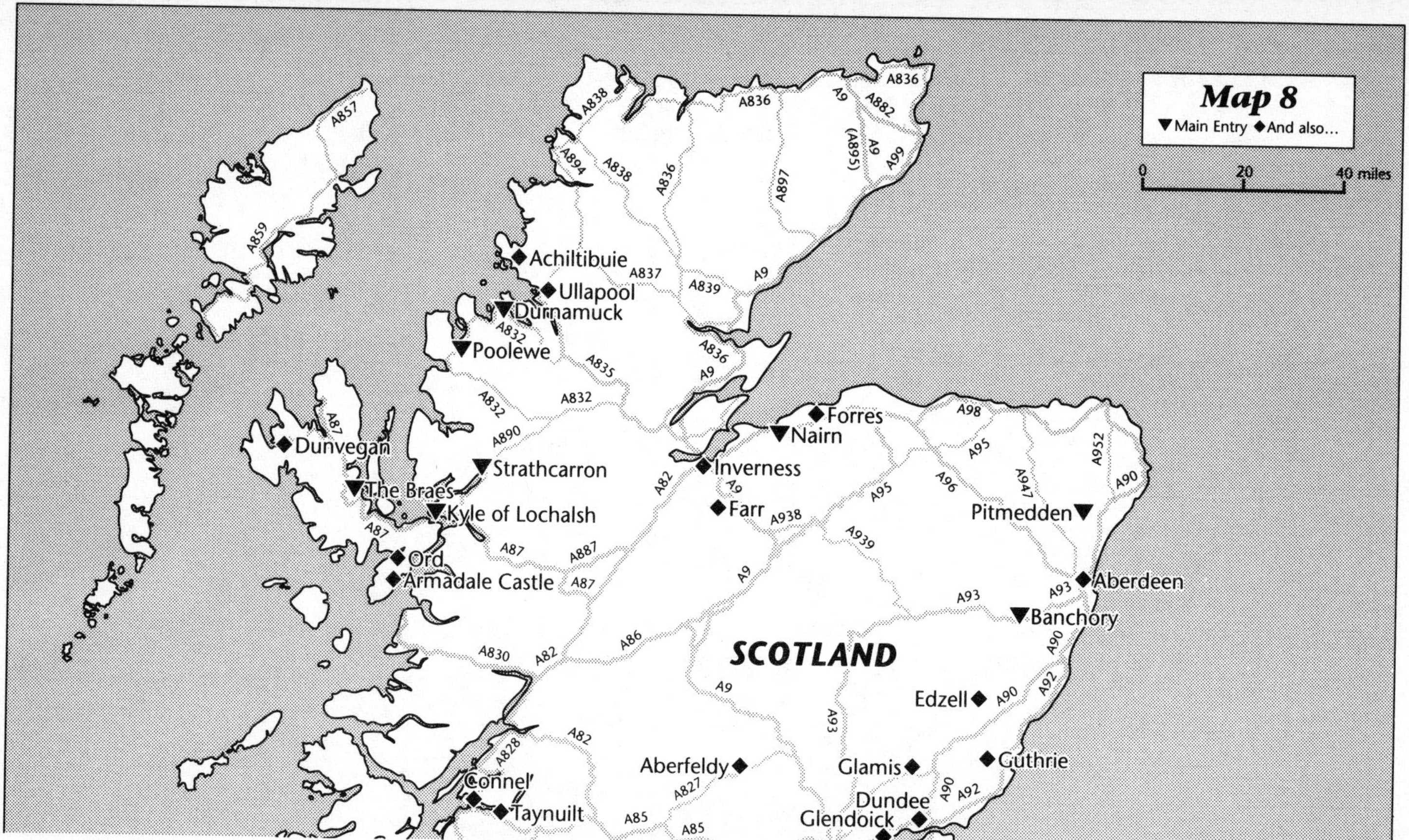
Map 8
▼Main Entry ◆And also...
0 20 40 miles
SCOTLAND
Achiltibuie
Ullapool
Durnamuck
Poolewe
Dunvegan
Strathcarron
The Braes
Kyle of Lochalsh
Ord
Armadale Castle
Inverness
Farr
Forres
Nairn
Pitmedden
Aberdeen
Banchory
Edzell
Guthrie
Glamis
Dundee
Glendoick
Aberfeldy
Connel
Taynuilt

Index